THE ANTIOCH BIBLE

The Syriac Peshiṭta Bible
with English Translation

Isaiah

Ṣurath Kthobh

Editors

George A. Kiraz

Andreas Juckel

The Syriac Peshiṭta Bible
with English Translation

Isaiah

English Translation by

Gillian Greenberg

Donald M. Walter

Text Prepared by

George A. Kiraz

Joseph Bali

gorgias press

2012

Gorgias Press LLC, 954 River Road, Piscataway, NJ, 08854, USA

www.gorgiaspress.com

2012

ISBN 978-1-4632-0155-5

Printed in the United States of America

My husband Morris, without whose unfailing support I could not have
entered this field of study
Morris Greenberg

My late friend and inspiring teacher
Michael P. Weitzman

Gillian Greenberg

My longtime friends: my chairman & colleague, and his wife
William E. and Martha Ann Phipps

Donald M. Walter

TABLE OF CONTENTS

FOREWORD TO THE EDITION

BY GEORGE A. KIRAZ

The primary objective of this edition is twofold: to provide a reliable text for scholars and students who are looking for a fully vocalized Syriac text, and to make available to religious communities, for whom this text is sacred, an English translation that can be used in various religious and cultural settings. As such, one had to navigate carefully between rigid scholarly principles and practical editorial choices.

Making of the Text

The current edition provides a West Syriac version of the 1887-91 Peshiṭta Mosul text.[1] While the Mosul text was prepared based on second millennium manuscripts, its text is substantially attested by manuscripts belonging to the first millennium. We are able to determine this with the help of three important tools: the apparatus criticus of the Leiden edition,[2] as well as two earlier collations made by Diettrich[3] and Running.[4] As ancient MSS are hardly vocalized, our text relies on the vocalization of the Mosul edition. In addition to full vocalization, our text is supplemented with complete Rukkākhā and Quššāyā pointing and other orthographic markings, keeping in mind the general orthographic principles adopted by Pusey and Gwilliam in their 1901 *Tetraeuangelium*.[5] Hence, while the

---

[1] Clemis Joseph David (ed.), *The Syriac Bible According to the Mosul Edition*, 3 volumes, with an introduction by Sebastian P. Brock (Piscataway, NJ, 2010), a reprint of the Mosul 1887-91 edition titled ܦܘܼܪܫܵܐ ܩܲܕ� ܐܝܟ ܡܒܥܐ ܕܡܬܐ ܕܟܬܒܐ ܕܝܬܩܐ.

[2] The Peshiṭta Institute, *The Old Testament in Syriac According to the Peshiṭta Version*, Part III, fascicle 1, Isaiah, prepared by S. P. Brock (Leiden, 1987).

[3] G. Diettrich, *Ein Apparatus criticus zur Pešiṭto zum Propheten Jesaia* (BZAW 8, 1905).

[4] L. G. Running, *An Investigation of the Syriac Version of Isaiah* (Ph.D. dissertation, John Hopkins University, Baltimore, 1964).

[5] P. E. Pusey and G. H. Gwilliam, *Tetraeuangelium Sanctum, the Fourfold Holy Gospel in the Peshitta Syriac Version with Critical Apparatus*, with an introduction by Andreas Juckel (Piscataway, NJ, 2003), a reprint of the 1901 edition.

consonantal tier is substantially ancient, the vocalism and orthographic tiers are quite late.

The departure point in preparing this text was an electronic version of the Mosul text, in East Syriac, that was kindly provided by Bethmardootha, Duhok, Iraq. This text was proof-read against the Mosul edition and corrected, in East Syriac, by Dayroyo Joseph Bali of Mor Ephrem Syriac Orthodox Seminary, Ma'arrat Saydnaya, Syria. The text was then converted by George Kiraz into the West Syriac Serṭo script and search-and-replace procedures were applied in order to approximate a West Syriac vocalization. The text was then proof read for a second and third time by Kiraz and Bali against the Mosul edition, adapting our text fully to the West Syriac orthographic tradition. Andreas Juckel checked the final text.

As the Mosul edition did not fully mark Rukkākhā and Quššāyā, these points were added and a regular expression[6] was applied to the text to ensure that all *bgādkpāt* letters are marked. When the consonantal orthography, and in many cases the vocalic orthography, of East and West Syriac diverged, use was made of Lee's 1823 edition[7] as well as linguistic resources including Audo,[8] Brockelmann,[9] Margoliouth,[10] and Smith.[11] As for Rukkākhā and Quššāyā pointing, analogies were made internally within other Mosul readings,[12] and externally with the Pusey and Gwilliam New Testament text, making use of my *Concordance*[13] as a tool and the guidelines presented in my introduction to spirantization.[14] The Mbaṭṭlānā and Marhṭānā were added systematically following current orthographic

---

[6] In computing, a regular expression provides a mechanism with which strings of text can be matched with a search criterion. In most notations, a bracket expression matches a single character inside that bracket (e.g., [ab] matches a single *a* or *b*). The exclamation mark denotes negation. Hence, the expression [bgdkpt][!RQ] (where R and Q represent the Rukkākhā and Quššāyā points, respectively) will match a single *bgādkpāt* letter that is *not* followed by a Rukkākhā or Quššāyā point. When this search fails, all *bgādkpāt* letters have been pointed (regardless of accuracy of course).

[7] S. Lee, *Vetus et Novum Testamentum Syriace* (London, 1823).

[8] T. Audo, ܣܝ̈ܡܐ ܕܠܫܢܐ ܣܘܪܝܝܐ (Mosul, 1897).

[9] C. Brockelmann, *Lexicon Syriacum* (1928).

[10] J. P. Smith (Mrs. Margoliouth), A *Compendious Syriac Dictionary Founded upon the Thesaurus Syriacus* (Oxford, 1903).

[11] P. Smith, *Thesaurus Syriacus* (Oxford, 1818-1895).

[12] For example, ܟ̈ܠܝ in Is. 15:8 is unmarked, but the *Taw* is marked with a Quššāyā point in ܟܠܝ̈ in the same verse.

[13] G. A. Kiraz, *A Computer Generated Concordance to the Syriac New Testament*, 6 volumes (Leiden, 1993).

[14] G. A. Kiraz, *Introduction to Syriac Spirantization, Rukkâkâ and Quššâyâ* (Losser, 1995).

conventions,[15] but the Mhaggyānā, Nāgudā, and Mṭappyānā, all ubiquitous in the Mosul text, were removed as they are alien to West Syriac orthography.[16]

The text was then collated against existing collations, most notably the Leiden apparatus but also the aforementioned collations of Diettrich and Running. It was interesting to note how close the Mosul text was to the readings of the manuscripts of the first millennium, in itself a testimony to the faithfulness of second millennium manuscripts, upon which Mosul was based, to the earlier text. Leiden and Mosul differed in ca. 185 readings; i.e., ca. three variants per chapter. In 41% of the time, the Mosul text was supported by a reading from the fifth, sixth, or seventh century (and 91% of those were sixth century readings). Recall that the Leiden text is based on MS 7a1 from the seventh century. In 80% of the time, the Mosul text was supported by a reading from the first millennium. It is also worth noting that 66 of the total 185 variants pertain to the addition or omission of *bdwl* prefixes, and 14 variants pertain to the existence or lack thereof of *Syāme*. Appendix 2 gives the variants of our text against the Leiden edition.

Orthographic Diversions from Leiden and Mosul

In terms of the consonantal tier, the present text differs orthographically from the Leiden and Mosul texts in two ways. Firstly, it intentionally replaces early Syriac orthographic conventions, most of which are also preserved in the East Syriac Mosul text, with West Syriac ones.[17] For example, Leiden and Mosul ܗܘܝ (perf. 3rd fem. pl.) is replaced in the present edition with ܗܘ̈ܝ adding *Syāme* and the suffix ܝ (Isa. 3:16); Leiden and Mosul ܣܡܟ is replaced with ܢܐܡܣ adding medial ܐ (Isa. 26:19); Leiden and Mosul ܪܝܫ is replaced with ܪܝܫ adding ܝ (Isa. 2:2 and elsewhere, Leiden has both forms). In some cases, the Leiden orthography is preserved against Mosul; e.g., ܘܡܟܘܠܬܗ against Mosul ܘܡܟܕܝܬܗ (Isa. 1:14).

---

[15] For instance, the Mbaṭlānā is used here to denote silent letters in verbal forms; e.g., ܗܘ̈ܝ (Isa. 3:16).

[16] On these symbols, see C. J. David, *Grammaire de la Langue Araméenne*, 2 volumes, (Mosul, 2nd ed., 1896) §62, §67.

[17] On orthography, see L. Van Rompay, 'Some Preliminary Remarks on the Origins of Classical Syriac as a Standard Langauge. The Syriac Version of Eusebius of Caesarea's Ecclesiastical History', in G. Goldenberg and S. Raz (eds.), *Semitic and Cushitic Studies* (Wiesbaden, 2004), 70-89; S. P. Brock, 'Some Diachronic Features of Classical Syriac', in M. F. J. Baasten and W. Th. Van Peursen (eds.), *Hamlet on the Hill. Semitic and Greek Studies Presented to Professor T. Muraoka on the Occasion of his Sixty-Fifth Birthday* (Louvain, 2003), 95-111.

Secondly, as one of the objectives of the present edition is to provide a functional text for religious communities, it was necessary to be systematic and to provide the reader with a standardized orthography. Hence, many contractions were systematically separated; e.g., Leiden ܕܣܟܝܢ ܗܘ was chosen over Mosul ܕܣܟܝܢܗܘ (Isa. 33:2), and Leiden ܘܐܠܘ ܠܐ over Mosul ܘܐܠܘܠܐ (Isa. 1:9). MS evidence and/or Lee's edition give support to most, if not all, of these changes.

Orthographic Diversions from Mosul

As for the vocalic tier, the present text differs from the Mosul text in a number of ways.

E. Syr. ◌ܶ was generally converted to the corresponding W. Syr. ◌ܶ except in lexemes where the E. and W. Syriac orthographies vary; e.g., E. Syr. ܬܘܣܦ̈ܬܐ vs. W. Syr. ܬܘܣܦܬܐ (Isa. 15:9).

E. Syr. ◌ܳ was generally converted to W. Syr. ◌ܳ except when followed by ܘ in which case it became ◌ܰ; e.g., E. Syr. ܒܝܘ̈ܡܝ vs. W. Syr. ܒܝܘ̈ܡܝ (Isa. 1:1). This also applies to nominal forms when followed by an enclitic demonstrative pronoun; e.g., E. Syr. ܛܠܐ ܗܘ vs. W. Syr. ܛܠܐ ܗܘ (Isa. 26:19). By extension, E. Syr. ܗܳܕܶܐ ܗܝ became W. Syr. ܗܳܕܶܐ ܗܝ (Isa. 14:26).

E. Syr. ◌ܺ was generally converted to W. Syr. ◌ܺ except in lexemes where the E. and W. orthographies vary; e.g., E. Syr. ܡܝ̈ܐ vs. W. Syr. ܡܝ̈ܐ (Isa. 15:6).

E. Syr. ◌ܻ was mapped to either ◌ܺ or ◌ܽ depending on the phonological, morphological or lexical context; e.g., ܝܶ became ܝܺ in ܬܐܘܪܚܘܢ (Isa. 34:14) but ܝܽ in ܬܐܠܚܘܢ (Isa. 34:13); ܡܩܦܝܢ became ܡܩܦܢܐ (Isa. 3:14). (See above for ܗܳܕܶܐ ܗܝ vs. ܗܳܕܶܐ ܗܝ.)

E. Syr. ܝܼ was converted to W. Syr. ◌ܽܝ, while E. Syr. ܘܿ and ܘܼ were collapsed into W. Syr. ܘ◌ܽ. The choice was made to place the vowel on the consonant preceding the matres lectionis.

Metathesis was applied to the sequence ʼV resulting in Vʼ; e.g., E. Syr. ܕܒܢܝ̈ܗܘܢ vs. W. Syr. ܕܒܢܝ̈ܗܘܢ (Isa. 1:1). In CʼV-initial stems prefixed with *bdwl* letters, this led to further vocalization changes on the prefixes; e.g., E. Syr. ܒܬܠܐ vs. ܒܬܠܐ (Isa. 50:2) where the ◌ܶ shifted to ܒ and the ◌ܰ was deleted.

The Mbaṭṭlānā was applied in the present text following the Pusey and Gwilliam tradition but with further extensions following contemporary orthographic conventions; e.g., ܘܪܒܝܬ (Isa. 1:2), ܘܪܒܝܬܘ (Isa. 1:10). In at least one case, E. and W. Syr. differ: E. ܠܒܘܢܬܐ vs. W. ܠܒܘܢܬܐ (Isa. 60:6 and elsewhere).

Only a few readings in Mosul were rejected, which seem to be typographical errors: Isa. 37:13 ܘܥܘܐ (M ܘܥܘܐ); Isa. 51:2 ܕܝܠܕܬܟܘܢ (M

ܘܕܚܝܠܬܐ); Isa. 58:10 ܘܪ̈ܬܐ (M ܘܪ̈ܬܐ). Additionally, verse 54:17 is numbered ܣܚ in M.

Text Organization

The division of the text into chapters and verses is a recent Western phenomenon. Early manuscripts divided the texts into chapters, called in Syriac ܩܦܠܐܘܢ, abbreviated ܩܦ, or ܨܚܚܐ, abbreviated ܨܚ. Having said that, ancient manuscripts do not always follow a systematic approach in these chapter divisions. The present text follows the recent Western division of chapters, naming each chapter in Syriac ܩܦܠܐܘܢ. Ancient Syriac chapter divisions are given in the outer margin preceded by the abbreviation ܨܚ for ܨܚܚܐ (they correspond to Roman numerals in the English translation). These were adapted from Brock's list of the system used in the majority of ancient manuscripts.[18]

The versification of the Mosul edition differs somewhat from the Leiden edition. The present edition follows the Mosul versification. See Appendix 1 for a list of differences.

Ancient manuscripts vary in the application of punctuation marks. The punctuation presented here follows the Mosul punctuation faithfully.

Acknowledgements

This text and translation project benefit from a number of scholars who were involved in its discussion and planning at various stages and in various capacities: Sebastian P. Brock, Terry Falla, Andreas Juckel, Alison Salvesen, Richard Taylor, Beryl Turner, Lucas Van Rompay, and Peter Williams.

Andreas Juckel, my co-editor in the Ṣurath Kthob series, played a major role in setting the textual policies of the edition and helped in the collation of readings. As this is the first volume in a larger project, the translation style and methodology adopted by Gillian Greenberg and Donald M. Walter will no doubt serve as a model for subsequent volumes.

This project would have taken much longer to complete if it were not for the electronic text provided by Fr. Shlimon Yesho Khoshaba of Beth Mardootha, Duhok, Iraq (not to be confused with Beth Mardutho The Syriac Institute, Piscataway, NJ, under whose auspices this project is carried out).

---

[18] The Peshiṭta Institute, *The Old Testament in Syriac According to the Peshiṭta Version*, Part III, fascicle 1, Isaiah, prepared by S. P. Brock (Leiden, 1987) xxvii-xxviii.

I am personally grateful to my wife Christine and three children: Tabetha Gabriella, Sebastian Kenoro, and Lucian Nurono. They always have to compete for my attention which I ought to give them rather than the various projects which take over my time. I most especially enjoyed proofing the text against Mosul for Isa. 1:1-15, 32:1-4, and 44:6-8 as ten-year-old Tabetha offered to help, maybe just to spend more time with ܟ݂ܐܒ݂ܐ. I would read the Mosul text, in Western pronunciation, and Tabetha would check the Serṭo text, always pointing out the number of Rukkākhā and Quššāyā marks, the existence or lack of *Syāme*, and any punctuation marks. On a long car trip to Long Island, seven-year-old Kenoro and Tabetha counted from a list the number of variants of the text against the various ancient manuscripts from the Leiden apparatus according to century, often checking their results against each other.

It is hoped that the current edition will be a motivation for further texts and translations of the Syriac Biblical tradition, and will stimulate the use of the Peshiṭta in educational and religious settings.

ABBREVIATIONS

ASV	American Standard Version (1901)
BCE	Before the Common Era
CE	Common Era
com.	common
ed.	editor
e.g.	exempli gratia
fem.	feminine
i.e.	id est
impf	imperfect
IO	Index Orthographicus
ISC	Inner-Syriac Corruption
lit.	literally
M	Mosul
masc.	masculine
ms	manuscript
mss	manuscripts
MT	Masoretic Text
om.	omit
P	Peshiṭta
part.	participle
pl.	plural
pr.	prior, before
sing.	singular
v.	verse
vol.	volume
1st	first person
2nd	second person
3rd	third person
√	Root (see the appropriate dictionary listed in the Bibliography for citations such as √II)

Introduction to the Translation

By Gillian Greenberg and Donald M. Walter

The Peshiṭta

The Peshiṭta, the Syriac translation of the Hebrew Bible, was made in Edessa in the second century CE. Most students of this text believe that it was translated not by a single man but by members of a 'Peshiṭta school'. The translators of the Peshiṭta wrote for Syriac speakers, whose main desire was to be able to access the Hebrew Old Testament in their own tongue. Their task was that of the great majority of translators: to produce a text which reads well, not as a stilted literal rendering of the source document, but which was at the same time a faithful translation of the Hebrew of their *Vorlage*. They succeeded admirably, and the Peshiṭta has been enormously important in the history of Syriac as a literary and liturgical language in Christianity in the East.

Whether these ancient translators were Jews or Christians is a much debated question; as yet, there is no universally accepted answer. A number of modern scholars believe that both Jews and Christians were involved at different times. According to this theory, at the time when the work began, the community in which the Peshiṭta school was based was Jewish. At this time, however, the young Christian church in the area was gaining strength, and during subsequent decades, as the translation progressed, the community converted to Christianity; so the work was begun by Jews and finished by Christians. Whatever the uncertainties pertaining to this work, one thing is clear: the Peshiṭta has stood the test of time. We hope that our translation will make the pleasure of reading it available to many more readers.

The Book of Isaiah

The Hebrew text of Isaiah has been well preserved both in the Masoretic Text and in a number of manuscripts, one almost complete and others fragmentary, found at Qumran. Most modern critics agree that the book can be divided into three main sections, chapters 1–39, 40–55, and 56–66. These divisions are largely based on reference to historical events and

individuals, and to differences in theological concepts and in the style of the Hebrew. The oracles of the first 39 chapters are today widely attributed to the eighth century prophet Isaiah whose name is given in the title of the book, who lived in Jerusalem. His prophetic ministry, according to the opening verse, lasted for approximately forty years, from about 740 to 700 BCE, in the reigns of the Judean kings Uzziah, Jotham, Ahaz, and Hezekiah. During this period Assyria was the dominant power in the area, threatening the existence of Judah, Israel, and neighboring states. Chapters 40–55 are currently attributed by most critics to a different prophet, 'Second' or 'Deutero'-Isaiah, writing in Babylon during the period of the exile. A third prophet, 'Trito'-Isaiah, resident in Palestine after 538 BCE, is today widely credited with the authorship of the final chapters 56–66. It must be emphasized, however, that this division of the biblical book is not universally accepted, and that even those critics who do accept the theory of multiple authorship are by no means in agreement concerning either the attribution of the various chapters or the sequence in which they were written.

Translation Policy

Our task was different from that which faced the scholars who wrote the Peshiṭta: our readership has different priorities. We were writing for people who want an English translation of the Syriac text, but who also want to be able to use this translation to help them follow and understand the Syriac, in which they are not all completely fluent. With this readership in mind we had to resist the strong temptation to try to write elegant and idiomatic English; rather, our English translation adheres as closely as possible to the Syriac text, facilitating a word-by-word comparison. It is not absolutely 'literal'; for instance, word order often cannot be preserved, for to do so would result in garbled English, but it is well to the 'literal' end of the scale of translation technique which ranges from 'free' to 'literal'.

Notes

The notes in the main text have two main purposes:

(i) At passages where a rendering close to the Syriac text would have resulted in unacceptable English, we have given a comparatively free rendering in the verse and a literal translation in the notes, e.g.

1:7. ܘܗܦܟܐ ܐܟܣܢܝܐ 'overthrown by strangers': lit. 'a ruin of strangers'.

32:13. ܒܬܐ ܕܚܕܘܬܐ 'joyful houses': lit. 'houses of joy'.

(ii) Sometimes, more than one translation is equally correct; here we have given the alternative in the notes, e.g.

21:2. ܛܠܘܡܐ ܛܠܡ 'the oppressor oppresses' or 'the deceiver deceives'.
38:3. ܡܫܰܠܡܐ 'perfect' or 'whole'.

Translation Technique

1. Additions. Some words in our translation have no equivalent in the Syriac text. These fall into two groups:

(i) Words shown between round brackets, added because the sense benefits from them, e.g.

- 1:22. ܣܘܚܪ̈ܢܝܟܝ ܚܠܛܝܢ ܡܝ̈ܐ 'your tavern-keepers mix water' rendered as 'your tavern-keepers mix (the wine with) water'.
- 4:1. ܠܚܡܢ ܢܐܟܘܠ 'we will eat our bread' rendered as 'we will eat our (own) bread'.
- 33:17. ܘܠܒܟ ܢܐܠܦ ܕܚܠܬܐ 'and your heart will learn the awe' rendered as 'and your heart will learn the awe (of him)'.
- 44:10. ܘܓܒܠܝܢ ܢܣܟ̈ܐ 'and fashioning molten', rendered as 'fashioning molten (images)'.
- 59:12. ܘܚܛܗ̈ܝܢ ܣܗܕܘܢ 'our sins testified us' rendered as 'our sins testified (against) us'.

(ii) Words added to conform to English idiom. These are not bracketed, e.g.

- 42:6. lit. ܘܝܗܒܬܟ ܩܝܡܐ ܠܥܡܐ lit. 'I gave you a covenant to the people': 'as' added: 'I gave you as a covenant to the people' .
- 42:22. ܦܚ̈ܐ ܐܢܘܢ ܟܠܗܘܢ ܓܪ̈ܘܐ lit. 'they are traps all their youths': 'for' added 'they are traps for all their youths'.
- 44:21. ܓܒܠܬܟ ܠܝ ܥܒܕܐ lit. 'I formed you a servant to me': 'to be' added: 'I formed you to be a servant to me'.

2. Consistency. We have given consistent translations wherever possible, but some exceptions were enforced either by the context or by differences between the range of meanings of some words in the two languages.

(i) More than one English word correctly translates one Syriac word, e.g.

- 1:4. ܙܪܥܐ 'seed' or 'offspring', which is given as an alternative at 45:25.
- 3:5. ܥܡܐ is translated as 'people', not as is more commonly the case in this translation as 'nation'. The context describes chaos on a small, personal, scale; in 42:6 ܥܡܐ, ܥܡ̈ܡܐ are rendered respectively as 'people' and 'nations'. The difference is not required by any difference between the singular and plural, but to give good sense.

- 3:14. ܕܝܢܐ ‘judgment’; 32:1. ‘justice’. This is an example of the process of ‘semantic borrowing’ in which the complete word already exists in the borrowing language, but its meaning in that language is extended to include an additional meaning which it already has in the lending language.
- 4:4. ܪܘܚܐ ‘wind’ or ‘spirit’.
- 13:12. ܐܢܫܐ ‘man’; 44:11. ܒܢܝ̈ܢܫܐ ‘sons of man’ or ‘mankind’.
- 14:7. ܒܬܫܒܘܚܬܐ ‘in praise’ or ‘in a hymn’.
- 63:1. √ܦܪܩ ‘salvation’ or ‘redemption’ as at 63:4.

(ii) One English word correctly translates more than one Syriac word, e.g.

- 36:2. ܘܩܡ ܒܡܣܩܬܐ ܕܒܪܟܬܐ ܥܠܝܬܐ ‘he was standing at the upper part of the upper pool’, ‘upper’ rendering roots ܣܠܩ and ܥܠ.
- 44:5. ܘܗܢܐ ܢܩܪܐ ܒܫܡܗ ܕܝܥܩܘܒ ... ܘܒܫܡ ܐܝܣܪܝܠ ܢܬܟܢܐ ‘this one will call on the name of Jacob … by the name of Israel he will be called’, ‘call’ rendering roots ܩܪܐ and ܟܢܐ.

(iii) Repetition of a Syriac word where repetition in English would be clumsy, e.g.

- 14:4. ܐܝܟܢܐ ܒܛܠ ܫܠܝܛܐ ܘܒܛܠ ܡܫܩܛܢܐ ‘How has the ruler come to naught, he who incites failed?’, ‘come to naught’ and ‘failed’ both rendering √ܒܛܠ.
- 44:20. ܘܡܛܥܝܢܐ ܗܘ ܛܥܝܢ ‘the wanderers go astray’, ‘wanderers’ and ‘go astray’ (an infinitive absolute) both rendering √ܛܥܐ.
- 60:7. ܘܒܝܬܐ ܕܬܫܒܘܚܬܝ ܐܫܒܚ ‘I will praise the house of my glory’, ‘praise’ and ‘my glory’ both rendering √ܫܒܚ.
- 66:5. ܫܡܥܘ ܦܬܓܡܗ ܕܡܪܝܐ ‘Hear the word of the Lord’; ܕܙܝܥܝܢ ܡܢ ܡܠܬܗ ‘those who tremble at his word’: ‘word’ is used both for ܦܬܓܡܐ and ܡܠܬܐ.

3. Syriac Usages. The following Syriac usages are noted:

(i) Singular and Plural:

a. Syriac singular rendered by English plural, e.g.

- 22:1. ܠܐܓܪܐ ‘onto the rooftop(s)’.
- 33:8. ܘܐܢܫܐ ܠܐ ܐܬܚܫܒܘ ‘men not respected’: collective noun, with plural verb.
- 52:15. ܢܐܚܕܘܢ ܡܠܟ̈ܐ ܦܘܡܗܘܢ ‘kings will shut their mouth(s)’.

b. Syriac plural rendered by English singular, e.g.

- 29:6. ܘܒܪ̈ܥܡܐ ‘with thunder’.

(ii) Syriac finite verb with *dālath* rendered by English infinitive, e.g.

– 5:2. ܘܣܟܝ ܕܢܥܒܕ ܥܢܒܐ ‘he waited for it to bear grapes’ lit. ‘he waited that it would bear grapes’.

(iii) √ܝܣܦ ‘to add’, e.g.

– 1:13. ܠܐ ܬܘܣܦܘܢ ܠܡܝܬܝܘ ܠܝ ‘do not again bring me ... ’ lit. ‘do not add to bring’.

(iv) ܡܢܐ ܠ ‘what to ... ’, e.g.

– 22:1. ܡܢܐ ܐܝܬ ܠܟܝ ‘what concerns you?’ lit. ‘what is to you?’.

(v) Regular Syriac equivalent, e.g.

– 3:15. ܡܪܝܐ ܚܝܠܬܢܐ ‘the mighty Lord’: in this context, this is the regular P rendering of יהוה צבאות ‘the Lord of hosts’.

(vi) *Waw* ܘ. This conjunction has a wide range of meanings, e.g.

a. Commonly omitted in translation, when used as an introduction to a verse or phrse:

– 56:7. ܩܘܪ̈ܒܢܝܗܘܢ ܘܕܒ̈ܚܝܗܘܢ ‘their offerings and their sacrifices’: the commonest usage.

– 4:1. ܘܢܐܚ̈ܕܢ ܫܒܥ ܢܫܝܢ lit. ‘And seven women will seize’: at the beginning of many verses *waw* does not fit well in the context, in English, and we have omitted it.

c. ‘yet’:

– 5:25. ܘܒܟܠܗܝܢ ܗܠܝܢ ܠܐ ܗܦܟ ܪܘܓܙܗ ‘yet for all these his anger has not turned away’.

d. ‘or’:

– 6:10. ܕܠܐ ܢܚܙܐ ܒܥܝ̈ܢܘܗܝ ܘܢܫܡܥ ܒܐܕ̈ܢܘܗܝ ‘it will not see with its eyes or hear with its ears’.

e. ‘so that’, ‘such that’:

– 10:19. ܠܡܢܝܢܐ ܢܗܘܘܢ ܘܛܠܝܐ ܢܟܬܘܒ ܐܢܘܢ ‘will be very few, so that a young child might write them down’.

f. ‘nor’:

– 17:8. ܘܠܐ ܢܚܘܪ ܒܦܬܟܪ̈ܐ ܘܒܡܬܟܠܬܐ ‘he will not look upon idols, nor upon false gods’.

g. ‘but’:

– 40:8. ܘܡܠܬܗ ܕܐܠܗܢ ܩܝܡܐ ܠܥܠܡܝܢ ‘but the word of our God stands firm for ever’.

(vii) ܠܡܐ: a composite of ܠ, and ܡܐ to form an interrogative particle, e.g.

– 49:24. ܠܡܐ ܡܬܕܒܪܐ ܕܒܪܬܗ ܕܓܢܒܪܐ ‘Shall the prey of the mighty be carried off?’

(viii) ܕܠܡܐ: a composite of ܕ, ܠ, and ܡܐ to mean 'lest', which is also used as an interrogative particle introducing a question to which a negative answer is expected, e.g.

– 45:9. ܕܠܡܐ ܐܡܪ ܛܝܢܐ ܠܦܚܪܐ ... ܘܠܐ ܗܘܝܬ ܥܒܕܐ ܕܐܝܕܝܟ 'Shall the clay say to the potter ... "I was not the work of your hands"?'

(ix) Ethical dative.

– 31:8. ܘܢܥܪܘܩ ܠܗ 'he will flee': lit. 'and he will flee himself'. Neither the *lāmadh* nor the objective pronoun can be rendered in acceptable English.

(ix) Attributive genitive.

– 11:9. ܒܟܠܗ ܛܘܪܐ ܕܩܘܕܫܝ 'on all my holy mountain', lit. 'the mountain of my holiness'.

(x) Imperfect or imperative.

– 2:9. ܘܠܐ ܬܫܒܘܩ ܠܗܘܢ 'do not forgive them' or 'you will not forgive them': the imperfect (with a negative) may also function as a negative imperative.

(xi) The verb 'to say'.

– 37:10. ܠܡܐܡܪ: this form, the infinitive construct, is regularly used to render MT לאמר 'to say' or 'saying'.

(xii) 'Other than'.

– 26:13. ܠܒܪ ܡܢܟ 'other than you', lit. 'outside from you', ܠܒܪ metaphorically used here to mean 'except, beyond'. This construction is often used of God, and also by God when it is written ܠܒܪ ܡܢܝ 'none other than me'. Sometimes ܠܝܬ ܬܘܒ or ܬܘܒ is included, adding emphasis, as at e.g. 45:5 ܘܠܝܬ ܬܘܒ ܠܒܪ ܡܢܝ lit. 'none again except me'.

Mistranslation

There are a number of passages where the difference between the Hebrew and the Syriac seems to be due to error by the translator. These are set out in Addendum 1.

Inner-Syriac Corruption

Passages where corruption of the text seems to have occurred during transmission are set out in Addendum 2. That section covers only passages where either all Syriac mss (cited in the Leiden Edition of the Peshiṭta of Isaiah) have the possible corruption, or only Mosul has the variant (as in 65:12). The Leiden Edition of the Peshiṭta of Isaiah gives many places

where only some mss, which were collated for that Edition, have an Inner-Syriac Corruption.

Meaning Obscure

There are a number of passages where although the meaning of individual words in the Hebrew is clear, the sense of the passage as a whole is obscure. The translator usually renders so as to arrive at an intelligible text, sometimes working more freely than usual, and sometimes even abdicates his responsibility and gives an atomistic rendering. There is an example at 8:21 where the referents in MT cannot be identified with certainty, and the lack of clarity in P 'He will pass over it, he will harden it, and he will hunger; when he has hungered he will be enraged, he will revile his king and his God' may reflect this difficulty. Chapter 28 includes several particularly difficult passages, with a good representative in the first verse: 'the garland which dishonors the might of his glory at the head of the fertile valley'. Some examples are set out in Addendum 3.

Names

The spelling of proper names in this translation normally follows that of the American Standard Version (ASV) of 1901. In this section names are considered where the Peshiṭta and the Hebrew differ consonantally. The citations are usually of the first occurrence of the name in Isaiah. These are set out in Appendix 3.

Addendum 1: Mistranslation

8:20 ܣܘܚܕܐ 'bribe'. MT שחר, either √III שחר where the root-meaning includes 'magic, malicious power,' or the noun 'dawn'. Both P and LXX have rendered שחד, suggesting either that this was the spelling in both *Vorlagen*, or that both translators made the same error. It is possible that P was influenced by the translation in LXX.

13:15 ܘܡܬܘܣܦܝܢ 'who are added'. √יסף 'to add' was wrongly perceived in MT הנספה 'who will be caught': the correct root ספה in the Niphal is 'to be caught'.

14:6 ܘܠܐ ܚܣܟܘ 'they did not resist'. √סרר 'to be stubborn' was wrongly perceived in MT בלתי סרה 'that did not cease': the correct root is סור 'to remove'.

14:10 ܐܬܐܫܠܡܬ ܠܢ 'been delivered up to us'. MT נמשלת אלינו 'be made like us'. A subconscious metathesis of *lamadh* and *mim* caused the error.

14:11 ܡܝܬ ܟܢܪܟ 'your harp has died'. √מות 'to die' was wrongly perceived in MT המית נבליך 'the music of your lutes': the correct root is המה 'to murmur'.

14:12 ܐܝܠܠ 'cry out'. MT הילל 'shining one'. √ילל 'to howl' was wrongly perceived in MT הילל 'shining one': the correct root is I הלל 'to shine'.

16:1 ܐܫܕܪ ܠܒܪ ܫܠܝܛܐ 'I will send the son of the ruler'. בר 'son' was wrongly perceived in MT כר 'lamb'.

16:4 ܕܡܫܚܩܐ 'reduced to dust' lit. 'minute' or 'dust'. MT המץ 'extortioner': probable guess at an unfamiliar Hebrew word.

17:9 ܐܝܟ ܓܘܒܐ ܕܫܬܩ 'like the silent well'. √II חרש 'to be dumb' was wrongly perceived in MT כעזובת החרש 'like forsaken places': the correct root is perhaps √III חרש, 'forest,' but inner-Hebrew corruption is possible. For MT כעזובת, √עזב 'to leave' the translator then needed a word which would fit his use of 'silent': a disused, abandoned well would be silent.

18:1 ܐܪܥܐ ܕܛܠܠܐ ܕܓܦܐ 'the land of the shadow of wings'. MT ארץ צלצל כנפים 'the land of whirring wings'. √III צלל 'to throw shadows' was wrongly perceived, rather than צלצל as a noun. Alternatively, the translator may have equated צ with ט, as is etymologically possible.

19:9 ܠܚܕܘܬܐ 'for joy'. ידה was wrongly perceived in MT חורי 'white (stuff)': the correct root is חור 'to be white'. The translator may have misread *resh* as *dalath*; he may also have been subconsciously influenced by the similarity of √II ידה 'to give thanks' to the Syriac √ܚܕܐ 'to be glad'.

19:10 ܟܠ ܕܥܒܕܝܢ ܫܟܪܐ ܠܡܫܬܝܐ ܕܢܦܫܐ 'all who make strong drink for the feast of the soul'. √שכר 'be or become drunk' was wrongly perceived in עשׂי שׂכר אגמי־נפשׁ, √שׂכר, 'the workers for hire sad of soul'. 'Feast' may be a guess, prompted by the theme of strong drink.

19:13 ܐܬܬܪܝܡܘ 'have become haughty'. √נשׂא 'to lift' was wrongly perceived in MT נשאו 'are deceived': the correct root is II נשא 'to deceive'.

21:5 ܕܣܟܘ ܣ̈ܟܘܝܐ 'watchmen, watch'. √I צפה 'to keep watch' was wrongly perceived in MT צפה הצפית 'spread the carpet': the correct root is II צפה 'to lay over, out'.

21:9 ܚܨܕ 'reaping': the translator seems to have read the initial מ in MT(21:10) מדשתי 'My threshed one' as מן 'from' and perhaps given 'reaping' as an approximate rendering of a mistakenly perceived דשא 'grass'. ܘܡܢ ܒܠܐ 'without' could perhaps come from a misreading of MT בן־גרני 'child of my threshing-floor' as בלי גרני. The sense is further obscured by the verse division which differs from that in MT, where the break occurs earlier, following 'shattered on the ground'.

22:3 ܟܠܗܘܢ ܡܫܠܛܢܝܟܝ ܒܗ ܐܣܛܝܘ 'all your rulers have staggered together'. Perhaps an example of 'Syromanie' in which the translator is subconsciously influenced by resemblance of the sound of a Hebrew root to a Syriac root. In MT כל־קציניך נדדו־יחד 'all your rulers have fled together' the root-meaning 'to stagger' is present in √I נדד though the more usual meaning is 'retreat, flee': the choice of √ܢܕ may show influence from the similarity of the sounds.

22:6 ܫܘܪܐ 'city wall'. MT קיר here probably a place-name, though the location is uncertain, rather than 'wall'.

24:6 ܡܛܠ ܗܠܝܢ ܒܐܒܠܐ ܬܬܒ ܐܪܥܐ 'Because of these things the earth will dwell in mourning'. In an unvocalized text, אֵלֶּה 'these' was wrongly perceived in MT אָלָה 'curse'. אבלה 'devoured' was misread as אבלה 'mourning'.

25:5 ܡܘܥܝܬܐ 'the shoot'. MT זמיר 'the song'. Possibly, √II זמר was perceived rather than √I זמר: √II זמר is used for the trimming of vines, which may have introduced the sense of 'shoot'.

26:10 ܡܟܣܢܘܬܐ ܒܐܪܥܐ ܡܬܩܢܐ 'reproof in the land corrects'. √נכה 'to smite' was wrongly perceived in MT בארץ נכחות יעול 'in an upright land he acts wickedly': the correct root is נכח 'front, straight'. The translator perceived not √נכח but √נכה 'to smite'. Having perceived 'reproof' he could not render the contrast of MT.

27:4 ܫܘܪܐ 'wall'. חומה was wrongly perceived in MT חמה 'wrath'.

27:8 ܒܣܐܬܐ 'by the seah'. סאה 'seah' was wrongly perceived in the difficult MT בסאסאה, probably 'by driving it away, by scaring it'. ܕܐܟܝܠ '(with) which he measured' is a mistranslation of MT בשלחה 'with sending away', presumably deliberate, determined by the misreading of בסאסאה. √II הגה in MT הגה 'he removed' was wrongly perceived as √I הגה which includes the sense 'to meditate', rendered as ܒܪܢܝܗ 'by that which he thought'.

28:1 ܘܠܟܠܝܠܐ ܕܡܨܥܪ 'and to the garland which dishonors'. MT וציץ נבל 'the fading blossom'. Rather than √I נבל 'to wither' the translator has read √II נבל 'to be foolish'.

28:21 ܒܡܥܒܪܬܐ 'in the pass'. MT פרצים is usually understood as the name of the mountain. The translator has understood the name as a noun פרץ 'breach' which suggested 'pass'.

29:10 ܥܠ ܥܝܢܝܗܘܢ ܘܥܠ ܢܒܝܐ 'upon their eyes and upon the prophets'. This differs from MT where the punctuation gives the sense that the prophets are the people's eyes: 'upon your eyes, upon the prophets'.

33:3 ܡܢ ܩܠܐ ܕܣܠܕܟ lit. 'At the sound of your awe, fear'. MT מקול המון 'At the sound of tumult'. The translator perhaps perceived not המון, but המן 'rage'.

48:17 ܕܠܐ ܠܥܘܠܐ 'that you will not do wrong'. √ܥܘܠ 'to do wrong' was wrongly perceived in MT להועיל 'to succeed', as √יעל 'to benefit'. Possible Syromanie; see 22:3.

51:14 ܒܚܒܠܐ 'by destruction'. √שחת 'to go to ruin' was wrongly perceived in MT לשחת. The correct understanding is 'to the pit': שחת is a noun.

51:20 ܣܠܩܐ ܕܟܡܝܫ 'flabby beet'. The translator did not understand the rare word תוא, and went for help to the LXX in which MT כתוא מכמר 'snared oryx' is rendered as 'half-cooked turnip', apparently taking מכמר as derived not from √II כמר 'to cast a net' but from √I כמר 'to be hot'.

54:7 ܒܪܘܓܙܐ ܙܥܘܪܐ 'small rage'. MT ברגע קטן 'small moment'. The translator misread רגע 'moment' as רגז 'rage'.

64:1 ܠܐ ܦܬܚܬ ܫܡܝܐ 'did you not open the heavens' or 'you did not open the heavens'. The conjunction לוא 'Oh that' in MT 63:19, לוא־קרעת שמים 'Oh that you had torn open the heavens', was misread as the negative לא.

65:5 ܒܪܘܓܙܝ 'in my anger'. The translation of אף as 'anger' in MT באפי 'in my nostrils' is technically correct but 'nostrils' fits the context better.

Addendum 2: Inner-Syriac Corruption.

1:5 ܘܬܘܣܦܘܢ ܠܡܬܪܕܝܘ 'again be chastised'. MT תוסיפו סרה 'rebel again'. √ܡܪܕ 'revolt' would render MT √סור. Miswriting, perhaps in a lapse of concentration perceiving the initial *mim* as the initial letter of an infinitive, could have resulted in the present form.

3:8 ܠܥܢܢܐ ܕܐܝܩܪܗ 'against the cloud of his glory' or 'to the cloud of his glory'. MT למרות עני כבודו 'to defy the cloud of his glory'. It is difficult to give an acceptable translation of the Syriac preposition *lāmadh* in this context; possibly a verb rendering למרות has been lost, giving the *lāmadh* the sense of an object marker rather than the initial letter of an infinitive construct.

8:14 ܛܪܢܐ 'flint'. MT צור 'rock'. An original ܛܘܪܐ 'rock' was possibly corrupted during transmission.

9:1 ܐܘܚܕܢܐ 'possession'. MT (8:23) והאחרון 'the last'. An original ܐܚܪܝܐ 'the last' possibly corrupted during transmission, writing *dālath nun* instead of *resh yodh*.

10:9 ܒܠܝܘ 'Balyo'. MT כלנו 'Calno'. At some point during transmission the initial *kaph* miswritten as *beth*, and *yodh* for *nun*.

10:14 ܒܢܬܐ ܕܡܫܒܩܢ 'forsaken daughters'. MT ביצים עזבות 'forsaken eggs'. Syriac does have an idiom ܒܥܐ ܡܫܒܩܬܐ 'forsaken eggs'; miswriting at some point during transmission is possible, as is deliberate word play.

11:14 ܘܢܦܠܚܘܢ 'they will labor'. MT ועפו 'they will fly'. An original √ܦܪܚ 'to fly' posssibly corrupted during transmission to √ܦܠܚ 'to labor'.

15:9 ܐܪܥܐ 'I will attend to'. MT אריה 'lion'. An original ܐܪܝܐ 'lion' possibly corrupted during transmission to ܐܪܥܐ.

21:4 ܘܡܘܬ̈ܪܐ ܕܪܓܬܝ 'virtues of my desire'. MT נשף חשקי 'twilight of my pleasure'. An original ܫܦܪܐ 'twilight before dawn' corrupted to ܡܘܬ̈ܪܐ.

23:13 ܐܩܝܡܘ ܒܨܘܝ̈ܐ 'they established inquirers'. MT הקימו בחיניו 'they erected its siege-towers'. Probable corruption of an original ܨܘܝܐ 'heap of stones, cairn' corrupted during transmission to ܒܨܘܝ̈ܐ. See also Addendum 3.

26:15 ܐܬܪܚܩܬ 'you have journeyed far away'. MT נכבדת 'you have glorified yourself'. P may be an imperfect dittography of the following word ܘܪܚܩܬ 'you have thrust out'.

27:4 ܒܩܘܪܒܐ 'shortly'. MT במלחמה 'in battle'. An original ܒܩܪܒܐ 'in battle' corrupted to ܒܩܘܪܒܐ.

37:13 ܥܘܐ Hebrew עוה; ܥܘܐ, a transliteration of the Hebrew.

65:12 ܐܬܒܪܟܘܢ 'I will break you'. MT תכרעו 'you will bow down'. Probably the original true form was ܬܒܪܟܘܢ, correctly translating the Hebrew; in Mosul it has become corrupted to a form which could be either a 1st com. sing. Peal perfect √ܬܒܪ 'to break' with a 2nd masc. pl. objective suffix, or, making less clear sense, a 3rd masc. pl. Ethpaal perfect of √ܒܪܟ with no suffix.

Addendum 3: Meaning Obscure

7:17 From 7:3 onwards, Isaiah reassures Ahaz and Jerusalem that the Syro-Ephraimitic threat in the persons of Rezin and Pekah, spelt out in 7:5, will be dealt with by Assyria. ܡܠܟܐ ܕܐܬܘܪ 'the king of Assyria' is a precise translation of MT מלך אשור, generally considered to be a gloss rather than a statement that the king of Assyria will be responsible for the division of Ephraim from Judah.

14:31 ܘܠܝܬ ܝܚܝܕܝ ܒܥܐ̈ܕܘܗܝ 'none at all at his feasts'. MT ואין בודד במועדיו 'no straggler in his ranks'. The translator saw the sense of 'alone' in MT √בדד 'be separate'. He probably reached 'feasts' from a correct perception of √יעד 'to appoint' which includes the senses of both 'appointed place', i.e. the position of a soldier, and of a festal assembly.

15:5 ܥܓܠܬܐ ܬܠܝܬܝܬܐ 'three year old heifer'. MT עגלת שלשיה: the meaning remains obscure.

16:4 ܫܠܡܘ ܕܐܬܕܩܩܘ ܘܫܚܝܩܐ 'for those who have been reduced to dust have come to an end'. MT כי־אפס המץ 'for the extortioner has come to an end'. Translation of the Hebrew has long presented a problem. MT

√מיץ 'press', giving מץ 'extortioner' is rare; the translator may have been guessing. In the context, a meaning akin to 'expel, disperse' would fit well. ܪܡܣܣܐ too is difficult. It could be a passive participle of the geminate root ܪܣ 'to pulverize'; but this makes poor sense, and the meaning 'to drive out' which fits the context is not attested for this root. √ܪܣܐ where the meaning 'to drive away' is attested would fit the context better but the form is grammatically incorrect.

23:1   ܐܬܒܙܬ ܡܢ ܒܝܬܐ ܡܢ ܡܝܬܐ 'for it has been plundered, from the house, (from) him who brings'. MT כי־שדד מבית מבוא perhaps 'so that there is no house, no entering in,' an atomistic rendering.

23:13   The Hebrew is very difficult, verging on the unintelligible. The translation is unusually free, in an attempt to give sense. See Addendum 2.

23:18   ܒܠܝܬܗ 'her old (clothing)'. MT עתיק 'stately'. 'clothing' is inferred from the context.

30:33   ܡܛܠ ܡܐܟܘܠܬܗ ܡܢ ܩܕܝܡ ܡܛܝܒܐ ܗܘܬ 'for his food was prepared from days of old'. MT כי־ערוך מאתמול תפתה 'for its hearth is prepared from of old'. The translator found תפתה difficult; he may have perceived the sense 'to burn', and stretched the sense to refer to sacrificial offerings. There are two nouns, 'food' and 'breath', which could be the subject of the fem. sing. verbs 'prepared … reign … dug'.

34:15 i.   ܘܐܬܢܦܨ 'been emptied' or 'shaken itself' or 'woken itself from sleep'. MT ותמלט 'and laid (eggs)' from √מלט 'to slip forth, slip away'.

34:15 ii.   ܨܪܝ ܒܛܠܠܗ 'pierced in its shadow'. MT בקעה 'pierced'; the order of the verbs has been changed in translation. The meaning remains obscure.

49:17   ܬܪܝܨܐܝܬ 'directly': MT מהרו is 3rd pl. perfect √I מהר 'to hasten'. The translator has rendered it adverbially with ܬܪܝܨܐܝܬ. The meaning remains obscure.

APPENDIX 1: VERSIFICATION

Leiden	Begins with Mosul	Mosul = MT	Change affects sense
1:17	4th word of 1:17	No	No
3:20	The last word of 3:19		
3:21	2nd word of 3:21		
7:6	2nd word of 7:6	No	
8:12	2nd word of 8:12	No	No
8:17	2nd word of 8:17	No	
8:22	3rd word of 8:22	No	No
8:23	Last 8 words of 8:22 + 9:1		No
9:1-20	9:2-21		
13:5	2nd word of 13:5	No	No
13:8	Last word of 13:7	No	No
14:10	4th word of 14:10	No	No
16:1	4th word of 16:1	No	No, but a bit odd
17:13	5th word of 17:13	No	No
21:10	Last 5 words of 21:9	No	MT better
23:3	2nd word of 23:3	No	Mosul better
25:5	7th word of 25:5	No	Mosul a bit better
26:3	Last 2 words of 26:2	No	No
28:3	4th word of 28:3	No	No
29:16	Last 2 words of 29:15	No	Mosul better
33:18	Last 3 words of 33:17	No	Mosul better
33:19	Last 2 words of 33:18	Possibly yes	

Leiden	Begins with Mosul	Mosul = MT	Change affects sense
34:1	3rd word of 34:1	An addition in P	Sums up 1st 4 verses
35:3	8th word of 35:3	An addition in P	Midpoint in book
37:19	2nd word of 37:19	No	MT better
38:3	Last word of 38:2	No	No
38:13	The Peshiṭta omits this verse due to a scribal error. Verse 12 ends in ܐܪܕܠܬܟܝܢ and verse 13, based on the Greek, Latin, and Hebrew texts, must have ended in the same word.		
38:16	Last 3 words of 38:15	No	No
38:22,21	38:21,22 (numbers, not text, reversed)	Numbers reversed	Text unaffected
40:20	Last 2 words of 40:19	No	No
41:9	Last word of 41:8	No	MT better
42:10	Last 2 words of 42:9	An addition in P	P adds a Title
43:10	2nd word of 43:10	No	Slight change in sense
44:10	4th word of 44:10	No	No
44:14	3rd word of 44:14	No	No
44:15	Last 3 words of 44:14	No	MT better
51:11	Last 2 words of 51:10	No	MT better
55:7	3rd word of 55:7	No	MT better
57:20,21	57:20		
64:1	9th word of 64:1 + 64:2		
64:2-11	64:3-12		

APPENDIX 2: VARIANT READINGS

The following table gives the variants of Mosul against Leiden. The last
column indicates the support for the Mosul reading as follows:

early	first millennium up to and including the tenth century.
late	post tenth century making use of the Leiden apparatus and of Diettrich.
Lee	only Lee's edition agrees with Mosul.
no support	Mosul's reading is unique.

Place	Mosul	Leiden	Support
1:3	ܐܗܝܡܢܐ	ܐܗܝܡܢܗ	Early
1:4	ܡܚܠܨܠܐ	ܡܚܠܠܡܐ	late
1:6	ܘܗܘ	om *waw*	early
1:13	ܘܡܚܡܠܐ	om *dālath*	late
3:14 1°	ܘܚܣ	om *waw*	late
5:2	ܘܗ ܒܪ	ܒܪܗܘ	early
5:2	ܘܗܘ	om *waw*	early
5:29 1°	ܘܗܘܡ	ܗܘܡ	late
5:30	ܘܗܘܡ	om *waw*	late
6:10	ܚܡ	ܚܡܪ	early
7:20	ܠܥܕܠܐ	ܕܥܕܠܐ	early
7:20	ܘܐ	pr *waw*	early
8:7	ܚܪܝܐ ܕܗܘܡܗܠܐ	tr	early
8:9	ܬܣܥܡܐ	ܬܣܡܐ	early
8:11	ܠܐ	pr *dālath*	late
8:12	ܘܗܘܡܠܣܒܚܘ	*seyāme*	early
9:14 (L 9:13)	ܘܘܒܚܠܐ ܘܘܒܚܠܐ	ܘܘܒܚܠܐ ܘܘܒܚܠܐ	early
9:15 (L 9:14)	ܘܒܚܠܐ	ܘܒܚܠܐ	early
10:4	ܐܗܙܢܐ	om *seyāme*	late
10:4	ܡܗܠܢܠܐ	om *seyāme*	late
10:10	ܘܐܡܘ	ܘܐܡܚܠܐ	early
10:12	ܘܡܚܠܐ	om *dālath*	early

Place	Mosul	Leiden	Support
10:27	ܡܘܡܝܐ	*seyāme*; 7a1 ܡܘܡ̈ܝܐ	Early
13:2	ܠܡܪ̈ܟܒ	ܠܡܪ̈ܟܒܬܟ	Early
13:9	ܠܗ	ܒܗ	Early
13:14	ܚܝ̈ܠܐ	ܚܝܠܐ	late
13:16	ܘܡܠܟܘ̈ܬܗܘܢ	om *waw* prefix	early
13:18	ܒܢ̈ܝܟܘܢ	ܒܢ̈ܝܗܘܢ	early
14:8	ܐܦ	pr *waw*	early
14:13	ܕܐܣܩ	om *dālath*	early
14:29	ܦܠܫܬ	ܦܠܫܬܝ	early
16:1	ܐܫܕܪ	7a1 ܫܕܪ; apparatus ܫܕܪܘ	late
17:9	ܒܝܘܡܐ	ܒܗ ܒܝܘܡܐ	early
17:10	ܕܛܥܝܬܝ	ܘܛܥܝܬܝ	early
19:11	ܘܡܠܟ̈ܐ	om *waw*	late
19:15 1º 2º	ܘܕܘܢܒܬܐ	ܘܕܢܘܒܬܐ	early
19:19	ܢܨܒܬܐ	omit	early
19:19	ܠܬܚܘܡ̈ܗ	ܠܬܚܘܡܗ	early
20:2	ܥܪܛܠܝ ܘܚܦܝ	ܚܦܝ ܘܥܪܛܠܝ	early
20:3	ܥܪܛܠܝ ܘܚܦܝ	ܚܦܝ ܘܥܪܛܠܝ	early
20:6	ܡܠܟܐ	ܩܕܡ ܡܠܟܐ	early
21:13	ܕܥܪܒܐ	ܕܥܪܒ	early
22:2 1º 2º	ܐܡܠܠܬܝ	ܐܬܡܠܠܬ	no support
22:4	ܘܠܐ	om *waw*	early
22:5	ܫܘܪ̈ܐ	om *seyāme*	early
22:13	ܘܡܐܟܘܠܬܐ	om *waw*	late
22:15	ܠܗܘܐ	omit	early
22:21	ܠܫܘܪ̈ܐ	ܠܫܘܪ̈ܝܗ	early
23:8	ܘܬܓܪ̈ܝܗ	ܘܬܓܪ̈ܗ	early
23:12	ܐܦ	pr *waw*	early
23:13	ܘܐܩܝܡܘ	ܘܐܩܝܡ	early
24:10	ܐܬܬܒܪܬ	ܐܬܒܪܬ	early
24:16	ܙܡܝ̈ܪܬܐ	om *seyāme*	late
24:21	ܒܗ	om	early
25:9	ܘܢܦܪܩ	om *waw*	no support
26:9	ܐܦ	pr *waw*	early
26:15	ܟܠܗܘܢ	pr *lāmadh*	early
26:19	ܠܐܫܝܦ	ܠܐܫܬܝܦ	early

Place	Mosul	Leiden	Support
27:10			late
27:12		pr *waw*	early
27:13		pr *beth*	early
28:7		pr *waw*	early
28:10			no support
28:18			early
28:26			late
28:27			early
28:27		*seyāme*	late
28:29		om *waw*	early
29:7			early
29:8			late
29:8			early
29:8		omit	late
30:6			early
30:12		omit	early
30:14		om *waw*	early
30:15			early
30:15		omit	early
30:17			early
30:19		om *waw*	early
30:29			early
30:33			late
31:3		om *seyāme*; 7a1	late
31:7			early
31:8	(impf.)	7a1 act. part.	no support
31:9			early
31:9			early
32:1		*seyāme*	early
32:11			early
33:5		om *seyāme*	early
33:6			Lee
33:7			early
34:7			late
34:11			no support
34:12 2°		omit	late

Place	Mosul	Leiden	Support
34:13			early
36:2		om *dālath*	early
36:11			no support
36:14		omit	early
36:18		pr *waw*	early
37:9			Lee
37:11			early
37:12			early
37:12			early
37:12			no support
37:27			early
37:30 2°		omit	early
37:36			early
37:36			early
38:2			early
38:4		omit	early
38:6		omit	early
38:17			late
38:18			early
40:9			early
40:12			early
40:13			early
40:20			late
40:23			early
41:4			no support
41:11	Peal	Aph'el	early
41:22		; 9d1	late
41:23			early
41:25			early
42:1			no support
42:7		om *seyāme*	early
42:7 1°		omit	early
42:8			early
42:11		pr *waw*	early
42:16 2°			late
43:1			early
43:2 2°		pr *waw*	early

Place	Mosul	Leiden	Support
43:10	ܩܬܘܗܝ	ܐܢܐ ܩܬܘܗܝ	early
43:13	ܘܐܦ	om *waw*	early
43:16	ܗܝܬܢܐ	ܚܬܢܐ	early
43:25	ܠܐ	ܐܘܬ ܠܐ	early
44:2	ܘܡܢܟ	ܒܝܚܡܐ	early
44:19	ܘܡܢܗ	ܘܡܢܕܗ	early
44:26	ܘܡܩܡ	om *waw*	late
45:5 2°	ܘܠܟ	om *waw*	Lee
45:11	ܗܘܡܘܗܝ	ܗܡܘܗܝ	early
45:19	ܘܐܢܐ	ܐܢܐ	no support; Lee ܘܐܢܐ
46:6	ܘܐܦ	om *waw*	early
46:10	ܘܡܣܘܐ	ܡܣܘܐ	late
46:11 1° 2°	ܘܬ	pr *waw*	early
47:1	ܐܘܬ	omit	early
47:5	ܐܘܬ	omit	early
48:1	ܡܬܢܐ	ܡܣܐ	late
48:3	ܕܚܡ	omit	early
48:5	ܘܣܡܝܡ	om *waw*	late
48:7	ܘܡܝ	om *waw*	early
49:1	ܡܡܕܬܝ	ܡܠܩܬܡܝ	early
49:12 3°	ܘܗܠܝܡ ܡܝ	ܘܡܝ	early
49:20	ܐܘܬ	om *waw*	early
50:8	ܘܐܝܕ	ܘܐܝܕ	early
51:4	ܘܪܩܐܡܣ	ܘܪܩܐܡܣ	early
51:9	ܘܡܠܟܠܡ	ܘܚܠܟܠܡ	early
51:11	ܘܢܘܩܣܡ	ܘܣܐܩܝܢ; ܒܘܩܣܡ 6h5	early
51:16	ܘܐܝܡܝ	*seyāme*	early
51:18	ܘܡܩܡܡ ܠܬܐ	omit	early
51:20	ܘܚܡܒ	ܘܚܡܢܙ	early (L against MSS)
55:5	ܘܐܡܙܐ	om *dālath*	early
55:5	ܘܡܝܡܐ	ܘܡܠܝܠܐ ܡܝܡܐ	early
55:12	ܐܣܚܡܐܘ	ܠܡܚܡܣܐܠ	early
55:12	ܘܡܠܣܘܝ	ܘܡܠܣܘܝ	early
56:6	ܐܡܚܐ	ܐܘ ܐܡܚܐ	early

Place	Mosul	Leiden	Support
56:7	ܒܐܚܕܐ	ܡܚܕܐ	early
56:11	ܘܐܢܐ	om *waw*	early
57:6	ܐܘ	pr *waw*	early
57:7	ܐܘ	pr *waw*	early
57:17	3rd fem. sing. ܘܐܦܢܝܬ ܐܦܝ	1st com. sing.	no support
58:1	ܘܟܪܙܡܠ	ܘܟܠܡܠ	early
58:6	ܡܝܙܐ	om *seyāme*	early
58:11	ܘܘܙܗܪ	ܘܘܙܗܪ	late
59:3	ܘܡܩܘܐܚܝ	ܡܩܘܐܚܝ	early
59:4	ܟܠܐ	ܕܘܠܐ	early
60:9	ܠܟܡܕܗ	om *lāmadh*	early
60:13	ܘܠܐܘܪܐ	ܐܪܘܐܪܐ	late
61:3 1°	ܘܡܠܟ	om *waw*	early
61:3 2°	ܘܡܠܟ	om *waw*	early
62:6	ܡܕܒܕܬܢܗ	ܡܕܒܕܬܢܐ	early
62:11	ܘܗܐ	om *dālath*	early
63:2	Perfect ܘܕܪܙ	ܘܕܪܙ	early
63:3	Perfect ܘܢܪܐ	ܘܢܪܐ	early
63:6	ܘܘܘܝܠܐ	ܘܐܘܝܠܐ	early
63:7	ܘܟܠܐ	om *dālath*	Lee
63:9	ܢܘܩܚܠܗ	ܡܘܩܚܠܐ	early
63:15	ܡܕܒܡܢܘ	ܡܕܒܬܡܘ	late
64:3 (L 64:2)	ܘܠܐ	om *dālath*	late
64:5 (L 64:4)	ܕܚܐܘܬܣܡܝ	pr *waw*	late
65:1 2°	ܗܘ ܐܢܐ	ܗܘ ܐܢܐ ܗܘ ܐܢܐ	late, 2nd hand
65:4	ܘܐܝܬܢܘܗܝ	ܘܐܝܬܢܘܗܝ ܠܟܡܙܐ ܝܥܘܘܡܐ ܘܟܡܚܒܡܚܐܗ ܡܝܥܐ ܡܕܒܡܐ ܘܢܙܚܪܗܝ ܠܟܡܙܝܠ	early
65:9	ܘܒܐܪܘܐܘܝܨ	ܘܒܐܪܘܐܘܝܨ	early
65:9	ܝܚܬ	ܝܚܬܣ	early
65:11	ܠܟܗܘܙܗ	om *lāmadh*	early
65:12	ܐܡܣܚܘܝ	ܐܡܣܚܘܝ	early
65:12	ܐܠܚܕܚܘܝ	ܠܐܚܕܚܘܝ	late
65:12	ܘܡܢܕܠܚܘܝ	ܘܡܢܕܠ	early
65:15	ܠܟܝܚܬ	ܠܟܬܝܚܣ	early

Place	Mosul	Leiden	Support
65:22	ܚܬܢ	ܚܣܡ	early
65:25	ܘܥܘܕܡ ܐܘܗܠ	ܠܥܡܝܢ ܬܘܗܠ	early
66:12	ܘܗܘ	om *dālath*	no support
66:12	ܐܪܥܐܬܗ	om *waw*	early
66:21	ܘܐ	pr *waw*	early

APPENDIX 3: NAMES

Common Syriac Proper Names

P regularly uses:

 ܐܘܪܫܠܡ for Hebrew ירושלם, e.g. 1:1.

 ܐܝܣܪܐܝܠ(ܠ) for Hebrew ישראל, e.g. 1:3.

 ܕܪܡܣܘܩ for Hebrew דמשק, e.g. 7:8.

 ܝܘܪܕܢ for Hebrew ירדן, e.g. 9:1 (MT 8:23).

 ܡܨܪܝܢ for Hebrew מצרים, e.g. 7:18.

 ܫܡܪܝܢ for Hebrew שמרון, e.g. 7:9.

 ܣܪܝܫܘܒ for Hebrew שאר ישוב, e.g. 7:3.

Replacement

In 10:26 P reads ܚܘܪܝܒ 'Horeb' for Hebrew עורב 'Oreb', which elsewhere in the Old Testament is only used as the name of Midianite princes.

 In 10:28 the obscure Hebrew מגרון is replaced by the well-known P ܡܟܡܫ. In 1 Samuel 14:2 the Hebrew is rendered with P ܟܡܫ.

 In 17:3 ܐܦܪܝܡ 'Ephraim' replaces Hebrew ארם 'Aram/Syria'. Elsewhere in the Peshiṭta of Isaiah, ܐܕܘܡ 'Edom' normally replaces this Hebrew. A special case is at 7:1 where P uses ܐܪܡ for Hebrew ארם (see Weitzman, *Syriac Version*, 62-67).

 In 37:38, P ܠܐܪܥܐ ܕܩܪܕܘܡܐ 'the land of Qardawaye' replaces Hebrew ארץ אררט 'land of Ararat', and P ܣܪܚܕܘܡ 'Sarhadom' replaces Hebrew אסר־חדן 'Esar-haddon'.

Initial Positions

Initial Hebrew *aleph* is omitted:

 10:9 P has ܪܦܕ for Hebrew ארפד.

 15:8 ܓܠܝܡ for Hebrew אגלים.

 37:38 ܣܪܚܕܘܡ for Hebrew אסר־חדן.

Initial Hebrew *yodh* is rendered with Syriac *ālaph*:

 1:1 ܐܫܥܝܐ for Hebrew ישעיהו.

 11:1 ܐܝܫܝ for Hebrew ישי.

 43:19 ܐܝܫܡܘܢ for Hebrew ישמון.

Of course regularly P has ܐܘܪܫܠܡ for Hebrew ירושלם.

Initial Hebrew *yodh* is omitted: in 8:2 ܒܪܟܝܐ renders Hebrew יברכיהו.

More interesting are:

(a) in 15:2 ܪܝܒܘܢ for Hebrew דיבן and in 15:9 for Hebrew דימון (found only in this verse). This rendering of Hebrew דיבון is the standard P equivalent of this common name.

(b) 37:12 ܕܬܠܣܪ for Hebrew תלשר (as also for the parallel 2 Kings 19:12 תלאשר).

(c) 37:13 ܗܢܥ renders Hebrew הנע, as in 2 Kings 18:34, 19:13.

Medial Positions

Replacements

Hebrew *dalath* is rendered with Syriac *resh*, as in 10:31 ܡܪܡܢܐ Hebrew מדמנה; 15:2 ܪܝܒܘܢ Hebrew דיבן; 21:13 ܕܘܪܢܝܡ Hebrew דדנים.

Hebrew *resh* is rendered with Syriac *dālath*, as in 17:2 ܥܕܘܥܝܪ Hebrew ערער.

Hebrew *nun* is rendered with Syriac *yodh*, as in10:9 ܟܠܝܘ Hebrew כלנו; 11:11 ܣܥܝܪ Hebrew שנער (and metathesis). The reverse occurs in 7:3 ܫܪܝܫܘܒ Hebrew שאר ישוב; 10:28 ܥܢܬ Hebrew עית.

Introductions and Deletions

P may introduce a *waw* where it is lacking in the orthography of the Hebrew: e.g. 1:1 ܥܘܙܝܐ Hebrew עזיהו; 1:9 ܣܕܘܡ Hebrew סדם; ܥܡܘܪܐ Hebrew עמרה; 2:3 ܝܥܩܘܒ Hebrew יעקב; 7:1 ܪܘܡܠܝܐ Hebrew רמליהו; 7:8 ܕܪܡܣܘܩ Hebrew דמשק; 9:1 ܝܘܪܕܢ Hebrew ירדן; 10:31 ܓܒܘܢ Hebrew גבים (where P also treats the Hebrew name as plural); 15:4 ܝܗܘܨ Hebrew יהץ; 21:13 ܕܘܪܢܝܡ Hebrew דדנים; 23:1 ܨܘܪ Hebrew צר; 34:6 ܒܘܨܪ Hebrew בצרה; 39:1 ܡܪܘܕܟ Hebrew מרדך; 54:9 ܢܘܚ Hebrew נח; 63:11 ܡܘܫܐ Hebrew משה.

The reverse may occur: e.g. 2:13 ܠܒܢܢ Hebrew לבנון; 23:2 ܨܝܕܢ Hebrew צידון; 65:10 ܥܟܪ Hebrew עכור.

P may introduce a *yodh* where it is lacking in the orthography of Hebrew: e.g. 2:13 P ܒܝܫܢ Hebrew בשן; 7:2 ܕܘܝܕ Hebrew דוד; 7:6 ܛܒܐܝܠ Hebrew טבאל; 8:8 ܥܡܢܘܐܝܠ Hebrew עמנו אל; 16:8 ܝܥܙܝܪ Hebrew יעזר; 46:1 ܒܝܠ Hebrew בל.

Naturally the reverse may occur: e.g. 7:1 ܪܨܢ Hebrew רצין; 15:8 ܐܠܡ Hebrew אילים; 49:12 ܣܝܢܡ Hebrew סינים; 60:6 ܥܝܦܐ Hebrew עיפה.

P may introduce both *waw* and *yodh*: e.g. 8:6 ܫܝܠܘܚܐ for Hebrew שלח; 17:2 ܥܕܘܥܝܪ Hebrew ערער; 66:19 ܬܘܒܝܠ for Hebrew תבל.

Aleph, Waw, and Yodh

These letters are sometimes interchanged, e.g. 1:3 ܐܝܣܪܝܠ Hebrew ישראל; 5:14 ܫܝܘܠ Hebrew שאול, where P *yodh* replaces Hebrew *aleph*. In 7:9 ܫܡܪܝܢ Hebrew שמרון, P *yodh* replaces Hebrew *waw*. The reverse occurs in e.g. 10:9 ܟܪܟܡܘܫ Hebrew כרכמיש. In 15:2 P *ālaph* replaces Hebrew *yodh* ܡܐܕܒܐ (ms 7a1 ܡܕܐܒܐ) Hebrew מידבא; in 60:7 the change is similar: ܢܒܐܘܬ Hebrew נביות.

An *ālaph* may be introduced where Hebrew lacks one: e.g. 20:1 ܬܐܪܬܢ Hebrew תרתן.

Of course it may be omitted as in 7:3 ܫܪܝܫܘܒ for Hebrew שאר ישוב; 29:1 ܐܪܝܠ Hebrew אריאל; 39:1 ܒܠܕܢ Hebrew בלאדן.

Inner-Syriac Corruptions

Of special interest are 15:8 ܒܠܝܡ Hebrew אילים (where the Syriac presumably reflects an ISC of ܒܠܝܡ) and 37:13 ܥܘܐ Hebrew עוה (where the Syriac presumably reflects an ISC of ܥܘܐ).

Endings

In many places a Syriac name ending in ܐ corresponds to a Hebrew name ending in Hebrew הו: e.g. 1:1 ܐܫܥܝܐ Hebrew ישעיהו; ܥܘܙܝܐ Hebrew עזיהו; and ܚܙܩܝܐ Hebrew יהזקיהו; 7:1 ܪܘܡܠܝܐ Hebrew רמליהו; 8:2 ܙܟܪܝܐ Hebrew זכריהו; ܒܪܟܝܐ Hebrew יברכיהו; 22:20 ܚܠܩܝܐ Hebrew חלקיהו.

Often P has a final ܐ where H has a final ה: e.g. 1:1 ܝܗܘܕܐ Hebrew יהודה; 1:9 ܥܡܘܪܐ Hebrew עמרה; 9:21 ܡܢܫܐ Hebrew מנשה; 10:31 ܡܕܡܢܐ Hebrew מדמנה; 15:4 ܐܠܥܠܐ Hebrew אלעלה; 16:8 ܫܒܡܐ Hebrew שבמה; 21:11 ܕܘܡܐ Hebrew דומה; 36:2 ܪܒ ܫܩܐ Hebrew רב־שקה; 37:8 ܠܒܢܐ Hebrew לבנה; 37:13 ܥܘܐ Hebrew עוה; 37:37 ܢܝܢܘܐ Hebrew נינוה; 51:2 ܣܪܐ Hebrew שרה; 60:6 ܥܝܦܐ Hebrew עיפה; 63:11 ܡܘܫܐ Hebrew משה.

P may add a final ܐ where Hebrew has nothing, e.g. 8:23 P ܓܠܝܠܐ Hebrew גליל; P 16:10 ܟܪܡܠܐ Hebrew כרמל; 21:13 ܥܪܒܐ (ms 7a1 ܥܪܒ) Hebrew ערב; 33:9 ܫܪܘܢܐ Hebrew שרון.

However, in e.g. 10:30 ܠܝܫ lacks the final Hebrew ה of the Hebrew לישה; similarly 34:6 ܒܘܨܪ Hebrew בצרה. So too at only 26:1 'Judah' is rendered ܝܗܘܕ Hebrew יהודה.

Changes without Pattern

In 37:38 ܐܣܪܚܕܘܡ Hebrew אסר־הדן: P replaces a Hebrew final ן with a ܡ.

Sibilants (Initial, Medial, Final)

Sin שׂ: a Hebrew שׂ may be represented by ܣ as in 1:3 ܐܝܣܪܝܠ Hebrew ישׂראל; 7:8 ܕܪܡܣܘܩ Hebrew דמשק; 10:28 ܡܟܡܣ Hebrew מכמשׂ; 16:8

ܣܘܒܡܐ Hebrew שׁבמה; 21:11 ܣܥܝܪ Hebrew שֵׂעִיר; 37:12 ܘܠܨܝ Hebrew תלשׂר; 51:2 ܣܪܐ Hebrew שׂרה.

Hebrew שׂ may also be represented by P ܣ as in 37:38 ܣܪܐܘܪ Hebrew שַׂראצר.

Hebrew *samech* ס may be represented by P ܣ as in 43:3 ܣܒܐ Hebrew סבא.

P *semkath* ܣ may replace a Hebrew שׁ as in 11:11 ܣܥܢܪ Hebrew שׁנער.

For the sake of completeness the common translations of 7:17 ܐܬܘܪ Hebrew אשׁור and 1:8 ܨܗܝܘܢ Hebrew ציון may be recalled.

Translation

In 7:19 Hebrew הבתות 'destruction' is translated as a proper noun: P ܒܬܐܠ. See also the note in the translation to 10:29.

BIBLIOGRAPHY

LEXICA AND DICTIONARIES

Koehler, L. and W. Baumgartner (1994), *The Hebrew and Aramaic Lexicon of the Old Testament,* revised by W. Baumgartner and J. J. Stamm. Leiden: Brill.

Payne Smith, J. (1903), *A Compendious Syriac Dictionary.* Oxford: Clarendon.

Payne Smith, R. (1879), *Thesaurus Syriacus.* Oxford: Clarendon.

Sokoloff, M. (2009) *A Syriac Lexicon.* Piscataway, New Jersey: Gorgias Press and Winona Lake, Indiana: Eisenbrauns.

REFERENCE

Brock, S. P. (1993), *Isaiah*, OTSy 3.1. Leiden: Brill.

GENERAL INTEREST

Albrektson, B. (1963), *Studies in the Text and Theology of the Book of Lamentations*, STL 21. Lund: Gleerup.

Carbajosa, I. (2008), *The Character of the Syriac Version of Psalms*, MPIL 17. Leiden: Brill.

Greenberg, G. (2002), *Translation Technique in the Peshiṭta to Jeremiah*, MPIL 13. Leiden: Brill.

Rignell, G. (1994), *The Peshiṭta to the Book of Job*, ed. K.-E. Rignell. Kristianstad [Sweden]: Monitor.

Walter, D. M. (2008), *Studies in the Peshiṭta of Kings*, T&S3 7. Piscataway, New Jersey: Gorgias Press.

Weitzman, M. P. (1999), *The Syriac Version of the Old Testament*, UCOP 56. Cambridge: Cambridge University Press.

Williams, P. J. (2001), *Studies in the Syntax of the Peshiṭta of 1 Kings*, MPIL 12. Leiden: Brill.

TEXT AND TRANSLATION

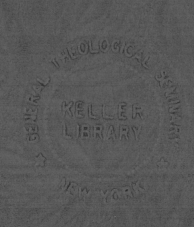

ܦܘܫܩ ܟܬܒܐ

ܐܘ ܣܘܟܠܐ ܦܫܝܛܐ ܥܡ ܡܚܘܝܢܘܬܐ ܐܪܬܘܕܘܟܣܝܐ

ܦܘܩܕܐ ܘܐܡܝܢܐ ܝܘܡܐ

ܦܘܪܫܐ ܬܒܝܥܐ

ܡܩܬܡܢ ܕܥܠܐ

ܝܘܦܝܫ ܕܢ ܐܝܠܗܝ ܘܚܕ ܚܢܙܐܪ   ܐܒܘܐܘܗܣ ܕܢ ܘܠܟܠܐܘ ܘܚܕ ܩܘܨܠܐ

ܪܘܩܐ ܒܓܗܢܡ܀

حداواو

سعحلا هلمحا اوا حزوزا هلمد ههحزا واهحلا بحما لههحا مههحمحا
وحلامحزنا هحسحلا: حم محدحزنهما ابيحسمحلا. الاهسحمحلا زوزا هلمد
هوا ملا ههحمحلا هحوزحملا: وحب هزب حلحمحسه ههحمس وهب
الاهزهحلا محزسملحه هحلد اهحز ـ اهزا: حملز هما وحسحلحه لحمزلحه هم
حزسحلا لحمحزحملا: واوهمحس بوهحزب زوهحلا وهحهما هحمزالحه: وسما
وحححللمحلا لههحا محمحمحسولا وحهحس.

هسمحس وحه حزوزا هلمد هحوزحملا حم ههحمحلا وللامحس وهحزنحلمحه
حلحزهما. واهحسس والحه هحزنهحلا حزنزا حمزنا: هوزا هلمحس: حملد
ههحمحلا هحوزحملا هوحه وللامحس: للاقب هزنه حهحسنا. واهحسس لحوحد وهقلا
حملا هم حزنملا وحهحزنه هحمحسس حهحزنحلحه حلحزهما وووزا حزنقملا: هم هوزا
سحمحمحسا اححز الا حزحلا حزوزا حهحسنا: وقلا حملا هم هحلحه حزنملا
هحمحسس حهحزنحلحه وهحه هوزا هلحلحلا. وزوحه لحححز وحهحلا وهحس
هزنه حزنملا وحهحمحمحا هحوزحملا هحمحسس هلحه حهم وللامحس: ههه
حهحسنا: وحملا هحمحسنا اه سحمحزنا الاقلا حزوحملحا الحس: هم حزنملا
وحملا هحمحسنا اه سحمحزنا هحلحلا الحس. هحوزا وهحس حزنملا حملا وقا
XXÍX هحمحس حزنحا ابيحسمحلا.

هلاوز حزوزا هلمد لههحا محمحمحسولا هحوسحملا محزسحلا وهحس
زوحلا. الحلا لحمامحز: هلاحس (وحس) هحلحمحس (حزوهزا)) لحححلحسا
هحسملحسا) هحه هحلحم امز حهحمحمحسولا حلحمحمحلا هوحه محزسحلا (سزب
لحمحلا حس:نه). وهملاحس نلانحس سحلد نحنحس (سزب لحمحلا هحه:نحلا). وهملاحس
نحس سحلد نحس (سزب لحمحلا حزحه: هحلا حزنز) وهحزنا.

ههلا وحه ههحلحلحمحمحلا هحمحزنحس لحهحسحملا حلحمحسم هحه سزحمحلا
وحزحملا وححزسحلا وهه هه سهه حم هلاحمحلا للحملازنسحلا وههحزا واهحلا بحما
حزسحلا: هحمحلحملا ابزوهحس هحمحلا وهحملحس هلحلحلاز وحزوه
حهحمسحلا حملا هحزنملحه حلحزهما. وحلحمحزنا لحوحه لحححلا حزحزنحلحلا حزنز
حزنا ـ هحس وهحمحمحلحس حزنزا حز نه هحس وهحملحه لحححزوزا
وهحمسحه حزنملا حمد ههحمحلا هحوزحملا وهحزنحس للامحس حملا حزنملا
لههحا وهه. وحلحمحزنا للحلا لاهحس ولا حهحقحس ٭ امز واهحس ٭
حسحلحلاه وهحز لحهحملا: و هحلحل حمد م
حهوزحلحه حز الحملحس وحملا حزنزا
وحزنا هحهم حللد

ܗܟܢܐ ܘܐܡܪ ܒܚܕ

ܩܦܠܐܘܢ: ܐ.

ܝܫ ܐ

1 ܐ ܚܙܘܐ ܕܐܫܥܝܐ ܒܪ ܐܡܘܨ: ܕܚܙܐ ܥܠ ܝܗܘܕ ܘܥܠ ܐܘܪܫܠܡ: ܒܝܘܡܝ ܥܘܙܝܐ:
ܘܝܘܬܡ: ܘܐܚܙ: ܘܚܙܩܝܐ: ܡܠܟܐ ܕܝܗܘܕܐ.

2 ܒ ܫܡܥܝ ܫܡܝܐ: ܘܨܘܬܝ ܐܪܥܐ: ܡܛܠ ܕܡܪܝܐ ܡܠܠ: ܒܢܝܐ ܪܒܝܬ ܘܐܪܝܡܬ:
ܘܗܢܘܢ ܐܥܠܘ ܒܝ.

3 ܓ ܝܕܥ ܬܘܪܐ ܩܢܝܗ: ܘܚܡܪܐ ܐܘܪܝܐ ܕܡܪܗ. ܘܐܝܣܪܝܠ ܠܐ ܝܕܥ: ܘܥܡܝ ܠܐ
ܐܣܬܟܠ.

4 ܕ ܘܝ ܠܥܡܐ ܚܛܝܐ: ܥܡܐ ܕܡܠܐ ܚܘܒܐ: ܙܪܥܐ ܒܝܫܐ. ܒܢܝܐ ܡܚܒܠܐ:
ܫܒܩܘܗܝ ܠܡܪܝܐ: ܘܐܪܓܙܘܗܝ ܠܩܕܝܫܐ ܕܐܝܣܪܝܠ: ܘܗܦܟܘ
ܠܒܣܬܪܗܘܢ.

5 ܗ ܠܡܢܐ ܬܘܒ ܬܬܡܚܘܢ: ܘܬܘܣܦܘܢ ܠܡܣܛܝܘ. ܟܠ ܪܫ ܠܟܐܒܐ: ܘܟܠ
ܠܒܐ ܠܟܘܪܗܢܐ.

6 ܘ ܡܢ ܦܣܬܐ ܕܪܓܠܐ ܘܥܕܡܐ ܠܪܫܐ: ܠܝܬ ܒܗ ܕܘܟܬܐ ܕܚܠܝܡܐ. ܡܚܘܬܐ:
ܘܡܟܬܫܬܐ: ܘܡܚܘܬܐ ܛܪܝܬܐ. ܠܐ ܠܡܥܨܪܘ: ܘܠܐ ܠܡܥܨܒܘ: ܘܐܦ ܠܐ ܠܡܪܟܟܘ
ܒܡܫܚܐ.

7 ܙ ܐܪܥܟܘܢ ܚܪܒܐ: ܘܩܘܪܝܟܘܢ ܝܩܝܕܢ ܒܢܘܪܐ. ܐܪܥܟܘܢ ܠܥܘܠܡܟܘܢ ܐܟܠܝܢ ܠܗ
ܢܘܟܪܝܐ. ܘܚܪܒܐ ܐܝܟ ܗܦܟܬܐ ܕܢܘܟܪܝܐ.

8 ܚ ܘܐܫܬܚܪܬ ܒܪܬ ܨܗܝܘܢ: ܐܝܟ ܡܛܠܬܐ ܒܟܪܡܐ: ܘܐܝܟ ܒܪܬܐ ܒܡܩܫܘܬܐ: ܘܐܝܟ
ܡܕܝܢܬܐ ܢܨܝܪܬܐ.

9 ܛ ܘܐܠܘ ܠܐ ܡܪܝܐ ܨܒܐܘܬ ܐܘܬܪ ܠܢ ܫܪܝܕܐ: ܐܝܟ ܣܕܘܡ ܗܘܝܢ ܗܘܝܢ: ܘܠܥܡܘܪܐ
ܡܬܕܡܝܢ ܗܘܝܢ.

10 ܝ ܫܡܥܘ ܦܬܓܡܗ ܕܡܪܝܐ: ܫܠܝܛܢܐ ܕܣܕܘܡ. ܘܨܘܬܘ ܢܡܘܣܗ ܕܐܠܗܢ ܥܡܐ
ܕܥܡܘܪܐ.

Chapter 1

I

1   The vision of Isaiah the son of Amoz, that he saw concerning Judah and concerning Jerusalem, in the days of Uzziah, and Jotham, and Ahaz, and Hezekiah, kings of Judah.

2   Hear, heaven,[1] and give ear, earth, for the Lord has spoken. I have brought up and raised children, yet they have wronged me.

3   The ox knew his owner, the ass his master's manger: yet Israel did not know, my people did not understand.

4   Woe to a sinful people, a people heavy with iniquity, a noxious seed, children acting corruptly. You have abandoned the Lord, you have provoked the Holy One of Israel to anger, you have regressed.[2]

5   Why will you again be wounded, again be chastised,[3] the whole head given over to pain, the whole[4] heart to distress?

6   From the sole of the foot as far as the brain, there is no sound place anywhere:[5] bruises, sores, swollen wounds, not to be bound up, not to be bandaged, not even soothed with oil.

7   Your land is desolate, your cities burnt with fire; strangers devour your land before you, it is deserted as if overthrown by strangers.

8   The daughter of Zion has been left, like a booth in a vineyard, like a lodge in a cucumber garden, like a besieged city.

9   Had the Lord of Hosts[6] not left us a remnant we would have been like Sodom, we would have become like Gomorrah.

10   Hear the word of the Lord, rulers of Sodom, give ear to the law of our God, people of Gomorrah.

---

[1] 'heaven'. ܫܡܝܐ consistently is singular in the Peshitta of Isaiah; it is variously translated in this translation by 'heaven' or 'the heavens'.

[2] 'you have regressed': lit. 'you have turned behind yourselves'.

[3] 'again be chastised'. See Introduction. Addendum 2.

[4] 'the whole … the whole' or 'every … every'.

[5] 'anywhere': lit. 'in it'.

[6] 'Lord of Hosts': lit. 'the Lord Sabaoth'.

11 ܝܐ ܠܡܢܐ ܗܘܝܢ ܠܝ ܣܘܓܐܐ ܕܕܒܚ̈ܝܟܘܢ: ܐܡܪ ܡܪܝܐ. ܣܒܥܬ ܥܠܘ̈ܬܐ ܕܕܟܪ̈ܐ: ܘܬܪܒܐ ܕܡܦܛܡ̈ܐ. ܘܕܡܐ ܕܬܘܪ̈ܐ: ܘܕܐܡܪ̈ܐ: ܘܕܓܕܝ̈ܐ: ܠܐ ܨܒܝܬ.

12 ܝܒ ܟܕ ܐܬܝܬܘܢ ܠܡܚܙܐ ܐܦܝ̈: ܡܢܘ ܒܥܐ ܗܠܝܢ ܡܢ ܐܝܕ̈ܝܟܘܢ ܠܡܕܫ ܕܪ̈ܬܝ.

13 ܝܓ ܠܐ ܬܘܣܦܘܢ ܠܡܝܬܝܘ ܠܝ ܩܘܪ̈ܒܢܐ ܣܪ̈ܝܩܐ: ܒܣܡܐ ܕܡܣܠܝܐ ܗܝ ܠܝ: ܪ̈ܝܫ ܝܪ̈ܚܐ ܘܫܒ̈ܬܐ: ܩܪܝܢ ܐܢܬܘܢ ܟܢܘܫܝܐ. ܠܐ ܐܟܠܐܢܐ ܕܥܘܠܐ ܘܨܘܡܐ.

14 ܝܕ ܪ̈ܝܫ ܝܪ̈ܚܝܟܘܢ ܘܥܐܕ̈ܝܟܘܢ: ܣܢܝܐ ܢܦܫܝ. ܗܘܘ ܥܠܝ ܠܡܥܩܬܐ. ܠܐܐܬ ܠܡܫܩܠ.

15 ܝܗ ܟܕ ܬܦܪܣܘܢ ܐܝܕ̈ܝܟܘܢ: ܐܟܣܐ ܥܝܢ̈ܝ ܡܢܟܘܢ. ܘܐܦ ܬܣܓܘܢ ܨܠܘܬܐ: ܠܐ ܫܡܥ ܐܢܐ. ܐܝܕ̈ܝܟܘܢ ܡܠܝܢ ܕܡܐ.

16 ܝܘ ܣܚܘ ܘܐܬܕܟܘ. ܘܐܥܒܪܘ ܒܝ̈ܫܬܐ ܕܥܒ̈ܕܝܟܘܢ ܡܢ ܩܕܡ ܥܝܢ̈ܝ.

17 ܝܙ ܫܠܘ ܡܢ ܒܝ̈ܫܬܐ: ܘܝܠܦܘ ܠܡܛܝܒܘ. ܒܥܘ ܕܝܢܐ: ܘܐܬܒܥܘ ܠܛܠܘܡܐ. ܕܘܢܘ ܝܬܡ̈ܐ: ܘܕܘܢܘ ܐܪܡܠܬܐ.

18 ܝܚ ܘܬܘ ܢܬܟܘܚ ܥܡ ܚܕ̈ܕܐ: ܐܡܪ ܡܪܝܐ. ܘܐܢ ܢܗܘܘܢ ܚܛܗ̈ܝܟܘܢ ܐܝܟ ܙܚܘܪܝܬܐ: ܐܝܟ ܬܠܓܐ ܢܚܘܪܘܢ. ܘܐܢ ܢܣܡܩܘܢ ܐܝܟ ܙܘܥܝܬܐ: ܐܝܟ ܥܡܪܐ ܢܗܘܘܢ.

19 ܝܛ ܘܐܢ ܬܬܛܦܝܣܘܢ ܘܬܫܬܡܥܘܢ: ܛܘܒܗ ܕܐܪܥܐ ܬܐܟܠܘܢ.

20 ܟ ܘܐܢ ܠܐ ܬܬܛܦܝܣܘܢ ܘܬܡܪܘܢ: ܚܪܒܐ ܬܐܟܠܟܘܢ. ܦܘܡܗ ܕܡܪܝܐ ܡܠܠ.

21 ܟܐ ܐܝܟܢܐ ܗܘܬ ܙܢܝܬܐ ܩܪܝܬܐ ܡܗܝܡܢܬܐ: ܕܡܠܝܐ ܗܘܬ ܕܝܢܐ. ܘܙܕܝܩܘܬܐ ܒܝܬܐ ܒܗ: ܘܗܫܐ ܩܛܘ̈ܠܐ.

22 ܟܒ ܣܐܡܟܝ ܐܣܬܠܝ. ܚܡܪ̈ܝܟܝ ܡܚܠܛ ܡܝ̈ܐ.

11   What are they to me, the multitude of your sacrifices, says the Lord? I have been satiated with burnt offerings of rams, the fat parts of fattened animals. I took no pleasure in the blood of bulls and lambs and goats.

12   When you come to see my face, who has sought these from your hands, to trample my courts?

13   Do not again bring me worthless offerings: the savor is an abomination to me. On the first of the months, and on the Sabbath, you assemble the congregation: I do not partake of deceit and distress.

14   The first days of your months, and your feast days, my soul hated; they were to me as baggage, I was wearied carrying them.[1]

15   When you spread out your hands I shall avert my eyes from you; even though you increase prayer, I am not listening: your hands are full of blood.

16   Wash, purify yourselves, remove the evils of your deeds from before my eyes,

17   Cease from evil deeds. Learn to do good, seek justice, do good to the oppressed, judge the orphans, judge the widows.

18   Come, let us speak with each other, says the Lord: if your sins should be as scarlet, they will be made white as snow; if they should turn red as scarlet dye, they will be like wool.

19   If you will obey and will listen to me, you will eat the good of the land.

20   But if you will not obey, and you dispute, you will be eaten by the sword: the mouth of the Lord has spoken.

21   How did she become a harlot, the faithful city, she who was filled with judgment, righteousness dwelt in her? And now, murderers!

22   Your silver has been rejected; your tavern-keepers mix (the wine with) water.

---

[1] 'carrying them': lit. 'to carry'.

23 ܟܓ ܪܘܪܒܢܝܟܝ ܡܪܘܕܝܢ. ܘܫܘܬܦܐ ܐܢܘܢ ܕܓܢܒܐ. ܟܠܗܘܢ ܪܚܡܝܢ ܫܘܚܕܐ.
ܘܡܫܬܪܓܪܓܝܢ ܠܡܦܪܥܘ ܦܘܪܥܢܐ. ܠܝܬܡܐ ܠܐ ܕܐܢܝܢ: ܘܕܝܢܐ ܕܐܪܡܠܬܐ ܠܐ
ܥܐܠ ܠܘܬܗܘܢ.

24 ܟܕ ܡܛܠ ܗܢܐ ܗܟܢܐ ܐܡܪ ܡܪܐ ܡܪܝܐ ܚܝܠܬܢܐ: ܚܣܝܢܐ ܕܐܝܣܪܐܝܠ: ܘܝ
ܡܬܦܪܥ ܐܢܐ ܡܢ ܣܢܐܝ: ܘܡܬܒܩܡ ܐܢܐ ܡܢ ܒܥܠܕܒܒܝ.

25 ܟܗ ܘܐܦܢܐ ܐܝܕܝ ܥܠܝܟܝ ܘܐܨܪܘܦ ܡܪܘܪܝܟܝ ܠܒܪܗ. ܘܐܥܒܪ ܒܘܟܠܝܟܝ ܟܠܗܘܢ.

26 ܟܘ ܘܐܩܝܡ ܕܝܢܝܟܝ ܐܝܟ ܕܡܢ ܩܕܝܡ: ܘܡܠܟܢܝܟܝ ܐܝܟ ܕܡܢ ܠܩܘܕܡܝܢ.
ܘܒܬܪܟܢ ܬܬܩܪܝܢ ܡܕܝܢܬܐ ܕܙܕܝܩܘܬܐ: ܘܡܕܝܢܬܐ ܕܗܝܡܢܘܬܐ.

27 ܟܙ ܨܗܝܘܢ ܒܕܝܢܐ ܬܬܦܪܩ: ܘܫܒܝܬܗ ܒܙܕܩܘܬܐ.

28 ܟܚ ܘܬܒܪܐ ܕܥܘܠܐ ܘܕܚܛܝܐ ܐܟܚܕܐ. ܘܐܝܠܝܢ ܕܫܒܩܘ ܠܡܪܝܐ ܢܫܘܦܘܢ.

29 ܟܛ ܡܛܠ ܕܢܒܗܬܘܢ ܡܢ ܦܬܟܪܐ ܕܨܒܘ. ܘܢܚܦܪܘܢ ܡܢ ܓܢܢܬܐ ܕܓܒܘ.

30 ܠ ܡܛܠ ܕܢܗܘܘܢ ܐܝܟ ܒܛܡܬܐ ܕܢܬܪܘܢ ܛܪܦܝܗ. ܘܐܝܟ ܓܢܬܐ ܕܡܝܐ ܠܝܬ
ܠܗ.

31 ܠܐ ܘܢܗܘܐ ܚܣܢܗܘܢ ܠܫܥܪܐ: ܘܥܒܕܝܗܘܢ ܠܓܒܠܘܪܝܬܐ. ܘܢܐܩܕܘܢ ܬܪܝܗܘܢ
ܐܟܚܕܐ. ܘܠܝܬ ܕܡܕܥܟ.

23   Your noblemen rebel, they are associates of thieves; they all love a bribe and hurry to requite interest. They do not judge orphans, the judgment of widows does not reach[1] them.

24   Because of this, thus says the Lord of lords, the mighty, the strong one of Israel: Ah! I take vengeance against those who hate me,[2] I am avenged on my enemies.

25   I will turn my hand against you, I will purge[3] your rebels to purity, remove all your evildoers.

26   I will establish your judges as of old, your counselors as from the first, and afterwards you will be called the city of righteousness, the city of faithfulness.

27   Zion will be redeemed by judgment, her captives by righteousness.

28   The crushing of the evildoers and of the sinners, together; and those who have forsaken the Lord will perish.

29   For they will be ashamed of the idols that they coveted, they will blush for the secret places that they chose.

30   For they will be like an oak whose leaves have fallen, like a garden in which there is no water.

31   Their strength will be as tow, their works as sparks, they will burn, the two of them together, and none will quench.[4]

---

[1] 'reach' or 'come to'.

[2] 'those who hate me': lit. 'my haters'.

[3] 'purge' or 'refine'.

[4] 'will quench': lit. 'who quenches'.

ܩܦܠܐܘܢ: ܒ.

1 ܐ ܦܬܓܡܐ ܕܚܙܐ ܐܫܥܝܐ ܒܪ ܐܡܘܨ: ܥܠ ܝܗܘܕܐ: ܘܥܠ ܐܘܪܫܠܡ.

2 ܒ ܢܗܘܐ ܒܚܪܬܐ ܕܝܘܡܬܐ: ܛܘܪ ܒܝܬܗ ܕܡܪܝܐ. ܡܬܩܢ ܒܪܝܫ ܛܘܪܐ: ܘܪܡ ܡܢ ܪܡܬܐ. ܘܢܗܦܟܘܢ ܠܗ ܟܠܗܘܢ ܥܡܡܐ.

3 ܓ ܘܢܐܙܠܘܢ ܥܡܡܐ ܣܓܝܐܐ: ܘܢܐܡܪܘܢ: ܬܘ ܢܣܩ ܠܛܘܪܗ ܕܡܪܝܐ: ܘܠܒܝܬ ܐܠܗܗ ܕܝܥܩܘܒ. ܘܢܠܦ ܡܢ ܐܘܪܚܬܗ. ܘܢܗܠܟ ܒܫܒܝܠܘܗܝ. ܡܛܠ ܕܡܢ ܨܗܝܘܢ ܢܦܩ ܢܡܘܣܐ: ܘܦܬܓܡܗ ܕܡܪܝܐ ܡܢ ܐܘܪܫܠܡ.

4 ܕ ܘܢܕܘܢ ܒܝܬ ܥܡܡܐ. ܘܢܟܣ ܠܥܡܡܐ ܣܓܝܐܐ ܕܪܚܘܩܐ. ܘܢܦܚܡܘܢ ܣܝܦܝܗܘܢ ܠܣܟܐ ܕܦܕܢܐ: ܘܪܘܡܚܝܗܘܢ ܠܡܓܙܠܐ. ܘܠܐ ܢܫܩܘܠ ܥܡܐ ܥܠ ܥܡܐ ܣܝܦܐ. ܘܬܘܒ ܠܐ ܢܐܠܦܘܢ ܩܪܒܐ.

5 ܗ ܕܒܝܬ ܝܥܩܘܒ: ܬܘ ܢܐܙܠ ܒܢܘܗܪܗ ܕܡܪܝܐ.

6 ܘ ܡܛܠ ܕܫܒܩܬܝܗܝ ܠܥܡܟ ܕܒܝܬ ܝܥܩܘܒ. ܡܛܠ ܕܐܬܡܠܝܘ ܐܝܟ ܕܡܢ ܩܕܡ. ܘܡܢܚܫܝܢ ܐܝܟ ܦܠܫܬܝܐ. ܘܒܝܠܕܐ ܕܒܢܝܐ ܢܘܟܪܝܐ ܪܚܡܘ.

7 ܙ ܘܐܬܡܠܝܬ ܐܪܥܗܘܢ ܣܐܡܐ ܘܕܗܒܐ. ܘܠܝܬ ܣܟܐ ܠܓܙܝܗܘܢ. ܘܐܬܡܠܝܬ ܐܪܥܗܘܢ ܪܟܫܐ: ܘܠܝܬ ܣܟܐ ܠܡܪܟܒܬܗܘܢ.

8 ܚ ܘܐܬܡܠܝܬ ܐܪܥܗܘܢ ܦܬܟܪܐ. ܠܥܒܕ ܐܝܕܝܗܘܢ ܣܓܕܘ: ܠܕܥܒܕ ܨܒܥܬܗܘܢ.

9 ܛ ܘܐܬܡܟܟ ܐܢܫܐ: ܘܐܫܬܦܠ ܓܒܪܐ. ܘܠܐ ܬܫܒܘܩ ܠܗܘܢ.

ܩܕ ܒ

10 ܝ ܥܘܠܘ ܒܟܐܦܐ: ܘܐܬܛܫܘ ܒܥܦܪܐ: ܡܢ ܩܕܡ ܕܚܠܬܗ ܕܡܪܝܐ: ܘܡܢ ܗܕܪܐ ܕܪܒܘܬܗ.

Chapter 2

1 The word which Isaiah son of Amos saw concerning Judah and concerning Jerusalem.

2 It will be, in the latter days, that the mountain of the house of the Lord will be established on the summit of the mountains, exalted above[1] the high places, and all the nations will look to it.

3 And they will go, many nations, and will say: Come, let us go up to the mountain of the Lord, and to the house of the God of Jacob; and he will teach us of his ways and we will walk in his paths, for the law comes forth from Zion, and the word of the Lord from Jerusalem.

4 He will judge among the nations, he will rebuke many distant nations; they will beat their blades into ploughshares, their spears into sickles, and nation will not lift up sword against nation, no more will they learn war.

5 (You) of the house of Jacob, come, and let us walk in the light of the Lord.

6 For you have abandoned your people of the house of Jacob: for they were filled as of old,[2] and practice divination like the Philistines, and they have brought up a multitude of foreign children.

7 And their land was filled with silver and gold, and there was no end to their treasures; their land was filled with horses, and there was no end to their chariots.

8 Their land was filled with idols, they worship the work of their hands, that which their fingers have made.

9 And man is humbled, the strong man is brought low; do not[3] forgive them.

II

10 Enter into the flinty rocks, hide yourselves in the dust, for[4] fear of the Lord and of the glory of his strength.

---

[1] 'exalted above': lit. 'higher from'.

[2] 'as of old': lit. 'as from before'.

[3] 'do not' or 'you will not'.

[4] 'for': lit. 'from before'.

11 He will humble the haughty eyes of man, the pride of the strong man will be humbled: the Lord alone will prevail on that day.

12 For the day of the Lord is upon all who exalt themselves and raise themselves up, upon everyone who lifts himself up, so that he will be humbled.

13 Upon all the cedars of Lebanon that are high and uplifted, and upon all the oaks of Bashan.

14 Upon all the high mountains, upon all the high hills.

15 Upon all the high towers, upon all the strong walls.

16 And on all the ships of Tarshish, and on all pleasant prospects.[1]

17 The pride of man will be humbled, the pride of the strong man laid low: the Lord alone will prevail on that day.

18 The idols will completely vanish.

19 And they will go into the caves in the rock, the clefts in the soil, for[2] fear of the Lord and of the glory of his strength, when he arises to subdue the land.

20 On that day, man will throw the idols of gold and of silver, that they made for themselves to worship, to vanity, to the bats.

21 To go into the caves of flinty rock, into the crags of rock, for[3] fear of the Lord and of the glory of his strength, when he arises to subdue the land.

22 Desist from man,[4] whose breath is in his nostrils: for how should he be valued?[5]

---

[1] 'prospects' or 'watchtowers'.

[2] 'for'. See v.10.

[3] 'for'. See v.10.

[4] 'Desist from man': i.e. put no reliance in man.

[5] 'how should he be valued': lit. 'as what is he valued'.

Chapter 3

1 For behold, the Lord of lords takes from Jerusalem and from Judah the stay, the support,[1] all who support with bread, all who support with water.

2 The mighty man, the warrior, the judge, the prophet, the diviner, and the elder.

3 The leader of fifty, the honorable man,[2] the counselor, the skillful carpenters, and the discerning in counsel.

4 I will appoint youths to be their noblemen; mockers will bear rule among them.

5 And the people will fall, man upon man, man upon his friend; young men will contend with the elders,[3] the contemptible with the honorable.

6 For a man will lay hold of, each his brother, of his father's house, and will say to him: You have clothes. Be our ruler, and may this scandal be under your hand.[4]

7 He will answer on that day, he will say: I am not head, for in my house there is no bread, nor even a garment. Do not make me a ruler over the people.

8 For Jerusalem has stumbled, Judah has fallen, for their tongue(s) and the work of their hands were bitter before the Lord, against the cloud[5] of his glory.

---

[1] 'the stay, the support': lit. 'the male supporter and the female supporter'.

[2] 'honorable man': lit. 'honored of face'.

[3] 'elders' or 'old'.

[4] 'may this scandal be under your hand': lit. 'this scandal under your hand'.

[5] 'against the cloud': it is difficult to give an acceptable translation of the Syriac preposition *lāmadh* in this context. See Introduction. Addendum 2.

9 ܛ ܡܣܒ ܒܐܦ̈ܝܗܘܢ ܣܗܕ ܒܗܘܢ. ܘܚܛܗ̈ܝܗܘܢ ܐܝܟ ܣܕܘܡ ܚܘܝܘ: ܘܠܐ
ܐܬܟܣܝܘ. ܘܝ ܠܢܦܫܗܘܢ: ܕܐܬܦܪܥܘ ܠܗܘܢ ܒܝ̈ܫܬܐ.

10 ܝ ܐܡܪܘ ܠܙܕܝܩܐ ܛܒ: ܡܛܠ ܗܢܐ ܦܐܪ̈ܐ ܕܥܒ̈ܕܝܗܘܢ ܢܐܟܠܘܢ.

11 ܝܐ ܘܝ ܠܪܫܝܥܐ ܒܝܫܐ: ܡܛܠ ܕܥܒܕ ܐܝ̈ܕܘܗܝ ܡܬܦܪܥ.

12 ܝܒ ܫܠܝ̈ܛܢܘܗܝ ܕܥܡܝ ܡܒܙܥܝܢ ܠܗ. ܘܢܫ̈ܐ ܐܫܬܠܛܘ ܒܗ. ܥܡܝ ܡܫܒ̈ܚܢܝܟ
ܐܛܥܝܘܟ. ܘܐܘܪܚܐ ܕܫܒ̈ܝܠܝܟ ܒܠܥܘ.

13 ܝܓ ܩܐܡ ܠܕܝܢ ܡܪܝܐ: ܘܩܐܡ ܠܕܝܢ ܠܥܡܗ.

14 ܝܕ ܡܪܝܐ ܒܕܝܢܐ ܢܥܘܠ: ܘܥܡ ܩܫܝ̈ܫܐ ܕܥܡܗ: ܘܥܡ ܪ̈ܘܪܒܢܘܗܝ. ܐܢܬܘܢ ܐܘܩܕܬܘܢ
ܟܪܡܐ. ܘܚܛܘܦܝܐ ܕܡܣܟ̈ܢܐ ܒܒ̈ܬܝܟܘܢ.

15 ܝܗ ܠܡܢܐ ܕܟܝܬܘܢ ܠܥܡܝ: ܘܐܦ̈ܐ ܕܡܣܟ̈ܢܐ ܐܛܚܢܬܘܢ: ܐܡܪ ܡܪܝܐ ܚܝܠܬܢܐ.

16 ܝܘ ܚܠܦ ܕܐܬܬܪܝܡ ܒ̈ܢܬ ܨܗܝܘܢ: ܘܗܠܟ̈ܝܢ ܒܨܘܪܐ ܙܩܝܦܐ. ܘܒܪܡܙܐ ܕܥܝ̈ܢܐ
ܡܗܠܟܢ ܗ̄ܘܝ. ܘܡܫܦܪ̈ܢ ܒܪ̈ܓܠܝܗܝܢ: ܘܡܩܫܩ̈ܢ.

17 ܝܙ ܢܩܪܚ ܡܪܝܐ ܩܘܕܩܕܐ ܕܒ̈ܢܬ ܨܗܝܘܢ. ܘܡܪܝܐ ܐܣܟܡܗܝܢ ܢܓܠܐ.

18 ܝܚ ܒܝܘܡܐ ܗܘ: ܢܥܒܪ ܡܪܝܐ ܫܘܒܚܐ ܕܡܣ̈ܐܢܝܗܝܢ. ܘܙܒ̈ܢܗܝܢ: ܘܙܪ̈ܘܠܝܗܝܢ.

9   Their hypocrisy[1] witnesses against them: they made manifest their sins like Sodom, they were not concealed. Alas for them![2] for they have brought[3] evil rewards upon themselves.[4]

10   Say to the righteous - Good: because of this they will eat the fruits of their works.

11   Alas! for the wicked - Evil: for the work of his hands is repaid.

12   The rulers of my people root him out, women bear rule over him; my people, your leaders have led you astray, they have disrupted the way of your paths.

13   The Lord stands up to judge, stands up to judge his people.

14   The Lord will enter into judgment with the elders of his people and with its noblemen. You have set the vineyard on fire, the spoil of the poor is in your houses.

15   Why have you harmed my people, shamed the faces of the poor? says the mighty Lord.

16   For they were haughty, the daughters of Zion: they walked haughtily,[5] as they walked they beckoned with their eyes,[6] with mincing feet,[7] exciting the imagination.

17   The Lord will lay low the heads of the daughters of Zion, the Lord will expose their form.

18   On that day the Lord will remove the ostentation of their garments, their ornaments, and their necklaces.

---

[1] 'Their hypocrisy': lit. 'their putting on an appearance'.

[2] 'Alas for them!': lit. 'Woe to their soul'.

[3] 'brought' or 'requited'.

[4] 'brought evil rewards upon themselves': lit. 'they have placed upon themselves evil rewards'.

[5] 'haughtily' or 'with a high neck'.

[6] 'as they walked they beckoned with their eyes': lit. 'with beckoning of eyes they were walking'.

[7] 'with mincing feet': lit. '(with) their feet mincing'.

19   The curls[1] of their hair, their plaits,[2] their temples.[3]

20   The decorations of their faces, their earrings, their necklaces,

21   Their anklets, their bracelets, and their bangles,[4]

22   Their coats, their long robes, their fine white linens, their purple garments,

23   Their long coats, their violet (garments), their scarlet (garments), the casket[5] (for) all their decorations.

24   And there will be dust[6] instead of their fragrant scent, and instead of the girdle round their waists they will tie on aprons, and instead of plaits there will be bald patches,[7] and instead of their violet (garments) they will cover themselves with sackcloth: for their beauty will be destroyed.

25   Your strong men will fall by the sword, your mighty men in battle.

26   They will lament, her gates will dwell in mourning, her victory[8] will fall to the ground.

---

[1] 'curls': lit. 'things of a round shape', so some sort of curling hair style may be meant. Alternatively, round decorative objects could be intended.

[2] 'plaits' or 'bracelets'.

[3] 'temples': probably 'the hair of their temples'.

[4] 'anklets … bangles' or 'bangles … anklets'.

[5] 'casket' or 'cloak, wrapper'.

[6] 'dust' or 'vinegar'.

[7] 'bald patches' or 'tearing out of the hair'.

[8] 'victory' or 'innocence'.

Chapter 4

1 Seven women will seize hold of one man on that day and they will say to him: We will eat our (own) bread, we will be clothed in our (own) garments, only let your name be given to us,[1] take away our shame.

2 On that day, the rising of the Lord will be for praise and for honor, and the fruits of the earth for pride and for praise, for that which remains of Israel.

3 And he that remains in Zion, and he who remains in Jerusalem, will be called holy, everyone who is written in Jerusalem for life.

4 The Lord will wash away the foulness of the daughters of Zion, he will remove the blood from the midst of Jerusalem, with a wind of judgment, with a burning wind.[2]

5 The Lord will create on its whole foundation, for the mountain of Zion on its surroundings, a cloud by day, and smoke and flashing of flame of fire by night, for upon all the glory it will form a covering.

6 And the shelter will be for shade during the day from the parching heat, to cover and to shelter from the downpour and from the rainfall.

---

[1] 'given to us': lit. 'called upon us'.

[2] 'wind … wind' or 'spirit … spirit'.

Chapter 5

1   I will sing praises for my beloved: the praise[1] of my beloved for his vineyard. My beloved had a vineyard, in a corner of a fertile place.

2   He labored over it and surrounded it with a hedge, he planted shoots in it, he built a tower in the middle of it, he also constructed a winepress in it: he waited for it to bear grapes, but it bore husks.

3   Now, men of Judah and inhabitants of Jerusalem: judge between me and my vineyard.

4   What more was it fitting to do for my vineyard, that I have not done for it? For I waited for it to bear grapes, but it bore husks.

5   Now I will show you something that I am doing to my vineyard. I am breaking down its tower, and it will be plundered,[2] I am breaking through its hedge, and it will be trodden down.[3]

6   I will lay it waste, it will not be pruned, it will not be cultivated, thorns and a tangle of briers will sprout in it, I will command the clouds not to send down rain upon it.

7   As for the vineyard of the mighty Lord, the house is that of the house of Israel, and the men who are from Judah are a new and cherished planting. I awaited justice but there was violence; and righteousness, but behold! a cry.

III

8   Woe to those who bring near house to house, join field with field! that you may seize a place, and may dwell, you alone, in the midst of the land.

9   In my ears the mighty Lord was heard: many houses will be desolate,[4] without inhabitant.

---

[1] 'praise' or 'chant'.

[2] 'plundered': lit. 'for spoil'.

[3] 'trodden down': lit. 'for treading down'.

[4] 'desolate': lit. 'a desolation'.

10 ܝ ܡܛܠ ܕܥܣܪ ܐܦܕ̈ܢܐ ܕܟܪܡܐ ܢܥܒܕܘܢ ܚܕܐ ܡܫܘܚܬܐ: ܘܙܪܥܐ ܕܟܘܪ ܢܥܒܕ ܓܪܒܐ.

11 ܝܐ ܘܝ ܠܕܡܩܕܡܝܢ ܒܨܦܪܐ: ܘܪܗܛܝܢ ܠܫܟܪܐ. ܘܡܘܚܪܝܢ ܒܪܡܫܐ: ܘܚܡܪܐ ܡܘܩܕ ܠܗܘܢ.

12 ܝܒ ܒܟܢܪ̈ܐ: ܘܒܩܝܬܪ̈ܐ: ܘܒܦܠܓܠܐ: ܘܒܙܡܪ̈ܐ: ܚܡܪܐ ܫܬܝܢ. ܘܒܥܒܕܘܗܝ ܕܡܪܝܐ ܠܐ ܡܣܬܟܠܝܢ. ܘܒܥܒܕ ܐܝܕܘܗܝ ܠܐ ܚܙܝܢ.

13 ܝܓ ܡܛܠ ܗܢܐ ܐܫܬܒܝ ܥܡܝ ܡܢ ܕܠܐ ܝܕܥܬܐ. ܘܐܣܓܝܘ ܡܝܬ̈ܝܗܘܢ ܡܢ ܟܦܢܐ. ܘܥܡܗܘܢ ܡܢ ܨܗܝܐ.

14 ܝܕ ܡܛܠ ܗܢܐ ܐܦܬܚܬ ܫܝܘܠ ܢܦܫܗ̇. ܘܦܬܚܬ ܦܘܡܗ̇ ܕܠܐ ܣܟ: ܘܢܚܬܘܢ ܠܗ̇ ܡܫܒܚ̈ܢܐ ܘܡܣܟ̈ܢܐ ܘܥܫܝ̈ܢܐ.

15 ܝܗ ܘܢܬܡܟܟ ܐܢܫܐ: ܘܢܬܡܫܦܠ ܓܒܪܐ. ܘܥܝ̈ܢܐ ܪ̈ܡܬܐ ܢܬܡܟܟܢ.

16 ܝܘ ܘܢܬܪܘܡ ܡܪܝܐ ܚܝܠܬܢܐ ܒܕܝܢܐ. ܘܐܠܗܐ ܩܕܝܫܐ ܢܬܩܕܫ ܒܙܕܝܩܘܬܐ.

17 ܝܙ ܘܢܪܥܘܢ ܐܡܪ̈ܐ ܒܕܒܪܗܘܢ. ܘܚܪ̈ܒܬܐ ܕܦܛܝܡ̈ܐ: ܓܝܘ̈ܪܐ ܢܐܟܠܘܢ ܐܢܝܢ.

18 ܝܚ ܘܝ ܠܕܢܓܕܝܢ ܚܛܗ̈ܝܗܘܢ ܐܝܟ ܚܒܠܐ ܐܪܝܟܐ. ܘܐܝܟ ܒܢܝܪܐ ܕܥܓܠܬܐ ܚܛܝܬܗܘܢ.

19 ܝܛ ܘܐܡܪܝܢ: ܢܣܬܪܗܒ ܢܥܒܕ ܡܪܝܐ ܥܒܕ̈ܘܗܝ ܕܢܚܙܐ ܐܢܝܢ. ܘܬܬܩܪܒ ܘܬܐܬܐ ܬܪܥܝܬܗ ܕܩܕܝܫܐ ܕܐܝܣܪܐܝܠ ܘܢܕܥܝܗ̇.

10   For ten yokes[1] of vineyard will make one bath[2] and the seed of a cor[3] will make one seah.[4]

11   Woe to those who rise early in the morning and run for strong drink; tarry in the evening, wine setting them on fire.

12   With harps, with lyres,[5] with tambourines, with timbrels, they drink wine; but they do not recognize the works of God, they give no heed to the work of his hands.

13   Therefore my people has been taken into captivity, for want of knowledge; their dead from hunger have multiplied, from thirst they have increased.

14   Therefore Sheol has enlarged herself, opened her mouth without limit;[6] they will descend into her, the glorious, the honorable, the powerful.

15   And man will be humbled, the strong man will be brought low, proud eyes will be humbled.

16   But the mighty Lord will be lifted up on high in judgment, the holy God sanctified in righteousness.

17   The lambs will feed as of their right;[7] the inhabitants will eat the wastelands that have been restored.[8]

18   Woe to those who lengthen their sins as a lengthened cord, as the rein of a calf their sin.

19   Saying: Quickly may the Lord hasten his works, so that we may see them; may the counsel of the Holy One of Israel come near, arrive, that we may know it.

---

[1] 'yokes': the area of a yoke is uncertain (one suggestion is about 2/3 of an acre), but the meaning of the prophecy is clear: the land will yield a poor crop.

[2] one 'bath': 40-45 liters, approximately eight gallons.

[3] a 'cor': approximately 11.5 bushels. A bushel is approximately 35 liters dry measure.

[4] a 'seah': approximately 1.5 pecks. A peck is approximately 9 liters dry measure.

[5] 'lyres' or 'cithers'.

[6] 'without limit': lit. 'that not an end'.

[7] 'as of their right': lit. 'in their rule'.

[8] 'the inhabitants will eat the wastelands that have been restored': lit. 'the restored wastelands, the inhabitants will eat them'.

20   Woe to those who call evil good, and good evil, who substitute light for darkness and darkness for light, who substitute[1] bitter for sweet and sweet for bitter.

21   Woe to those who are wise in their own eyes,[2] prudent in their own opinion.[3]

22   Woe to those who are mighty to drink wine, to the strong men who mix strong drink.

23   Who acquit the guilty because of his bribe, but who set aside the acquittal of the innocent.[4]

24   Because of this, as the stubble is consumed by the tongue of fire that kindles (it), by the flame that sets on fire they will be consumed, their root will be like fine dust, their bud will rise up like chaff, because they despised the law of the mighty Lord, they provoked to anger the speech of the Holy One of Israel.

25   Therefore the anger of the Lord has raged against his people, he has raised his hand against them, he struck them, the mountains trembled, their dead bodies were as refuse in the midst of the markets: yet for all these his anger has not turned away, his hand is yet high.

26   He will raise a sign to the nations from far away, he will whistle to them from the ends of the earth, and quickly and speedily they will come.

27   They will not be weary, they will not stumble, they will not slumber nor will they sleep; they will not loosen the girdle round their loins, nor will their sandal-straps be broken.

28   Their arrows are sharp, their bows are strung,[5] the hooves of their horses will seem like flints, their wheels like a whirlwind.

29   Their roaring like that of a roaring lion, like a roaring lion's whelp, who seizes the prey and carries (it) off: and there is none who saves.

---

[1] 'substitute … substitute': lit. 'set … set'. The Syriac of 10:33 is different.

[2] 'in their own eyes': lit. 'in the eyes of their soul'.

[3] 'in their own opinion': lit. 'before their faces'.

[4] 'the innocent': lit. 'innocent from them'.

[5] 'strung': lit. 'full'.

30 ܀ ܘܢܣܒ ܚܟܡܬܗ ܚܢܦܘܬܐ ܗܘ: ܐܝܢ ܢܥܩܒܝܗ ܦܡܐ. ܡܢܫܘܬܗ ܟܠܘܟܐ: ܘܢܗܘܐ
ܣܩܘܒܠܐ ܘܐܘܚܕܢܐ. ܘܢܗܘܐ ܢܣܒ ܚܢܦܚܝܘܬܗ.

30   He will roar at them on that day, like the roaring of the sea; they will look upon the land and there will be darkness and distress, the light will grow dim in their thick darkness.

ܡܦܩܬܐ: ܘ.

1 ܐ ܒܫܢܬܐ ܕܡܝܬ ܥܘܙܝܐ ܡܠܟܐ: ܚܙܝܬ ܠܡܪܝܐ ܝܬܒ ܥܠ ܟܘܪܣܝܐ ܪܡܐ.
ܘܫܘܠܐ ܕܡܦܘܠܘܗܝ ܡܠܐ ܗܝܟܠܗ.

2 ܒ ܘܣܪܦܐ ܩܝܡܝܢ ܠܥܠ ܡܢܗ: ܫܬ ܫܬ ܓܦܝܢ ܠܚܕ ܡܢܗܘܢ. ܒܬܪܬܝܢ
ܡܟܣܝܢ ܦܪܨܘܦܗ: ܘܒܬܪܬܝܢ ܡܟܣܝܢ ܪܓܠܝܗܘܢ: ܘܒܬܪܬܝܢ ܦܪܚܝܢ.

3 ܓ ܘܩܪܝܢ ܗܢܐ ܠܗܢܐ: ܘܐܡܪܝܢ: ܩܕܝܫ: ܩܕܝܫ: ܩܕܝܫ: ܡܪܝܐ ܚܝܠܬܢܐ: ܕܡܠܝܐ
ܟܠܗ ܐܪܥܐ ܬܫܒܘܚܬܗ.

4 ܕ ܘܙܥ ܐܣܩܘܦܬܐ ܕܬܪܥܐ ܡܢ ܩܠܐ ܕܩܪܐ: ܘܒܝܬܐ ܐܬܡܠܝ ܬܢܢܐ.

5 ܗ ܘܐܡܪܬ ܘܝ ܠܝ ܕܬܘܝܪ ܐܢܐ: ܡܛܠ ܕܓܒܪܐ ܐܢܐ ܛܡܐ ܣܦܘܬܐ: ܘܒܝܬ ܥܡܐ
ܕܛܡܐ ܣܦܘܬܗ ܥܡܪ ܐܢܐ. ܘܠܡܠܟܐ ܡܪܝܐ ܚܝܠܬܢܐ ܚܙܝ ܥܝܢܝ.

6 ܘ ܘܦܪܚ ܠܘܬܝ ܚܕ ܡܢ ܣܪܦܐ: ܘܒܐܝܕܗ ܓܘܡܪܬܐ ܢܣܒ ܡܢ ܡܕܒܚܐ:
ܒܡܘܠܚܬܐ.

7 ܙ ܘܩܪܒ ܠܦܘܡܝ: ܘܐܡܪ ܠܝ: ܗܐ ܩܪܒܬ ܗܕܐ ܠܣܦܘܬܟ: ܘܢܥܒܪ ܥܘܠܟ:
ܘܚܛܗܝܟ ܢܫܬܒܩܘܢ.

8 ܚ ܘܫܡܥܬ ܩܠܗ ܕܡܪܝܐ ܕܐܡܪ: ܠܡܢ ܐܫܕܪ: ܘܡܢ ܢܐܙܠ. ܘܐܡܪܬ ܗܐ ܐܢܐ
ܫܕܪܝܢܝ.

9 ܛ ܘܐܡܪ ܠܝ: ܙܠ ܐܡܪ ܠܥܡܐ ܗܢܐ: ܫܡܥܘ ܡܫܡܥ: ܘܠܐ ܬܣܬܟܠܘܢ. ܘܚܙܘ
ܡܚܙܐ: ܘܠܐ ܬܕܥܘܢ.

10 ܝ ܐܬܥܒܝ ܠܗ ܠܒܗ ܕܥܡܐ ܗܢܐ: ܘܐܕܢܝܗܘܢ ܐܝܩܪ: ܘܥܝܢܝܗܘܢ ܥܡܨ. ܕܠܐ
ܢܚܙܐ ܒܥܝܢܝܗܘܢ: ܘܢܫܡܥ ܒܐܕܢܝܗܘܢ: ܘܢܣܬܟܠ ܒܠܒܗ: ܘܢܬܘܒ ܘܢܫܬܒܩ
ܠܗ.

Chapter 6

1   In the year that Uzziah the king died, I saw the Lord sitting upon a high throne, and the robe, with the train of his skirts, filled his temple.

2   And seraphim standing above him, each of them with six wings,[1] covering his face with two, covering his feet with two, and flying with two.

3   Calling, this one to that one,[2] and saying: Holy, holy, holy, the mighty Lord, for all the earth is filled with his praises.

4   The doorposts of the doors shook at the voice that was calling,[3] and the house was filled with smoke.

5   I said: Woe is me, for I am confounded, for I am a man of unclean lips,[4] and among a people of unclean lips I live, and my eyes have seen the king, the mighty Lord.

6   One of the seraphim flew towards me; and in his hand a coal he had carried from the altar with tongs.

7   He touched my mouth and said to me: See! This has touched your lips so that your iniquity may pass away, your sins may be forgiven

8   I heard the voice of the Lord that said: Whom shall I send, and who will go? I said: See! I (am here), send me.

9   He said to me: Go, say to this people 'Listen! Listen with care[5] - but you will not understand. See! Look closely[6] - but you will not know'.

10   So, harden the heart of this people, make its ears heavy, its eyes dull,[7] so that it will not see with its eyes or hear with its ears, or understand with its heart, and repent, and it would be forgiven it.

---

[1] 'each of them with six wings': lit. 'six, six wings to one of them'.

[2] 'this one to that one': lit. 'this one to this one'. A standard idiom.

[3] 'voice that was calling' or 'voice of one who was calling'.

[4] 'a people of unclean lips': lit. 'a people which unclean are its lips'.

[5] 'Listen! listen with care': lit. 'Hear, hearing'.

[6] 'See! look closely': lit. 'See, seeing'.

[7] 'make … its eyes dull': lit. 'stop up its eyes'.

11 ܝܐ ܘܐܡܪܬ ܥܕܡܐ ܠܐܡܬܝ ܡܪܝܐ: ܘܐܡܪ ܥܕܡܐ ܕܢܚܪ̈ܒܢ ܩܘܪ̈ܝܐ ܡܢ ܥܡܘܪ ܕܝܬܒ:
ܘܒ̈ܬܐ ܡܢ ܥܡܘܪ ܐܢܫܐ: ܘܐܪܥܐ ܬܫܬܐܪ ܚܪܒܐ.

12 ܝܒ ܘܢܪܚܩ ܡܪܝܐ ܠܐܢܫܐ: ܘܬܣܓܐ ܡܫܒܩܘܬܐ ܒܓܘܗ̇ ܕܐܪܥܐ.

13 ܝܓ ܘܢܦܫܘܢ ܒܗ̇ ܚܕ ܡܢ ܥܣܪܐ: ܘܬܬܘܒ: ܘܬܗܘܐ ܠܡܪܥܝܬܐ: ܐܝܟ ܒܘܛܡܬܐ ܘܐܝܟ
ܒܠܘܛܐ ܕܢܦܠ ܡܢ ܩܘܪܡܗ. ܙܪܥܐ ܗܘ ܩܕܝܫܐ ܢܨܒܬܗ.

11   I said: Until when, Lord? He said: Until the cities are laid waste, uninhabited,[1] the houses empty of people,[2] and the land becomes waste, deserted.

12   The Lord will drive man away, and in the midst of the land the wasteland will increase.

13   But those remaining in it (will be) one tenth; and it will return and it will be burnt, like a terebinth, like an oak that fell from its acorn-cup:[3] the seed is holy, its planting.

---

[1] 'uninhabited': lit. 'without an inhabitant'.

[2] 'empty of people' or 'without a man'.

[3] 'acorn-cup' or 'root'.

ܡܓܠܬܐ: ܙ.

1 ܐ ܘܗܘܐ ܒܝܘܡܬܗ ܕܐܚܙ: ܒܪ ܝܘܬܡ: ܒܪ ܥܘܙܝܐ ܡܠܟܐ ܕܝܗܘܕܐ: ܣܠܩ ܪܨܝܢ ܡܠܟܐ ܕܐܪܡ: ܘܦܩܚ ܒܪ ܪܘܡܠܝܐ ܡܠܟܐ ܕܐܝܣܪܐܝܠ ܠܐܘܪܫܠܡ: ܠܡܬܟܬܫܘ ܥܡܗ: ܘܠܐ ܐܫܟܚܘ ܕܢܬܟܬܫܘܢ ܥܡܗ.

2 ܒ ܘܐܬܐܡܪ ܠܒܝܬܗ ܕܕܘܝܕ: ܘܐܫܬܘܝܘ ܐܪܡ ܥܡ ܐܦܪܝܡ. ܘܙܥ ܠܒܗ ܘܠܒܐ ܕܥܡܗ: ܐܝܟ ܕܙܝܥܝܢ ܐܝܠܢܐ ܕܥܒܐ ܡܢ ܩܕܡ ܪܘܚܐ.

ܣܕ ܓ.

3 ܓ ܘܐܡܪ ܡܪܝܐ ܠܐܫܥܝܐ: ܦܘܩ ܠܐܘܪܥܗ ܕܐܚܙ: ܐܢܬ ܘܫܐܪܝܫܘܒ ܒܪܟ: ܥܠ ܓܢܒ ܢܩܒܐ ܒܪܟܬܐ. ܕܒܐܘܪܚܐ ܕܚܩܠܗ ܕܩܨܪܐ.

4 ܕ ܘܐܡܪ ܠܗ: ܐܙܕܗܪ ܘܫܠܝ: ܘܠܐ ܬܕܚܠ. ܘܠܒܟ ܠܐ ܢܬܪܟ. ܡܢ ܩܕܡ ܬܪܝܢ ܙܢܒܐ: ܐܘܕܐ ܡܬܢܢܢܐ: ܡܢ ܚܡܬܐ ܕܪܘܓܙܗ ܕܪܨܝܢ ܘܕܒܪ ܪܘܡܠܝܐ.

5 ܗ ܚܠܦ ܕܐܬܡܠܟܘ ܥܠܝܟ ܒܝܫܬܐ: ܐܪܡ: ܘܐܦܪܝܡ: ܘܒܪ ܪܘܡܠܝܐ.

6 ܘ ܘܐܡܪܘ. ܢܣܩ ܠܝܗܘܕ ܘܢܥܩܪܝܗ: ܘܢܬܪܥܝܗ. ܘܢܡܠܟ ܒܗ ܡܠܟܐ ܠܒܪ ܛܒܐܝܠ.

7 ܙ ܗܟܢܐ ܐܡܪ ܡܪܝܐ ܐܠܗܐ: ܠܐ ܬܩܘܡ ܘܠܐ ܬܗܘܐ.

8 ܚ ܡܛܠ ܕܪܫܐ ܕܐܪܡ ܕܪܡܣܘܩ: ܘܪܫܐ ܕܕܪܡܣܘܩ ܪܨܝܢ: ܘܒܥܘܕ ܫܬܝܢ ܘܚܡܫ ܫܢܝܢ: ܢܬܒܪ ܐܦܪܝܡ ܡܢ ܥܡܐ.

9 ܛ ܘܪܫܐ ܕܐܦܪܝܡ ܫܡܪܝܢ: ܘܪܫܐ ܕܫܡܪܝܢ ܒܪ ܪܘܡܠܝܐ. ܘܐܢ ܠܐ ܬܗܝܡܢܘܢ: ܐܦ ܠܐ ܬܫܬܪܪܘܢ.

10 ܝ ܘܐܘܣܦ ܬܘܒ ܡܪܝܐ ܠܡܐܡܪ ܠܐܚܙ.

Chapter 7

1 And it happened, in the days of Ahaz son of Jotham son of Uzziah king of Judah that Rezin king of Aram went up, and Pekah son of Remaliah king of Israel, to Jerusalem to fight against it; but they were unable to fight[1] against it.

2 It was told to those of the house of David that Aram has conspired with Ephraim; his heart shook, and the heart of his people as the trees of a forest shake before the wind.

IV

3 The Lord said to Isaiah: Go out to meet Ahaz,[2] you and Sharnashub your son, to the bank of the upper pool that is in the path of the field of the fuller.

4 Say to him: Take care, be still, do not fear, let not your heart[3] be confounded by these two tails, brands singed by the fury of the anger of Rezin and of the son of Remaliah.

5 For they have taken evil counsel against you, Aram, Ephraim, and the son of Remaliah.

6 They have said: Let us go up against Judah, and break her down, make a breach in her, and make king over her[4] the son of Tabeel.

7 Thus says the Lord God: It will not stand, it will not be.

8 For the head of Aram is Damascus, and the head of Damascus is Rezin, and after 65 years Ephraim will waste away from nationhood.[5]

9 The head of Ephraim is Samaria, and the head of Samaria is the son of Remaliah. If you do not believe you will also not understand.

10 And the Lord spoke again to Ahaz saying:

---

[1] 'unable to fight': lit. 'not able that they might fight'.

[2] 'to meet Ahaz': lit. 'to the meeting of Ahaz'.

[3] 'do not fear, let not your heart …' or 'you shall not fear, your heart shall not …': either imperfects in a modal sense, or negative imperatives (pl.).

[4] 'make king over her': lit. 'make king over her a king'.

[5] 'waste away from nationhood': lit. 'waste from a nation'.

11 ܝܐ ܫܐܠ ܠܟ ܐܬܐ ܡܢ ܡܪܝܐ ܐܠܗܟ: ܒܥܘܡܩ: ܫܐܠ : ܐܘ ܐܪܝܡ ܠܥܠ.

12 ܝܒ ܘܐܡܪ ܐܚܙ. ܠܐ ܐܫܐܠ : ܘܠܐ ܐܢܣܐ ܠܡܪܝܐ ܐܠܗܝ.

13 ܝܓ ܘܐܡܪ. ܫܡܥܘ ܒܝܬܗ ܕܕܘܝܕ: ܙܥܘܪܐ ܗܝ ܠܟܘܢ ܕܡܠܐܝܢ ܐܢܬܘܢ ܠܒܢܝܢܫܐ:
ܐܠܐ ܕܡܠܐܝܢ ܐܦ ܠܐܠܗܝ.

14 ܝܕ ܡܛܠ ܗܢܐ ܢܬܠ ܠܟܘܢ ܡܪܝܐ ܗܘ ܐܬܐ: ܗܐ ܒܬܘܠܬܐ ܒܛܢܐ ܘܝܠܕܐ
ܒܪܐ: ܘܬܩܪܐ ܫܡܗ ܥܡܢܘܐܝܠ.

15 ܝܗ ܚܐܘܬܐ ܘܕܒܫܐ ܢܐܟܘܠ : ܕܢܕܥ ܠܡܣܠܝܘ ܒܒܝܫܬܐ: ܘܠܡܓܒܐ ܛܒܬܐ.

16 ܝܘ ܡܛܠ ܕܥܕܠܐ ܢܕܥ ܛܠܝܐ ܠܡܣܠܝܘ ܒܒܝܫܬܐ: ܘܠܡܓܒܐ ܛܒܬܐ:
ܬܫܬܒܩ ܐܪܥܐ ܕܕܚܠ ܐܢܬ ܡܢܗ ܡܢ ܩܕܡ ܬܪܝܢ ܡܠܟܝܗ̈.

17 ܝܙ ܡܪܝܐ ܢܝܬܐ ܥܠܝܟ: ܘܥܠ ܥܡܟ: ܘܥܠ ܒܝܬ ܐܒܘܟ: ܝܘܡܬܐ ܕܠܐ ܐܬܘ ܡܢ
ܝܘܡܐ ܕܐܥܒܪ ܠܐܦܪܝܡ ܡܢ ܝܗܘܕܐ ܡܠܟܐ ܕܐܬܘܪ.

18 ܝܚ ܘܢܗܘܐ ܒܝܘܡܐ ܗܘ: ܢܫܪܩ ܡܪܝܐ ܠܕܒܒܐ: ܕܒܣܘܦܝ ܢܗܪܘܬܐ ܕܡܨܪܝܢ:
ܘܠܕܒܘܪܝܬܐ ܕܒܐܪܥܐ ܕܐܬܘܪ.

19 ܝܛ ܘܢܐܬܘܢ ܘܢܬܢܝܚܘܢ ܟܠܗܘܢ ܒܢܚܠܐ ܕܚܘܪܒܐ: ܘܒܢܩܥܬܐ ܕܟܐܦܐ: ܘܒܟܠܗܘܢ
ܢ̈ܚܠܐ.

20 ܟ ܒܝܘܡܐ ܗܘ: ܢܓܪܘܥ ܡܪܝܐ ܒܡܣܦܪܐ ܪܒܐ: ܒܥܒܪܘܗܝ ܕܢܗܪܐ ܠܡܠܟܐ
ܕܐܬܘܪ: ܡܢ ܪܫܗ ܘܠܡܙܥܪܐ ܕܪ̈ܓܠܘܗܝ. ܐܦ ܕܩܢܗ ܢܣܦܘܠ.

21 ܟܐ ܘܢܗܘܐ ܒܝܘܡܐ ܗܘ: ܢܚܐ ܓܒܪܐ ܥܓܠܬܐ ܕܬܘܪܐ: ܘܬܪܬܝܢ ܥܢܐ.

22 ܟܒ ܘܢܗܘܐ ܡܢ ܣܘܓܐܐ ܕܥܒܕܝܢ ܚܠܒܐ: ܢܐܟܘܠ ܚܐܘܬܐ: ܡܛܠ ܕܕܒܫܐ ܘܚܐܘܬܐ
ܢܐܟܘܠ ܡܢ ܕܡܫܬܚܪ ܒܓܘܗ ܕܐܪܥܐ.

11 Ask for a sign for yourself from the Lord your God: Go deep, ask, or go high above.

12 But Ahaz said: I will not ask, I will not test the Lord my God.

13 He said: Listen, house of David, it is a small thing to you, that you weary man: but will you also weary my God?

14 Therefore the Lord God will give you a sign: see! a virgin conceives and bears a son, and he will be called: 'His name is Emmanuel'.

15 Butter[1] and honey he will eat, when he will know to reject evil and to choose good.

16 For, before the child will know to reject evil and to choose good it will be deserted, the land which you loathe,[2] because of[3] its two kings.

17 The Lord will bring upon you, upon your people, and upon the house of your father, days which have not come since the day when I will make Ephraim pass away from Judah: the king of Assyria.

18 It will be on that day that the Lord will whistle to the flies that are in the lower parts of the rivers of Egypt, and the bees that are in the land of Assyria.

19 They will come, they will settle, all of them, in the valley of Yatot, in the chasms of the rock, in all the holes.

20 On that day the Lord will shave with a razor the watered (region), on the further shores of the river, the king of Assyria: from his head to the hair of his feet;[4] he will also carry off his beard.

21 And it will be on that day, a strong man will support a heifer and two flocks of sheep.[5]

22 And it will be, from the abundance of milk they have made, he will eat butter, for honey and butter they will eat, who remain in the midst of the land.

---

[1] 'Butter' or 'Curds'.

[2] 'which you loathe' or 'in which you are weary/distressed'.

[3] 'because of': lit. 'from before'.

[4] 'hair of his feet': euphemistic.

[5] 'two flocks of sheep' or 'two sheep'.

23 And it will be, on that day, every place in which there are a thousand vines worth[1] a thousand pieces of silver, will be a tangle of briars and thorns.

24 With arrows and with bows they will enter there, for with a tangle of briars and thorns all the land will be filled.

25 And all the hills which used to be ploughed,[2] will be ploughed; the fear of a tangle of briars and thorns will not enter there,[3] and it will be a place of pasture for oxen, a place which sheep will tread.[4]

---

[1] 'worth': lit. 'at (the price of)'.

[2] 'which used to be ploughed' or 'in which the plough was ploughing'.

[3] 'the fear of a tangle of briars and thorns will not enter there' or 'you will not enter there (for) fear of the tangle of briars and thorns'.

[4] 'place which sheep will tread': lit. 'a place of treading for the sheep'.

ܩܦܠܐܘܢ: ܚ.

1 ܐ ܘܐܡܪ ܠܝ ܡܪܝܐ ܣܒ ܠܟ ܓܠܝܘܢܐ ܪܒܐ: ܘܟܬܘܒ ܒܓܘܗ ܒܟܬܒܐ ܕܐܢܫܐ: ܠܡܣܪܗܒ ܫܒܝܐ: ܘܠܡܒܙܒܙ ܒܙܬܐ.

2 ܒ ܘܣܗܕܘ ܠܝ ܣܗܕܐ ܕܡܗܝܡܢܝܢ: ܠܐܘܪܝܐ ܟܗܢܐ: ܘܠܙܟܪܝܐ ܒܪ ܒܪܟܝܐ.

3 ܓ ܘܩܪܒܬ ܠܢܒܝܬܐ: ܘܒܛܢܬ ܘܝܠܕܬ ܒܪܐ. ܘܐܡܪ ܠܝ ܡܪܝܐ: ܩܪܝ ܫܡܗ ܡܣܪܗܒ ܫܒܝܐ: ܘܡܒܙܒܙ ܒܙܬܐ.

4 ܕ ܡܛܠ ܕܥܕܠܐ ܢܕܥ ܛܠܝܐ ܠܡܩܪܐ ܐܒܐ ܘܐܡܐ: ܢܫܩܘܠ ܚܝܠܐ ܕܕܪܡܣܘܩ: ܘܒܙܬܐ ܕܫܡܪܝܢ: ܩܕܡ ܡܠܟܐ ܕܐܬܘܪ.

5 ܗ ܘܐܘܣܦ ܬܘܒ ܡܪܝܐ ܠܡܐܡܪ ܠܝ.

6 ܘ ܚܠܦ ܕܐܣܠܝܘ ܥܡܐ ܗܢܐ ܡܝܐ ܕܫܝܠܘܚܐ ܕܪܕܝܢ ܒܫܠܝܐ: ܘܚܕܝܘ ܒܪܨܝܢ ܘܒܒܪ ܪܘܡܠܝܐ.

7 ܙ ܡܛܠ ܗܢܐ ܡܣܩ ܥܠܝܗܘܢ ܡܪܝܐ: ܡܝܐ ܕܢܗܪܐ ܥܫܝܢܐ ܘܣܓܝܐܐ: ܠܡܠܟܐ ܕܐܬܘܪ: ܘܠܟܠܗ ܐܝܩܪܗ. ܘܢܣܩ ܥܠ ܟܠܗܘܢ ܦܨܝܕܝܗܘܢ: ܘܢܗܠܟ ܥܠ ܟܠܗܘܢ ܫܘܪܝܗܘܢ.

8 ܚ ܘܢܥܒܪ ܒܝܗܘܕܐ: ܘܢܫܛܘܦ ܘܢܥܒܪ: ܘܥܕܡܐ ܠܨܘܪܐ ܢܡܛܐ. ܘܢܗܘܐ ܦܘܫܛܐ ܕܓܦܘܗܝ: ܡܠܐ ܦܬܝܗ ܕܐܪܥܟ ܥܡܢܘܐܝܠ.

9 ܛ ܙܘܥܘ ܥܡܡܐ: ܘܐܬܬܒܪܘ. ܘܨܘܬܘ ܟܠܗܘܢ ܪܘܚܩܝܗ ܕܐܪܥܐ. ܐܬܚܝܠܘ ܘܐܬܬܒܪܘ.

10 ܝ ܐܬܡܠܟܘ ܡܠܟܬܐ: ܘܬܬܒܛܠ. ܡܠܠܘ ܡܠܬܐ: ܘܠܐ ܬܬܩܝܡ ܡܛܠ ܥܡܢܘܐܝܠ.

Chapter 8

1   The Lord said to me: Take a large writing tablet and write on it, in the script of man: 'To hasten the captivity and to press hard upon the spoil'.

2   I called to witness for me[1] trustworthy witnesses, Uriah the priest and Zechariah the son of Berechiah.

3   I touched the prophetess, and she conceived and bore a son; the Lord said to me: Call his name 'Hastening the Captor, the Spoiler Pressing Hard'.

4   For before the child will know how to call 'Father' and 'Mother' he will take away the possession of Damascus and the spoil of Samaria, before the king of Assyria.

5   The Lord spoke to me again:

6   Because this people have rejected the waters of Shiloah that flow calmly,[2] and have rejoiced in Rezin and the son of Remaliah,

7   Because of this, the Lord will bring up upon them the waters of the river, many and strong, the king of Assyria and all his glory, and it will go up upon all their watercourses, it will flow[3] over all their city walls.

8   It will pass over Judah, overflow and pass over, it will come as far as the neck, and with the spread[4] of its wings the breadth of your land will be filled, Emmanuel.

9   Tremble, nations, and be broken; give ear, all distant ones of the earth, strengthen yourselves: yet be broken.

10 Take counsel - it will be brought to naught; speak a word - it will not be established: for God is with us.[5]

---

[1] 'I called to witness for me … witnesses': lit. 'There witnessed (sing.) for me witnesses'.

[2] 'calmly': lit. 'in silence'.

[3] 'flow': lit. 'go'.

[4] 'spread': lit. 'height'.

[5] 'God is with us': the meaning of the name 'Emmanuel' which in the Peshitta is written as a single word.

11 ܝܐ ܗܟܢܐ ܐܡܪ ܠܝ ܡܪܝܐ: ܐܝܟ ܚܣܝܢ ܐܝܕܐ: ܘܐܪܕܝܢܝ: ܠܐ ܐܗܠܟ ܒܐܘܪܚܗ ܕܥܡܐ ܗܢܐ.

12 ܝܒ ܘܐܡܪ: ܠܐ ܬܐܡܪܘܢ ܡܪܕܐ: ܐܝܟ ܕܐܡܪ ܥܡܐ ܗܢܐ ܡܪܕܐ: ܘܒܕܚܠܬܗܘܢ ܠܐ ܬܕܚܠܘܢ: ܘܠܐ ܬܙܘܥܘܢ.

13 ܝܓ ܠܡܪܝܐ ܚܝܠܬܢܐ ܩܕܫܘ: ܘܗܘܝܘ ܕܚܠܬܟܘܢ: ܘܗܘܝܘ ܡܙܝܥܢܟܘܢ.

14 ܝܕ ܘܢܗܘܐ ܠܡܩܕܫܐ: ܘܠܟܐܦܐ ܕܬܘܩܠܬܐ: ܘܠܫܘܥܐ ܕܬܘܩܠܬܐ: ܠܬܪܬܝܗܘܢ ܒܬܐ ܕܐܝܣܪܐܝܠ: ܠܦܚܐ ܘܠܡܬܩܠܢܘܬܐ ܠܥܡܘܪܘܗܝ ܕܐܘܪܫܠܡ.

15 ܝܗ ܘܢܬܬܩܠܘܢ ܒܗܘܢ ܣܓܝܐܐ: ܘܢܦܠܘܢ: ܘܢܬܬܒܪܘܢ: ܘܢܬܬܨܝܕܘܢ: ܘܢܬܬܐܚܕܘܢ.

16 ܝܘ ܨܘܪ ܣܗܕܘܬܐ: ܘܚܬܘܡ ܢܡܘܣܐ.

17 ܝܙ ܒܬܠܡܝܕܝ ܐܣܟܐ ܠܡܪܝܐ ܕܐܗܦܟ ܐܦܘܗܝ ܡܢ ܕܒܝܬ ܝܥܩܘܒ: ܘܐܣܟܐ ܠܗ.

18 ܝܚ ܗܐ ܐܢܐ ܘܒܢܝܐ ܕܝܗܒ ܠܝ ܡܪܝܐ: ܠܐܬܐ ܘܠܬܕܡܘܪܬܐ ܒܐܝܣܪܐܝܠ: ܡܢ ܩܕܡ ܡܪܝܐ ܚܝܠܬܢܐ ܕܫܪܐ ܒܛܘܪܐ ܕܨܗܝܘܢ.

19 ܝܛ ܘܐܢ ܢܐܡܪܘܢ ܠܟܘܢ: ܕܫܐܠܘ ܡܢ ܐܣܘܬܐ ܘܡܢ ܚܪܫܐ: ܕܡܨܦܨܦܝܢ: ܘܡܗܓܝܢ: ܠܐ ܗܘ ܥܡܐ ܕܠܐܠܗܗ ܐܠܐ ܕܫܐܠܝܢ ܠܡܝܬܐ ܥܠ ܚܝܐ.

20 ܟ ܠܢܡܘܣܐ ܘܠܣܗܕܘܬܐ: ܕܠܐ ܢܐܡܪܘܢ ܐܝܟ ܡܠܬܐ ܗܕܐ: ܕܠܝܬ ܠܗ ܠܡܠܬܐ ܗܕܐ ܫܘܚܕܐ.

21 ܟܐ ܘܢܥܒܪ ܒܗ: ܘܢܬܩܫܐ: ܘܢܟܦܢ. ܘܡܐ ܕܟܦܢ ܢܪܓܙ: ܘܢܨܚܐ ܠܡܠܟܗ ܘܠܐܠܗܗ.

22 ܟܒ ܘܢܚܘܪ ܠܥܠ: ܘܒܐܪܥܐ ܢܚܘܪ: ܘܗܐ ܐܘܠܨܢܐ ܘܚܫܘܟܐ: ܘܥܩܬܐ ܘܥܡܛܢܐ ܢܬܕܚܐ. ܡܛܠ ܕܠܐ ܢܬܦܢܐ ܠܐܝܢܐ ܕܡܥܩ: ܐܝܟ ܕܒܙܒܢܐ ܩܕܡܝܐ.

11 Thus spoke the Lord to me, as (one who) firmly holds the hand: he will turn me aside so that I shall not walk in the way of this people,

12 And he said: Do not say 'a conspiracy' as this people said 'a conspiracy'; do not fear their fear,[1] do not tremble.

13 Sanctify the mighty Lord: he is your fear, he is your helper.

14 May he be as a sanctuary, a stone of affliction, a stumbling flint, to the two houses of Israel, as snares and as nets to the inhabitants of Jerusalem.

15 Many will stumble on them; they will fall and be broken, hunted and seized.

16 Bind fast the testimony, seal the law.

17 With my teaching, I will wait for the Lord who has turned away his face from the house of Jacob, I will look for him.

18 See, I and the children whom the Lord has given me are for a sign and a wonder in Israel, from the mighty Lord who dwelt on Mount Zion.

19 When they say to you: 'Ask of the diviners and the soothsayers who chirp and murmur', (reply:) 'They were not God's people, these who ask of the dead concerning the living'.

20 On account of the law and on account of the testimony, they should not speak thus,[2] there is none to give a bribe concerning it.

21 He will pass over it, he will harden it, and he will hunger; when he has hungered he will be enraged, he will revile his king and his God.

22 He will turn to the heavens,[3] he will gaze upon the land, but adversity and darkness and sadness and gloom will drive him away: for he will not harass the one who is distressed as in former time.

---

[1] 'fear' or 'false god', 'idol', or 'dreaded one'.

[2] 'thus': lit. 'as this word'.

[3] 'the heavens': lit. 'above'.

ܦܨܠܐ: ܛ.

ܝܕ ܫ

1 ܐ ܡܙܒܢ ܐܪܥܐ ܕܙܒܘܠܘܢ܆ ܘܐܪܥܐ ܕܢܦܬܠܝ. ܘܐܚܪܝܬܐ ܝܩܪ܆ ܐܘܪܚܐ ܕܝܡܐ܆
ܥܒܪܗ ܕܝܘܪܕܢܢ ܗܘܐ܆ ܓܠܝܠܐ ܕܥܡܡܐ.

2 ܒ ܥܡܐ ܕܡܗܠܟ ܒܚܫܘܟܐ܆ ܚܙܘ ܢܘܗܪܐ ܪܒܐ. ܘܝܬܒܝ ܒܐܬܪܐ ܕܛܠܠܝ ܡܘܬܐ܆
ܢܘܗܪܐ ܕܢܚ ܥܠܝܗܘܢ.

3 ܓ ܐܣܓܝܬ ܥܡܐ܆ ܘܠܗ ܐܘܪܒܬ ܚܕܘܬܐ. ܚܕܝܘ ܩܕܡܝܟ ܐܝܟ ܗܢܘܢ ܕܚܕܝܢ
ܒܚܨܕܐ܆ ܘܐܝܟ ܗܢܘܢ ܕܕܝܨܝܢ ܡܐ ܕܡܦܠܓܝܢ ܒܙܬܐ.

4 ܕ ܡܛܠ ܕܢܝܪܐ ܕܫܘܥܒܕܗܘܢ܆ ܘܫܘܛܐ ܕܟܬܦܗܘܢ܆ ܘܫܒܛܐ ܕܡܫܥܒܕ ܗܘܐ
ܠܗܘܢ܆ ܬܒܪܬ ܐܝܟ ܝܘܡܐ ܕܡܕܝܢ.

5 ܗ ܡܛܠ ܕܟܠ ܡܐܢܐ ܡܣܐܢ ܒܪܘܥܬܐ. ܘܠܒܘܫܐ ܡܥܓܠܠ ܒܕܡܐ. ܘܢܗܘܐ
ܠܝܩܕܐ ܘܠܡܐܟܘܠܬܐ ܕܢܘܪܐ.

6 ܘ ܡܛܠ ܕܛܠܝܐ ܐܬܝܠܕ ܠܢ܆ ܘܒܪܐ ܐܬܝܗܒ ܠܢ. ܘܗܘܬ ܫܘܠܛܢܗ ܥܠ
ܟܬܦܗ. ܘܐܬܩܪܝ ܫܡܗ ܬܕܡܘܪܐ ܘܡܠܟܐ܆ ܐܠܗܐ ܓܢܒܪܐ ܕܥܠܡܐ܆ ܡܠܟܗ
ܕܫܠܡܐ.

7 ܙ ܠܡܣܓܝܘ ܫܘܠܛܢܗ. ܘܠܫܠܡܗ ܠܝܬ ܣܟܐ܆ ܥܠ ܟܘܪܣܝܗ ܕܕܘܝܕ܆
ܘܥܠ ܡܠܟܘܬܗ. ܕܢܬܩܢܝܗ ܘܢܣܡܟܝܗ ܒܕܝܢܐ ܘܒܙܕܝܩܘܬܐ܆ ܡܢ ܗܫܐ ܘܥܕܡܐ
ܠܥܠܡ. ܛܢܢܗ ܕܡܪܝܐ ܚܝܠܬܢܐ ܢܥܒܕ ܗܕܐ.

8 ܚ ܦܬܓܡܐ ܫܕܪ ܡܪܝܐ ܒܝܥܩܘܒ܆ ܘܢܦܠ ܒܐܝܣܪܝܠ.

9 ܛ ܘܢܕܥܘܢ ܥܡܡܐ ܟܠܗܘܢ܆ ܐܦܪܝܡ ܘܥܡܘܪܘܗܝ ܕܫܡܪܝܢ܆ ܒܓܐܝܘܬܐ ܘܒܪܡܘܬ
ܠܒܐ܆ ܘܐܡܪܝܢ.

Chapter 9

V

1   The land of Zebulun has hastened, (so has) the land of Naphtali, and the possession has prevailed: the way of the sea, the other side of the river Jordan, Galilee of the nations.

2   The people who walk in darkness have seen a great light; those who dwell in the land of the shadows of death, light has risen upon them.

3   You have increased the nation, have made it rejoice greatly;[1] they have rejoiced before you as those who rejoice in the harvest, as those who exult when they divide the spoil.

4   For the yoke of their subjugation, the staff of their shoulder, and the rod of the one who subjugated them, you have broken as the day of Midian.

5   For every voice heard in trembling, and the garment soaking in blood, is to be burnt,[2] for fuel[3] for the fire.

6   For a child has been born to us, a son has been given to us, and its government has been upon his shoulder, and his name has been called the Wondrous One, the Counselor, God the Mighty One of Eternity, the Ruler of Peace.

7   To increase his government, and (may there be) no end[4] to his peace, upon the throne of David and unto his kingdom; so that he will establish it, and he may support it with justice and with righteousness, from now and forever: the zeal of the mighty Lord brings this to pass.

8   The Lord has sent a word to Jacob, and it has fallen on Israel.

9   They will know (it), all the peoples, Ephraim and the inhabitants of Samaria, with pride and with arrogant heart,[5] saying:

---

[1] 'have made it rejoice greatly': lit. 'have magnified gladness for it'.

[2] 'to be burnt': lit. 'for burning'.

[3] 'fuel': lit. 'food'.

[4] '(may there be) no end': lit. 'there is no end'.

[5] 'arrogant heart': lit. 'with grandeur of heart'.

10 ܝ ܠܒ̈ܢܐ ܢܦܠܘ: ܘܢܒܢܐ ܒܟܐܦ̈ܐ. ܘܢܦܣܘܩ ܫܩ̈ܡܐ: ܘܐܪ̈ܙܐ ܢܫܚܠܦ.

11 ܝܐ ܘܢܥܫܢ ܡܪܝܐ ܠܐܠܨ̈ܘܗܝ ܕܪܨܝܢ ܥܠܘܗܝ. ܘܠܒܥܠܕܒ̈ܒܘܗܝ ܢܚܪܘܒ.

12 ܝܒ ܐܪܡ ܡܢ ܡܕܢܚܐ: ܘܦܠܫ̈ܬܝܐ ܡܢ ܡܥܪܒܐ. ܘܢܐܟܠܘܢܗ ܠܐܝܣܪܐܝܠ ܒܟܠܗ
ܦܘܡܗܘܢ. ܘܒܗܠܝܢ ܟܠܗܝܢ ܠܐ ܗܦܟ ܪܘܓܙܗ. ܘܐܦ ܐܝܕܗ ܪܡܐ.

13 ܝܓ ܘܥܡܐ ܠܐ ܐܬܦܢܝܘ: ܠܡܢ ܕܡܚܝܗܝ. ܘܠܡܪܝܐ ܚܝܠܬܢܐ ܠܐ ܒܥܘ.

14 ܝܕ ܘܢܦܣܘܩ ܡܪܝܐ ܡܢ ܐܝܣܪܐܝܠ: ܪܫܐ ܘܕܘܢܒܬܐ: ܘܕܘܢܒܬܐ ܘܪܫܐ: ܒܝܘܡܐ ܚܕ.

15 ܝܗ ܣܒܐ ܘܢܣܝܒ ܐܦ̈ܐ ܗܘܝܘ ܪܫܐ. ܘܢܒܝܐ ܕܡܠܦ ܫܘܩܪܐ ܗܘܝܘ ܕܘܢܒܬܐ.

16 ܝܘ ܘܢܗܘܘܢ ܡܛܥܝܢ̈ܘܗܝ ܕܥܡܐ ܗܢܐ: ܡܛܥܝܢ ܘܡܬܛܥܝܢ ܒܗ.

17 ܝܙ ܡܛܠ ܗܢܐ ܠܐ ܢܚܕܐ ܡܪܝܐ ܥܠ ܥܠܝܡ̈ܝܗܘܢ. ܘܥܠ ܝܬܡ̈ܝܗܘܢ
ܘܥܠ ܐܪ̈ܡܠܬܗܘܢ ܠܐ ܢܪܚܡ. ܡܛܠ ܕܟܠܗܘܢ ܚܢܦܝܢ ܘܒܝܫܝܢ. ܘܟܠ
ܦܘܡ ܡܡܠܠ ܣܟܠܘܬܐ. ܘܒܗܠܝܢ ܟܠܗܝܢ ܠܐ ܗܦܟ ܪܘܓܙܗ. ܘܐܦ ܐܝܕܗ
ܪܡܐ.

18 ܝܚ ܡܛܠ ܕܝܩܕܐ ܪܘܫܥܐ ܐܝܟ ܢܘܪܐ: ܘܬܐܟܘܠ ܟܘܒ̈ܐ ܘܩܘ̈ܪܐ. ܘܬܐܚܕ ܒܥܒ̈ܐ
ܕܥܒܐ. ܘܢܬܥܩܒܘܢ ܐܝܟ ܥܛܪܐ ܕܬܢܢܐ.

19 ܝܛ ܒܚܡܬܗ ܕܡܪܝܐ ܚܝܠܬܢܐ ܐܬܚܪܒܬ ܐܪܥܐ. ܘܗܘܐ ܥܡܐ ܐܝܟ ܗܘ ܕܐܟܝܠܬܗ ܢܘܪܐ.
ܘܓܒܪ ܥܠ ܐܚܘܗܝ ܠܐ ܢܚܘܣ.

20 ܟ ܘܢܓܙܘܪ ܥܠ ܝܡܝܢܗ ܘܢܟܦܢ. ܘܢܐܟܘܠ ܥܠ ܣܡܠܗ. ܘܠܐ ܢܣܒܥܘܢ. ܓܒܪ
ܒܣܪܐ ܕܕܪܥܗ ܢܐܟܘܠ.

10   We will lay bricks, we will hew stones,[1] we will cut down the sycamores and exchange them for cedars.[2]

11   The Lord will strengthen the oppressors of Rezin against him, he will provoke his enemies,

12   Edom from the east, and the Philistines from the west. They will devour Israel with wide open[3] mouth: yet despite all these his anger has not turned away, his hand is yet high.

13   The people did not repent[4] until they were beaten; they did not seek the mighty Lord.

14   The Lord cast out from Israel, the head and the tail, the tail and the head, in a single day.

15   The elder, and the honorable man[5], he is the head; the prophet who teaches falsehood, he is the tail.

16   The leaders of this people will be (those) leading (it) astray, submerging it.

17   Therefore the Lord will not rejoice in their young men, he will not cherish their orphans and their widows, for they are all impious and evil, and every mouth speaks folly. Yet despite all these his anger has not turned away, his hand is yet high.

18   For sin smoldered like a fire: it will devour the tangle of briars and thorns, it will burn the boughs of the forest; the chosen will be enveloped in the smoke.

19   At the rebuke of the mighty Lord the land trembled, the people were as the fuel of the fire:[6] no man will spare his brother.[7]

20   He will tear at his right hand yet be hungry, he will devour at his left hand yet not be satisfied; each will eat the flesh of his arm.

---

[1] 'hew stones': lit. 'hew hewn stones'.

[2] 'exchange them for cedars': lit. 'cedars we will exchange'.

[3] 'wide open': lit. 'whole, all'.

[4] 'repent': lit. 'turn, turn back'.

[5] 'honorable man': lit. 'honorable of face'.

[6] 'the fuel of the fire': lit. 'as he whom the fire devoured'.

[7] 'no man will spare his brother': lit. 'a man will not spare his brother'.

21 مܢ ܡܢܬܐ ܠܐܚܪ̈ܢܐ: ܘܐܚܪ̈ܢܐ ܟܡܢܬܐ: ܘܐܚܣܪܐ ܚܠܐ ܣܘܗܘܐ. ܘܒܗܘܟܡ ܩܠܗܡ
ܠܐ ܗܘܝ ܙܘܚܪܗ. ܘܒܐܘܒ ܐܝܪܗ ܙܘܢܐ.

21   Manasseh against Ephraim, Ephraim against Manasseh, together against Judah: yet despite all these his anger has not turned away, his hand is yet high.

48

Chapter 10

1   Woe to those who promulgate unfair precepts,[1] who write iniquity.

2   To pervert the justice of the needy, to plunder the lawsuit of the poor of my people, that they may take captive the widows, plunder the orphans.

3   What will you do on the day of retribution, at the tumult that comes from far away; to whom will you flee for help,[2] to whom will you leave your honor?

4   So that you may not kneel beneath the prisoners, fall beneath the slain. Yet despite all these his anger has not turned away, his hand is yet high.

5   Ah Assyria![3] he is the rod of my anger; he is, in their hand, the staff of my scourge.[4] I will send him against the profane people.

6   I will give him command of a wrathful people, so that he may take captives,[5] plunder the spoil, make it trodden down[6] like the mire in the streets.

7   But he was not made like this,[7] and in his heart it was not purposed thus; but he would destroy in his heart, bring to an end many peoples.

8   For he said: See! the noblemen likewise are kings.

9   See! Balyo is like Carchemish, Hamath like Arpad, Samaria like Damascus.

10   And as my hand has found the kingdoms of idols, of graven images, from Jerusalem and from Samaria,

---

[1] 'promulgate unfair precepts': lit. 'declare declarations of deceit'.

[2] 'for help': lit. 'that you may be helped'.

[3] 'Ah Assyria!' or 'Woe to Assyria!'.

[4] 'the staff in their hand is my scourge': lit. 'it is in their hand, the staff of my scourge'.

[5] 'take captives': lit. 'take captive captivity'.

[6] 'trodden down': lit. 'a treading down'.

[7] 'made like this' or 'likened thus'.

11 ܝܐ ܘܐܝܟ ܕܥܒܕܬ ܠܫܡܪܝܢ ܘܠܦܬܟܪܝܗ̇: ܗܟܢܐ ܐܥܒܕ ܠܐܘܪܫܠܡ ܘܠܦܬܟܪܝܗ̇.

12 ܝܒ ܘܢܗܘܐ ܡܐ ܕܫܠܡ ܡܪܝܐ ܟܠܗܘܢ ܥܒܕܘܗܝ ܒܛܘܪܐ ܕܨܗܝܘܢ: ܘܒܐܘܪܫܠܡ: ܐܦܩܘܕ ܥܠ ܦܐܪܘܗܝ ܕܠܒܐ ܪܒܐ ܕܡܠܟܐ ܕܐܬܘܪ: ܘܥܠ ܫܘܒܗܪܐ ܕܪܘܡܐ ܕܥܝܢܘܗܝ.

13 ܝܓ ܡܛܠ ܕܐܡܪ ܕܒܚܝܠܐ ܕܐܝܕܝ ܥܒܕܬ: ܘܒܚܟܡܬܝ. ܡܛܠ ܕܡܣܬܟܠܢ ܐܢܐ. ܐܥܒܪܬ ܬܚܘܡܝܗܘܢ ܕܥܡܡܐ. ܘܒܙܒܙܬܗܘܢ ܒܙܬ. ܘܐܚܬܬ ܡܕܝܢܬܐ ܕܝܬܒܢ.

14 ܝܕ ܘܐܫܟܚܬ ܐܝܕܝ ܐܝܟ ܩܢܐ ܠܚܝܠܐ ܕܥܡܡܐ: ܘܐܝܟ ܕܟܢܫܝܢ ܒܝܥܐ ܕܫܒܝܩܢ: ܟܢܫܬܗ ܠܟܠܗ ܐܪܥܐ. ܘܠܐ ܗܘܐ ܕܡܢܝܕ ܓܦܐ: ܘܦܬܚ ܦܘܡܗ ܘܨܦܪ.

15 ܝܗ ܕܠܡܐ ܡܫܬܒܗܪ ܢܪܓܐ ܥܠ ܡܢ ܕܦܣܩ ܒܗ. ܐܘ ܡܫܬܐܪܡ ܡܣܪܐ ܥܠ ܡܢ ܕܢܣܪ ܒܗ. ܐܘ ܡܫܬܥܠܐ ܫܒܛܐ ܥܠ ܡܢ ܕܡܪܝܡ ܠܗ.

16 ܝܘ ܡܛܠ ܗܢܐ ܢܫܕܪ ܡܪܝܐ ܐܠܗܐ ܚܝܠܬܢܐ: ܐܒܕܢܐ ܥܠ ܡܫܡܢܘܗܝ. ܘܬܚܝܬ ܐܝܩܪܗ ܬܐܩܕ ܝܩܕܢܗ ܐܝܟ ܝܩܕܢܐ ܕܢܘܪܐ.

17 ܝܙ ܘܢܗܘܐ ܢܘܗܪܗ ܕܐܝܣܪܐܝܠ ܠܢܘܪܐ: ܘܩܕܝܫܘܗܝ ܠܫܠܗܒܝܬܐ. ܘܬܐܩܕ ܘܬܐܟܘܠ ܟܘܒܗ ܘܦܩܘܠܘܗܝ ܒܝܘܡܐ ܚܕ.

18 ܝܚ ܘܫܘܒܚܐ ܕܥܒܗ ܘܕܟܪܡܠܗ: ܡܢ ܢܦܫܐ ܘܥܕܡܐ ܠܒܣܪܐ ܢܣܦܪ. ܘܢܗܘܐ ܐܝܟ ܕܠܐ ܗܘܐ.

19 ܝܛ ܘܫܪܟܐ ܕܩܝܣܐ ܕܥܒܗ: ܠܡܢܝܢܐ ܢܗܘܘܢ. ܘܛܠܝܐ ܢܟܬܘܒ ܐܢܘܢ.

11   As I did to Samaria and to her idols, so I will do to Jerusalem and to her idols.

12   And it will come to pass, when the Lord will have completed all his works on Mount Zion and in Jerusalem, I will punish the fruits of the great heart of the king of Assyria, and the glory of the pride of his eyes.

13   For he said: By the might of my hand I have done it, and by my wisdom, for I am prudent; I have set aside the borders[1] of the nations, I have plundered their riches, I have subdued the inhabited cities.

14   My hand has acquired the might of the nations, like a nest; as those who gather the forsaken daughters[2] I have gathered the whole land; there was not one raising a wing, who opened his mouth, or was chirping.

15   Should the axe should be praised more than the man who hews with it? Or the saw be exalted over him who saws with it? or the rod be raised above him who raises it?

16   Therefore the mighty Lord God will send destruction upon his fat ones; instead of his glory his fuel will burn like the fuel of a fire.

17   And the light of Israel will be the fire, and his holy ones the flame,[3] and it will set on fire and devour its tangle of briars and thorns in a single day.

18   The glory of his dense forest and of his fertile place,[4] from the soul even to the flesh, he will lay waste: it will be as if it had never been.[5]

19   The remnant of the trees of his forest will be very few,[6] so that[7] a young child might write them down.

---

[1] 'have set aside the borders': lit. 'have made the borders … pass away'.

[2] 'daughters' or 'young'.

[3] 'the fire … the flame': lit. 'for fire … for flame'.

[4] 'fertile place' or 'Carmel'; 'fertile place' is a semantic borrowing from the Hebrew. So too 29:17, 32:15,16.

[5] 'as if it had never been': lit. 'as that which was not'.

[6] 'very few': lit. 'for number'.

[7] 'so that': lit. 'and'.

20 ܟ ܘܢܗܘܐ ܒܝܘܡܐ ܗܘ: ܠܐ ܢܘܣܦ ܬܘܒ ܫܪܟܗ ܕܐܝܣܪܝܠ: ܘܐܝܠܝܢ ܕܐܫܬܘܙܒܘ
ܡܢ ܕܒܝܬ ܝܥܩܘܒ ܠܡܬܬܟܠܘ ܥܠ ܡܢ ܕܡܚܐ ܐܢܘܢ. ܐܠܐ ܢܬܬܟܠܘܢ
ܒܩܘܫܬܐ ܥܠ ܡܪܝܐ ܩܕܝܫܐ ܕܐܝܣܪܝܠ.

21 ܟܐ ܘܫܪܟܐ ܢܬܦܢܘܢ: ܫܪܟܗ ܕܝܥܩܘܒ ܠܘܬ ܐܝܠ ܓܢܒܪܐ.

ܩܦ ܗ

22 ܟܒ ܐܢ ܢܗܘܐ ܥܡܟ ܐܝܣܪܝܠ: ܐܝܟ ܚܠܐ ܕܝܡܐ: ܫܪܟܐ ܢܬܦܢܘܢ ܡܢܗܘܢ. ܓܙܝܡ
ܘܦܣܩ: ܘܫܛܦ ܒܙܕܝܩܘܬܐ.

23 ܟܓ ܡܛܠ ܕܓܡܝܪܘܬܐ ܘܦܣܩܬܐ ܥܒܕ ܡܪܝܐ ܚܝܠܬܢܐ ܒܟܠܗ ܐܪܥܐ.

24 ܟܕ ܗܟܢܐ ܐܡܪ ܡܪܝܐ ܚܝܠܬܢܐ: ܠܐ ܬܕܚܠ ܥܡܝ ܕܥܡܪ ܒܨܗܝܘܢ: ܡܢ ܐܬܘܪܝܐ
ܕܡܚܐ ܠܟ ܒܫܒܛܗ: ܘܫܒܛܗ ܡܪܝܡ ܥܠܝܟ ܒܐܘܪܚܐ ܕܡܨܪܝܢ.

25 ܟܗ ܡܛܠ ܕܥܕ ܩܠܝܠ ܙܥܘܪ: ܘܢܫܬܠܡ ܪܘܓܙܝ ܘܚܡܬܝ ܥܠ ܚܒܠܗܘܢ.

26 ܟܘ ܘܢܥܝܪ ܥܠܘܗܝ ܡܪܝܐ ܚܝܠܬܢܐ ܫܘܛܐ: ܐܝܟ ܡܚܘܬܐ ܕܡܕܝܢ ܕܒܛܘܪܐ ܕܥܘܪܒ:
ܘܫܒܛܗ ܥܠ ܝܡܐ: ܘܢܪܝܡܝܗ ܒܐܘܪܚܐ ܕܡܨܪܝܢ.

27 ܟܙ ܘܢܗܘܐ ܒܝܘܡܐ ܗܘ: ܢܥܒܪ ܫܘܥܒܕܗ ܡܢ ܟܬܦܟ: ܘܢܝܪܗ ܡܢ ܨܘܪܟ.
ܘܢܬܚܒܠ ܢܝܪܐ ܡܢ ܩܕܡ ܡܫܚܐ.

28 ܟܚ ܐܬܐ ܠܥܝܬ: ܘܥܒܪ ܒܡܓܪܘܢ. ܘܒܡܟܡܣ ܣܡ ܡܐܢܘܗܝ.

29 ܟܛ ܥܒܪ ܠܡܥܒܪܬܐ ܕܓܒܥ ܠܓܒܥ ܒܝܬ ܒܠܢ: ܕܪܡܬ ܙܥܬ: ܘܓܒܥܬ ܫܐܘܠ
ܥܪܩܬ.

20 It will come to pass on that day that he will no more increase the remnant of Israel, and those of the house of Jacob who are delivered, to put their trust in him who smote them; but they will put their trust in the truth, in the Lord, the Holy One of Israel.

VI

21 The remnant will return, the remnant of Jacob, to El Shaddai.[1]

22 And (even) if your people Israel will be like the sand of the sea, a remnant of them shall return, cut short, hewn down: it has overflowed in righteousness.

23 For the destruction,[2] and the judgments,[3] the mighty Lord makes in all the earth.

24 Thus says the mighty Lord: Do not be afraid, my people who dwell in Zion, of the Assyrian who strikes you with his rod, raising his staff upon you in the way of Egypt.

25 Because in a little while my anger and my fury at their corruption[4] will be completed.

26 The mighty Lord will stir up a whip against him, like the scourge of Midian at Mount Horeb: his rod was over the sea, he raised it in the way of Egypt.

27 And it will come to pass on that day: his servitude will pass from your shoulder, his yoke from your neck, the yoke will be completely destroyed.[5]

28 He has come to Anat, passed over Megiddo, he has put his baggage in Michmash.

29 He has passed, by the pass of Geba, to the place of our lodging for the night;[6] Ramath was afraid, Gibat-Saul fled.

---

[1] 'El Shaddai' or 'Almighty God'.

[2] 'destruction' or 'end'.

[3] 'judgments' or 'things decided/decreed'.

[4] 'corruption' or 'destruction'.

[5] 'completely destroyed': lit. 'from measure'.

[6] 'the place of our lodging for the night' or 'Beth-Bytan'.

54

30   Neigh out loud,[1] daughter of Gallim; give ear, Laishah; answer, Anathoth.

31   Madmenah has fled, the inhabitants of Gebim have become strong.

32   Until today he halts at Nob; he menaces[2] the mountain of the daughter of Zion and the heights of Jerusalem.

33   See! The Lord, the mighty God, overthrows the glorious in strength; the elevated[3] will be humbled, the high will be brought down.

34   He will lop off the boughs of the forest with iron, and Lebanon in its glory will fall.

---

[1] 'out loud': lit. 'with your voice'.

[2] 'menaces': lit. 'moves his hand against'.

[3] 'elevated': lit. 'high in stature'.

ܩܦܠܐܘܢ: ܝܐ.

1 ܐ ܘܢܦܘܩ ܫܒܛܐ ܡܢ ܥܩܪܗ ܕܐܝܫܝ. ܘܢܦܪܥ ܢܘܪܒܐ ܡܢ ܫܪܫܗ.

2 ܒ ܘܬܬܢܝܚ ܘܬܫܪܐ ܥܠܘܗܝ ܪܘܚܐ ܕܐܠܗܐ: ܪܘܚܐ ܕܚܟܡܬܐ ܘܕܣܘܟܠܐ: ܪܘܚܐ ܕܡܠܟܐ ܘܕܓܢܒܪܘܬܐ: ܪܘܚܐ ܕܝܕܥܬܐ ܘܕܕܚܠܬܗ ܕܡܪܝܐ.

3 ܓ ܘܢܕܢܚ ܒܕܚܠܬܗ ܕܡܪܝܐ. ܘܠܐ ܐܝܟ ܕܚܙܝܢ ܥܝܢܘܗܝ ܢܕܘܢ: ܘܠܐ ܐܝܟ ܕܫܡܥܢ ܐܕܢܘܗܝ ܢܟܣ.

4 ܕ ܢܕܘܢ ܒܟܐܢܘܬܐ ܠܡܣܟܢܐ: ܘܢܟܣ ܒܬܪܝܨܘܬܐ ܠܡܟܝܟܐ ܕܐܪܥܐ. ܢܡܚܐ ܠܐܪܥܐ ܒܫܒܛܐ ܕܦܘܡܗ. ܘܒܪܘܚܐ ܕܣܦܘܬܗ ܢܩܛܘܠ ܠܪܫܝܥܐ.

5 ܗ ܬܗܘܐ ܙܕܝܩܘܬܐ ܐܣܪ ܚܨܘܗܝ: ܘܗܝܡܢܘܬܐ ܚܙܩܐ ܕܚܨܘܗܝ.

6 ܘ ܢܪܥܐ ܕܐܒܐ ܥܡ ܐܡܪܐ. ܘܢܡܪܐ ܥܡ ܓܕܝܐ ܢܪܒܘܥ. ܘܥܓܠܐ ܘܓܘܪܝܐ ܕܐܪܝܐ ܘܬܘܪܐ: ܐܟܚܕܐ ܢܪܥܘܢ. ܘܛܠܝܐ ܙܥܘܪܐ ܢܕܒܪ ܐܢܘܢ.

7 ܙ ܬܘܪܬܐ ܘܕܒܐ ܐܟܚܕܐ ܢܪܥܝܢ. ܘܒܢܝܗܘܢ ܐܟܚܕܐ ܢܪܒܥܘܢ. ܘܐܪܝܐ ܐܝܟ ܬܘܪܐ ܢܐܟܘܠ ܬܒܢܐ.

8 ܚ ܘܢܫܬܥܐ ܝܠܘܕܐ ܒܚܪܘܪܐ. ܘܒܚܘܪܐ ܕܐܣܦܣ ܢܘܫܛ ܐܝܕܗ ܚܣܝܠܐ.

9 ܛ ܘܠܐ ܢܒܐܫܘܢ: ܘܠܐ ܢܚܒܠܘܢ ܒܟܠܗ ܛܘܪܐ ܕܩܘܕܫܝ. ܡܛܠ ܕܐܬܡܠܝܬ ܐܪܥܐ ܝܕܥܬܗ ܕܡܪܝܐ: ܐܝܟ ܡܝܐ ܕܡܟܣܝܢ ܠܝܡܐ.

10 ܝ ܘܢܗܘܐ ܒܝܘܡܐ ܗܘ: ܫܪܫܗ ܕܐܝܫܝ ܕܩܐܡ: ܐܬܐ ܠܥܡܡܐ ܘܥܠܘܗܝ ܥܡܡܐ ܢܣܒܪܘܢ. ܘܬܗܘܐ ܢܝܚܬܗ ܐܝܩܪܐ.

Chapter 11

1   And a staff will come forth from the stump[1] of Jesse, and a shoot will spring up[2] from its root.

2   The spirit of God will settle, will dwell, upon him: a spirit of wisdom and of understanding; a spirit of intelligence and of might; a spirit of knowledge and of the fear of the Lord.

3   He will shine forth[3] in the fear of the Lord; he will not judge as his eyes see, nor will he rebuke as his ears hear.

4   With truth he will judge the wretched; with integrity he will rebuke the poor of the earth; with the rod of his mouth he will strike the earth, with the breath of his lips he will slay the impious.

5   Righteousness will be the belt of his loins, faithfulness the girdle of his waist.[4]

6   The wolf will dwell with the lamb; the leopard will lie down with the kid; the calf, the lion's whelp, and the bull will feed together; and a little child will lead them.

7   The cow and the bear will feed together, their young[5] will lie down together; the lion will eat straw, like the ox.

8   The child will play with the basilisk;[6] on the asp's hole the weaned infant will stretch out his hand.

9   They will do no evil, they will not destroy, on all my holy mountain: for the earth will be filled with the knowledge of the Lord, as the waters that cover the sea.

10   And it will be, on that day, the root of Jesse will stand firm,[7] a sign to the nations: and the nations will seek him out, and his resting-place will be glorious.

---

[1] 'stump' or 'trunk'.

[2] 'spring up' or 'bring forth fruit'.

[3] 'shine forth' or 'rise'.

[4] 'waist': lit. 'sides'.

[5] 'young' or 'offspring'.

[6] 'basilisk' or 'cockatrice'.

[7] 'will stand firm': lit. 'which stands firm'.

11 ܝܐ ܘܢܗܘܐ ܒܝܘܡܐ ܗܘ: ܢܘܣܦ ܡܪܝܐ ܬܢܝܢܐ ܕܐܝܕܗ: ܘܢܩܢܐ ܫܪܟܐ ܕܥܡܗ
ܕܐܫܬܚܪܘ: ܡܢ ܐܬܘܪ: ܘܡܢ ܡܨܪܝܢ: ܘܡܢ ܦܬܪܘܣ: ܘܡܢ ܟܘܫ: ܘܡܢ
ܥܝܠܡ: ܘܡܢ ܫܢܥܪ: ܘܡܢ ܚܡܬ: ܘܡܢ ܓܙܪܬܐ ܕܝܡܐ.

12 ܝܒ ܘܢܙܩܘܦ ܐܬܐ ܠܥܡܡܐ: ܘܢܟܢܫ ܠܛܪܝܕܐ ܕܐܝܣܪܝܠ: ܘܠܡܒܕܪܬܐ ܕܝܗܘܕܐ
ܢܟܢܫ ܡܢ ܐܪܒܥ ܟܢܦܝܗ ܕܐܪܥܐ.

13 ܝܓ ܘܬܥܒܪ ܛܢܢܐ ܡܢ ܐܦܪܝܡ: ܘܒܥܠܕܒܒܘܗܝ ܕܝܗܘܕܐ ܢܬܒܕܪܘܢ. ܐܦܪܝܡ ܠܐ ܢܛܢ
ܒܝܗܘܕܐ: ܘܝܗܘܕܐ ܠܐ ܢܐܠܘܨ ܠܐܦܪܝܡ.

14 ܝܕ ܘܢܦܪܚܘܢ ܒܟܬܦܐ ܕܦܠܫܬܝܐ ܥܠ ܝܡܐ. ܘܐܟܚܕܐ ܢܒܙܘܢ ܠܒܢܝ ܡܕܢܚܐ.
ܠܐܕܘܡ ܘܠܡܘܐܒ ܢܘܫܛܘܢ ܐܝܕܝܗܘܢ. ܘܒܢܝ ܥܡܘܢ ܢܫܬܡܥܘܢ ܠܗܘܢ.

15 ܝܗ ܘܢܚܪܒ ܡܪܝܐ ܠܫܢ ܝܡܐ ܕܡܨܪܝܢ: ܘܢܪܝܡ ܐܝܕܗ ܥܠ ܢܗܪܐ ܒܬܘܩܦܐ
ܕܪܘܚܗ: ܘܢܡܚܝܘܗܝ ܠܫܒܥܐ ܢܚܠܝܢ: ܘܢܥܒܪ ܒܡܣܢܐ.

16 ܝܘ ܘܢܗܘܐ ܫܒܝܠܐ ܠܫܪܟܐ ܕܥܡܗ: ܕܐܫܬܚܪܘ ܡܢ ܐܬܘܪ: ܐܝܟ ܕܗܘܬ ܠܐܝܣܪܝܠ:
ܒܝܘܡܐ ܕܣܠܩܘ ܡܢ ܐܪܥܐ ܕܡܨܪܝܢ.

11   It will be on that day that the Lord will again, for a second time, by his hand, gain the remnant of his people who have remained, from Assyria, from Egypt, from Patros, and from Cush, from Elam, from Seir, from Hamath, and from the islands of the sea.

12   He will raise up a sign to the nations, he will gather the wanderers of Israel, he will gather the scattered of Judah, from the four corners of the earth.

13   Envy will depart from Ephraim, the oppressors of Judah will perish; Ephraim will not envy Judah, Judah will not oppress Ephraim.

14   They will labor[1] upon the shoulders of the Philistines to the sea; together they will despoil the children of the east; they will lay their hands upon[2] Edom and Moab; the children of Ammon will obey them.

15   The Lord will dry up the stretch[3] of sea that is in Egypt, he will lift up his hand over the river with the power of his wind: he will smite it, making[4] seven streams,[5] that a man may cross over it[6] in sandals.

16   There will be a highway for the remnant of his people who have remained from Assyria, as there was for Israel on the day that they came up from the land of Egypt.

---

[1] 'labor': does not translate MT 'fly'. Possible Inner-Syriac corruption (ISC). See Introduction. Addendum 2.

[2] 'lay their hands upon': lit. 'stretch out their hands to'.

[3] 'stretch': lit. 'tongue'.

[4] 'making': lit. 'to'.

[5] 'streams' or 'valleys'.

[6] 'a man may cross over it': lit. 'that it may be crossed over'.

ܩܦܠܐܘܢ: ܡܒ.

1 ܐ ܘܬܐܡܪ ܒܝܘܡܐ ܗܘ: ܐܘܕܐ ܠܟ ܡܪܝܐ ܕܪܓܙܬ ܥܠܝ: ܘܐܬܦܢܝ ܪܘܓܙܟ ܘܒܝܐܬܢܝ.

2 ܒ ܗܐ ܐܝܠ ܐܠܗܐ ܦܪܘܩܝ ܐܬܬܟܠܬ: ܘܠܐ ܐܙܘܥ. ܡܛܠ ܕܬܘܩܦܝ ܘܫܘܒܚܝ ܡܪܝܐ ܗܘ: ܘܗܘܐ ܠܝ ܠܦܘܪܩܢܐ.

3 ܓ ܘܬܡܠܘܢ ܡܝܐ ܒܚܕܘܬܐ ܡܢ ܡܒܘܥܐ ܕܦܘܪܩܢܐ.

4 ܕ ܘܬܐܡܪܘܢ ܒܝܘܡܐ ܗܘ: ܐܘܕܘ ܠܡܪܝܐ ܘܩܪܘ ܒܫܡܗ: ܘܚܘܘ ܒܥܡܡܐ ܨܒܘܬܗ. ܐܬܕܟܪܘ ܕܪܡ ܗܘ ܫܡܗ.

5 ܗ ܙܡܪܘ ܠܡܪܝܐ ܡܛܠ ܕܓܐܘܬܐ ܥܒܕ. ܝܕܝܥܐ ܗܝ ܗܕܐ ܒܟܠܗ ܐܪܥܐ.

6 ܘ ܙܘܥܝ ܘܫܒܚܝ ܥܡܘܪܬܐ ܕܨܗܝܘܢ. ܡܛܠ ܕܪܒ ܗܘ ܕܒܓܘܟܝ: ܩܕܝܫܐ ܕܐܝܣܪܝܠ.

Chapter 12

1   You will say on that day: I will give thanks to[1] you, Lord, for you were angry with me, but you have turned away your anger, and you have comforted me.

2   See! I trust in God my savior, I will not be moved, for the Lord is my strength and my praise, he will be salvation[2] for me.

3   You will draw water with rejoicing from the spring of redemption.

4   You will say on that day: Give thanks to the Lord, call on his name, declare his skill among the peoples, remember that powerful is his name.

5   Sing (praise) to the Lord, for he has made magnificent things:[3] this is known throughout the[4] earth.

6   Exult, sing praises, inhabitant of Zion, for that which is in your midst is great: the Holy One of Israel.

---

[1] 'give thanks to' or 'praise'.

[2] 'salvation' or 'redemption'.

[3] 'magnificent things': lit. 'magnificence, stateliness'.

[4] 'throughout the earth': lit. 'in the whole earth'.

ܡܩܠܬܗ: ܝܚ.

1 ܐ ܡܫܩܠܐ ܕܒܒܠ ܕܚܙܐ ܐܫܥܝܐ ܒܪ ܐܡܘܨ

2 ܒ ܥܠ ܛܘܪܐ ܩܪܝܚܐ ܐܪܝܡܘ ܐܬܐ. ܐܪܝܡܘ ܠܗܘܢ ܩܠܐ. ܐܢܝܦܘ ܐܝܕܐ. ܢܥܠܘܢ ܒܬܪܥܝ ܫܠܝܛܢܐ.

3 ܓ ܐܢܐ ܦܩܕܬ ܠܡܩܕܫܝ. ܘܩܪܝܬ ܠܓܢܒܪܐ ܒܪܘܓܙܝ. ܘܡܫܬܒܗܪܝܢ ܒܬܘܕܝ.

4 ܕ ܩܠܐ ܕܪܓܘܫܝܐ ܒܛܘܪܐ: ܕܘܡܝܐ ܕܥܡܡܐ ܣܓܝܐܐ: ܩܠܐ ܕܪܓܘܫܝܐ ܕܡܠܟܘܬܐ ܕܥܡܡܐ ܕܡܬܟܢܫܝܢ. ܡܪܝܐ ܚܝܠܬܢܐ ܦܩܕ ܚܝܠܐ.

5 ܗ ܡܬܝܬܝܬܐ ܐܬܝܢ ܡܢ ܪܘܚܩܐ: ܘܡܢ ܣܘܦܝ ܫܡܝܐ ܡܪܝܐ: ܘܡܐܢܝ ܕܪܘܓܙܗ: ܠܡܚܒܠܘ ܠܟܠܗ ܐܪܥܐ.

6 ܘ ܐܝܠܠܘ ܡܛܠ ܕܩܪܝܒ ܗܘ ܝܘܡܗ ܕܡܪܝܐ: ܘܐܝܟ ܒܙܬܐ ܡܢ ܫܕܝܐ ܢܐܬܐ.

7 ܙ ܡܛܠ ܗܢܐ ܟܠܗܝܢ ܐܝܕܝܐ ܢܬܪܦܝܢ. ܘܟܠܗ ܠܒܐ ܕܐܢܫܐ ܢܬܡܣܐ. ܘܢܬܕܠܚܘܢ.

8 ܚ ܘܙܘܥܐ ܘܡܚܒܠܐ ܐܝܟ ܕܝܠܕܬܐ ܢܐܚܕܘܢ ܐܢܘܢ. ܘܢܬܡܗܘܢ ܓܒܪ ܒܚܒܪܗ. ܘܐܦܐ ܕܡܫܠܗܒܐ ܐܦܝܗܘܢ.

9 ܛ ܗܐ ܝܘܡܗ ܕܡܪܝܐ ܐܬܐ: ܕܐܟܙܪܝ ܟܠܗ ܠܗ. ܐܟܙܪܝ ܘܡܠܝܐ ܪܘܓܙܗ. ܕܢܚܪܒܝܗ ܠܐܪܥܐ ܠܚܘܪܒܐ: ܘܚܛܝܗ ܢܘܒܕ ܡܢܗ.

10 ܝ ܡܛܠ ܕܟܘܟܒܐ ܕܫܡܝܐ ܘܡܢܬܘܬܗܘܢ ܠܐ ܢܢܗܪܘܢ. ܢܚܫܟ ܫܡܫܐ ܒܡܕܢܚܗ. ܘܢܘܗܪܗ ܕܣܗܪܐ ܠܐ ܢܢܗܪ.

Chapter 13

1   The burden of Babylon, which Isaiah the son of Amos saw.

2   Upon the bare mountains lift up a sign, call out[1] to them, beckon with the hand: they will enter by the rulers' gates.

3   I have commanded[2] my sanctuary; I have called to the mighty men in my anger, and to those who wax strong in my magnificence.

4   A sound of tumult on the mountain, as of[3] many peoples, a sound of the tumult of kingdoms of peoples gathered together: the mighty Lord visits the armies.[4]

5   Warriors come from afar, the Lord from the uttermost ends of heaven, (with) the instruments of his anger, to destroy all the earth.

6   Howl! for it is near, the day of the Lord: it will come suddenly, like robbery.

7   Because of this all hands weaken, every heart of man will melt away, will be disquieted.

8   Terrors and travails like those of a woman in labor will seize them, they will be struck dumb, each man with his companion,[5] their faces aflame.[6]

9   See! The day of the Lord is coming, for which there is no healing; wrathful and hot his anger, so that he will make the land a waste place, and cast out[7] from it its sinners.

10 For the stars of the heavens and their hosts will give no[8] light; the sun in its going forth will be darkened, the light of the moon will not shine.

---

[1] 'call out': lit. 'raise a voice'.

[2] 'commanded' or 'visited'.

[3] 'as of': lit. 'the similitude of'.

[4] 'visits the armies' or 'performs mighty acts'.

[5] 'they will be struck dumb, each man with his companion' or 'they will be amazed, each man by his companion'.

[6] 'their faces aflame': lit. 'faces of flame their faces'.

[7] 'cast out' or 'destroy'.

[8] 'give no': lit. 'not give'.

11 ܝܐ ܐܦܩܘܕ ܒܝܫܬܐ ܥܠ ܬܒܝܠ: ܘܥܠ ܪܫܝܥܐ ܚܘܒܝܗܘܢ. ܐܒܛܠ ܙܗܘܬܐ
ܕܡܒܗܪܢܐ. ܘܓܐܘܬܐ ܕܥܫܝܢܐ ܐܡܟܟ.

12 ܝܒ ܐܘܩܪ ܓܒܪܐ ܡܢ ܕܗܒܐ: ܘܐܢܫܐ ܡܢ ܕܗܒܐ ܕܐܘܦܝܪ.

13 ܝܓ ܡܛܠ ܗܢܐ ܫܡܝܐ ܐܪܓܙ. ܘܬܙܘܥ ܐܪܥܐ ܡܢ ܕܘܟܬܗ: ܒܚܡܬܗ ܕܡܪܝܐ
ܚܝܠܬܢܐ: ܒܝܘܡܐ ܕܚܡܬܐ ܕܪܘܓܙܗ.

14 ܝܕ ܢܗܘܘܢ ܐܝܟ ܛܒܝܐ ܕܪܕܝܦ: ܘܐܝܟ ܥܢܐ ܕܠܝܬ ܠܗ ܡܟܢܫܢܐ. ܐܢܫ ܠܥܡܗ
ܢܬܦܢܘܢ: ܘܓܒܪ ܠܐܪܥܗ ܢܥܪܩܘܢ.

15 ܝܗ ܟܠ ܕܢܫܬܟܚ: ܢܬܕܩܪ. ܘܟܠ ܕܢܬܐܚܕ: ܢܦܠ ܒܚܪܒܐ.

16 ܝܘ ܘܥܘܠܠܝܗܘܢ ܢܬܪܛܫܘܢ ܠܥܝܢܝܗܘܢ. ܘܢܬܒܙܙܘܢ ܒܬܝܗܘܢ. ܘܢܫܝܗܘܢ ܢܬܛܢܦܢ.

17 ܝܙ ܗܐ ܡܥܝܪ ܐܢܐ ܥܠܝܗܘܢ ܠܡܕܝܐ: ܕܟܣܦܐ ܠܐ ܚܫܒܝܢ ܠܗܘܢ: ܘܕܗܒܐ ܠܐ
ܨܒܝܢ.

18 ܝܚ ܩܫܬܐ ܕܥܠܝܡܐ ܢܬܒܪܢ. ܘܥܠ ܦܐܪܐ ܕܟܪܣܐ ܠܐ ܢܪܚܡܘܢ. ܘܥܠ ܒܢܝܗܘܢ
ܠܐ ܚܝܣܐ ܥܝܢܝܗܘܢ.

19 ܝܛ ܘܬܗܘܐ ܒܒܠ ܚܝܠܐ ܕܡܠܟܘܬܐ: ܘܫܘܒܚܐ ܕܬܫܒܘܚܬܐ ܕܟܠܕܝܐ: ܐܝܟ ܕܗܦܟ
ܐܠܗܐ ܠܣܕܘܡ ܘܠܥܡܘܪܐ.

20 ܟ ܠܐ ܬܬܝܬܒ ܠܥܠܡ: ܘܠܐ ܬܬܥܡܪ ܠܕܪܕܪܝܢ. ܘܠܐ ܢܫܪܘܢ ܬܡܢ ܥܪܒܝܐ: ܘܪܥܘܬܐ ܠܐ
ܢܪܒܥܘܢ ܬܡܢ.

VII

11   I will visit evil upon the world, and their iniquity upon the wicked; I will bring to an end the pride of the boastful, I will humble the pomp of the powerful.

12   I will make man more precious than gold, mankind[1] more than the gold of Ophir.

13   Therefore I will enrage the heavens, the earth will be moved from its place, at the rebuke of the mighty Lord on the day of the heat of his anger.

14   They will be like fleeing gazelles, like sheep without a shepherd;[2] each person will turn to his (own) people, each man will flee to his (own) land.

15   Everyone who is found will be stabbed; all who are added[3] will fall by the sword.

16   Their infants will be beaten before their eyes, their houses despoiled, their women dishonored.

17   See! I am arousing against them the Medes, to whom silver is of no account, who take no pleasure[4] in gold.

18   The bows of the young men will be broken, they will have no mercy on the fruits of the womb, their eyes will not take pity on your children.

19   And Babylon, the might of kingdoms, the praise of the pomp of the Chaldeans, will be as when God overthrew Sodom and Gomorrah.

20   It will never be inhabited, nor lived in forever and ever, the Arabs will not dwell there, shepherds will not feed (their flocks) there.

---

[1] 'mankind': lit. 'a man'.

[2] 'without a shepherd': lit. 'which have no-one gathering'.

[3] 'who are added'. MT 'who will be caught'. See Introduction. Addendum 1.

[4] 'take no pleasure in gold': lit. 'in gold they do not desire'.

21   But the beasts will lie down there, their houses will be filled with echoes;[1] ostriches[2] will live there, demons will dance there.

22   Screech-owls will answer in their palaces, jackals in the temples of their pleasures: it is near, her time to come, her days will be prolonged no more.

---

[1] 'echoes': lit. 'daughters of voices'.

[2] 'ostriches': ܒܬ appears to mean 'the young of …', but ܒܬ ܩܠܐ is an idiom for the name of the bird.

ܡܓܠܬܐ: ܚ.

1 ܐ ܡܛܠ ܕܡܪܚܡ ܡܪܝܐ ܥܠ ܥܡܗ: ܘܡܬܪܥܐ ܠܒܝܬ ܐܝܣܪܐܝܠ.
ܘܢܦܩܘܢ ܐܢܘܢ ܡܢ ܐܘܪܚܗܘܢ. ܘܢܬܒܠܘܢ ܒܠܒܗܘܢ ܥܡܘܪܐ. ܘܢܬܐܣܦܘܢ ܥܠ
ܕܥܡܗ ܢܥܡܘܕ.

2 ܒ ܘܢܒܥܘܢ ܐܢܘܢ ܒܥܡܡܐ. ܘܢܥܠܘܢ ܐܢܘܢ ܠܐܘܪܚܗܘܢ. ܘܢܬܪܘܢ ܐܢܘܢ ܕܥܡܗ
ܐܝܣܪܐܝܠ: ܒܐܘܪܚܗ ܕܡܪܝܐ: ܒܥܒܕܐ ܘܠܐܡܗܬܐ. ܘܢܗܘܘܢ ܫܒܝܢ ܠܫܒܝܗܘܢ:
ܘܢܫܠܛܘܢ ܒܡܫܥܒܕܢܝܗܘܢ.

3 ܓ ܘܢܗܘܐ ܒܝܘܡܐ ܕܢܢܝܚ ܡܪܝܐ ܡܢ ܥܡܠܟ: ܘܡܢ ܪܘܓܙܟ: ܘܡܢ ܦܘܠܚܢܐ
ܩܫܝܐ ܕܐܫܬܥܒܕܬ.

4 ܕ ܬܫܩܘܠ ܡܬܠܐ ܗܢܐ ܥܠ ܡܠܟܐ ܕܒܒܠ: ܘܬܐܡܪ. ܐܝܟܢܐ ܒܛܠ ܡܫܥܒܕܐ:
ܘܒܛܠ ܡܫܩܠܢܐ.

5 ܗ ܬܒܪ ܡܪܝܐ ܚܘܛܪܐ ܕܪܫܝܥܐ: ܘܫܒܛܐ ܕܫܠܝܛܐ.

6 ܘ ܕܡܚܐ ܗܘܐ ܠܥܡܡܐ ܒܚܡܬܐ: ܡܚܘܬܐ ܕܠܐ ܡܫܪܝܐ. ܘܪܕܐ ܗܘܐ ܒܪܘܓܙܐ ܠܥܡܡܐ.
ܘܪܕܦ ܠܗܘܢ ܕܠܐ ܚܘܣ.

7 ܙ ܐܬܬܢܝܚܬ ܘܫܠܝܬ ܟܠܗ ܐܪܥܐ: ܘܪܢܝ ܒܬܫܒܘܚܬܐ.

8 ܚ ܐܦ ܒܪܘܬܐ ܚܕܝ ܥܠܝܟ ܘܐܪܙܐ ܕܠܒܢܢ. ܡܢ ܟܕ ܫܟܒܬ: ܠܐ ܣܠܩ ܩܛܘܥܐ
ܥܠܝܢ.

Chapter 14

1   For the Lord has mercy on Jacob, and is well pleased with[1] Israel; he will leave them in their land, and the inhabitants will join with them, and be added to those of the house of Jacob.

2   The peoples will guide them, and bring them to their land; they will possess them, those of the house of Israel, in the land of the Lord, as servants and as maidservants; they will take captive their captors, and they will rule over their oppressors.[2]

3   It will be, on the day that the Lord will give you rest from your distress and from your anger, and from the harsh servitude to which you were subjected,

4   That you will utter[3] this proverb concerning the king of Babylon, and you will say: How has the ruler come to naught,[4] he who incites failed?'

5   The Lord has broken the rod of the wicked, the scepter of the ruler.

6   Who smote the nations with lasting anger, a blow that they did not resist,[5] chastised the nations with anger, pursued[6] them without pity.

7   All the earth is at rest, dwells in peace; it has exulted, in praise.[7]

8   Even the cypress, and the cedars of Lebanon, rejoice at you: From the time that you lay down, they have not gone up to us to cut (us) down'.

---

[1] 'well pleased with' or 'chooses'.

[2] 'oppressors' or 'taskmasters'.

[3] 'utter': lit. 'take up'.

[4] 'come to naught ... failed': the √ ܫܠܐ is used for both verbs.

[5] 'they did not resist': lit. 'they did not rebel'. MT 'a blow that did not cease'. See Introduction. Addendum 1.

[6] 'smote ... chastised ... pursued': participles.

[7] 'at rest, dwells in peace': lit. 'has taken rest and been silent'.

9 ܛ ܫܝܘܠ ܡܢ ܠܬܚܬ ܐܬܪܓܙܬ ܠܘܩܒܠ ܡܐܬܝܟ. ܐܥܝܪܬ ܥܠܝܟ ܓܢܒܪܐ: ܘܟܠܗܘܢ ܫܠܝܛܢܐ ܕܐܪܥܐ ܕܐܩܝܡܬ ܡܢ ܟܘܪܣܘܬܗܘܢ.

10 ܝ ܟܠܗܘܢ ܡܠܟܐ ܕܥܡܡܐ ܢܥܢܘܢ ܘܢܐܡܪܘܢ ܠܟ: ܐܦ ܐܢܬ ܐܬܡܚܝܬ ܐܟܘܬܢ: ܘܠܘܬܢ ܐܬܡܬܠܬ.

11 ܝܐ ܘܐܬܡܟܟ ܢܚܬ ܠܫܝܘܠ: ܘܩܠ ܟܢܪܟ. ܬܚܘܬܝܟ ܢܬܡܟܟܘܢ ܪܡܫܐ: ܘܡܟܣܝܬܟ ܬܘܠܥܐ.

12 ܝܒ ܐܝܟܢܐ ܢܦܠܬ ܡܢ ܫܡܝܐ. ܐܝܠܠ ܒܪ ܨܦܪܐ. ܢܦܠܬ ܠܐܪܥܐ ܡܚܪܒܢܐ ܕܥܡܡܐ.

13 ܝܓ ܐܢܬ ܐܡܪܬ ܒܠܒܟ. ܕܐܣܩ ܠܫܡܝܐ: ܘܠܥܠ ܡܢ ܟܘܟܒܘܗܝ ܕܐܠܗܐ ܐܪܝܡ ܟܘܪܣܝ: ܘܐܬܒ ܒܛܘܪܐ ܪܡܐ ܕܒܣܘܦܝ ܓܪܒܝܐ.

14 ܝܕ ܘܐܣܩ ܥܠ ܪܘܡܐ ܕܥܢܢܐ: ܘܐܬܕܡܐ ܠܥܠܝܐ.

15 ܝܗ ܡܟܝܠ ܠܫܝܘܠ ܬܚܘܬ: ܘܠܫܘܠܝ ܕܓܘܒܐ.

16 ܝܘ ܟܠ ܚܙܝܟ ܥܠܝܟ ܢܒܩܘܢ. ܘܒܟ ܢܣܬܟܠܘܢ: ܘܢܐܡܪܘܢ: ܗܢܘ ܓܒܪܐ ܕܡܪܓܙ ܗܘܐ ܐܪܥܐ: ܘܐܙܝܥ ܡܠܟܘܬܐ.

17 ܝܙ ܘܥܒܕ ܬܒܝܠ ܚܘܪܒܐ. ܘܩܘܪܝܗ̇ ܣܚܦ: ܘܐܣܝܪܘܗܝ ܠܐ ܫܪܐ.

9   Sheol from below was angered[1] at[2] your coming; she aroused mighty men against you, all the rulers of the earth whom you raised up[3] from their thrones.

10   All the kings of the nations will answer and say to you: Have you too grown weak like us, been delivered up to us?[4]

11   Your glory has descended to Sheol, your harp has died.[5] Worms[6] are spread out below you, worms[7] will cover you.

12   How you have fallen from the heavens! Cry out[8] at the dawn! You have fallen to the earth, disgraced of the nations.

13   You said in your heart: I will ascend to the heavens, I will raise my throne higher than the stars of God, I will dwell on the high mountains in the uttermost parts of the north,

14   I will ascend to the height of the clouds, I will be like the exalted one.

15   Thence to Sheol you will descend, to the bottom of the pit.

16   All who see you will stare,[9] they will understand,[10] they will say: This is the man who saddens[11] the earth, who terrified kingdoms.

17   He has made the inhabitable world as desolate as a wilderness, ruined its cities; he has not released its prisoners.

---

[1] 'angered' or 'embittered' or 'saddened'.

[2] 'at': lit. 'before'.

[3] 'whom you raised up': The consonantal text can be translated 'whom she raised up'; so MT.

[4] 'been delivered up to us' or 'have you handed us over'. MT 'become like us'. See Introduction. Addendum 1.

[5] 'your harp has died'. MT 'the music of your lutes'. See Introduction. Addendum 1.

[6] 'Worms' or 'dust'.

[7] 'Worms … worms': lit. 'The worm … worm' using two different nouns for 'worm'.

[8] 'Cry out'. See Introduction. Addendum 1.

[9] 'stare': lit. 'gaze'.

[10] 'they will understand': lit. 'by you they will understand'.

[11] 'saddens' or 'embitters'.

18 ܝܚ ܟܠܗܘܢ ܡܠܟܐ ܕܥܡܡܐ: ܫܟܝܒܝܢ ܒܐܝܩܪܐ: ܐܢܫ ܒܒܝܬܗ.

19 ܝܛ ܘܐܢܬ ܐܫܬܕܝܬ ܡܢ ܩܒܪܟ: ܐܝܟ ܢܘܪܒܐ ܡܣܠܝܐ: ܠܒܘܫܐ ܕܩܛܝܠܐ
ܘܕܡܚܝܢ ܒܣܝܦܐ: ܕܢܚܬܝܢ ܠܟܐܦܐ ܕܓܘܒܐ ܐܝܟ ܦܓܪܐ ܕܕܝܫܐ.

20 ܟ ܘܠܐ ܬܬܚܒܪ ܥܡܗܘܢ ܒܩܒܘܪܬܐ. ܡܛܠ ܕܐܪܥܟ ܚܒܠܬ: ܘܥܡܟ ܩܛܠܬ. ܠܐ
ܢܩܘܡ ܠܥܠܡ ܙܪܥܐ ܒܝܫܐ.

21 ܟܐ ܛܝܒܘ ܠܒܢܘܗܝ ܩܛܠܐ ܒܚܘܒܐ ܕܐܒܘܗܘܢ. ܕܠܐ ܢܩܘܡܘܢ ܘܢܐܪܬܘܢ ܐܪܥܐ: ܘܢܡܠܘܢ
ܐܦܝ ܬܐܒܝܠ ܩܘܪܝܐ.

22 ܟܒ ܐܩܘܡ ܥܠܝܗܘܢ: ܐܡܪ ܡܪܝܐ ܚܝܠܬܢܐ. ܘܐܘܒܕ ܫܡܗ ܕܒܒܠ: ܘܫܪܟܗ
ܘܛܘܗܡܗ ܘܫܪܒܬܗ: ܐܡܪ ܡܪܝܐ.

23 ܟܓ ܘܐܣܝܡܝܗ ܝܪܬܘܬܐ ܠܩܘܦܕܐ: ܘܐܓܡܐ ܕܡܝܐ. ܘܐܟܢܫܝܗ ܒܡܟܢܫܬܐ ܕܐܒܕܢܐ:
ܐܡܪ ܡܪܝܐ ܚܝܠܬܢܐ.

24 ܟܕ ܝܡܐ ܡܪܝܐ ܚܝܠܬܢܐ ܘܐܡܪ: ܕܐܝܟ ܕܐܬܚܫܒܬ: ܗܟܢܐ ܢܗܘܐ. ܘܐܝܟ ܕܐܬܪܥܝܬ:
ܬܬܩܝܡ.

25 ܟܗ ܕܐܬܒܪ ܠܐܬܘܪܝܐ ܒܐܪܥܝ: ܘܥܠ ܛܘܪܝ ܐܕܘܫܝܘܗܝ. ܘܢܥܒܪ ܢܝܪܗ ܡܢܗܘܢ:
ܘܫܘܩܠܗ ܡܢ ܟܬܦܝܗܘܢ ܢܥܒܪ.

26 ܟܘ ܗܕܐ ܗܝ ܬܪܥܝܬܐ ܕܐܬܪܥܝܬ ܥܠ ܐܪܥܐ ܟܠܗ. ܘܗܕܐ ܗܝ ܐܝܕܐ ܕܐܬܬܪܝܡܬ ܥܠ
ܟܠܗܘܢ ܥܡܡܐ.

27 ܟܙ ܡܪܝܐ ܚܝܠܬܢܐ ܐܬܪܥܝ: ܡܢܘ ܢܒܛܠ. ܘܐܝܕܗ ܪܡܝܐ ܡܢܘ ܢܗܦܟ.

28 ܟܚ ܡܫܩܠܐ ܕܦܠܫܬ: ܒܫܢܬܐ ܕܡܝܬ ܐܚܙ ܡܠܟܐ ܗܘܐ ܡܫܩܠܐ ܗܢܐ.

18 All the kings of the nations have lain down in glory, each[1] in his house.

19 But you have been thrown from your grave, like a rejected shoot, (dressed in) the garment of the slain, the slain with the sword, who go down into the stones of the pit, like dead bodies trodden (under foot).

20 You will not rejoice with them in the grave, for you have ravaged your land, slain your people: the evil seed will never arise.

21 Prepare slaughter for his children, for the iniquity of their father, such that they will not rise up, they will not possess the land, not cover[2] the face of the inhabitable world with war.

22 I will rise up against them, says the mighty Lord: I will destroy the name of Babylon, its seed, its stock, its generation, says the Lord.

23 I will make it an inheritance for porcupines,[3] and pools of water. I will gather it up with the broom of destruction, says the mighty Lord.

24 The mighty Lord has sworn and said: As I have planned, so will it be; as I have purposed, so will it come to pass.[4]

25 I will break the Assyrian in my land; I will tread him down upon my mountains; his yoke will pass away from them, his oppression will pass from their shoulder(s).

26 This is the meaning which was purposed for the whole earth; this is the hand which was raised up upon all the nations.

27 The mighty Lord has purposed: who will bring (his purpose) to naught? Who will turn back[5] his high hand?

28 The burden of Philistia. In the year that Ahaz the king died there was this prophecy.[6]

---

[1] 'each': lit. 'a man'.

[2] 'cover': lit. 'fill'.

[3] 'porcupines' or 'owls'.

[4] 'come to pass' or 'be established'.

[5] 'turn back' or 'overthrow'.

[6] 'prophecy': lit. 'burden, load', with special reference to prophecy.

29   Do not rejoice, all Philistia,[1] because the rod of your oppressor is broken! for from the root of the serpent an asp emerges - and its fruits, the flying basilisk.

30   Then the firstborn of the poor will feed, the needy will lie down in peace; I will starve your root to death,[2] and that which remains of you will be slain.

31   Wail, city! Cry, city! All Philistia has been disturbed, for from the north comes smoke; none at all at his feasts.[3]

32   What will he reply to the messenger of the nations: The Lord establishes the foundations of Zion; the needy of his people are sheltered in her.

---

[1] 'all Philistia': lit. 'all of you, Philistia'.

[2] 'starve your root to death': lit. 'kill your root by hunger'.

[3] 'none at all at his feasts'. MT 'no straggler in his ranks'. See Introduction. Addendum 3.

76

Chapter 15

VIII

1   The burden of Moab. The city of Moab was plundered by night: they were struck dumb; the walls of Moab were plundered by night: they were confounded.

2   They went up to the house of Ribon, to the high places to weep, over Nebo, over Medeba. Moab howls, all heads bald,[1] every beard shorn.

3   In its streets they gird themselves with sackcloth,[2] upon the rooftops, in the streets everyone wails, weeping they descend.[3]

4   Heshbon will howl, and Elealeh; their voice was heard as far as Yasot; because of this the strong men of Moab will cry out, his soul will cry out to him.

5   My heart (cries out) for[4] Moab, it will cry out with its breath as far as Zoar, (like) a three year old heifer;[5] for weeping (will they go) in the ascent of Luhith, they will go up by it; on the way to Horonaim they will raise[6] a shout of destruction.

6   For the waters of Nimrin will fail, for the grass has dried up, the tender grass has withered away, there was no green herb.

7   Because of this all that remained[7] has passed away; they will carry away their possessions to the valley of the willows.

8   For wailing has gone around the border of Moab, his wailing (reaches) as far as Eglaim, his wailing (reaches) to the well of Elim.

9   For the waters of Ribon were filled with blood: for I will bring yet more[8] upon Ribon, I will attend to[9] those who escape from Moab.

---

[1] 'all heads bald': lit. 'on all his heads bald spots'.

[2] 'sackcloth': pl.

[3] 'descend': sing. verb.

[4] '(cries out) for' or 'is (set) against'.

[5] 'three year old heifer'. See Introduction. Addendum 3.

[6] 'raise': lit. 'make'.

[7] 'all that remained': lit. 'whatever remained'.

[8] 'bring yet more': lit. 'set an addition'.

[9] 'I will attend to': possible ISC. See Introduction. Addendum 2.

ܩܦܠܐܘܢ: ܗ.

1 ܐ ܘܟܠ ܡܢܘܬܐ ܕܐܪܥܐ: ܐܡܪܘ ܠܒܪ ܡܫܠܛܢܐ ܕܐܪܥܐ: ܡܢ ܟܐܦܐ ܕܡܕܒܪܐ ܠܛܘܪܐ
ܕܒܪܬ ܨܗܝܘܢ.

2 ܒ ܘܢܗܘܐ ܐܝܟ ܦܪܚܬܐ ܕܡܫܢܝܐ ܩܢܗ. ܘܒ̈ܢܬܗ ܕܡܘܐܒ: ܡܥܒ̈ܪܢܝܬܐ ܢܗܘܝܢ
ܒܡܥܒܪ̈ܬܐ ܕܐܪܢܘܢ.

3 ܓ ܐܥܠܝ ܬܪܥܝܬܐ: ܘܥܒܕܝ ܬܘܟܠܢܐ. ܣܝܡܝ ܐܝܟ ܠܠܝܐ ܛܠܠܟܝ ܒܡܨܥܬ ܛܗܪܐ.
ܛܫܝ ܠܡܒܕ̈ܪܐ. ܘܠܡܬܢܕܕܢܐ ܠܐ ܬܓܠܝܢ.

4 ܕ ܢܥܡܪܘܢ ܒܟܝ ܡܒܕ̈ܪܐ ܕܡܘܐܒ. ܗܘܝ ܠܗܘܢ ܡܛܫܝܬܐ ܡܢ ܩܕܡ ܒܙܘܙܐ.
ܡܛܠ ܕܫܠܡ ܚܡܣܐ: ܘܫܠܡ ܒܙܘܙܐ: ܘܕܝܫܐ ܡܢ ܐܪܥܐ.

5 ܗ ܘܢܬܩܢ ܟܘܪܣܝܐ ܒܛܝܒܘܬܐ. ܘܢܬܒ ܥܠܘܗܝ ܒܩܘܫܬܐ ܒܡܫܟܢܗ ܕܕܘܝܕ:
ܕܝܢܐ ܘܡܚܒܒ ܕܝܢܐ: ܘܡܣܪܗܒ ܙܕܝܩܘܬܐ.

6 ܘ ܫܡܥܢ ܫܘܒܗܪܗ ܕܡܘܐܒ: ܕܛܒ ܐܬܝܩܪ ܫܘܒܗܪܗ ܘܪܘܪܒܘܬܗ ܘܥܘܠܗ. ܠܐ ܗܘܐ
ܗܟܢܐ ܒܕ̈ܝܠܗ ܠܟܘܢ ܡܫ̈ܘܚܬܗ.

7 ܙ ܡܛܠ ܗܢܐ ܢܝܠܠ ܡܘܐܒ. ܘܟܠ ܡܘܐܒ ܟܠܗ ܢܝܠܠ: ܥܠ ܫܬܐܣ̈ܐ ܕܩܝܪܐ
ܕܚܪܣܬ. ܬܗܓܘܢ ܐܝܟ ܟܪ̈ܝܗܐ.

Chapter 16

1   To the remnant of the land,[1] I will send the son of the ruler[2] of the land, from the rock of the wilderness to the mountain of the daughter of Zion.

2   It will be like a bird that moves (from) its nest; the daughters of Moab will be abandoned at the crossing of the Arnon.

3   Bring reflection (to bear), meditate deeply;[3] make your shadow like night, at the height of noon;[4] hide those who wander, do not disclose those who scatter.

4   May they dwell with you, the dispersed of Moab; be a shelter for them, from the presence of the plunderer, for those who have been reduced[5] to dust[6] have come to an end,[7] the plunderer has perished, and the oppressor has been removed[8] from the earth.

5   The throne will be established in grace;[9] he will sit on it in truth, in the tent of David: the judge, he who seeks judgment, and he who hastens righteousness.

6   We have heard of the pomp of Moab, that he bore himself with his great pomp, his pride, his ill-will. It was not thus[10] that his diviners searched on his behalf.

7   Therefore Moab will wail, he will wail for all Moab; for the foundations of the city walls which are ruined, you will moan like the weak.

---

[1] 'To the remnant of the land': this phrase closes the previous verse in MT; in Mosul it opens the chapter, perhaps intended to be read as a heading.

[2] 'I will send the son of the ruler'. See Introduction. Addendum 1.

[3] 'meditate deeply': lit. 'make profound meditation'.

[4] 'height of noon': lit. 'middle of the midday'.

[5] 'have been reduced': sing. verb.

[6] 'those who have been reduced to dust'. See Introduction. Addendum 3.

[7] 'have come to an end': sing. verb.

[8] 'been removed': lit. 'come to an end'.

[9] 'grace' or 'goodness' or 'loving kindness'.

[10] 'It was not thus …' or 'Was it not thus …'.

8 ܚ ܡܛܠ ܕܚܩܠܬܐ ܕܚܫܒܘܢ ܚܪܒ. ܓܦܬܐ ܕܣܒܡܐ: ܡܪ̈ܘܬܐ ܕܥܡ̈ܡܐ ܥܩܪܘ
ܫܒܘܫܝܬܗ: ܘܥܕܡܐ ܠܝܥܙܪ ܡܛܬ. ܘܛܥܬ ܠܡܕܒܪܐ ܫܘܒܛܝܗ. ܦܫܛܘ ܘܥܒܪܘ
ܝܡܐ.

9 ܛ ܡܛܠ ܗܢܐ ܐܒܟܐ ܒܒܟܝܐ ܕܝܥܙܪ ܓܦܬܐ ܕܣܒܡܐ. ܐܪܘܝܟܝ ܡܢ
ܕܡܥܝ̈ ܚܫܒܘܢ: ܘܐܠܥܠܐ: ܡܛܠ ܕܥܠ ܚܨܕܟܝ ܘܥܠ ܩܛܝܦܟܝ ܕܘܢܐ
ܢܦܠ.

10 ܝ ܘܐܬܟܢܫ ܚܕܘܬܐ ܘܕܝܨܐ ܡܢ ܟܪܡܠܐ. ܘܒܟܪܡܠܐ ܠܐ ܢܚܕܘܢ. ܘܠܐ ܢܕܪܟܘܢ ܚܡܪܐ
ܒܡܥܨܪ̈ܬܐ. ܘܠܐ ܢܕܘܫ ܕܝܘܫܐ: ܡܛܠ ܕܒܛܝܠܐ ܐܥܠܝܠ.

11 ܝܐ ܡܛܠ ܗܢܐ ܒܢܝ ܥܠ ܡܘܐܒ: ܐܝܟ ܟܢܪܐ ܢܐܠܠ. ܘܟܪܣܝ ܥܠ ܩܘܪܐ
ܕܚܕܬܘܒܝܢ.

12 ܝܒ ܘܗܘܐ ܕܚܙܐ ܕܠܐܝ ܡܘܐܒ ܥܠ ܥܠܘܬܐ: ܢܐܬܐ ܠܡܩܕܫܗ ܠܡܨܠܝܘ: ܘܠܐ
ܢܫܟܚ.

13 ܝܓ ܗܢܐ ܦܬܓܡܐ ܕܡܠܠ ܡܪܝܐ ܥܠ ܡܘܐܒ ܡܢ ܗܝܕܝܢ.

14 ܝܕ ܘܗܫܐ ܡܠܠ ܡܪܝܐ ܘܐܡܪ: ܒܬܠܬ ܫܢܝ̈ܢ ܐܝܟ ܫܢܝ̈ ܐܓܝܪܐ: ܢܨܛܥܪ ܐܝܩܪܗ
ܕܡܘܐܒ: ܥܠ ܣܘܓܐܐ ܕܥܡܗ. ܘܢܫܬܐܪ ܫܪܟܐ ܙܥܘܪ: ܘܠܐ ܫܒܝܚ.

8   For the fields of Heshbon were laid waste; the strong men of the nations have lopped off the shoots of the vine of Sibmah:[1] they reached as far as Jazer, her offshoots perished[2] in the wilderness, they stretched out, they passed across the sea.

9   Therefore I will make you weep, with weeping for Jazer, the vine of Sibmah; I will water you with your tears, Heshbon and Elealeh: for upon your harvest, upon your vintage, will fall the oppressor.[3]

10   Rejoicing and exultation will pass away from Carmel, they will not rejoice in Carmel, they will not trample the wine in the wine press, the treader will not tread underfoot, for I will bring the treader to naught.

11   Therefore my being (mourns) for Moab, it will speak like the harp, my being[4] (mourns) for the ruined city wall.

12   And when he saw that Moab was weary, on[5] the high places, he would come to the sanctuary to pray, but he would be unable.

13   This is the word the Lord spoke concerning Moab, from then.

14   And now the Lord has spoken and said: In three years, like the years of a hired servant, the glory of Moab will be dishonored, by the multitude of his people; very little will remain, and nothing[6] great.

---

[1] 'the strong men of the nations have lopped off the shoots of the vine of Sibmah': lit. 'the vine of Sibmah, the mighty men of the nations, have lopped off her shoots'.

[2] 'perished' or 'were forgotten'.

[3] 'oppressor' or 'he who treads'.

[4] 'being … being': lit. 'belly … inward parts'.

[5] 'on' or 'on account of'.

[6] 'nothing': lit. 'not'.

ܩܦܠܐܘܢ: ܒ.

1 ܐ ܡܫܩܠܐ ܕܕܪܡܣܘܩ. ܗܐ ܕܪܡܣܘܩ ܡܬܥܒܪܐ ܡܢ ܩܪܝܬܐ. ܘܬܗܘܐ ܠܚܘܪܒܐ ܘܠܡܦܘܠܬܐ.

2 ܒ ܘܢܗܘܝܢ ܫܒܝܩܢ ܩܘܪܝܐ ܕܥܪܘܥܝܪ. ܘܢܗܘܝܢ ܠܓܙܪܐ ܕܢܪܒܥܘܢ ܒܗܝܢ. ܘܠܐ ܢܗܘܐ ܠܗܘܢ ܡܙܝܥܢܐ.

3 ܓ ܘܢܬܒܛܠ ܥܘܫܢܐ ܡܢ ܐܦܪܝܡ: ܘܡܠܟܘܬܐ ܡܢ ܕܪܡܣܘܩ. ܘܫܪܟܐ ܕܐܪܡ ܐܝܟ ܐܝܩܪܐ ܕܒܢܝ ܐܝܣܪܝܠ ܢܗܘܘܢ: ܐܡܪ ܡܪܝܐ ܚܝܠܬܢܐ.

4 ܕ ܘܢܗܘܐ ܒܝܘܡܐ ܗܘ: ܢܬܡܟܟ ܐܝܩܪܗ ܕܝܥܩܘܒ. ܘܫܘܡܢܐ ܕܒܣܪܗ ܢܬܒܙܙ.

5 ܗ ܘܢܗܘܐ ܐܝܟ ܗܘ ܕܟܢܫ ܚܨܕܐ ܕܩܡܚܐ: ܘܕܪܥܗ ܫܒܠܐ ܢܚܨܕ. ܘܢܗܘܐ ܐܝܟ ܗܘ ܕܡܠܩܛ ܫܒܠܐ ܒܥܘܡܩܐ ܕܪܦܐܝܡ.

6 ܘ ܘܢܫܬܚܪ ܒܗ ܥܘܠܠܐ ܐܝܟ ܙܝܬܐ ܕܢܦܨܘܗ: ܬܪܬܝܢ ܬܠܬ ܙܝܬܝܢ ܒܪܝܫ ܩܢܝܐ ܒܣܘܟܘܗܝ: ܐܪܒܥܐ ܘܚܡܫܐ: ܐܡܪ ܡܪܝܐ ܐܠܗܐ ܕܐܝܣܪܝܠ.

7 ܙ ܒܗ ܒܝܘܡܐ ܗܘ: ܢܬܬܟܝܠܘܢ ܥܠ ܥܒܘܕܗ. ܘܥܝܢܘܗܝ ܢܚܘܪܢ ܠܩܕܝܫܐ ܕܐܝܣܪܝܠ.

8 ܚ ܘܠܐ ܢܬܬܟܠ ܥܠ ܡܕܒܚܐ ܕܥܒܕ ܐܝܕܘܗܝ ܘܥܒܕ ܨܒܥܬܗ. ܘܠܐ ܢܚܙܐ ܐܫܝܪܬܐ ܘܕܒܚܘܢܐ.

9 ܛ ܒܝܘܡܐ ܗܘ: ܢܗܘܝܢ ܩܘܪܝܐ ܕܥܘܫܢܗ ܐܝܟ ܫܘܒܩܐ ܕܚܘܪܫܐ: ܘܐܡܝܪܐ ܕܐܫܬܒܩܘ ܡܢ ܩܕܡ ܒܢܝ ܐܝܣܪܝܠ. ܘܬܗܘܐ ܠܚܘܪܒܐ.

10 ܝ ܕܛܥܝܬܝ ܠܐܠܗܐ ܦܪܘܩܟܝ. ܘܠܬܩܝܦܐ ܡܥܫܢܢܟܝ ܠܐ ܐܬܕܟܪܬܝ. ܡܛܠ ܗܢܐ ܐܢܨܒܝ ܢܨܒܐ ܢܨܝܒܐ. ܒܚܩܠܐ ܢܘܟܪܝܐ ܐܙܪܥܝܗ.

Chapter 17

1   The burden of Damascus. See! Damascus is no longer[1] a city. It will be a waste place, a ruin.

2   The cities of Aroer will be deserted: they will be taken over by[2] the flocks which will lie down in them, there will be no danger for them.[3]

3   Strength will cease from Ephraim, and the kingdom from Damascus. The remnant of Ephraim will be as the glory of the children of Israel, says the mighty Lord.

4   And it will be on that day that the glory of Jacob will grow weak, and the fat of his body will be wasted away.

5   It will be like him who gathers the harvest of standing corn, and (with) his arm reaps the ears of wheat, like him who gleans the ears of wheat in the vale of Rephaim.

6   A gleaning will be left in it, as in the beaten olive tree, two (or) three olives at the top of the trunk, in its boughs, and four or five, says the Lord God of Israel.

7   And it will be on that day that man will put trust in his maker, and his eyes will look to the Holy One of Israel.

8   He will not put trust in the altars which his hands have made, his fingers have made; he will not look upon idols, nor upon false gods.

9   On that day his strong cities will be like the silent well,[4] belonging to the emir, that was left before the children of Israel; you will be destroyed.[5]

10 For you forgot[6] God, your savior; your powerful defender you did not call to mind; because of this you will plant a beautiful plant, you will propagate it with foreign shoots.

---

[1] 'is no longer': lit. 'passes away from'.

[2] 'taken over by': lit. 'for'.

[3] 'there will be no danger for them': lit. 'for which there will be nothing injurious'.

[4] 'silent well'. See Introduction. Addendum 1.

[5] 'destroyed': lit. 'for destruction'.

[6] 'forgot' or 'wandered away from'.

11   On the day that you will plant it, a shoot[1] will go forth, your seed will spring up at dawn, like the servitude[2] of the ingathering[3] on the sad day, like the pain of man.

12   Woe to the might of many nations: their clamor like[4] the clamor of the seas, like the tumult of the peoples,

13   Like the clamor of many waters; and he will rebuke it; he will flee far away, he will run like the dust of the mountains before the wind, like straw before the whirlwind.

14   At the time of evening - See! Violence; before it is dawn, he will not be left. This is the portion of our oppressor, the lot of our plunderer.

---

[1] 'shoot' or 'blossom'.

[2] 'servitude' or 'yoke'.

[3] 'ingathering' or 'vintage '.

[4] 'like': lit. 'goes… like'.

Chapter 18

IX

1   Oh, for the land of the shadow of wings,[1] which is on the far shore of the rivers of Cush,

2   Which sends envoys by sea, in vessels of papyrus upon the face of the waters: Go, swift messengers, to a people plucked up and rooted out, to a people stronger than it, and beyond; a people base and down-trodden, whose land the rivers have plundered.

3   All inhabitants of the world, who dwell in the land: when the mountains have lifted up the standard, you will see; when the trumpet has sounded, you will hear.

4   For thus said the Lord to me: I will bring calm; look on my preparation, as the burning[2] heat above the river, as the cloud of dew on the day of harvest.

5   For before the harvest, the bud has been perfected, and the flower ripened, and there will be a bloom; but he will cut off luxuriant growth with a sickle, the shoot will die,[3] and he will throw (it) away.

6   They will be left, together, for the bird(s) of prey of the mountains, and for the beast(s) of the earth; the bird(s) of prey will gather together upon it, and every beast of the earth will rage against it.

7   On that day he will bring gifts to the mighty Lord: a people plucked up and rooted out, a people stronger than it, and beyond; a people base and down-trodden, whose land the rivers have plundered, to the place of the name of the mighty Lord, to the mountain of Zion.

---

[1] 'the land of the shadow of wings'. MT 'the land of whirring wings'. See Introduction. Addendum 1.

[2] 'burning' or 'glowing'.

[3] 'die': lit. 'pass away'.

ܩܦܠܐܘܢ: ܝܛ.

1 ܐ ܡܫܩܠܐ ܕܡܨܪܝܢ. ܗܐ ܡܪܝܐ ܪܟܝܒ ܥܠ ܥܢܢܐ ܩܠܝܠܬܐ: ܘܐܬܐ ܠܡܨܪܝܢ.
ܘܢܙܘܥܘܢ ܦܬܟܪܐ ܕܡܨܪܝܢ ܡܢ ܩܕܡܘܗܝ. ܘܠܒܗ ܕܡܨܪܝܐ ܢܬܡܣܐ ܒܓܘܗ.

2 ܒ ܘܐܓܪܐ ܡܨܪܝܐ ܒܡܨܪܝܐ. ܘܢܬܟܬܫܘܢ ܓܒܪܐ ܥܡ ܐܚܘܗܝ: ܘܓܒܪܐ ܥܡ ܚܒܪܗ:
ܡܕܝܢܬܐ ܥܡ ܡܕܝܢܬܐ: ܘܡܠܟܘܬܐ ܥܡ ܡܠܟܘܬܐ.

3 ܓ ܘܬܬܦܫܩ ܪܘܚܗ ܕܡܨܪܝܐ ܒܓܘܗ: ܘܬܪܥܝܬܗ ܐܒܠܥ. ܘܢܫܐܠܘܢ ܡܢ ܦܬܟܪܐ
ܘܡܢ ܡܓܕܫܢܐ: ܘܡܢ ܙܟܘܪܐ ܘܡܢ ܚܪܫܐ.

4 ܕ ܘܐܫܠܡ ܠܡܨܪܝܐ ܒܐܝܕܝ ܕܡܪܐ ܩܫܝܐ. ܘܡܠܟܐ ܥܫܝܢܐ ܢܫܠܘܛ ܒܗܘܢ: ܐܡܪ
ܡܪܝܐ ܚܝܠܬܢܐ.

5 ܗ ܘܢܚܪܒܘܢ ܡܝܐ ܡܢ ܝܡܐ. ܘܢܗܪܐ ܢܚܪܒ ܘܢܝܒܫ.

6 ܘ ܘܢܚܪܒܘܢ ܢܗܪܘܬܐ: ܘܢܬܡܣܟܢܘܢ. ܘܢܚܪܒܘܢ ܢܗܪܘܬܐ ܥܡܝܩܬܐ. ܩܢܝܐ ܘܐܘܪܒܝܐ
ܘܦܩܪܘܗܝ ܢܝܒܫܘܢ.

7 ܙ ܘܥܘܒܐ ܕܥܠ ܢܗܪܐ: ܘܥܠ ܦܘܡܗ ܕܢܗܪܐ: ܘܟܠ ܕܡܙܕܪܥ ܥܠ ܓܢܒܗ
ܕܢܗܪܐ ܢܝܒܫ. ܘܢܫܬܩܦ ܘܠܐ ܢܫܬܟܚ.

8 ܚ ܘܢܐܠܘܢ ܨܝܕܐ. ܘܢܬܒܟܘܢ ܟܠܗܘܢ ܕܪܡܝܢ ܨܢܪܬܐ ܒܢܗܪܐ. ܘܕܦܪܣܝܢ ܡܨܝܕܬܐ
ܥܠ ܐܦܝ ܡܝܐ ܢܬܒܨܪܘܢ.

9 ܛ ܘܢܒܗܬܘܢ ܦܠܚܝ ܟܬܢܐ: ܕܣܪܩܝܢ ܘܙܩܪܝܢ ܠܚܙܘܬܐ.

10 ܝ ܘܢܬܡܟܟܘܢ ܟܠ ܕܥܒܕܝܢ ܫܟܪܐ: ܠܢܦܫܬܐ ܕܢܘܢܐ.

Chapter 19

1   The burden of Egypt. See! The Lord is mounted upon swift clouds, he enters Egypt: the idols of Egypt will tremble in his presence, the heart of Egypt will melt away in its midst.

2   I will set Egypt against[1] Egypt: a man will fight with his brother, a man with his neighbor, a city with a city, and a kingdom with a kingdom.

3   The spirit of the Egyptian will be cut off in its midst, I will drown its counsel: they will inquire of the idols, the magicians, the diviners, and the soothsayers.

4   I will deliver the Egyptians into the hand of harsh lords; a strong king will have dominion over them, says the mighty Lord.

5   The waters will fail from the sea; the river will lie waste, be dried up.

6   The rivers will fail, become weak; the mighty rivers will lie waste; cane and reed and papyrus will be dried up.

7   The pond-weed by the river, and by the mouth of the river, and everything which is sown on the bank of the river will be dried up, will be blighted, will disappear.[2]

8   The fishermen will lament, those who cast fishing rods in the river will sit in mourning; those who spread out nets upon the surface[3] of the waters have grown weak.

9   Those who work with flax will be ashamed, those who comb cotton (cloth) and weave for joy.[4]

10   They will be brought low, all who make strong drink for the feast of the soul.[5]

---

[1] 'set … against': lit. 'incite … with'.

[2] 'disappear': lit. 'not be present'.

[3] 'surface': lit. 'face'.

[4] 'for joy'. MT 'white (stuff)'. See Introduction. Addendum 1.

[5] 'all who make strong drink for the feast of the soul'. MT 'all the workers for hire sad of soul'. See Introduction. Addendum 1.

11 ܝܐ ܫܛܘ ܪ̈ܘܪܒܢܐ ܕܨܘܥܢ. ܘܚ̈ܟܝܡܐ ܕܡܠܟܝܢ ܠܦܪܥܘܢ ܡܠܟܐ ܡܠܟܐ ܣܟܠܬܐ.
ܐܝܟܢܐ ܬܐܡܪܘܢ ܠܦܪܥܘܢ ܕܚܟܝ̈ܡܐ ܚܢܢ: ܘܒܢ̈ܝ ܡܠ̈ܟܐ ܩܕ̈ܡܝܐ.

12 ܝܒ ܐܝܟܐ ܐܢܘܢ ܚܟܝ̈ܡܝܟܝ: ܢܚܘܘܢܟܝ: ܘܢܕܥܘܢ ܡܢܐ ܐܬܪܥܝ ܡܪܝܐ ܚܝܠܬܢܐ ܥܠ
ܡܨܪܝܢ.

13 ܝܓ ܫܛܘ ܪ̈ܘܪܒܢܐ ܕܨܘܥܢ. ܐܬܛܥܝܘ ܪ̈ܘܪܒܢܐ ܕܡܦܝܣ: ܘܐܛܥܝܘ ܠܡܨܪܝܢ ܒܪ̈ܘܫܝܗ
ܕܫ̈ܒܛܝܗ.

14 ܝܕ ܡܪܝܐ ܡܙܓ ܒܓܘܗ ܪܘܚܐ ܕܛܘܥܝܝܐ: ܘܐܛܥܝܘ ܠܡܨܪܝܢ ܒܟܠܗܘܢ ܒܥܒ̈ܕܝܗܘܢ:
ܐܝܟ ܕܛܥܐ ܪܘܝܐ ܒܬܘܝܬܗ.

15 ܝܗ ܘܠܐ ܢܗܘܐ ܠܡܨܪܝܢ ܥܒܕܐ ܕܢܥܒܕ ܪ̈ܫܐ ܘܕܘܢܒܬܐ: ܘܣܘܦܐ.

16 ܝܘ ܒܝܘܡܐ ܗܘ: ܢܗܘܘܢ ܡܨܪ̈ܝܐ ܐܝܟ ܢܫ̈ܐ. ܘܢܕܚܠܘܢ ܘܢܙܘܥܘܢ ܡܢ ܩܕܡ ܢܘܦܐ ܕܐܝܕܗ
ܕܡܪܝܐ ܚܝܠܬܢܐ ܕܡܢܝܦ ܥܠܝܗܘܢ.

17 ܝܙ ܘܬܗܘܐ ܐܪܥܐ ܕܝܗܘܕܐ ܠܡܨܪ̈ܝܐ ܠܚܓܐ. ܘܟܠ ܕܢܥܗܕܝܗ ܠܗ: ܢܬܪܗܒ: ܡܢ
ܩܕܡ ܬܪܥܝܬܗ ܕܡܪܝܐ ܚܝܠܬܢܐ ܕܐܬܪܥܝ ܥܠܝܗܘܢ.

18 ܝܚ ܒܝܘܡܐ ܗܘ: ܢܗܘ̈ܝܢ ܚܡܫ ܡܕ̈ܝܢܢ ܒܐܪܥܐ ܕܡܨܪܝܢ: ܕܡܡܠܠܢ ܒܠܫܢܐ ܟܢܥܢܝܐ.
ܘܝܡܝܢ ܠܡܪܝܐ ܚܝܠܬܢܐ. ܘܚܕܐ ܡܢܗܝܢ ܩܪܝܢ ܠܗ ܐܬܐܡܪ.

19 ܝܛ ܒܝܘܡܐ ܗܘ: ܢܗܘܐ ܡܕܒܚܐ ܠܡܪܝܐ ܚܝܠܬܢܐ ܒܓܘܗ ܕܐܪܥܐ ܕܡܨܪܝܢ:
ܘܩܝܡܬܐ ܠܡܪܝܐ ܥܠ ܬܚܘܡܗ.

11 The great men of Zoan played the fool,[1] and (also) the wise men who counsel Pharaoh the king with crazy counsels: how will you say to Pharaoh 'We are wise, the sons of ancient kings'?

12 Where are your wise men? let them show you, let them know, what the mighty Lord has purposed regarding Egypt.

13 The great men of Zoan played the fool;[2] the great men of Memphis have become haughty,[3] they have led Egypt astray with the chiefs[4] of her tribes.

14 The Lord has mingled in her midst a wandering spirit; he[5] has led the Egyptian astray in all his works, as a drunkard wanders in his vomit.

15 There will be no man who will make for the Egypt the head or the tail, or the tail or the head.

16 On that day the Egyptian will be like a woman,[6] he will fear and tremble before the height of the hand of the mighty Lord which he lifts up against him.

17 The land of Judah will be an object of terror to the Egyptian; all who may remember it will dread[7] the purpose of the mighty Lord which he has purposed against him.

18 In that day there will be five cities in the land of Egypt which speak in the Canaanite tongue and swear by the mighty Lord, and one of them will be called 'Hares'.[8]

19 On that day there will be an altar to the mighty Lord in the midst of the land of Egypt, and a monument to the Lord near its border.

---

[1] 'played the fool': lit. 'were contemptuous'.

[2] 'played the fool': lit. 'were contemptuous'.

[3] 'have become haughty'. MT 'are deceived'. See Introduction. Addendum 1.

[4] 'chiefs': lit. 'corners', a semantic borrowing of the Hebrew metaphorical use of 'corner' as 'chief, ruler'.

[5] 'he' or 'it'.

[6] 'a woman': pl.

[7] 'dread': lit. 'be afraid before'.

[8] 'Hares': P transliterates the Hebrew חרס 'Destruction'.

20 ܟ ܘܬܗܘܐ ܠܐܬܐ ܘܠܣܗܕܘܬܐ ܠܡܪܝܐ ܚܝܠܬܢܐ ܒܐܪܥܐ ܕܡܨܪܝܢ: ܡܛܠ ܕܢܩܥܘܢ
ܩܕܡ ܡܪܝܐ ܡܢ ܩܕܡ ܐܠܘܨܐ. ܘܢܫܕܪ ܠܗܘܢ ܦܪܘܩܐ: ܘܕܝܢܐ: ܘܢܦܨܐ ܐܢܘܢ.

21 ܟܐ ܘܢܬܝܕܥ ܡܪܝܐ ܠܡܨܪܝܐ: ܘܢܕܥܘܢܗ ܡܨܪܝܐ ܠܡܪܝܐ ܒܝܘܡܐ ܗܘ. ܘܢܩܪܒܘܢ
ܕܒܚܐ ܘܩܘܪܒܢܐ. ܘܢܢܕܪܘܢ ܢܕܪܐ ܠܡܪܝܐ: ܘܢܫܠܡܘܢ.

22 ܟܒ ܘܢܡܚܐ ܡܪܝܐ ܠܡܨܪܝܐ ܡܚܘܬܐ: ܘܢܐܣܐ ܐܢܘܢ. ܘܢܬܦܢܘܢ ܠܘܬ ܡܪܝܐ: ܘܢܥܢܐ
ܐܢܘܢ: ܘܢܐܣܐ ܐܢܘܢ.

23 ܟܓ ܒܝܘܡܐ ܗܘ: ܢܗܘܐ ܫܒܝܠܐ ܡܢ ܡܨܪܝܢ ܠܐܬܘܪ: ܘܡܢ ܐܬܘܪ ܠܡܨܪܝܢ.
ܘܢܥܠܘܢ ܐܬܘܪܝܐ ܠܡܨܪܝܢ: ܘܡܨܪܝܐ ܠܐܬܘܪ. ܘܢܦܠܚܘܢ ܡܨܪܝܐ ܠܐܬܘܪܝܐ.

24 ܟܕ ܒܝܘܡܐ ܗܘ ܢܗܘܐ ܐܝܣܪܐܝܠ ܚܕ ܡܢ ܬܠܬܐ: ܠܡܨܪܝܐ ܘܠܐܬܘܪܝܐ ܒܘܪܟܬܐ
ܒܓܘ ܐܪܥܐ.

25 ܟܗ ܕܠܗ ܒܪܟ ܡܪܝܐ ܚܝܠܬܢܐ: ܘܐܡܪ: ܒܪܝܟ ܥܡܝ ܕܒܡܨܪܝܢ: ܘܥܒܕ ܐܝܕܝ
ܕܒܐܬܘܪ. ܘܝܪܬܘܬܝ ܐܝܣܪܐܝܠ.

20   It will be for a sign and for a testimony to the mighty Lord in the land of Egypt, for they will call upon the Lord from the presence of the oppressor, and he will send to them a savior and a judge, and he will deliver them.

21   The Lord will be recognized by the Egyptians, the Egyptians will know the Lord on that day; they will bring sacrifices and fine flour; they will take[1] vows to the Lord and they will fulfill (them).

22   The Lord will strike the Egyptians a blow; and he will heal them: they will turn to the Lord and he will answer them, he will heal them.

23   On that day there will be a highway from Egypt to Assyria, and from Assyria to Egypt; the Assyrian will enter into Egypt, and the Egyptian into Assyria; and the Egyptians will serve the Assyrians.

24   On that day Israel will be the third[2] with the Egyptians and with the Assyrians: a blessing in the midst of the earth.

25   Which the mighty Lord has blessed and said: Blessed are[3] my people who are in Egypt, and the work of my hands that is in Assyria, and my inheritance, Israel.

---

[1] 'take': lit. 'vow'.

[2] 'the third': lit. 'one of three'.

[3] 'are': sing. verb.

1 حَمَيَدَا وَاٰلِاٰ بِاٰۥزَاٰ لَحمزۡهو: حُبِ عَبزۡهُ هَنزۡحٖیم مَحدَا وِٱلَاٰهو: وَاٰلِاٰحَکَمه حُم اَمزۡهو ودَٕحجمُۃ.

2 دۡه حَرَجَنَا هَه: مَحْلَلَا مُدنَا حۡمَ اَمَعنَا بجُنَا جَد اَمُهز: وَاٰحَد حَده: زِلَا عنَد هَعُمَا هٖی مَرۡزَتِی: ودۡحمَهَۃنَتۡی هٖی ڒۡحكۡمٖی. ودَۡحجَی وَجُنَا: ووَهَكۡحِ حَدَلَا ومۡحۡجَۃَ.

3 وَاٰحَد مُدنَا: اَمَدَلَا ووَهَكۡحِ حَجبٖی اَمَعنَا حَدَلَا ومۡحۡجَۃ: وَوَجُنَا نَوَقۡمِ اَبَاٰقِبَاٰلِا ومۡاوۡحَتۡبَاٰلِا بِاٰحۡكِ عنَتۡی نَحَلَا مَۡزۡوِی ودَحَلَا تُه.

4 وَوَجُنَا نَبَحَد مَحدَا وِٱلَاٰهو عجَحۡجَا وِمۡزۡوِی: ومۡعجَحۡجَا ووّۡهم: وحُكۡتنَحَا ووَهَجَا حَدَلَا ومۡحۡجَۃ. وۡنَلِی حِلَا قُهوۡمَهُنَۃ ومۡزۡوِی.

5 وۡنَلَاۡاٰجزۡهی وۡنَجهۡبَاٰهی: هٖی تُهم اَوۡمۡكۡنَهَهی: ومۡم مۡزۡوِی اَحۡتۡحۡمۡسۡحَلَاهَهی.

6 وۡنَلَاۡحَد حُعۡحۡدوۡاٰ وِحۡزۡزَنَاٰلِا هُوِاٰ جمۡوۡعَحۡا هَه: هُووۡحَا بوه اَوۡمۡكۡنَبِ: وَحَدزَمِ حۡحۡحۡجۡحَبۡوۡه ومۡحۡحۡجۡحۡجۡقۡزۡیۡه هٖی مَحدَا وِٱلَاٰهو. ومۡحۡبِی اَمَعنَا نَبۡقۡزۡاٰ.

Chapter 20

1　In the year that Tartan came to Ashdod, when Sargon king of Assyria sent him, when he fought with Ashdod and subdued it,

2　At that time the Lord spoke through the mouth of[1] Isaiah the prophet, the son of Amoz, and said to him: Go, loosen the sackcloth from your loins, and your sandals from your feet; he did so, and went[2] stripped bare and unshod.

3　And the Lord said: Just as my servant Isaiah has gone, stripped bare and unshod, so there will be signs and wonders for three years, against Egypt and against Cush.

4　Thus the king of Assyria will take the captives of Egypt and the captives of Cush, young men and old, stripped bare and unshod, and the nakedness of Egypt will be revealed.

5　They will be broken-hearted and ashamed, of Cush (the source of) their confidence and of Egypt, their glory.

6　And the inhabitant(s) of this island will say[3] on that day: Here is (the source of) our confidence, from which[4] we have fled, to be helped, to be saved from the king of Assyria; and we, how shall we be saved?

---

[1] 'through the mouth of': lit. 'by the hand of'.

[2] 'went': lit. 'walked'.

[3] 'say': sing. verb.

[4] 'from which': lit. 'that'.

Chapter 21

1   The burden of the wilderness of the sea. As the whirlwind of the south will go swiftly from the wilderness and will come from a distant land,

2   A grievous vision has appeared to us: the oppressor oppresses,[1] and the plunderer plunders. Go up, Elam, keep guard;[2] Media, I have brought to an end all her sighs.

3   Because of this I was seized with trembling,[3] terrors gripped me like the terrors of a woman giving birth; I trembled so (much that) I could not hear, I was (so) distressed that I could not see.

4   My heart wanders, terrors shake me, and the virtues[4] of my desire have put me to fright.

5   Prepare the tables; watchmen, watch;[5] eat and drink; rise up, rulers; oil the shields.

6   For thus said the Lord to me: Go, set up a watchman who will make known everything that he sees.

7   He saw a company of horsemen in pairs,[6] (some) riding a mule or riding a camel; he listened carefully[7] to a great report.

8   And the watchman cried in my ears, and said: Lord, I stand (guard) constantly by day, and I stand on my watch every night.[8]

9   See! A man came, from the riders, of the horsemen; he answered and said: She has fallen, she has fallen, Babylon, and all her graven gods (lie) shattered on the ground, from the reaping,[9] without the granary.

---

[1] 'oppressor oppresses' or 'deceiver deceives'.

[2] 'keep guard': in the sense 'to lay siege'.

[3] 'I was seized with trembling': lit. 'my loins (or back) were filled with trembling'.

[4] 'virtues' or 'beauties'. See Introduction. Addendum 2.

[5] 'watchmen, watch'. See Introduction. Addendum 1.

[6] 'a company of horsemen in pairs': lit. 'a riding of two horsemen'.

[7] 'listened carefully' or 'gave heed'.

[8] 'every night': lit. 'all the nights'.

[9] 'reaping' or 'harvest'.

10 ܝ ܡܕܡ ܕܫܡܥܬ ܡܢ ܡܪܝܐ ܐܠܗܐ ܕܐܝܣܪܝܠ: ܚܘܝܬܟܘܢ.

11 ܝܐ ܡܫܩܠܐ ܕܕܘܡܐ. ܠܝ ܩܪܐ ܡܢ ܣܥܝܪ ܢܛܘܪܐ ܕܒܠܠܝܐ.

12 ܝܒ ܐܡܪ ܢܛܘܪܐ: ܐܬܐ ܨܦܪܐ ܐܦ ܠܠܝܐ. ܐܢ ܒܥܝܢ ܐܢܬܘܢ ܒܥܘ: ܬܘܒ ܐܬܘ ܐܢܬܘܢ.

13 ܝܓ ܡܫܩܠܐ ܕܥܪܒܐ ܒܪܡܫܐ ܒܥܒܐ ܬܒܘܬܘܢ: ܒܫܒܝܠܐ ܕܕܘܕܢܝܡ.

14 ܝܕ ܠܐܘܪܥ ܨܗܝܐ ܐܝܬܘ ܡܝܐ: ܥܡܘܪܐ ܕܐܪܥܐ ܕܬܝܡܢܐ. ܒܠܚܡܗܘܢ ܐܘܪܥܘ ܠܥܪܝܩܐ.

15 ܝܗ ܡܛܠ ܕܡܢ ܩܕܡ ܣܝܦܐ ܐܬܥܪܩܘ: ܘܡܢ ܩܕܡ ܚܪܒܐ ܕܫܠܝܦܬܐ: ܘܡܢ
ܩܕܡ ܩܫܬܐ ܕܡܬܝܚܐ: ܘܡܢ ܩܕܡ ܩܘܫܝܐ ܕܩܪܒܐ.

16 ܝܘ ܡܛܠ ܕܗܟܢܐ ܐܡܪ ܠܝ ܡܪܝܐ: ܒܫܢܬܐ ܚܕܐ ܐܝܟ ܫܢܝ ܐܓܝܪܐ: ܢܫܠܡ
ܟܠܗ ܐܝܩܪܐ ܕܩܕܪ.

17 ܝܙ ܘܫܪܟܐ ܕܡܢܝܢܐ ܕܩܫܬܐ: ܓܢܒܪܐ ܕܒܢܝ ܩܕܪ ܢܒܨܘܢ: ܡܛܠ ܕܡܪܝܐ ܐܠܗܐ
ܕܐܝܣܪܝܠ ܡܠܠ.

10   That which I have heard from the Lord God of Israel, I have made known to you.

11   The burden of Dumah. He called to me from Seir, the watchman of the night (watch).[1]

12   The watchman said: Dawn has come, as has[2] the night. If you are seeking, seek: you are coming again. [3]

13   The burden of Arabah. In the evening you will lodge in the forest, on the road to Dedanim.

14   To meet the thirsty, bring water, inhabitants of the land of the south; with your bread meet the scattered.

15   For they were scattered by the blade, by the sharpened sword, by the drawn bow, by[4] the force of the war.

16   For thus said the Lord to me: When a year is completed, as the years of a hired servant, all the glory of Kedar will come to an end.[5]

17   And the remnant of the number of the archers, the men of the sons of Kedar, will be diminished: for the Lord God of Israel has spoken.

---

[1] 'of the night (watch)': lit. 'that (was) in the night', i.e. the watchman called to the speaker. Alternatively, a vocative is intended, i.e. 'Watchman of the night!'.

[2] 'as has': lit. 'also'.

[3] 'you are coming again' or 'turn back, you who are coming'.

[4] 'by'[1,2,3,4]: lit. 'before'.

[5] 'come to an end' or 'perish'.

مَ.

100

Chapter 22

X

1 The burden of the valley of Hezyon.[1] What concerns you[2] now, that you have gone up, all of you, onto the rooftop(s)?

2 You have filled the city with tumult, you have filled the strong city with clamor; your slain were not slain by the sword, nor (your) dead in battle.

3 All your rulers have staggered[3] together; those who remained with you have been taken captive by the bow(men),[4] they have been taken captive[5] together, they have fled far away.

4 Therefore I said: Leave me, I shall weep bitterly; do not strive[6] to comfort me concerning the ruin of the daughter of my people.

5 For (there) is a day of tumult, of trampling under foot, of weeping, to the mighty Lord God in the valley of Hezyon: he has searched the city walls, cried out upon the mountains.

6 Elam bore the quiver, with the riders,[7] the horsemen;[8] the city wall[9] revealed the targets.[10]

7 The choicest of the deep valleys will be filled with chariots; horsemen will draw up in line of battle against the gates.

8 Judah will reveal (its) ranks: on that day you will see the weapons of the house of the forest.

9 You saw that the breaches of the city of David were many; you gathered the waters of the lower pool.

---

[1] 'Hezyon': here and in v.5 P transliterates the Hebrew noun 'vision'.

[2] 'concerns you': lit. 'is to you'.

[3] 'staggered': MT 'fled'. See Introduction. Addendum 1.

[4] 'bow(men)': lit. 'bow'.

[5] 'taken captive … taken captive' or 'bound … bound'.

[6] 'strive': lit. 'be pressing'.

[7] 'riders' or 'chariotry'.

[8] 'the riders, the horsemen': lit. 'riders of the man horsemen'

[9] 'city wall': MT 'Kir'. See Introduction. Addendum 1.

[10] 'targets' or 'bucklers, round shields'.

10 ܝ ܘܡܢܝܬܘܢ ܒܬܐ ܕܐܘܪܫܠܡ. ܘܣܬܪܬܘܢ ܒܬܐ: ܕܬܚܣܢܘܢ ܫܘܪܐ.

11 ܝܐ ܘܡܥܝܢܬܐ ܥܒܕܬܘܢ ܒܝܢ ܫܘܪܐ ܠܡܝܐ ܕܢܩܥܬܐ ܥܬܝܩܬܐ. ܘܠܐ ܚܪܬܘܢ ܠܥܒܘܕܗ. ܘܠܓܒܘܠܗ ܡܢ ܪܘܚܩܐ ܠܐ ܚܙܝܬܘܢ.

12 ܝܒ ܘܩܪܐ ܡܪܝܐ ܐܠܗܐ ܚܝܠܬܢܐ ܒܝܘܡܐ ܗܘ: ܠܒܟܝܐ ܘܠܡܪܩܕܐ ܘܠܩܪܝܚܘܬܐ: ܘܠܚܓܪܐ ܕܣܩܐ.

13 ܝܓ ܘܗܐ ܚܕܘܬܐ ܘܪܘܙܐ: ܢܟܣܝܢ ܕܬܘܪܐ: ܘܢܟܣܝܢ ܕܥܢܐ: ܘܡܬܒܣܡܝܢ ܕܒܣܪܐ: ܘܫܬܝܢ ܕܚܡܪܐ. ܢܐܟܘܠ ܘܢܫܬܐ: ܡܛܠ ܕܡܚܪ ܢܡܘܬ.

14 ܝܕ ܓܠܝܐ ܗܘ ܒܐܕܢܝ ܡܪܝܐ ܚܝܠܬܢܐ: ܘܐܡܪ: ܠܐ ܢܫܬܒܩ ܠܟܘܢ ܚܛܗܐ ܗܢܐ ܥܕܡܐ ܕܬܡܘܬܘܢ: ܐܡܪ ܡܪܝܐ ܐܠܗܐ ܚܝܠܬܢܐ.

15 ܝܗ ܗܟܢܐ ܐܡܪ ܡܪܝܐ ܐܠܗܐ ܚܝܠܬܢܐ: ܙܠ ܠܘܬ ܣܘܟܢ ܗܢܐ: ܠܘܬ ܫܒܢܐ ܪܒܝܬܐ: ܘܐܡܪ ܠܗ.

16 ܝܘ ܡܢܐ ܠܟ ܐܝܟ ܗܪܟܐ: ܘܡܢܐ ܐܝܬ ܠܟ ܗܪܟܐ. ܕܢܩܪܬ ܠܟ ܗܪܟܐ ܩܒܪܐ. ܢܩܪ ܒܪܘܡܐ ܩܒܪܗ: ܘܓܠܦ ܒܟܐܦܐ ܡܫܪܝܗ.

17 ܝܙ ܗܐ ܡܪܝܐ ܡܫܕܐ ܫܕܝܐ ܠܟ ܓܒܪܐ: ܘܡܥܛܦ ܥܛܦܐ ܠܟ.

18 ܝܚ ܢܟܪܟܟ ܟܘܪܟܝܐ ܐܝܟ ܟܘܪܝܐ ܕܐܣܦܪܐ: ܠܐܪܥܐ: ܘܪܘܝܚܬܐ ܕܐܝܕܝܐ. ܬܡܢ ܬܡܘܬ: ܘܬܡܢ ܡܪܟܒܬܐ ܕܐܝܩܪܟ: ܨܥܪܐ ܕܒܝܬ ܡܪܟ.

19 ܝܛ ܘܐܕܚܝܟ ܡܢ ܐܬܪܟ: ܘܐܣܚܦܟ ܡܢ ܩܝܡܟ.

10   You filled the houses of Jerusalem; you pulled down houses so that you might strengthen the city wall.

11   You made reservoirs between the city wall(s) for the waters of the old pool: but you did not look to its maker, you did not see its founder of long ago.[1]

12   The mighty Lord God called on that day for weeping, for mourning, for tearing out of hair, for putting on sackcloth.

13   But see! Pleasure and rejoicing, slaughter of bulls and slaughter of sheep,[2] eating meat,[3] drinking wine: let us eat and let us drink, for tomorrow we will die!

14   It was revealed in my ears (by) the mighty Lord, he said: You shall not take away this sin from yourselves[4] until you die, says the mighty Lord God.

15   Thus says the mighty Lord God: Go to this steward,[5] to Shebna who is in charge of the household,[6] and say to him:

16   What are you doing here? what concerns you here? that you should hew out a grave for yourself here, hewing out his grave on high, engraving his dwelling in the stone?

17   See! The Lord indeed hurls you (around), mighty man - and indeed forgets you.

18   He will afflict you with suffering like the suffering of a cohort in a broad land;[7] there you will die, and there will be the chariot of your glory, the shame of the house of your lord.

19   And I will overthrow you, from your glory; I will pull you down from your position.

---

[1] 'long ago' or 'afar'.

[2] 'sheep' or 'the flock'.

[3] 'eating meat': lit. 'food of flesh'.

[4] 'from yourselves': lit. 'to yourselves'.

[5] 'steward': an approximate transliteration of the Hebrew סכן.

[6] 'who is in charge of the household': lit. 'the great one of the house'. The same Syriac title is also found in 36:3,22, 37:2. Although this title may be rendered 'steward' this is not the same term for 'steward' as was used earlier in this verse transliterating the Hebrew סכן.

[7] 'broad land': lit. 'open of hands', i.e. a land stretching far in both directions.

20 ܟ ܘܢܗܘܐ ܒܝܘܡܐ ܗܘ: ܐܡܪ ܡܪܝܐ: ܐܩܪܐ ܠܥܒܕܝ ܐܠܝܩܝܡ ܒܪ ܚܠܩܝܐ.

21 ܟܐ ܘܐܠܒܫܝܘܗܝ ܟܘܬܝܢܟ. ܘܒܗܡܝܢܟ ܐܚܣܢܝܘܗܝ. ܘܫܘܠܛܢܟ ܐܬܠ ܒܐܝܕܘܗܝ. ܘܢܗܘܐ ܐܒܐ ܠܥܡܘܪ̈ܐ ܕܐܘܪܫܠܡ: ܘܠܒܢ̈ܝܐ ܕܒܝܬ ܝܗܘܕܐ.

22 ܟܒ ܘܐܣܝܡ ܩܠܝܕܐ ܕܒܝܬ ܕܘܝܕ ܥܠ ܟܬܦܗ. ܘܢܦܬܚ: ܘܠܝܬ ܕܢܐܚܘܕ. ܘܢܐܚܘܕ. ܘܠܝܬ ܕܢܦܬܚ.

23 ܟܓ ܘܐܩܒܥܝܘܗܝ ܣܟܬܐ ܒܐܬܪܐ ܡܗܝܡܢܐ. ܘܢܗܘܐ ܟܘܪܣܝܐ ܕܐܝܩܪܐ ܠܒܝܬ ܐܒܘܗܝ.

24 ܟܕ ܘܢܬܠܘܢ ܥܠܘܗܝ ܟܠܗ ܐܝܩܪܐ ܕܒܝܬ ܐܒܘܗܝ: ܡܢܟܣܐ ܘܡܫܡܫܢܐ: ܘܟܠ ܡܐܢܐ ܙܥܘܪܐ: ܡܢ ܡܐܢܐ ܕܟܣܐ: ܘܥܕܡܐ ܠܡܐܢܐ ܕܟܢܪ̈ܐ.

25 ܟܗ ܒܝܘܡܐ ܗܘ: ܐܡܪ ܡܪܝܐ ܚܝܠܬܢܐ: ܢܬܥܩܪ ܣܟܬܐ ܕܩܒܝܥܐ ܒܐܬܪܐ ܡܗܝܡܢܐ. ܘܬܬܬܒܪ ܘܬܦܠ. ܘܢܐܒܕ ܡܘܒܠܐ ܕܥܠܝܗ: ܡܛܠ ܕܡܪܝܐ ܡܠܠ.

20   And it will be on that day, says the Lord, I will call to my servant Eliakim son of Hilkiah.

21   I will clothe him with your tunic, with your belt I will gird him; I will put your government into his hands, and he will be a father to the inhabitants of Jerusalem and to the men of the house of Judah.

22   And I will put the keys of the house of David upon his shoulder; he will open and none will shut, he will shut and none will open.

23   I will fix him as a peg in a safe[1] place, and he will be a throne of glory for his father's house.

24   And they will lay upon him all the glory of his father's house, the venerable and the praiseworthy; and every small vessel:[2] of musical instrument, even the instrument of the harp.[3]

25   On that day, says the mighty Lord, the peg which was struck in a safe place will be uprooted, it will be pulled down, it will fall; and the burden which was set upon it will come to naught: for the Lord has spoken.

---

[1] 'safe' or 'enduring'.

[2] 'vessel': it is uncertain whether musical instruments or containers used in the temple service are intended.

[3] 'of musical instrument, even the instrument of the harp': lit. 'from the musical instrument even unto the instrument of the harp'.

Chapter 23

XI

1   The burden of Tyre. Howl, ships of Tarshish: for it has been plundered, from the house, (from) him who brings;[1] from the land of the Kittim it has been revealed to us.

2   Be silent,[2] inhabitants of the island; the merchant of Sidon who passes on by the sea.

3   They have filled you with many waters; the seed of the merchant was the harvest of the river; his ingathering was the commerce with the nations.

4   Be ashamed, Sidon, for the sea has spoken, and the strength of the sea: I have not labored, nor have I given birth, nor have I reared youths,[3] nor have I brought up[4] virgins.

5   When it was heard in Egypt: pains will seize hold of them, as the report of Tyre.

6   Pass over to Tarshish; howl, inhabitants of the island.

7   Is this yours,[5] strong one, that is from days of old?[6] Her feet will go before her, so that she may dwell far away.

8   Who counseled thus against Tyre, the crowned one?[7] her merchants are princes, her Canaanites[8] the honored of the earth.

9   The mighty Lord has purposed to bring to naught the honor of every army, to dishonor all the honored of the earth.

---

[1] 'for it has been plundered, from the house, (from) him who brings'. MT is difficult. See Introduction. Addendum 3.

[2] 'Be silent' or 'Be still'.

[3] 'youths': lit. 'unmarried youths' (boys aged between ten and eighteen years).

[4] 'brought up': lit. 'lifted up'.

[5] 'Is this yours' or 'This is for you'.

[6] 'days of old': lit. 'former days'.

[7] 'the crowned one' or 'who gives crowns'.

[8] 'Canaanites': as in Hebrew, the root also means 'merchant, tradesman'.

108

10   Pass on to your land like the river, daughter of Tarshish; no more is there anyone who will drive you away.

11   He has lifted up his hand over the sea, he has provoked the kingdoms; the Lord has commanded concerning Canaan, that he will destroy its strong places.

12   He said: You will not again wax strong, oppressed one, virgin daughter of Sidon. Rise up, pass over to Kittim; there too there will be no rest for you.

13   See the land of the Chaldeans: this is the people which the Assyrian was not, he made it for the wind; they established inquirers, they searched into its walled enclosures,[1] they made it a ruin.[2]

14   Howl, ships of Tarshish, for your strength has been plundered.

15   For it will be, on that day, Tyre shall be forgotten for seventy years, like the days of one king, and after seventy years they will sing to Tyre the song of the harlot.

16   Take a harp, and go around (in) the city, harlot who has been forgotten; play a sweet melody,[3] make more music so that you may be remembered.

17   It will be, after seventy years, (that) the Lord will visit Tyre: he will return to her the money of her hiring,[4] and she will play the harlot with all the kingdoms on the face of the earth.

18   Her commerce and the money of her hiring will be holy to the Lord; they will not be put (in) the treasure house, they will not be guarded, but her commerce will be for those who dwell before the Lord, to eat, and to be satisfied, and to cover her old (clothing).[5]

---

[1] 'walled enclosures' or 'palaces'.

[2] MT is difficult. See Introduction. Addenda 2 and 3.

[3] 'a sweet melody': lit. '(what is) fair'.

[4] 'money of her hiring': pl.

[5] 'her old (clothing)'. See Addendum 3.

ܩܦܠܐܘܢ: ܒ.

1 ܐ ܗܐ ܡܪܝܐ ܡܣܪܩ ܠܐܪܥܐ: ܘܡܚܪܒ ܠܗ. ܘܡܗܦܟ ܐܦܝܗ: ܘܡܒܕܪ ܠܥܡܘܪܝܗ.

2 ܒ ܘܢܗܘܐ ܥܡܐ ܐܝܟ ܟܗܢܐ: ܘܥܒܕܐ ܐܝܟ ܡܪܗ: ܘܐܡܬܐ ܐܝܟ ܡܪܬܗ: ܩܢܝܐ ܐܝܟ ܡܙܒܢܢܐ: ܘܡܘܙܦܐ ܐܝܟ ܡܘܙܦܢܐ: ܐܝܟ ܡܪܐ ܚܘܒܬܗ ܕܚܝܒ ܠܗ.

3 ܓ ܡܣܬܪܩܘ ܬܣܬܪܩ ܐܪܥܐ: ܘܡܬܒܙܙܘ ܬܬܒܙܙ. ܡܛܠ ܕܡܪܝܐ ܡܠܠ ܦܬܓܡܐ ܗܢܐ.

4 ܕ ܐܒܠܬ ܘܚܪܒܬ ܬܒܝܠ ܐܪܥܐ. ܐܒܠܬ ܘܚܪܒܬ: ܘܐܬܐܒܠܬ ܬܒܝܠ. ܐܠܐ ܪܘܡܗ ܕܐܪܥܐ.

5 ܗ ܘܐܪܥܐ ܐܬܛܢܦܬ ܠܥܡܘܪܝܗ. ܡܛܠ ܕܥܒܪܘ ܢܡܘܣܐ: ܘܫܚܠܦܘ ܦܘܩܕܢܐ: ܘܒܛܠܘ ܩܝܡܐ ܕܥܠܡ.

6 ܘ ܡܛܠ ܗܟܢ ܐܟܠܬ ܠܘܛܬܐ ܐܪܥܐ. ܘܢܬܚܝܒܘܢ ܟܠܗܘܢ ܥܡܘܪܝܗ. ܡܛܠ ܗܢܐ ܢܬܡܣܟܢܘܢ ܟܠܗܘܢ ܥܡܘܪܝܗ ܕܐܪܥܐ: ܘܢܫܬܚܪܘܢ ܐܢܫܐ ܩܠܝܠ.

7 ܙ ܐܒܠ ܬܐܒܠ ܚܡܪܐ. ܘܟܠܬ ܓܘܦܢܐ. ܘܐܬܬܢܚܘ ܟܠ ܚܕܝ ܠܒܐ.

8 ܚ ܒܛܠܬ ܚܕܘܬܐ ܕܩܠܚܬܐ ܘܫܠܝ ܩܠܐ ܕܙܡܪܐ. ܒܛܠܬ ܚܕܘܬܐ ܕܟܢܪܐ.

9 ܛ ܒܙܡܪܐ ܠܐ ܢܫܬܘܢ ܚܡܪܐ. ܢܡܪ ܫܟܪܐ ܠܫܬܘܗܝ.

10 ܝ ܐܬܬܒܪܬ ܩܪܝܬܐ: ܘܐܬܬܚܕ ܟܠ ܒܝܬ ܡܥܠܢܐ.

11 ܝܐ ܝܠܠܬܐ ܥܠ ܚܡܪܐ ܒܫܘܩܐ. ܒܛܠܬ ܟܠܗ ܚܕܘܬܐ. ܘܥܒܪ ܕܘܨܗ ܕܐܪܥܐ.

12 ܝܒ ܘܐܫܬܚܪܬ ܒܩܪܝܬܐ ܚܪܒܐ. ܘܬܘܗܝܐ ܢܦܩܘܢ ܬܪ̈ܥܝܗ.

13 ܝܓ ܗܟܢܐ ܢܗܘܐ ܒܓܘܗ ܕܐܪܥܐ ܒܝܢܝ ܥܡܡܐ: ܐܝܟ ܢܩܦܬܐ ܕܙܝܬܐ: ܘܐܝܟ ܥܘܠܠܬܐ ܡܐ ܕܫܠܡ ܩܛܦܐ.

Chapter 24

1   Behold! The Lord destroys the earth, makes a breach in it, casts down its face, scatters its inhabitants.

2   The people will be like the priest, the servant like his master, the maidservant like her mistress, the purchaser like the vendor, the borrower like the lender, the creditor like his debtor.

3   The earth will be completely destroyed,[1] completely despoiled, for the Lord has spoken this word.

4   The earth mourned, it dwelt in mourning, it mourned and dwelt, the world made lamentation, the pride of the earth mourned.

5   The earth has become like its inhabitants: for they have transgressed the law, changed the commandment, brought to naught the eternal covenant.

6   Because of these things the earth will dwell in mourning,[2] all its inhabitants will be found guilty; because of this all the inhabitants of the earth will be brought to destruction, few men will remain.

7   The crop(s) dwelt in lamentation, the vines mourned, all the joyful of heart groaned.

8   Joy has ceased, the tambourines (too), the sound of delight has stilled, joy has ceased, the harps (too).

9   They will not drink wine with music; strong drink will be bitter to those who drink it.

10   The city has been plundered, all the wine-cellars have been closed up.

11   An outcry over the wine in the streets! all joy has ceased, the delight of the earth has passed away.

12   Destruction is left in the city, misery will break her gates to pieces.

13   So will it be in the midst of the earth among the peoples, as the beating of the olive (tree), as the gleaning when the harvest is finished.

---

[1] 'destroyed' or 'corrupted'.

[2] 'Because of these things the earth will dwell in mourning'. See Introduction. Addendum 1.

14 ܝܕ ܗܢܘܢ ܢܪܝܡܘܢ ܩܠܗܘܢ. ܘܢܫܒܚܘܢ ܒܪܒܘܬܗ ܕܡܪܝܐ. ܘܢܙܘܥܘܢ ܡܢ ܝܡܐ.

15 ܝܗ ܡܛܠ ܗܢܐ ܒܬܫܒ̈ܚܬܐ ܫܒܚܘ ܠܡܪܝܐ: ܘܒܓܙܪ̈ܬܐ ܕܝܡܐ ܫܡܗ ܕܡܪܝܐ
ܐܠܗܐ ܕܐܝܣܪܝܠ.

16 ܝܘ ܡܢ ܟܢܦ̈ܝܗ̇ ܕܐܪܥܐ ܬܫܒ̈ܚܬܐ ܫܡܥܢ: ܚܝܠܐ ܕܙܕܝܩܐ ܘܐܡܪܬ: ܐܪܙܝ ܠܝ: ܐܪܙܝ ܠܝ: ܐܘܝ
ܠܝ: ܢܟ̈ܠܐ ܐܢܟܠܘ: ܢܟ̈ܠܐ ܐܢܟܠܘ.

17 ܝܙ ܕܚܠܬܐ ܘܓܘܡܨܐ: ܘܦܚܐ ܥܠܝܟ: ܥܡܘܪܐ ܕܐܪܥܐ.

18 ܝܚ ܘܡܢ ܕܢܥܪܘܩ ܡܢ ܩܠܐ ܕܕܚܠܬܐ: ܢܦܠ ܒܓܘܡܨܐ. ܘܡܢ ܕܢܣܩ ܡܢ ܓܘ
ܓܘܡܨܐ: ܢܬܐܚܕ ܒܦܚܐ. ܡܛܠ ܕܟܘ̈ܘܐ ܡܢ ܡܪܘܡܐ ܐܬܦܬܚܘ: ܘܙܥ
ܫܬܐܣ̈ܘܗ̇ ܕܐܪܥܐ.

19 ܝܛ ܡܙܥ ܐܙܘܥ ܐܪܥܐ: ܘܡܙܠ ܐܙܘܠ ܐܪܥܐ: ܘܡܬܡܛ ܐܬܡܛܠ ܐܪܥܐ.

20 ܟ ܘܡܙܥ ܐܙܘܥ ܐܪܥܐ ܐܝܟ ܪܘܝܐ. ܘܐܬܢܝܕ ܐܝܟ ܡܛܠܠܐ. ܘܬܬܩܠ ܥܠܝܗ̇ ܥܘܠܗ̇:
ܘܬܦܠ. ܘܠܐ ܬܘܣܦ ܠܡܩܡ.

21 ܟܐ ܒܗ ܒܝܘܡܐ ܗܘ: ܢܣܥܘܪ ܡܪܝܐ ܥܠ ܚܝܠܐ ܕܪܘܡܐ ܒܪܘܡܐ: ܘܥܠ ܡܠܟ̈ܐ
ܕܐܪܥܐ ܒܐܪܥܐ.

22 ܟܒ ܘܢܟܢܫܘܢ ܟܢܘܫܬܐ ܠܐܣܝܪ̈ܐ ܒܓܘܒܐ. ܘܢܬܚܒܫܘܢ ܥܠ ܚܒܫܐ. ܘܠܣܘܓܐܐ
ܕܝܘ̈ܡܬܐ ܢܬܦܩܕܘܢ.

23 ܟܓ ܘܢܚܦܪ ܣܗܪܐ: ܘܢܒܗܬ ܫܡܫܐ. ܡܛܠ ܕܐܡܠܟ ܡܪܝܐ ܚܝܠܬܢܐ: ܒܛܘܪܐ
ܕܨܗܝܘܢ: ܘܒܐܘܪܫܠܡ. ܘܩܕܡ ܩܫܝ̈ܫܘܗܝ ܢܫܬܒܚ.

14 They will raise up their voice, they will praise the stateliness of the Lord, they will neigh from the sea.

15 Therefore with a hymn praise the Lord, in the islands of the sea the name of the Lord God of Israel.

16 From the ends of the earth we have heard chants,[1] the might of the righteous who say: (It has) mystical significance for me! (It has) mystical significance for me! woe is me, the unjust have committed injustice, the unjust have (perpetrated) iniquity, committed injustice.

17 Fear, the pit, and the snare (have come) upon you, inhabitants of the earth.

18 He who would flee from the sound of fear will fall into the pit, and he who would climb up[2] from the midst of the pit will be taken by the snare: for the floods from on high[3] were opened, the foundations of the earth were moved.

19 Indeed, the earth will be moved; indeed, the earth will quake; indeed, the earth will totter!

20 The earth will indeed be moved, like a drunkard; it will shake like a hut, its iniquity will weigh heavily[4] upon it, it will fall and rise[5] no more.

21 On that day the Lord will visit[6] the hosts of the height on high,[7] and the kings of the earth on the earth.

22 They will gather an assembly concerning the prisoner in the well; they will plot against the confined; after many days they will be redeemed.

23 The moon will be put to shame, the sun will be ashamed, for the mighty Lord has reigned[8] on the mountain of Zion and in Jerusalem, and before his holy ones he will sing praises.

---

[1] 'chants' or 'songs, hymns, psalms'.

[2] 'climb up': lit. 'go up'.

[3] 'on high': lit. 'the height'.

[4] 'weigh heavily' or 'be heavy, grievous'.

[5] 'rise': lit. 'stand'.

[6] 'visit' or 'punish'.

[7] 'high': lit. 'the height'.

[8] 'reigned' or 'begun to reign'.

ܩܦܠܐܘܢ: ܟܗ.

1 ܐ ܡܪܝܐ ܐܠܗܝ ܐܢܬ: ܐܪܘܡܡܟ: ܘܐܘܕܐ ܠܫܡܟ. ܕܥܒܕܬ ܕܘܡܪܐ ܘܡܠܟܐ ܡܗܝܡܢܬܐ. ܡܢ ܪܘܚܩܐ ܐܡܝܢ.

2 ܒ ܡܛܠ ܕܥܒܕܬ ܩܪܝܬܐ ܠܓܠܐ: ܘܩܪܝܬܐ ܚܣܝܢܬܐ ܠܡܦܘܠܬܐ. ܒܝܬܐ ܕܢܘܟܪܝܐ ܠܥܠܡ ܡܢ ܩܪܝܬܐ ܠܐ ܢܬܒܢܐ.

3 ܓ ܡܛܠ ܗܢܐ ܢܫܒܚܘܢܟ ܥܡܡܐ ܥܫܝܢܐ. ܘܩܪܝܬܐ ܕܥܡܡܐ ܥܫܝܢܐ ܢܕܚܠܘܢ ܡܢܟ.

4 ܕ ܡܛܠ ܕܗܘܝܬ ܡܥܫܢܐ ܠܡܣܟܢܐ: ܘܥܘܕܪܐ ܠܒܝܫܐ ܒܐܘܠܨܢܗ:

ܡ̈ܢ ܡܕ

ܫܘܪܐ ܡܢ ܪܘܡܬܐ: ܘܛܠܠܐ ܡܢ ܚܘܡܐ.

5 ܗ ܡܛܠ ܕܪܘܚܐ ܕܥܫܝܢܐ ܐܝܟ ܪܘܡܬܐ ܕܫܘܪܐ: ܘܐܝܟ ܛܠܠܐ ܒܨܗܝܐ. ܘܫܘܒܚܐ ܕܢܘܟܪܝܐ ܬܡܟܟ: ܘܚܘܡܐ ܒܛܠܠܐ ܕܥܢܢܐ. ܫܘܒܚܐ ܕܥܫܝܢܐ ܬܡܟܟ.

6 ܘ ܘܢܥܒܕ ܡܪܝܐ ܚܝܠܬܢܐ ܠܟܠܗܘܢ ܥܡܡܐ ܒܛܘܪܐ ܗܢܐ: ܡܫܬܘܬܐ ܡܫܚܢܬܐ: ܘܡܫܬܘܬܐ ܕܚܡܪܐ ܘܡܫܚܐ: ܕܡܚܝܢ ܡܫܚܐ ܘܚܡܪܐ.

7 ܙ ܘܢܬܒܠܥ ܒܛܘܪܐ ܗܢܐ: ܐܦܝ ܡܟܣܝܬܐ ܕܡܟܣܝܐ ܗܘܐ ܥܠ ܟܠܗܘܢ ܥܡܡܐ. ܘܦܪܣܬܐ ܕܐܬܦܪܣܬ ܥܠ ܐܦܝ ܟܠܗܘܢ ܥܡܡܐ.

8 ܚ ܘܢܬܒܠܥ ܡܘܬܐ ܠܙܟܘ ܠܥܠܡܝܢ. ܘܢܥܒܪ ܡܪܝܐ ܐܠܗܐ ܚܝܠܬܢܐ ܕܡܥܬܐ ܡܢ ܐܦܝܢ. ܘܚܣܕܐ ܕܥܡܗ ܢܥܒܪ ܡܢ ܟܠܗ ܐܪܥܐ: ܡܛܠ ܕܡܪܝܐ ܡܠܠ.

Chapter 25

1   Lord, you are my God: I will exalt you, I will praise[1] your name, for you have made marvelous things,[2] a faithful purpose, from afar. Amen.

2   For you have made the city a heap of stones, the strong city a ruin, a temple of foreigners forever, a city no more:[3] it will not be rebuilt.

3   Therefore many nations will praise you, a city of strong peoples will fear you.

4   For you were a support for the needy, a helper of the poor in his affliction, a shelter from the downpour, a shade from the parching heat.

XII

5   For the spirit of the mighty is like a downpour against a wall, like a shade from the parching heat; you will lay low the pride of the foreigners, as the parching heat is weakened by[4] the shelter of the clouds; he will lay low the shoot[5] of the mighty ones.

6   The mighty Lord will prepare, among all people on this mountain, a feast of fat dishes, a protected feast of fat dishes,[6] from our giver of life, heavenly and mighty.

7   The face of the ruler who bore rule over all peoples will be devoured on this mountain, and the sacrifice which was slain for the sake of all peoples.

8   Death will be devoured by victory forever; the mighty Lord God will take away tear(s) from all faces, take away[7] the reproach of his people from the whole earth: for the Lord has spoken.

---

[1] 'praise' or 'confess'.

[2] 'marvelous things': sing.

[3] 'a city no more': lit. 'from a city'.

[4] 'as the parching heat is weakened by …': lit. 'and the parching heat in …'.

[5] 'shoot'. See Introduction. Addendum 1.

[6] 'a feast of fat dishes, a protected feast of fat dishes': lit. 'a feast fat/rich, a feast guarded and fat/rich'.

[7] 'take away'[1]: lit. 'make pass away'.

9 ܛ ܘܢܐܡܪ ܒܝܘܡܐ ܗܘ: ܗܢܘ ܡܪܝܐ ܐܠܗܢ: ܕܣܟܝܢ ܠܗ ܘܢܦܪܩܢ. ܗܢܘ ܡܪܝܐ
ܐܠܗܢ ܕܣܟܝܢ ܠܗ: ܢܕܘܨ ܘܢܚܕܐ ܒܦܘܪܩܢܗ.

10 ܝ ܡܛܠ ܕܬܬܢܝܚ ܐܝܕܗ ܕܡܪܝܐ ܒܛܘܪܐ ܗܢܐ: ܘܢܬܕܝܫ ܡܘܐܒ ܬܚܘܬܘܗܝ:
ܐܝܟ ܕܡܬܕܝܫ ܬܒܢܐ ܒܓܪܓܪܐ.

11 ܝܐ ܘܢܦܪܘܣ ܐܝܕܘܗܝ ܒܓܘܗ: ܐܝܟ ܕܡܦܪܣ ܣܚܝܐ ܠܡܣܚܐ. ܘܢܡܟܟ ܫܘܒܗܪܗ
ܥܡ ܢܟܘܠܐ ܕܐܝܕܘܗܝ.

12 ܝܒ ܘܟܠܗ ܥܘܫܢܐ ܕܫܘܪܝܟܝ ܢܡܟܟ: ܘܢܫܦܠ: ܘܢܡܚܗ̇ ܠܐܪܥܐ ܥܕܡܐ
ܠܥܦܪܐ.

9   You will say on that day: This is the Lord our God; we have waited for him, he will save us; this is the Lord our God; we have waited for him; we will exult and rejoice in his salvation.

10   For the hand of the Lord will rest on this mountain, Moab will be trodden beneath him as straw is trodden at threshing.[1]

11   He will stretch out his hands in its midst as the swimmer stretches to swim; he will lay low its strength with the spreading out of his hands.

12   He will lay low the stronghold[2] of the strength of your walls; he will cast (it) down, bring (it) to the ground, even to the dust.

---

[1] 'at threshing': lit. 'by the threshing sled'.

[2] 'stronghold' or 'citadel'. The vocalization in Mosul is unusual.

Chapter 26

1   On that day this song will be sung in the land of Judah: The city whose redemption has prevailed, set up the wall and the rampart.[1]

2   Open the gates; the righteous people who keep faith, who stand firm,[2] will enter.

3   You will keep peace for us, for in you, Lord, we have put our trust, forever and ever.

4   For the Lord God is powerful forever.

5   For he will lay low those who dwell on the height(s); he will lay low the strong city, to the ground - he will bring it (down) to the dust.

6   The foot of the poor will trample it, the steps[3] of the needy.

7   The path is straight for the needy: straight, a plain,[4] (is) the way of the righteous.

8   We have also hoped for[5] the way of your judgments, Lord: for your name and for your remembrance our soul longs.[6]

9   My soul has desired you at night, my spirit too within me seeks to be with you;[7] for as your judgments are upon the earth, (so) the inhabitants of the world[8] have learnt righteousness.

10   The unjust has fled far away so that he will not learn righteousness; reproof in the land corrects;[9] they will not see the magnificence of the Lord.

---

[1] 'rampart': lit. 'son of the wall'.

[2] 'stand firm': lit. 'keep assent'.

[3] 'steps': lit. 'walking'.

[4] 'a plain' or 'clear'.

[5] 'hoped for' or 'awaited'.

[6] 'our soul longs': lit. 'the desire of our soul'.

[7] 'seeks to be with you': lit. 'anticipates'.

[8] 'world': lit. 'the habitable earth'.

[9] 'reproof in the land corrects'. See Introduction. Addendum 1.

11 ܝܐ ܡܪܝܐ ܒܪܘܡܬܐ ܕܐܝܕܟ ܠܐ ܢܚܙܘܢ. ܢܚܙܘܢ ܘܢܒܗܬܘܢ ܛܢܢܗ ܕܥܡܐ. ܘܐܝܟ ܢܘܪܐ ܬܐܟܘܠܝܢܘܢ ܠܒܥܠܕܒܒܝܟ.

12 ܝܒ ܡܪܝܐ ܐܠܗܢ ܗܒ ܠܢ ܫܠܡܐ: ܡܛܠ ܕܐܝܟ ܟܠܗܘܢ ܥܒܕܝܢ ܥܒܕܬ ܠܢ.

13 ܝܓ ܡܪܝܐ ܐܠܗܢ: ܗܘܘ ܥܠܝܢ ܡܪ̈ܘܬܐ ܠܒܪ ܡܢܟ. ܠܚܘܕܝܟ ܫܡܟ ܕܡܟܝܠ ܢܬܕܟܪ.

14 ܝܕ ܡܝ̈ܬܐ ܠܐ ܢܚܘܢ: ܘܓܢܒܪ̈ܐ ܠܐ ܢܩܘܡܘܢ. ܡܛܠ ܗܢܐ ܦܩܕܬ ܘܐܘܒܕܬ ܐܢܘܢ. ܘܐܘܒܕܬ ܟܠܗ ܕܘܟܪܢܗܘܢ.

15 ܝܗ ܐܘܣܦܬ ܡܪܝܐ ܥܠ ܥܡܐ: ܐܘܣܦܬ ܥܠ ܥܡܐ. ܐܬܝܩܪܬ ܘܪܚܩܬ ܟܠܗܘܢ ܣܘܦܝܗ ܕܐܪܥܐ.

16 ܝܘ ܡܪܝܐ ܒܐܘܠܨܢܐ ܥܩܒܘܟ: ܘܒܫܘܥܝܐ ܠܚܫܘ ܡܪܕܘܬܟ.

17 ܝܙ ܐܝܟ ܒܛܢܬܐ ܕܩܪܝܒܐ ܠܡܐܠܕ: ܘܡܚܒܠܐ ܘܡܨܘܚܐ ܒܚܒ̈ܠܝܗ: ܗܟܢܐ ܗܘܝܢ ܡܢ ܩܕܡܝܟ ܡܪܝܐ.

18 ܝܚ ܒܛܢܢ ܘܚܒܠܢ ܐܝܟ ܗܘܝܢ ܕܝܠܕܢ ܪܘܚܐ. ܦܘܪܩܢ ܕܠܐ ܥܒܕܢ ܒܐܪܥܐ: ܘܠܐ ܢܦܠܘܢ ܥܡܘܪܝܗ ܕܬܒܝܠ.

11 Lord, they will not see when you raise[1] your hands; they will see the ardent desire of the people, and be ashamed; as a furnace you will consume your enemies.[2]

12 Lord, you will keep peace for us: for as all our deeds, (so) you have made ready for us.

13 Lord our God, lords other than you were over us; your name[3] only we will remember.[4]

14 The dead do not give life; the mighty do not raise up; because of this you have visited,[5] you have made them look contemptible, you have destroyed all their remembrance.

15 You have increased, Lord, the people; you have increased the people; you have journeyed far away,[6] you have enlarged[7] the borders of the world.

16 Lord, in suffering they entreated you, in distress they murmured (under) your chastisement.

17 Like the pregnant woman near to giving birth, writhing, crying out in the pains of her labor: thus were we before you, Lord.

18 We conceived, we labored in birth as those who give birth to the winds: save us, that we may not be lost[8] from the earth, that the inhabitants of the world may not fall.[9]

---

[1] 'when you raise': lit. 'in the height of'.

[2] 'you will consume your enemies'. Less likely (but perhaps closer to MT) 'it will consume your enemies'.

[3] 'your name': lit. 'your name which is yours'.

[4] 'your name only we will remember' or if the Ethpeel can be rendered as passive 'your name only will be remembered'.

[5] 'visited' or 'punished'.

[6] 'journeyed far away'. See Introduction, Addendum 2.

[7] 'enlarged': lit. 'thrust out, driven away'.

[8] 'be lost' or 'perish'.

[9] 'fall' or 'fail'.

19   Your dead will live, their dead bodies will arise; they will awake, they will sing praise(s),[1] those who lie down in the dust: for your dew is the dew of light, and you will overthrow the land of the mighty.

20   Come, my people: go into your inner chambers, shut your doors around you,[2] hide yourself a little while, until my wrath passes by.

21   For see! The Lord goes forth from his place, he visits the iniquity of the inhabitant of the earth upon him: the earth will reveal its blood, it will conceal its slain no more.

---

[1] '… will live, … will arise; … will awake, … will sing praise(s)' or 'May … live, may … arise; may … awake, may … offer praises'.

[2] 'around you': lit. 'against/in your faces'.

ܩܦܠܐܘܢ: ܟܙ.

1 ܐ ܒܝܘܡܐ ܗܘ: ܢܬܒܥ ܡܪܝܐ ܒܣܝܦܗ ܩܫܝܐ ܘܪܒܐ ܘܚܣܝܢܐ: ܥܠ ܠܘܝܬܢ ܚܘܝܐ ܥܪܘܩܐ: ܘܥܠ ܠܘܝܬܢ ܚܘܝܐ ܥܩܠܬܢܐ. ܘܢܩܛܘܠ ܠܬܢܝܢܐ ܕܒܝܡܐ.

2 ܒ ܒܝܘܡܐ ܗܘ: ܟܪܡܐ ܕܚܡܪܐ ܥܢܘ ܠܗ.

3 ܓ ܐܢܐ ܡܪܝܐ ܢܛܪ ܐܢܐ ܠܗ. ܐܡܝܢܐܝܬ ܐܫܩܝܘܗܝ: ܘܐܦܩܘܕ ܥܠܘܗܝ. ܒܠܠܝܐ ܘܒܐܝܡܡܐ ܐܛܪܘܗܝ.

4 ܕ ܫܘܪܐ ܠܝܬ ܠܝ: ܡܢ ܪܡ ܢܬܠ ܠܝ ܚܘܪܐ ܘܟܘܒܐ. ܒܩܪܒܐ ܐܦܘܫ ܒܗ: ܘܐܘܩܕܝܘܗܝ ܐܟܚܕܐ.

5 ܗ ܐܘ ܢܐܚܘܕ ܒܥܘܫܢܝ: ܘܐܥܒܕ ܠܗ ܫܠܡܐ. ܫܠܡܐ ܐܥܒܕ ܠܗ.

6 ܘ ܐܝܟ ܕܡܢ ܒܥܩܪܗ ܕܝܥܩܘܒ. ܢܦܪܥ ܘܢܦܪܘܚ ܐܝܣܪܝܠ. ܘܢܡܠܘܢ ܐܦܝ ܬܒܝܠ ܦܐܪܐ.

7 ܙ ܐܝܟ ܡܚܘܬܐ ܕܡܚܝܢܘܗܝ: ܡܚܝܗܝ. ܘܐܝܟ ܩܛܠܐ ܕܩܛܠܘܗ: ܩܛܠܗ.

8 ܚ ܒܡܬܐܐ ܕܐܬܝܠ: ܬܕܘܢܘܢܝܗܝ: ܒܪܘܚܐ ܒܪܘܚܗ ܩܫܝܐ ܒܝܘܡܐ ܩܝܛܐ.

9 ܛ ܡܛܠ ܗܢܐ: ܒܗܕܐ ܢܫܬܒܩ ܥܘܠܗ ܕܝܥܩܘܒ. ܘܗܢܘܢ ܦܐܪܘܗܝ ܦܐܪܐ ܕܢܥܒܪ ܚܛܝܬܗ: ܡܐ ܕܢܣܝܡ ܟܠܗܘܢ ܟܐܦܐ ܕܡܕܒܚܐ. ܐܝܟ ܟܐܦܐ ܕܓܝܪܐ ܕܡܬܦܪܟܢ: ܘܐܫܝܪܐ ܠܐ ܢܬܩܝܡܘܢ ܦܬܟܪܐ ܘܚܡܢܐ.

Chapter 27

1   On that day the Lord will visit,[1] with his harsh, great, and powerful sword, Leviathan the basilisk,[2] Leviathan the crooked serpent, and he will kill the dragon which is in the sea.

2   On that day, a vineyard of wine: raise (a song) to it.

3   I the Lord, I guard it, I will water it continually, I will visit it, I will guard it by night and by day.

4   You have no wall;[3] who then has given you a tangle of briars and thorns? shortly[4] I will breathe upon it, I will set it on fire at once.

5   Or let him lay hold on my strength: I will make peace for him, peace I will make for him.

6   Those who are from the root of Jacob: Israel will bloom, will bud, they will cover[5] the face of the world with fruit.

7   As the blow that he struck him, he struck him; as the slaying (with) which he slew him, he slew him.

8   By the seah (with) which he measured, you will judge him; by that which he thought,[6] in his harsh spirit on the hot day.

9   Therefore, by this, the iniquity of Jacob will be forgiven;[7] by all these fruits, his sin will pass away; when he sets all the stones of the altar like stones of chalk which are ground to powder: so they will not stand, the idols and the false gods.

---

[1] 'visit' or 'punish'.

[2] 'basilisk': the two words, ܚܪܡܢܐ ܚܘܝܐ, the second from a root including the meaning 'cruel', and ܚܘܝܐ 'snake' together mean 'basilisk'. Sometimes ܚܪܡܢܐ is used alone, as at 11:8.

[3] 'wall'. MT 'wrath'. See Introduction. Addendum 1.

[4] 'shortly'. MT 'in battle'. See Introduction. Addendum 2.

[5] 'cover': lit. 'fill'.

[6] 'By the seah ... by that which he thought'. MT 'by driving it away ... he removed'. See Introduction. Addendum 1.

[7] 'forgiven' or 'taken away'.

10 ܝ ܡܛܠ ܕܡܕܝܢܬܐ ܥܫܝܢܬܐ܇ ܥܡܘܪܝܗ ܚܪܒܐ ܘܡܫܬܒܩܐ܇ ܘܚܪܒܐ ܐܝܟ
ܡܕܒܪܐ. ܬܡܢ ܢܪܥܐ ܥܓܠܐ܇ ܘܬܡܢ ܢܪܥܐ ܘܢܓܡܪ ܫܘܟܝܗ.

11 ܝܐ ܒܝܒܫܐ ܕܚܪܐ܇ ܢܬܬܒܪܘܢ ܢܫܐ ܕܐܬܝܢ ܡܢܗܪܢ ܠܗ܇ ܡܛܠ ܕܠܐ ܗܘܐ ܥܡܐ
ܡܣܬܟܠܢܐ. ܡܛܠ ܗܢܐ ܠܐ ܢܪܚܡ ܥܠܘܗܝ ܥܒܘܕܗ. ܘܓܒܘܠܗ ܠܐ ܢܚܘܣ
ܥܠܘܗܝ.

12 ܝܒ ܘܢܗܘܐ ܒܝܘܡܐ ܗܘ܇ ܢܚܒܘܛ ܡܪܝܐ ܡܢ ܡܥܒܪܬܐ ܕܢܗܪܐ܇ ܥܕܡܐ ܠܢܚܠܐ
ܕܡܨܪܝܢ. ܘܐܢܬܘܢ ܬܬܠܩܛܘܢ ܚܕ ܠܘܬ ܚܕ܇ ܒܢܝ ܐܝܣܪܐܝܠ.

13 ܝܓ ܘܢܗܘܐ ܒܝܘܡܐ ܗܘ܇ ܢܬܩܥ ܫܝܦܘܪܐ ܪܒܐ܇ ܘܢܐܬܘܢ ܕܐܒܕܘ ܒܐܪܥܐ ܕܡܨܪܝܢ܇
ܘܕܐܬܒܕܪܘ ܒܐܪܥܐ ܕܐܬܘܪ. ܘܢܣܓܕܘܢ ܒܐܪܥܗ ܕܡܪܝܐ ܠܡܪܝܐ܇ ܒܛܘܪܗ ܩܕܝܫܐ
ܒܐܘܪܫܠܡ.

10   For the powerful city, alone, desolate, and deserted, (will be) desolate like the wilderness; there the calf will feed, there he will feed and consume its tender grass.

11   In the dry land of the harvest, the women will be broken who come to make it light; for this was not an intelligent people: because of this its maker will not take pity on it, he who fashioned it will not cherish it.

12   It will be on that day (that) the Lord will thresh, from the spike[1] of the river to the torrent of Egypt; and you will be gathered together, one to another, children of Israel.

13   It will be on that day (that) the great trumpet will be sounded, and they will come, those who perished in the land of Egypt, and were scattered in the land of Assyria, and they will worship the Lord in the land of the Lord; in his holy mountain, in Jerusalem.

---

[1] 'spike' or 'blade, ear of wheat'. The Hebrew original may also mean 'flowing stream'.

ܩܦܠܐܘܢ: ܟܚ.

1 ܐ ܘܝ ܠܟܠܝܠܐ ܓܐܝܐ ܕܪܘܝܐ ܐܦܪܝܡ: ܘܠܗܒܠܐ ܡܪܒܪܐ ܚܝܠܐ ܕܫܘܒܚܗ ܕܪܝܫ ܢܚܠܐ ܕܫܡܝܢܐ: ܕܐܬܪܡܝܢ ܒܚܡܪܐ.

2 ܒ ܗܐ ܚܝܠܐ ܘܥܘܫܢܐ ܕܡܪܝܐ: ܐܝܟ ܪܘܡܒܐ ܕܒܪܕܐ: ܘܐܝܟ ܥܠܥܠܐ ܕܬܒܪܐ: ܘܐܝܟ ܪܘܡܒܐ ܕܡܝܐ ܣܓܝܐܐ ܕܓܪܦܝܢ.

3 ܓ ܐܢܚܬ ܠܐܪܥܐ ܒܐܝܕܝ. ܘܒܪܓܠܐ ܢܬܕܝܫ ܟܠܝܠܐ ܓܐܝܐ ܕܪܘܝܐ ܐܦܪܝܡ.

4 ܕ ܘܢܗܘܐ ܗܒܠܐ ܡܪܒܪܐ: ܚܝܠܐ ܕܫܘܒܚܗ ܕܪܝܫ ܢܚܠܐ ܕܫܡܝܢܐ: ܐܝܟ ܒܟܘܪܬܐ ܕܩܕܡ ܩܝܛܐ: ܕܡܐ ܕܚܙܝܗ ܡܢ ܕܚܙܐ ܠܗ: ܥܕ ܗܝ ܒܐܝܕܗ: ܒܠܥ ܠܗ.

5 ܗ ܒܝܘܡܐ ܗܘ: ܢܗܘܐ ܡܪܝܐ ܚܝܠܬܢܐ ܠܟܠܝܠܐ ܕܚܝܠܐ: ܘܠܗܒܠܐ ܡܫܒܚܐ ܠܫܪܟܐ ܕܥܡܗ.

6 ܘ ܠܪܘܚܐ ܕܕܝܢܐ: ܠܡܢ ܕܝܬܒ ܥܠ ܕܝܢܐ ܘܠܓܢܒܪܘܬܐ: ܕܡܗܦܟܝܢ ܩܪܒܐ ܡܢ ܬܪܥܐ.

7 ܙ ܐܦ ܗܢܘܢ ܒܚܡܪܐ ܛܥܘ: ܘܒܫܟܪܐ ܛܥܘ. ܟܘܡܪܐ ܘܢܒܝܐ ܛܥܘ ܒܫܟܪܐ. ܐܬܒܠܥܘ ܡܢ ܚܡܪܐ. ܐܬܘ ܡܢ ܫܟܪܐ. ܛܥܘ ܒܚܙܘܬܐ. ܐܦܟܘ ܐܦܘܛܩܝ.

8 ܚ ܡܛܠ ܕܦܬܘܪܝܗܘܢ ܟܠܗܘܢ ܐܬܡܠܝܘ ܬܝܘܒܐ ܘܨܐܬܐ ܡܢ ܟܠܗ ܐܬܪܐ.

9 ܛ ܠܡܢ ܢܠܦ ܝܕܥܬܐ. ܘܠܡܢ ܢܫܡܥ ܫܡܥܐ: ܠܕܫܠܝܢ ܡܢ ܚܠܒܐ: ܘܕܦܪܝܫܝܢ ܡܢ ܬܕܝܐ.

10 ܝ ܡܛܠ ܦܩܕܐ ܥܠ ܦܩܕܐ: ܘܦܩܕܐ ܥܠ ܦܩܕܐ. ܘܣܒܪܐ ܥܠ ܣܒܪܐ: ܘܣܒܪܐ ܥܠ ܣܒܪܐ. ܩܠܝܠ ܬܡܢ: ܘܩܠܝܠ ܬܡܢ.

11 ܝܐ ܡܛܠ ܕܒܡܡܠܠܐ ܥܡܠܐ ܘܒܠܫܢܐ ܐܚܪܢܐ ܐܡܠܠ ܥܡܗ ܥܡ ܥܡܐ ܗܢܐ.

Chapter 28

XIII

1　Woe to the proud crown of the drunkard Ephraim, and to the garland which dishonors the might of his glory at the head of the fertile valley, of those who are dazed with wine.

2　See! The might and the strength of the Lord, like a torrent of hail, like a destroying whirlwind, like a torrent of many overflowing waters.

3　I will give rest to the land by your hand; by foot the proud crown of the drunkard Ephraim will be trodden down.

4　And it will be the garland which dishonors, the might of his glory at the head of the fertile valley, like the first-ripe (fruit) before summer, which when he has seen it, he who sees it, he devours it while it is (yet) in his hand.

5　On that day the mighty Lord will be as a crown of might, as a glorious garland, for the remnant of his people.

6　As a spirit of judgment, for him who sits in judgment and fortitude, who turn[1] war from the gate.

7　Also, these went astray in wine, went astray in strong drink; priests and prophets went astray in strong drink; they were swallowed up by wine, shaken by strong drink; they went astray in drunkenness; they ate intemperately.

8　For all the tables were filled with vomit and excrement, from lack of a place.[2]

9　To whom will he teach knowledge, whom will he make understand the report? To those weaned from milk, withdrawn from the breasts?

10　For excrement upon excrement, and excrement upon excrement, and vomit upon vomit, and vomit upon vomit; a little there and a little there-.

11　For with difficult speech, and in another tongue, I will speak with him, with this people.

---

[1] 'turn': pl. part.

[2] 'from lack of a place': i.e., with no clean area.

12 ܝܒ ܕܐܡܪܬ ܠܗܘܢ: ܗܕܐ ܗܝ ܢܝܚܬܝ: ܐܢܝܚܘ ܠܡܠܐ̈ܝܐ. ܘܗܕܐ ܫܠܝܐ. ܘܠܐ ܨܒܘ
ܠܡܫܡܥ.

13 ܝܓ ܘܗܘܐ ܠܗܘܢ ܡܠܬܗ ܕܡܪܝܐ: ܢܓܕܐ ܥܠ ܢܓܕܐ: ܘܢܓܕܐ ܥܠ ܢܓܕܐ:
ܘܢܛܘܒܐ ܥܠ ܢܛܘܒܐ: ܘܢܛܘܒܐ ܥܠ ܢܛܘܒܐ: ܩܠܝܠ ܠܬܡܢ: ܘܩܠܝܠ
ܠܬܡܢ. ܕܢܗܦܟܘܢ ܘܢܫܬܪܥܘܢ ܠܒܣܬܪܗܘܢ: ܘܢܬܬܒܪܘܢ ܘܢܬܬܨܝܕܘܢ
ܘܢܬܬܐܚܕܘܢ.

14 ܝܕ ܡܛܠ ܗܢܐ ܫܡܥܘ ܦܬܓܡܗ ܕܡܪܝܐ ܓܒܪ̈ܐ ܡܡܝܩܢܐ: ܫܠܝܛܢܘܗܝ ܕܥܡܐ
ܗܢܐ ܕܒܐܘܪܫܠܡ.

15 ܝܗ ܡܛܠ ܕܐܡܪܬܘܢ ܕܐܩܝܡܢ ܩܝܡܐ ܥܡ ܡܘܬܐ. ܘܥܡ ܫܝܘܠ ܥܒܕܢ ܚܙܘܐ.
ܫܘܛܐ ܕܪܘܓܙܐ ܟܕ ܢܥܒܪ: ܠܐ ܢܐܬܐ ܥܠܝܢ. ܡܛܠ ܕܣܡܢ ܕܓܠܘܬܐ
ܬܘܟܠܢ: ܘܒܫܘܩܪܐ ܐܬܛܫܝܢ.

16 ܝܘ ܡܛܠ ܗܢܐ ܗܟܢܐ ܐܡܪ ܡܪܝܐ ܐܠܗܐ: ܗܐ ܐܢܐ ܡܩܝܡ ܐܢܐ ܒܨܗܝܘܢ ܟܐܦܐ:
ܟܐܦܐ ܒܚܝܪܬܐ ܒܩܪܢܐ ܝܩܝܪܬܐ: ܫܬܐܣܬܐ ܕܫܬܐܣܬܐ. ܕܡܗܝܡܢ ܠܐ ܢܙܘܥ.

17 ܝܙ ܘܐܣܝܡ ܕܝܢܐ ܠܡܫܘܚܬܐ: ܘܙܕܝܩܘܬܐ ܠܡܬܩܠܐ. ܘܢܚܛܘܦ ܒܪܕܐ ܠܣܒܪܐ
ܕܓܠܐ. ܘܠܡܛܠܬܐ ܡܝܐ ܢܓܪܦܘܢ.

18 ܝܚ ܘܢܬܒܛܠ ܩܝܡܟܘܢ ܕܥܡ ܡܘܬܐ. ܘܚܙܘܟܘܢ ܕܥܡ ܫܝܘܠ ܠܐ ܢܩܘܡ. ܫܘܛܐ
ܕܪܘܓܙܐ ܟܕ ܢܥܒܪ: ܬܗܘܘܢ ܠܗ ܠܕܘܫܐ.

19 ܝܛ ܘܒܙܒܢܐ ܕܥܒܪ ܢܕܒܪܟܘܢ. ܡܛܠ ܕܒܨܦܪܐ ܒܨܦܪܐ ܢܥܒܪ. ܒܐܝܡܡܐ ܘܒܠܠܝܐ
ܬܗܘܐ ܙܘܥܬܐ. ܟܠܢܫ ܐܣܬܟܠ ܫܡܘܥܬܐ.

20 ܟ ܡܛܠ ܕܩܛܢ ܡܫܟܒܐ ܠܡܫܬܪܥܘ. ܘܡܟܣܝܬܐ ܥܠܝܒܐ: ܘܠܐ ܡܬܟܢܫܐ.

12   For I said to them: This is my rest: give rest to the harassed; this is the calm; but they did not want to listen.

13   The word of the Lord to them was: excrement upon excrement, excrement upon excrement, and vomit upon vomit, and vomit upon vomit; a little there and a little there, so that they might return, be overthrown backwards,[1] be broken, hunted, and seized.

14   Therefore hear the word of the Lord, O scornful men, rulers of this people which is in Jerusalem.

15   For you said: We have made a covenant with death, with Sheol we have made an appearance; the scourge of the overwhelming flood, when it passes over, will not come upon us, for we have put our trust in falsehood, sheltered ourselves with a lie.

16   Therefore thus says the Lord God: See! I prepare a stone in Zion, a stone tried as an honorable corner(stone), the head of the foundation wall: he who trusts (in it) will not fear.

17   I will set judgment as the measurement, righteousness as the balance: hail will beat down false hope, waters will dash against the refuge.

18   And your covenant with death will be declared null, your appearance with Sheol will not stand firm; the scourge of the overwhelming flood, when it passes over - you will be for it to tread down.[2]

19   During the time when it passes over it will take you: for it will pass over morning after morning;[3] by day and by night it moved;[4] only the listener will understand.

20   For the garment is too short to cover him, the thread[5] is meager, incomplete.[6]

---

[1] 'overthrown backwards': lit. 'overthrown behind them'.

[2] 'to tread down': lit. 'for treading down'.

[3] 'morning after morning': lit. 'in the dawn in the dawn'.

[4] 'moved' or 'was moved'.

[5] 'thread' or 'warp'.

[6] 'incomplete': lit. 'not full'.

21 ܟܐ ܡܛܠ ܕܒܛܘܪܐ ܒܬܘܪܒܬܐ ܢܩܘܡ ܡܪܝܐ: ܐܝܟ ܥܘܡܩܐ ܕܓܒܥܘܢ ܢܪܓܙ
ܠܡܥܒܕ ܥܒܕܘܗܝ: ܢܘܟܪܝܢ ܥܒܕܘܗܝ. ܘܠܡܥܒܕ ܥܒܕܝܬܗ: ܢܘܟܪܝܢ
ܥܒܕܝܬܗ.

22 ܟܒ ܘܗܫܐ ܠܐ ܬܡܝܩܘܢ: ܕܠܐ ܢܬܚܝܠܢ ܡܪܘܬܟܘܢ. ܡܛܠ ܕܓܡܘܪܐ ܘܦܣܩܬܐ
ܫܡܥܬ ܡܢ ܡܪܝܐ ܚܝܠܬܢܐ: ܥܠ ܟܠܗ ܐܪܥܐ.

23 ܟܓ ܨܘܬܘ ܘܫܡܥܘ ܩܠܝ: ܨܘܬܘ ܘܫܡܥܘ ܡܐܡܪܝ.

24 ܟܕ ܕܠܡܐ ܝܘܡܐ ܟܠܗ ܕܪܐ ܐܟܪܐ ܠܡܙܪܥ: ܘܪܦܕ ܘܡܦܩ ܐܪܥܗ.

25 ܟܗ ܠܐ ܗܘܐ ܡܐ ܕܐܫܘܝ ܐܦܬܗ: ܙܪܥ ܩܨܚܐ: ܘܟܡܘܢܐ ܙܪܩ. ܘܣܡܐ ܚܛܐ ܘܣܥܪܐ
ܘܟܘܢܬܐ ܒܬܚܘܡܗ.

26 ܟܘ ܢܪܕܝܘܗܝ ܒܕܝܢܐ ܕܐܠܗܐ ܘܢܠܦܝܘܗܝ.

27 ܟܙ ܡܛܠ ܕܠܐ ܗܘܐ ܒܡܘܪܓܐ ܡܬܕܝܫ ܩܨܚܐ. ܘܐܦܠܐ ܡܬܗܦܟ ܓܝܓܠܐ ܥܠ
ܟܡܘܢܐ. ܡܛܠ ܕܒܚܘܛܪܐ ܡܬܢܦܨ ܩܨܚܐ: ܘܟܡܘܢܐ ܒܫܒܛܐ.

28 ܟܚ ܒܟܘܪܐ ܡܬܕܝܫ ܡܬܐܟܠ. ܡܛܠ ܕܠܐ ܗܘܐ ܠܥܠܡ ܡܕܝܫ ܐܕܪܝܗܘܢ.
ܘܒܩܠܐ ܕܓܝܓܠܐ ܕܥܓܠܬܗܘܢ: ܘܒܦܪܫܗܘܢ ܢܕܩܘܢܗ.

29 ܟܛ ܘܐܦ ܗܕܐ ܡܢ ܩܕܡ ܡܪܝܐ ܚܝܠܬܢܐ ܢܦܩܬ. ܕܡܪܐ ܕܬܪܥܝܬܐ ܐܘܪܒ ܬܪܥܝܬܐ.

21 For in the mountain, in the pass,[1] the Lord will arise: as in the valley of Gibeon he will do his deeds in anger[2] - strange are his deeds; to do his deeds - strange are his deeds.

22 And now, do not mock, lest you should be severely chastised,[3] for destruction, decisions, I have heard from the mighty Lord, concerning all the earth.

23 Give ear and hear my voice; give ear, hear my speech.

24 Does[4] the ploughman plough all day to sow? lifts up and harrows his land?

25 Does he not,[5] when he has leveled its surface,[6] scatter fennel, sow cummin, cast wheat, barley, and rye, within its borders?

26 He will instruct him in the judgment of God; he will praise him.

27 For it was not by threshing that the fennel was threshed, nor is the threshing machine driven round upon the cummin, for the fennel is beaten out with a staff, the cummin with a rod.

28 Grain is threshed for our sake, for not for victory[7] would I thoroughly thresh it;[8] with the many wheels of his threshing machine, and with the hooves (of his oxen) they will pound it.

29 This too has gone out from the presence of the mighty Lord, the wonderful in counsel,[9] excelling in guidance.[10]

---

[1] 'pass'. See Introduction. Addendum 1.

[2] 'he will do his deeds in anger': lit. 'he will be angry to do his deeds'.

[3] 'lest you should be severely chastised': lit. 'that your chastisements may not be grievous'.

[4] The opening word, ܠܡܐ, is used where a negative answer is expected.

[5] 'Does he not': lit. 'Was it not'.

[6] 'surface': lit. 'face'.

[7] 'victory' or 'justification'.

[8] 'for not for victory would I thoroughly thresh it': lit. 'for it was not for victory I would thoroughly thresh it'.

[9] 'in counsel': lit. 'of counsel'.

[10] 'excelling in guidance': lit. 'he has increased education'.

ܩܦܠܐܘܢ: ܟܛ.

1 ܐ ܘܝ ܐܪܝܐܝܠ ܐܪܝܐܝܠ ܩܪܝܬܐ ܕܫܪܐ ܕܘܝܕ. ܐܘܣܦܘ ܫܢܬܐ ܥܠ ܫܢܬܐ: ܥܐܕܐ ܢܬܢܩܦܘܢ.

2 ܒ ܘܐܥܝܩ ܠܐܪܝܐܝܠ: ܘܬܗܘܐ ܥܘܩܬܐ ܘܐܘܠܝܬܐ: ܘܬܗܘܐ ܐܝܟ ܐܪܝܐܝܠ.

3 ܓ ܘܐܫܪܐ ܐܝܟ ܐܣܦܝܪܐ ܥܠܝܟܝ. ܘܐܠܒܟܝ ܒܟܡܝܢܐ. ܘܐܩܝܡ ܥܠܝܟܝ ܡܫܪܝܬܐ.

4 ܕ ܘܬܬܡܟܟܝܢ. ܘܡܢ ܥܦܪܐ ܬܡܠܠܝ. ܘܡܢ ܥܦܪܐ ܢܨܦܨܦ ܡܠܬܟܝ. ܘܢܗܘܐ ܩܠܟܝ ܡܢ ܐܪܥܐ ܐܝܟ ܐܘܒܐ. ܘܡܢ ܥܦܪܐ ܢܨܦܨܦ ܡܠܬܟܝ.

5 ܗ ܘܢܗܘܐ ܐܝܟ ܕܩܐ ܕܥܦܪܐ ܣܘܓܐܐ ܕܢܘܟܪܝܐ. ܘܐܝܟ ܥܘܪܐ ܕܥܒܪ ܣܘܓܐܐ ܕܥܫܝܢܐ. ܘܢܗܘܐ ܡܢ ܫܠܝܐ ܒܫܠܝܐ.

6 ܘ ܡܢ ܩܕܡ ܡܪܝܐ ܚܝܠܬܢܐ: ܬܬܦܩܕܝ ܒܪܥܡܐ: ܘܒܙܘܥܐ ܘܒܩܠܐ ܪܒܐ: ܘܒܥܘܪܥܠܐ: ܘܒܥܠܥܠܐ: ܘܒܫܠܗܒܝܬܐ ܕܢܘܪܐ ܕܡܘܩܕܐ.

7 ܙ ܘܢܗܘܐ ܐܝܟ ܚܠܡܐ ܒܚܙܘܐ ܕܠܠܝܐ: ܣܘܓܐܐ ܕܟܠܗܘܢ ܥܡܡܐ ܕܡܬܟܬܫܝܢ ܥܠ ܨܗܝܘܢ: ܘܟܠ ܚܝܠܐ ܘܩܪܒܐ ܕܡܥܝܩܝܢ ܠܗ.

8 ܚ ܘܢܗܘܐ ܐܝܟ ܟܦܢܐ ܕܚܠܡ ܒܚܠܡܗ ܕܐܟܠ. ܘܡܐ ܕܐܬܬܥܝܪ: ܣܪܝܩ ܘܣܪܝܩܐ ܢܦܫܗ. ܘܐܝܟ ܨܗܝܐ ܕܚܠܡ ܒܚܠܡܗ ܕܫܬܐ. ܘܡܐ ܕܐܬܬܥܝܪ: ܣܪܝܩ ܘܣܪܝܩܐ ܢܦܫܗ. ܗܟܢܐ ܢܗܘܐ ܣܘܓܐܐ ܕܟܠܗܘܢ ܥܡܡܐ ܕܡܬܟܬܫܝܢ ܥܠ ܛܘܪܐ ܕܨܗܝܘܢ.

Chapter 29

1   Woe! Ariel, Ariel, the city where David dwelt; add year to year, feast days will be celebrated.

2   I will distress Ariel, there[1] will be moaning and lamentation; she will be like Ariel.

3   I will besiege you like a company of soldiers, I will hem you in with a siege-engine,[2] I will raise a garrison[3] against you.

4   You will be laid low, you will speak from the dust, your words will shriek from the dust, your voice will be heard from the ground like (the voice of) a diviner: your words will shriek[4] from the dust.

5   And the multitude of your oppressors will be like fine sand, the multitude of your mighty ones like the chaff which passes away: it will happen[5] suddenly, in an instant.[6]

6   From the presence of the mighty Lord you will be visited with earthquakes, with thunder, with great noise, with baldness, with storm wind, with a burning flame of fire.

7   It will be as a dream in a vision of the night, the multitude of all the nations strengthening themselves against Zion, all the hosts and crowds of those who distress her.

8   It will be like a famished (man) who dreams that he is eating, but when he wakes is harassed, his spirit empty; like a thirsty man who dreams that he is drinking, but when he wakes is harassed, his spirit[7] empty; thus will be the multitude of all the nations strengthening themselves against the mountain of Zion.

---

[1] 'there' or 'she'.

[2] 'siege-engine': from a root 'to bore, pierce', so perhaps equipment for boring holes through fortifying walls.

[3] 'garrison' or 'guard'.

[4] 'shriek': the words are likened to the shrill speech of magicians.

[5] 'happen': lit. 'be'.

[6] 'in an instant': lit. 'immediately'.

[7] 'spirit'[1], the Syriac word is often translated into English as 'soul' but that does not fit the context here.

9 ܛ ܐܬܡܗܘ ܘܐܬܕܡܪܘ: ܘܐܬܛܥܝܘ ܘܐܬܪܘܝܘ: ܪܘܝܘ ܠܐ ܡܢ ܚܡܪܐ: ܘܐܬܛܥܝܘ ܠܐ ܡܢ ܫܟܪܐ.

10 ܝ ܡܛܠ ܕܢܣܟ ܒܟܘܢ ܡܪܝܐ ܪܘܚܐ ܕܫܢܬܐ. ܘܡܥܡܨ ܥܠ ܥܝܢܝܟܘܢ ܘܥܠ ܢܒܝܐ: ܘܥܠ ܪܝܫܝܟܘܢ ܕܚܙܝܢ ܚܙܘܢܐ.

11 ܝܐ ܘܬܗܘܐ ܠܟܘܢ ܚܙܘܐ ܕܟܠܗܘܢ ܐܝܟ ܡܠܐ ܕܟܬܒܐ ܕܚܬܝܡ. ܕܡܐ ܕܢܬܠܘܢܝܗܝ ܠܡܢ ܕܝܕܥ ܣܦܪܐ: ܢܐܡܪܘܢ ܠܗ ܩܪܝ ܗܢܐ: ܘܢܐܡܪ ܠܐ ܡܫܟܚ ܐܢܐ: ܡܛܠ ܕܚܬܝܡ ܗܘ.

12 ܝܒ ܘܢܬܠܘܢܝܗܝ ܠܟܬܒܐ ܠܡܢ ܕܠܐ ܝܕܥ ܣܦܪܐ. ܘܢܐܡܪܘܢ ܠܗ ܩܪܝ ܗܢܐ. ܘܢܐܡܪ ܠܐ ܝܕܥ ܐܢܐ ܣܦܪܐ.

ܩܕ ܗ.

13 ܝܓ ܘܐܡܪ ܡܪܝܐ: ܡܛܠ ܕܩܪܒ ܥܡܐ ܗܢܐ ܒܦܘܡܗ: ܘܒܣܦܘܬܗ ܡܝܩܪܝܢ ܠܝ: ܘܠܒܗ ܪܚܝܩ ܡܢܝ: ܘܗܘܬ ܕܚܠܬܗܘܢ ܡܢܝ ܒܦܘܩܕܢܐ ܘܒܝܘܠܦܢܐ ܕܐܢܫܐ.

14 ܝܕ ܡܛܠ ܗܢܐ: ܗܐ ܡܘܣܦ ܐܢܐ ܠܡܬܕܡܪܘ ܠܥܡܐ ܗܢܐ: ܒܬܕܡܘܪܬܐ ܘܒܬܡܗܐ. ܘܬܐܒܕ ܚܟܡܬܐ ܕܚܟܝܡܘܗܝ. ܘܣܘܟܠܐ ܕܣܘܟܠܬܢܘܗܝ ܢܬܛܫܐ.

15 ܝܗ ܘܝ ܠܡܬܥܡܩܝܢ ܡܢ ܡܪܝܐ: ܠܡܛܫܝܘ ܬܪܥܝܬܐ. ܘܗܘܝܢ ܒܚܫܘܟܐ ܥܒܕܝܗܘܢ. ܘܐܡܪܝܢ ܡܢܘ ܚܙܐ ܠܢ: ܐܘ ܡܢܘ ܝܕܥ ܡܢܐ ܡܬܗܦܟܝܢ.

16 ܝܘ ܐܝܟ ܛܝܢܐ ܕܦܚܪܐ ܚܫܝܒܝܢ ܐܢܘܢ. ܕܠܡܐ ܐܡܪ ܥܒܕܐ ܠܥܒܘܕܗ ܠܐ ܥܒܕܬܢܝ. ܘܓܒܝܠܬܐ ܐܡܪܐ ܠܓܒܘܠܗ: ܕܡܣܟܠܐܝܬ ܠܐ ܓܒܠܬܢܝ.

17 ܝܙ ܗܐ ܒܪ ܩܠܝܠ ܙܒܢ: ܘܢܬܗܦܟ ܠܒܢܢ ܠܟܪܡܠܐ: ܘܟܪܡܠܐ ܠܥܒܐ ܢܬܚܫܒ.

18 ܝܚ ܘܢܫܡܥܘܢ ܒܝܘܡܐ ܗܘ ܚܪܫܐ ܡܠܐ ܕܟܬܒܐ. ܘܡܢ ܚܫܘܟܐ ܘܡܥܡܛܢܐ: ܥܝܢܐ ܕܣܡܝܐ ܢܚܙܝܢ.

9   Be speechless, be amazed, be harassed, be dazed, those who are drunk (but) not from wine, who go astray (but) not from strong drink.

10   For the Lord has poured out upon them a spirit sound asleep, and it has been heavy upon their eyes and upon the prophets, upon the heads of those who see what is concealed.

11   And it will be, for them, the vision of them all, like the words of a sealed book which, when they gave it to one who could read,[1] they said to him: Read this; but he will say: I cannot, for it is sealed.

12   They will give the book to him who cannot read, and they will say to him: Read this; but he will say: I cannot read.

XIV

13   And the Lord said: Because this people has drawn near with its mouth, and honored me with its lips - but its heart is far from me, and their awe of me (was) by commandment, instructed by man,

14   Because of this, See! I am again setting this people apart, with a wonder, with a marvel, and the wisdom of its wise men will come to naught, and the understanding of its intelligent men will be taken away.

15   Woe to those who turn perversely from the Lord, to hide the intent;[2] their deeds are in darkness, saying: Who sees us? or who knows where we turn?

16   You are reckoned as potter's clay. Does[3] the work say to its maker: You did not make me? or the matter that was formed say to him who forms it: You did not form me wisely?

17   See! A very little time, and Lebanon will become a fruitful field,[4] and the fruitful field will be reckoned as a dense forest.

18   On that day the deaf will hear the words of the book, and from darkness, and thick darkness, the eyes of the blind will see.

---

[1] 'who could read': lit. 'who knows a book'.

[2] 'intent': lit. 'opinion'.

[3] The word ܪܠܡܐ is used where a negative answer is expected.

[4] 'become a fruitful field': lit. 'be turned into Carmel'. See note to 10:18.

138

19   The lowly will rejoice yet more in the Lord,[1] the poor will exult in the Holy One of Israel.

20   For the oppressor has passed on, the scornful man has finished, all who stir up iniquity have perished.

21   For they make a man sin by a word, they set a stumbling-block for him who admonishes, they turn the righteous aside, into darkness.

22   Therefore thus says the Lord, concerning the house of Jacob, who redeemed Abraham: no more will Jacob be ashamed, no more will his face blush.

23   When his children have seen the work of my hands, they will sanctify my name, in his midst, and they will sanctify the Holy One of Jacob, they will magnify the God of Israel.

24   And these foolish ones will know that their spirit has gone astray, and those who go wrong will learn to obey.

---

[1] 'rejoice yet more in the Lord': lit. 'increase in the Lord with joy'.

ܩܦܠܐܘܢ: ܠ.

1 ܐ ܘܝ ܠܒܢܝܐ ܡܪܘܕܐ: ܐܡܪ ܡܪܝܐ: ܕܥܒܕܝܢ ܬܪܥܝܬܐ ܘܠܐ ܡܢܝ. ܘܢܣܟܘ ܢܘܣܟܐ: ܘܠܐ ܡܢ ܪܘܚܝ. ܕܢܘܣܦܘܢ ܚܛܗܐ ܥܠ ܚܛܗܐ.

2 ܒ ܕܐܙܠܝܢ ܠܡܚܬ ܠܡܨܪܝܢ: ܘܡܢ ܦܘܡܝ ܠܐ ܫܐܠܘ. ܕܢܬܥܫܢܘܢ ܒܥܘܫܢܗ ܕܦܪܥܘܢ. ܘܢܬܟܣܘܢ ܒܛܠܠܗ ܕܡܨܪܝܢ.

3 ܓ ܢܗܘܐ ܠܟܘܢ ܥܘܫܢܗ ܕܦܪܥܘܢ ܠܒܗܬܬܐ: ܘܬܟܣܝܬܐ ܕܛܠܠܗ ܕܡܨܪܝܢ ܠܚܣܕܐ.

4 ܕ ܡܛܠ ܕܗܘܘ ܒܨܥܢ: ܪܘܪܒܢܘܗܝ ܘܡܠܐܟܘܗܝ ܥܕܡܐ ܠܚܢܣ.

5 ܗ ܠܘܬ ܥܡܐ ܕܠܐ ܡܘܬܪ ܠܗܘܢ: ܠܐ ܠܡܥܕܪܢܘܬܐ ܘܠܐ ܠܡܘܬܪܢܘܬܐ: ܐܠܐ ܠܒܗܬܬܐ ܘܠܚܣܕܐ.

6 ܘ ܡܫܩܠܐ ܕܒܥܝܪܐ ܕܒܝܥܐ ܒܐܪܥܐ ܕܐܘܠܨܢܐ ܘܕܥܩܬܐ. ܐܪܝܐ ܘܓܘܪܝܐ ܕܐܪܝܐ: ܘܚܘܘܬܐ ܐܟܕܢ ܘܫܪܦܐ ܕܦܪܚ. ܢܫܩܠܘܢ ܥܠ ܚܨܐ ܕܥܝܪܐ ܥܘܬܪܗܘܢ: ܘܥܠ ܓܒܐ ܕܓܡܠܐ ܓܙܝܗܘܢ: ܠܘܬ ܥܡܐ ܕܠܐ ܡܘܬܪ ܠܗܘܢ.

7 ܙ ܘܡܨܪܝܐ ܒܣܪܝܩܘܬܐ ܘܒܣܪܝܩܘܬܐ ܡܥܕܪܝܢ. ܡܛܠ ܗܢܐ ܩܥܝܬ ܠܗܘܢ: ܕܫܪܝܪ ܗܘ ܬܘܒܠܬܗܘܢ ܗܢܐ.

8 ܚ ܗܫܐ ܬܐ ܟܬܘܒ ܥܠ ܠܘܚܐ ܗܠܝܢ: ܘܥܠ ܦܢܟܐ ܪܫܘܡܝܗܘܢ: ܕܢܗܘܐ ܠܝܘܡܐ ܐܚܪܝܐ ܠܣܗܕܘܬܐ ܠܥܠܡ ܥܠܡܝܢ.

9 ܛ ܡܛܠ ܕܥܡܐ ܗܘ ܡܡܪܡܪܢܐ: ܒܢܝܐ ܐܢܘܢ ܕܓܠܐ: ܒܢܝܐ ܕܠܐ ܨܒܘ ܠܡܫܡܥ ܢܡܘܣܗ ܕܡܪܝܐ.

Chapter 30

1 Woe to the rebellious children, says the Lord, who have formed belief, but not from me; who have poured out libations, that are not from my spirit: so that they may add sins to sins.

2 Who went to go down[1] to Egypt, but did not consult me,[2] so that they might strengthen themselves in the strength of Pharaoh, take refuge in the shadow of Egypt.

3 The strength of Pharaoh will be a disgrace to you, the refuge of the shadow of Egypt (will be) a disguise.

4 For he is in Zoan, and his nobles and his perverted[3] messengers will grow weary.

5 To a people who are no use to them, not with help, not with profit, but with shame, with reproach.

6 The burden of the beasts of the south, in a land oppressed and grieved: the lion and the lion's whelp, and from them the asp, and the flying basilisk, will carry their riches on the back(s) of foals, their treasures on the hump(s) of camels, to a people who are no use to them.

7 The Egyptians help in vanity and in falsehood; therefore I have proclaimed to them that this in which they trust[4] is empty.

8 Now go, write upon these tablets, and upon the book of their covenant, that it may be, in the last day(s), as a witness forever and ever.

9 For it is a rebellious people, they are deceitful children, children who did not wish to hear[5] the law of the Lord.

---

[1] 'Who went to go down' or 'Who prepared to go down'. The verb ܐܙܠ when directly preceding another verb, as here, may signify intention.

[2] 'consult me': lit. 'ask from my mouth'.

[3] 'perverted' or 'impious'.

[4] 'in which they trust': lit. 'their trust'.

[5] 'hear' or 'obey'.

ـ ١٠ وَأَهَدِهِ حِيـزَّبُمُا ولَا بُمِنَّهُ: مَحَـٰٓنَجتُا ولَا بُإِمنّٰهُ كُ مَحصفبِداً. مَحِّحٰ كُ
فَحَىْدِجِدا. مَمِنَّهُ كُ ذَبُبُدا.

ـ ١١ مَأهِنِهُلَّمُ فُمَ أَمزَسُا. مَأمفقُمُ فَمَ حِجتُلا. مَجُهُحِمُ فِنَّ حمَّبِمُا
وَأَمحَبُّمَلَا .

ـ ١٢ مَهُـٰٓبَمَ مُبُلا: مُجَّنُا أَهَـٰ مُحزَنُا مَبُّمُا وَأَمحَبُّمَلَا: هَلَا وَأَمحَكَمُمُ
مَحِّحُا مُؤْا: مَآماَٰجَحِّمُمُ ـَحُهُحَمَّمُا: مَمِّنَّحُمُ مَآماَٰجَحِّمُمُ حكَّمُمِ..

ـ ١٣ مَهُـٰٓبَمَ مُبُلا بُؤُمَا حِجفُمُ سَبُبُدا مُؤْا أَمِن مَأَمُحَدًا مَتِحَحِّكُمُ: مَأَمِن فُمَؤْا
مُمُا مِفُمَ هَحمُدا مُمَا بُأَدَّمُ.

ـ ١٤ مَبُأَدَّمُ أَمِن مَأَجُدُا مَمُدَانُا مِحمُدُا مَبُأَجَمُ ولَا مَمُّمَّمُ. ولَا مَحَمَحِّمُ حِجَبَحِّمُؤُمِ
مَنِّفُا حَمحَمَحِّمَ مُؤَ مَمَؤُا فَمَ مِمَبُنُا: مَأَجِلَا حَحفَيُّمَبُّؤ مُؤَ مُمُنُا فَمَ
ذُهَذُا.

ـ ١٥ مَهُـٰٓبَمَ مُبُلا مُجَّنُا أَهَـٰ مُحزَنُا مَبُّمُا وَأَمحَبُّمَلَا: مُمُا مِبَأَجِّمُمُ
مَآماَٰنَّمَحِّمُمُ: مَآماَقُنَّمُمُ. مَجِمُّحَمُا مَجِمُّحِجَذُا بُؤُمَا حَبُّحِجُّمَبُأَجِّمُمُ. ولَا
آماَٰلَّمُحمحَمَّمُمُ.

ـ ١٦ مَأَهَـٰذُنَّأُمُ. لَا مُجَّنُا: هَلَا مَجِّمُا بُمَجُّ. مَهَلَا مَحِّمَتَلَا بُمَنُّمَمُ. مَهُـٰٓبَمَ مُبُلا
بُأَحمُمُ: مَنُمَمُمُ مَحِّمَحِّمُ مَّمَمِّحمُمُ.

ـ ١٧ حُحُجِ فُمَ مُلابُلا مِمَبِ: مَفُمَ مُلابُلا مِمَمَحمُا بُأَحمُمُ: حِبُمُا مِبِأَحُحَاَّمِمَنُّمُ. أَمِن
حَبُؤَا هَلَا بُمَمَ بُهَمَؤُا: مَأَمِن أَبُلا هَلَا بُمَحَدًا.

ـ ١٨ مَهُـٰٓبَمَ بُمَبُزُأ مُحزَنُا حَمحَزَنُّمَفُؤ حكَّمَمُمُ. مَآماَٰلَأُمِّحِم حَمحَزَنُّمَفُؤ حكَّمَمُمُ.
مَهُـٰٓبَمَ بُأَحكُؤَا مَؤَ بُمُنُا مُحزَنُا. مَحُمَجَّمَّمَمُ حِبُجِلَا بُمَمَفُمَ حُمَ.

10 Who said to the seers: Do not foretell;[1] to the prophets: Do not prophesy[2] reproof to us; speak deception to us, foretell falsehood to us.

11 Turn aside from the way, return from the paths, withdraw from us the Holy One of Israel.

12 Therefore, thus says the Lord, the Holy One of Israel: Because you despised this word, and put your trust in violence, complained and put your trust in it,

13 Therefore this sin will be for you like a ruin[3] which has fallen, like a high wall which suddenly broke.[4]

14 Its breaking like the breaking of a potter's vessel, which is broken pitilessly, no vessel found in its fragments in which coals[5] could be taken[6] from a fire, nor water drawn in it[7] from a well.

15 Therefore thus says the Lord, the Holy One of Israel: When you have returned and rested, you will be saved; in quietness and in trust[8] will be your fortitude - but you would not be persuaded.

16 But you said: Not so; we will ride on horses, we will flee with the swift: therefore you will flee, and your pursuers will be swift.

17 A thousand from the rebuke of one, from the rebuke of five you will flee, until you remain as a beacon on the mountain top, as a sign upon the height.

18 For the Lord will begin to take pity on you, exalt himself to have compassion on you, for the Lord is a God of judgment, and blessed are all they who wait for him.

---

[1] 'Do not foretell' or 'You will not see'.

[2] 'Do not prophesy' or 'You will not prophesy'.

[3] 'ruin' or 'breach'.

[4] 'which suddenly broke': lit. 'its breaking was sudden'.

[5] 'coals': lit. 'fire' using ܢܘܪܐ instead of ܓܘܡܖ̈ܐ.

[6] 'could be taken': lit. 'to take up'.

[7] 'drawn in it': lit. 'to draw with it'.

[8] 'trust' or 'hope'.

19 ܝܛ ܡܛܠ ܕܥܡܐ ܒܨܗܝܘܢ ܢܥܡܪ: ܘܒܐܘܪܫܠܡ. ܒܟܝܐ ܠܐ ܬܒܟܘܢ. ܡܪܚܡܘ
ܢܪܚܡ ܥܠܝܟ ܩܠܐ ܕܒܥܘܬܟܘܢ: ܘܡܐ ܕܫܡܥ ܢܥܢܝܟܘܢ.

20 ܟ ܘܢܬܠ ܠܟܘܢ ܡܪܝܐ ܠܚܡܐ ܕܐܘܠܨܢܐ: ܘܡܝܐ ܕܐܘܠܨܢܐ. ܘܠܐ ܢܬܛܫܘܢ ܬܘܒ
ܠܡܠܦܢܝܟܘܢ. ܘܢܚܙܝܢ ܥܝܢܝܟܘܢ ܠܡܠܦܢܝܟܘܢ.

21 ܟܐ ܘܐܕܢܝܟܘܢ ܢܫܡܥܢ ܡܠܬܐ ܡܢ ܒܣܬܪܟܘܢ: ܕܐܡܪܐ: ܗܢܐ ܗܘ ܐܘܪܚܐ: ܗܠܟܘ
ܒܗ. ܘܠܐ ܬܣܛܘܢ ܠܝܡܝܢܐ ܘܠܣܡܠܐ.

22 ܟܒ ܘܬܛܡܘܢ ܨܠܡܐ ܕܣܐܡܐ ܕܦܬܟܪܝܟܘܢ: ܘܦܪܙܠܐ ܕܢܣܟܐ ܕܕܗܒܟܘܢ. ܘܬܕܪܘܢ
ܐܢܘܢ ܐܝܟ ܡܝܐ ܕܕܘܬܢܝܬܐ. ܘܐܝܟ ܟܦܬܐ ܬܦܩܘܢ ܐܢܘܢ.

23 ܟܓ ܘܢܬܠ ܡܛܪܐ ܠܙܪܥܟܘܢ: ܕܬܙܪܥܘܢ ܒܐܪܥܐ: ܘܠܚܡܐ ܕܥܠܠܬܐ ܕܐܪܥܐ. ܢܗܘܐ
ܕܫܡܝܢ ܘܡܫܡܢ: ܪܥܝܐ ܕܒܥܝܪܟܘܢ ܒܝܘܡܐ ܗܘ ܒܐܬܪܐ ܪܘܝܚܐ.

24 ܟܕ ܘܒܥܝܪܐ ܘܬܘܪܐ ܕܦܠܚܝܢ ܒܐܪܥܐ: ܒܠܝܠܐ ܡܠܝܚܐ ܢܐܟܠܘܢ: ܕܡܕܪܝܢ ܒܪܦܫܐ
ܘܒܡܕܪܘܢܐ.

25 ܟܗ ܘܬܗܘܐ ܥܠ ܟܠ ܛܘܪ ܪܡ: ܘܥܠ ܟܠ ܪܡܬܐ ܪܡܬܐ: ܢܗܪܘܢ ܦܠܓܐ ܕܡܝܐ
ܒܝܘܡܐ ܕܩܛܠܐ ܪܒܐ: ܘܒܡܦܠܬܐ ܕܡܓܕܠܐ.

26 ܟܘ ܘܬܗܘܐ ܢܘܗܪܗ ܕܣܗܪܐ ܐܝܟ ܢܘܗܪܗ ܕܫܡܫܐ. ܘܢܘܗܪܗ ܕܫܡܫܐ ܢܗܘܐ ܚܕ
ܒܫܒܥܐ: ܐܝܟ ܢܘܗܪܐ ܕܫܒܥܐ ܝܘܡܝܢ: ܒܝܘܡܐ ܕܢܚܒܘܫ ܡܪܝܐ ܠܬܒܪܐ ܕܥܡܗ:
ܘܟܐܒܐ ܕܡܚܘܬܗ ܢܐܣܐ.

ܟܕ ܩܗ

27 ܟܙ ܗܐ ܫܡܗ ܕܡܪܝܐ ܐܬܐ ܡܢ ܪܘܚܩܐ. ܝܩܕ ܪܘܓܙܗ: ܘܝܩܝܪ ܡܫܩܠܗ.
ܘܣܦܘܬܗ ܡܠܝܢ ܪܘܓܙܐ. ܘܠܫܢܗ ܐܝܟ ܢܘܪܐ ܕܐܟܠܐ.

19   For the people dwell in Zion and in Jerusalem, and indeed you will not weep; indeed he will take pity on the sound of your cry, and having heard he will answer you.

20   The Lord will give you bread in affliction, and water in affliction; no more will he assemble those who lead you astray, and your eyes will look upon those who lead you astray.

21   Your ears will hear a word from behind you which says: This is the way, Go in it; and you will not turn aside[1] to the right or to the left.

22   You will defile the silver which plates your idols, and the ephod made from their molten gold;[2] you will scatter them like menstruous waters, throw them out[3] like refuse.

23   Rain will be given for your seed, which you will sow in the land, and the produce of the seed in the land will be fat and fertile, a pasture for your animals on that day, in a fertile place.

24   And oxen and young bullocks which labor on the land will eat mixed[4] dry fodder, which has been tossed up with the winnowing-fan and with the winnowing-shovel.

25   And upon[5] every high mountain, upon every high hill, will flow streams of water on the day of the great slaughter, of the overthrow of the towers.

26   And the light of the moon will be as the light of the sun; and the light of the sun will be sevenfold,[6] like the light of seven days; on the day that the Lord will bind up the wound of his people, will heal the pain of his affliction.

XV

27   See! The name of the Lord comes from afar, his anger burns, his burden[7] glorious, his lips full of anger, his tongue like a burning fire.

---

[1] 'and you will not turn aside' or 'and do not turn aside'.

[2] 'made from their molten gold': lit. 'which is poured of their gold'.

[3] 'throw them out': lit. 'take them out'.

[4] The term for 'mixed' also implies 'clean'.

[5] 'And upon': lit. 'it will be upon'.

[6] 'sevenfold': lit. 'one with seven'.

[7] 'burden' or 'exaltation'.

28 His breath like an overflowing river: it will break off at the neck, to distress the nations on account of their worthless wandering, and for the bridle on the cheeks of the nations which leads them astray.

29 There will be praise for you, a crown sanctified at the festival, gladness of heart like him who walks in gladness, to come to the mountain of the Lord, to the Mighty One of Jacob.

30 The Lord will make the glory of his voice heard, the blow of his arm he will make manifest in the heat of anger and in the consuming flame of fire, in the battering downpour, in the hailstones.

31 For in the presence of the greatness of the Lord the Assyrian will be broken, struck with the rod.

32 And it will be, in all his deeds, the staff of servitude that the Lord will lay upon him; with tambourines, with harps, in a mighty battle he will fight against him.

33 For his food was prepared from days of old,[1] even prepared that it might reign; he dug deep,[2] he enlarged its dwelling house;[3] many were the trees, and the fire: the breath of the Lord is like a river of brimstone which sets it on fire.

---

[1] 'days of old': lit. 'before days'.

[2] 'was prepared … it might reign … dug deep': these verbs are fem. sing. See Introduction. Addendum 3.

[3] 'its dwelling house': lit. 'her dwelling house'.

ܩܦܠܐܘܢ: ܠܐ.

1 ܐ ܘܝ ܠܕܢܚܬܝܢ ܠܡܨܪܝܢ ܠܡܥܕܪܢܘܬܗ: ܘܥܠ ܪ̈ܟܫܐ ܡܬܬܟܠܝܢ: ܘܡܬܬܟܠܝܢ ܥܠ ܡܪ̈ܟܒܬܐ ܣܓܝ̈ܐܬܐ: ܘܥܠ ܦܪ̈ܫܐ ܕܛܒ ܥܫܝܢ. ܘܠܐ ܐܬܬܟܠܘ ܥܠ ܩܕܝܫܐ ܕܐܝܣܪܝܠ: ܘܠܡܪܝܐ ܠܐ ܒܥܘ.

2 ܒ ܘܚܟܝܡܘܬܗ ܐܝܬܝ ܒܝܫܬܐ: ܘܡܠ̈ܘܗܝ ܠܐ ܐܥܒܪ. ܘܩܡ ܥܠ ܒܝܬܐ ܕܒ̈ܝܫܐ: ܘܥܠ ܥܘܕܪܢܐ ܕܥܒ̈ܕܝ ܥܘܠܐ.

3 ܓ ܘܡܨܪ̈ܝܐ ܐ̱ܢܫܐ ܐܢܘܢ: ܘܠܐ ܗܘܘ ܐܠܗܐ. ܘܣܘܣܘܬܗܘܢ ܕܒܣܪܐ ܐܢܘܢ: ܘܠܐ ܗܘܘ ܕܪܘܚܐ. ܘܡܪܝܐ ܢܪܡܐ ܐܝܕܗ: ܘܢܬܬܚܠܨ ܡܥܕܪܢܐ. ܘܢܬܩܠ ܗܘ ܕܡܬܥܕܪ. ܘܟܠܗܘܢ ܐܟܚܕܐ ܢܣܘܦܘܢ.

4 ܕ ܡܛܠ ܕܗܟܢܐ ܐܡܪ ܠܝ ܡܪܝܐ: ܐܝܟ ܕܢܗܡ ܐܪܝܐ ܘܓܘܪܝܐ ܕܐܪܝܐ ܥܠ ܛܪܦ ܕܐܬܐ: ܘܡܩܪܝܢ ܠܗ ܣܘܓܐܐ ܕܪ̈ܥܘܬܐ. ܘܡܢ ܩܠܗܘܢ ܠܐ ܕܚܠ: ܘܡܢ ܣܘܓܐܗܘܢ ܠܐ ܡܬܬܙܝܥ. ܗܟܢܐ ܢܚܘܬ ܡܪܝܐ ܚܝܠܬܢܐ ܠܡܬܟܬܫܘ ܥܠ ܛܘܪܐ ܕܨܗܝܘܢ: ܘܥܠ ܪܡܬܗ.

5 ܗ ܐܝܟ ܨܦܪ̈ܐ ܕܦܪ̈ܚܢ: ܗܟܢܐ ܢܓܢ ܡܪܝܐ ܚܝܠܬܢܐ ܥܠ ܐܘܪܫܠܡ: ܢܓܢ ܘܢܦܨܐ: ܘܢܚܘܣ ܘܢܦܪܘܩ.

6 ܘ ܬܘܒܘ ܒܢ̈ܝ ܐܝܣܪܝܠ: ܕܐܥܡܩܬܘܢ ܡܪܘܕܘܬܐ.

7 ܙ ܡܛܠ ܕܒܝܘܡܐ ܗܘ: ܢܫܠܘܢ ܐ̱ܢܫܐ ܦܬܟܪ̈ܐ ܕܕܗܒܐ ܘܕܣܐܡܐ: ܕܥܒܕ ܠܟܘܢ ܐܝܕ̈ܝܟܘܢ ܚܛܗܐ.

8 ܚ ܘܢܦܠ ܐܬܘܪܝܐ ܒܚܪܒܐ: ܚܪܒܐ ܠܐ ܕܓܒܪܐ: ܘܚܪܒܐ ܠܐ ܕܒܢܝ̈ܢܫܐ ܬܐܟܠܝܘܗܝ. ܘܢܥܪܘܩ ܠܗ ܡܢ ܩܕܡ ܚܪܒܐ: ܘܥܠܝܡ̈ܘܗܝ ܠܡܕܐܬܐ ܢܗܘܘܢ.

9 ܛ ܘܫܠܝܛܐ ܕܡܕܝܢܬܗ ܢܥܒܪ. ܘܢܬܬܒܪܘܢ ܡܢ ܐܬܐ ܪ̈ܘܪܒܢܘܗܝ. ܐܡܪ ܡܪܝܐ ܕܢܘܗܪܗ ܒܨܗܝܘܢ: ܘܐܬܘܢܗ ܒܐܘܪܫܠܡ.

Chapter 31

1   Woe to those who go down to Egypt to be helped, putting their trust in horses, putting their trust in many chariots, in horsemen who are very strong, but who did not trust in the Holy One of Israel, did not seek the Lord.

2   In his wisdom he brought evil, he did not set aside his words; he arose against the house of evil men, against the help of evil-doers.

3   For the Egyptians are men, they were not gods; their horses are flesh, not spirit; the Lord will stretch out his hand, and the helper will be overthrown, even the one who is helped will fall, all of them together will come to an end.

4   For thus the Lord said to me: As the lion, and the lion's whelp, roar over the prey,[1] and many shepherds cry out against him, but he does not fear their voice, and he does not tremble at their number: so will the mighty Lord descend to gather his strength upon the mountain of Zion, upon her high places.

5   As the birds which fly, so will the mighty Lord protect Jerusalem; he will protect, he will deliver, he will support, and he will help.

6   Return, children of Israel, who have been so rebellious.[2]

7   For on that day men[3] will despise the idols of gold and of silver which your hands made for you for a sin.

8   And the Assyrian will fall by the sword - a sword not of men; and the sword - not of warriors - will consume him; he will flee[4] from the sword, and his young men will be a sign.

9   He will dwell on the crag of his dwelling-place, his noblemen broken by the sign, says the Lord, whose light is in Zion, his furnace in Jerusalem.

---

[1] 'the prey': lit. 'something that he tears'.

[2] 'been so rebellious': lit. 'strengthened rebellion'.

[3] 'men': sing.

[4] 'flee': lit. 'flee himself'.

Chapter 32

1 See! A king with righteousness, and noblemen with justice, will rule.

2 And man will be as a shelter against the wind, as a refuge against the downpour, as a stream of water in a dry place, as the shadow of a mighty stone in a weary land.

3 The eyes of those who see will not be stopped up, and the ears of those who listen will take heed.

4 The heart of the foolish will understand knowledge, and the tongue of the stutterer will be ready[1] to speak peace.[2]

5 No more will they call the madman 'Ruler', nor will they call the worthless 'Savior'.

6 For the madman speaks madness, his heart devises iniquity, so that he may act impiously, may speak error, lay waste the spirit[3] of the hungry, deprive the thirsty of drink.

7 The instruments[4] of the worthless[5] are evil: he plots a purpose[6] to destroy the needy by lying words, and the word of the poor by judgment.

8 But the great man aims at greatness, he will take his stand upon greatness.

9 Rich women, arise, hear my voice; daughters who have heard good tidings,[7] hear my words.

10 After one year[8] they will be angry, those who have heard good tidings: for the harvest is finished, gathered in - but it will have failed.[9]

---

[1] 'be ready': lit. 'hasten'.

[2] 'peace' or 'peaceably'.

[3] 'spirit': lit. 'soul, self'.

[4] 'instruments' or 'vessels'.

[5] 'worthless' or 'empty'.

[6] 'purpose' or 'opinion, mind'.

[7] 'have heard good tidings': lit. 'who have good tidings brought'.

[8] 'After one year': lit. 'The days of a year'.

[9] 'will have failed': lit. 'has not come'.

11   Tremble, rich women, be angry, those who have heard good tidings, strip yourselves bare, gird sackcloth on your loins.

12   Beat your breasts[1] for the tender grass of the field, for the vine of her fruits.

13   On the land of my people thorns and briars will shoot up, and in all your joyful houses, in the strong city.

14   For the temple was forgotten, the strength of the city deserted, the beautiful houses became (animals') dens forever, thorns and a delight for wild asses, a pasturage for the flock of sheep.

15   Until a wind from the height(s) is stirred up over us, and the wilderness will become a fertile place, and the fertile place[2] will resemble[3] a forest.

16   And justice will dwell in the wilderness, and righteousness be bestowed on the fertile place.[4]

17   And the work of righteousness will be peace, and the labor of righteousness calm, with trust[5] forever and ever.

18   And my people will dwell in a habitation of peace, in a tent of trust, a lodging-place of trust.

19   And hail will fall on the forest, and the city be laid low like a plain.

20   Blessed are you who sow beside all the waters, where the bull and the ass tread.

---

[1] 'Beat your breasts': lit. 'mourn upon your breasts'.

[2] 'fertile place'[1,2] or 'Carmel'[1,2]. See note to 10:18.

[3] 'will resemble': lit. 'be counted as'.

[4] 'fertile place' or 'a Carmel'. See note to 10:18.

[5] 'trust' or 'hope'.

Chapter 33

1 Woe to the plunderer: you shall not plunder; and may he who is false not deceive you; when you have wished to plunder, you will be plundered; and when you wish to deceive, deceit will be suspected in you.

2 Lord, have mercy on us, for we trust in you;[1] be our help at dawn, and our savior in the time of adversity.

3 At the sound of the awe of you[2] the nations trembled; from your height the nations were scattered.

4 After this your spoil will be collected as the gathering of the crawling locust, and as the gathering of the locust which is gathered.

5 The Lord who dwells on high[3] is lifted up; he has filled Zion with justice and righteousness.

6 Your time will be truth,[4] your salvation in a refuge: wisdom, knowledge, the fear of the Lord, is his treasure.

XVI

7 Were he to be seen[5] by them, they would cry out grievously, and the messengers of peace would weep bitterly.

8 The highways are[6] deserted, the wayfarers have come to an end, the covenant has come to an end, the cities are despised, men[7] not respected.[8]

9 The land lamented, dwelt in mourning; Lebanon blushed and was ashamed, Sharon became a plain, Bashan and Carmel lay waste.[9]

---

[1] 'we trust in you': lit. 'our hope is upon you'.

[2] 'awe of you': lit. 'your awe, fear'. See Introduction. Addendum 2.

[3] 'high': lit. 'the heights'.

[4] 'truth' or 'faithfulness, firmness'.

[5] 'Were he to be seen': lit. 'If he would appear'.

[6] 'are'[!]: lit. 'were'.

[7] 'men': sing.

[8] 'respected' or 'thought much of'.

[9] 'lay waste': sing. verb.

 ـ .

 ـ .

 ـ .

 ـ .

 ـ .

 ـ .

 ـ .

 ـ .

 ـ .

 ـ .

 ـ .

10   After this I will arise, says the Lord, after this I will exalt myself, after this I will be raised up.

11   You will bear thorns, you will bring forth stubble with your breath; fire will consume you.

12   The nations will burn up as with quicklime; as thorns collected for the fire they will be burnt.

13   Hear, (you who are) distant, everything which I have done; know, (you who are) near, my might.

14   The sinners in Zion were afraid; trembling will seize[1] the godless; who among us will live[2] with the devouring fire, who among us will live with the eternal burning?

15   He who walks in righteousness, and speaks (with) integrity, who hates deceit and robbery, who refuses to take a bribe,[3] who stops up his ears that he may not hear (evil), closes his eyes that he may not see evil.

16   This one will dwell on the height(s), his dwelling-place on the stronghold of the crag; his bread given, his water assured.

17   Your eyes will see the king in his grace, in distant lands; and your heart will learn the awe (of him).

18   Where is the scribe? where the banker? where is he who counts the towers for the strong people?

19   He will not consider a people slow of tongue, hesitant of speech, not understood.

20   Look to Zion, the city of our festivals: your eyes will behold Jerusalem, the prepared dwelling, the tent which is not moved, its pegs never uprooted, none of its tent-cords broken off.[4]

---

[1] 'seize': lit. 'fall on'.

[2] 'who among us will live'¹: lit. 'who will dwell for us'.

[3] 'refuses to take a bribe': lit. 'shakes his hand from taking a bribe'.

[4] 'none of its tent-cords broken off': lit. 'all its tent-cords not broken off'.

21 ܟܐ ܡܛܠ ܕܡܪܝܐ ܫܡܐ ܗ̱ܘ ܠܢ ܡܫܒܚܢܐ. ܘܗܘ ܢܗܘܐ ܠܢ ܐܬܪܐ ܢܗܪܐ: ܘܢܗܪ̈ܘܬܐ
ܦܘܬܝܐ ܕܐܝ̈ܕܝܐ. ܕܠܐ ܬܐܙܠ ܒܗ ܡܪܘܒܬܐ ܕܡܫܘܛܐ. ܘܚܝܠܐ ܕܢܫܬܒܚ: ܠܐ ܢܥܒܪ
ܒܗ.
22 ܟܒ ܡܛܠ ܕܡܪܝܐ ܗ̱ܘ ܕܝ̈ܢܢ. ܘܡܪܝܐ ܗ̱ܘ ܡܦܪܫܢܢ. ܘܡܪܝܐ ܗ̱ܘ ܡܠܟܢ: ܘܗܘܝܘ
ܦܪܘܩܢ.
23 ܟܓ ܐܫܬܪܝܘ ܚܒ̈ܠܝܟܝ ܕܠܐ ܐܫܬܪܪܘ. ܘܐܬܪܦܝܘ ܐܣܛܘܪ̈ܘܢܝܟܝ ܕܠܐ ܢܦܪܣܘܢ ܐܬܐ: ܗܝܕܝܢ
ܢܬܦܠܓܘܢ ܒܙܬܐ. ܘܚܓܝܪ̈ܐ ܢܒܙܘܢ ܒܙܬܐ.
24 ܟܕ ܘܠܐ ܢܐܡܪ ܫܒܒܐ ܕܟܪܝܗ ܐܢܐ. ܥܡܐ ܕܝܬܒ ܒܗ: ܫܒܝܩܝܢ ܚܛܗ̈ܘܗܝ.

21   For the Lord is a glorious name for us, he will be a shining place for us, a splendor, a spacious place,[1] where the authority of the ruler will not reign, and the powerful one, who is present, will not pass over it.[2]

22   For the Lord is the judge, and the Lord is the lawgiver, and the Lord is our king, and he is our savior.

23   Your lines are loosened so that they may not be firmly fixed, your columns bent down so that they may not spread out the sign, until they have divided the spoil, and the multitude of the lame has carried off the prey.

24   The inhabitant will not say: I am sick; the people who dwell in it were punished for sin.[3]

---

[1] 'spacious place': lit. 'an open place of hands'.

[2] 'over it': lit. 'over in it'.

[3] 'were punished for sin': lit. 'received punishment for sin'; idiomatic.

ܩܦܠܐܘܢ: ܟܒ.

1 ܐ ܐܬܐ ܕܝܢܐ. ܩܪܘܒܘ ܥܡ̈ܡܐ ܠܡܫܡܥ: ܘܐܨܬܘܬܘ ܐܡ̈ܘܬܐ. ܬܫܡܥ ܐܪܥܐ ܒܡܠܝܗ: ܬܒܝܠ ܘܟܠܗܘܢ ܝܠܝܕܝܗ.

2 ܒ ܡܛܠ ܕܪܘܓܙܗ ܕܡܪܝܐ ܥܠ ܟܠܗܘܢ ܥܡ̈ܡܐ. ܘܚܡܬܗ ܥܠ ܟܠܗ ܚܝܠܗܘܢ. ܕܢܚܪܘܒ ܐܢܘܢ: ܘܢܫܠܡ ܐܢܘܢ ܠܩܛܠܐ.

3 ܓ ܘܢܫܬܕܘܢ ܩܛܝ̈ܠܝܗܘܢ. ܘܢܣܩ ܣܪܝܐ ܕܫܠܕ̈ܝܗܘܢ. ܘܢܬܡܣܘܢ ܛܘܪ̈ܐ ܡܢ ܕܡܗܘܢ.

4 ܕ ܘܢܬܡܣܘܢ ܟܠ ܚܝ̈ܠܘܬܐ ܕܫܡܝܐ. ܘܢܬܟܪܟܘܢ ܫܡܝܐ ܐܝܟ ܡܓܠܬܐ. ܘܟܠܗ ܚܝܠܗܘܢ ܢܬܪ: ܐܝܟ ܛܪܦܐ ܕܢܬܪ ܡܢ ܓܦܬܐ: ܘܐܝܟ ܦܐܘܬܐ ܡܢ ܬܐܬܐ.

5 ܗ ܡܛܠ ܕܐܬܪܘܝܬ ܚܪܒܝ ܒܫܡܝܐ. ܗܐ ܥܠ ܐܕܘܡܝܐ ܬܚܘܬ: ܥܠ ܥܡܐ ܕܐܬܚܪܡ ܠܕܝܢܐ.

6 ܘ ܚܪܒܗ ܕܡܪܝܐ ܡܠܝܐ ܕܡܐ. ܐܬܕܗܢܬ ܡܢ ܕܡܐ ܘܡܢ ܬܪܒܐ ܕܐܡܪ̈ܐ: ܘܕܥܬܘ̈ܕܐ: ܘܬܪܒܐ ܕܟܘܠܝ̈ܬܐ ܕܕܟܪ̈ܐ. ܡܛܠ ܕܕܒܚܬܐ ܠܡܪܝܐ ܒܒܘܨܪ: ܘܩܛܠܐ ܪܒܐ ܒܐܪܥܐ ܕܐܕܘܡ.

7 ܙ ܘܢܚܬܘܢ ܪ̈ܝܡܐ ܥܡܗܘܢ: ܘܬܘܪ̈ܐ ܥܡ ܬܘܪ̈ܐ. ܘܬܪܘܐ ܐܪܥܐ ܡܢ ܕܡܗܘܢ. ܘܥܦܪܐ ܡܢ ܬܪܒܗܘܢ ܢܪܘܐ.

8 ܚ ܡܛܠ ܕܝܘܡܐ ܕܬܒܥܬܐ ܠܡܪܝܐ: ܘܫܢܬܐ ܕܦܘܪܥܢܐ ܠܕܝܢܐ ܕܨܗܝܘܢ.

9 ܛ ܘܢܬܗܦܟܘܢ ܢܚ̈ܠܝܗ ܠܙܦܬܐ: ܘܥܦܪܗ ܠܟܒܪܝܬܐ. ܘܬܗܘܐ ܐܪܥܗ ܙܦܬܐ ܕܝܩܕܐ.

10 ܝ ܠܐ ܬܕܥܟ ܠܠܝܐ ܘܐܝܡܡܐ. ܠܥܠܡ ܢܣܩ ܬܢܢܗ. ܘܬܚܪܒ ܠܕܪ̈ܕܪܝܢ. ܘܠܥܠܡ ܥܠܡܝܢ ܐ̱ܢܫ ܠܐ ܢܥܒܪ ܒܗ.

Chapter 34

1   The place of judgment. Come near, nations, to hear; give ear, peoples; let the earth hear in its multitude,[1] the world[2] and all its inhabitants.

2   For the anger of the Lord is against all the nations, his fury is against all their host, so that he may lay them waste, deliver them to slaughter.

3   Their slain will be cast out, the stench of their corpses will spread, the mountains will rot[3] with their blood.

4   And all the hosts of heaven will rot, and the heavens will be bound up like a scroll, and all their host will fall off, like a leaf which falls off the vine, like an unripe fig from the fig-tree.

5   For my sword will be drunken in heaven: See! it will descend upon the Edomites, upon the people which has been found guilty in law.[4]

6   The sword of the Lord is filled with blood, it has been fattened with blood, with the fat parts of fattened animals, of kids, with the fat of rams' kidneys, for there is a sacrifice to the Lord in Bozrah, and great slaughter in the land of Edom.

7   Wild bulls will fall down with them, and bulls with young bullocks, and the land will be drunken with their blood, and the soil will be fattened by their fat.

8   For there is a day of vengeance for the Lord, and a year of retribution for the judgment of Zion.

9   Her torrents will be turned into pitch, her soil into brimstone, her land will become burning pitch.

10   It will not be extinguished by night or by day; its smoke will rise up forever, it will lie waste for generations, man will never again pass[5] through it.

---

[1] 'multitude' or 'fullness'.

[2] 'world': lit. 'inhabited world'.

[3] 'rot with' or 'melt from'.

[4] 'law' or 'judgment'.

[5] 'man will never again pass': lit. 'forever and ever a man will not pass'.

162

11   Pelicans and porcupines will inherit[1] it, owls and ravens will live in it.

12   He will stretch out over it the measuring line of desolation;[2] there will be no gladness there, nor will they call (it) a kingdom there; all its noblemen will be ruined.[3]

13   Thorns will shoot up in its palaces, thorn-bushes and thistles in its stronghold; it will be a dwelling-place for jackals, a pasturage for ostriches.

14   Specters will meet in it, in hostile encounters, the demon will call to his companion; the night-specter has settled there, has found her rest.

15   The owl will nest there, it has shaken itself,[4] crept,[5] pierced in its shadow;[6] vultures were gathered there, one to another.

16   Seek in the book of the Lord, and read: not one of them will be forgotten;[7] they did not seek one another,[8] but he spoke his command,[9] and his spirit gathered them.

17   He cast lots for them, and his hand distributed the measures for them, so that they will possess it forever, dwell in it for generations.

---

[1] 'inherit' or 'take possession of'.

[2] 'desolation' or 'the sword'.

[3] 'ruined': lit. 'a ruin'.

[4] 'shaken itself' or 'woken itself from sleep'. See Introduction. Addendum 3.

[5] 'crept'. MT 'brood'. √II חלד means 'to dig, hollow out'; possibly the translator was thinking of the process of nesting. See Introduction. Addendum 3.

[6] 'pierced in its shadow'. See Introduction. Addendum 3.

[7] 'not one of them will be forgotten': lit. 'one of them will not be forgotten'.

[8] 'one another': lit. 'one to one'.

[9] 'spoke his command': lit. 'commanded by his mouth'.

Chapter 35

1   The thirsty wilderness will rejoice, the plain will leap for joy, it will blossom as the autumn crocus.

2   It will leap for joy like the rock-goat; the glory of Lebanon will be given to it with praise, and the honor of Carmel and of Sharon: they will see the glory of the Lord and the honor of our God.

3   An admonition and an encouragement of the weak: the savior is coming and redeems them.[1] Strengthen the weakened hands, the trembling knees make firm.

4   Say to the faint-hearted: Strengthen yourselves, do not fear. See! your God, the avenger, comes; God the redeemer comes, and redeems you.

5   Then the eyes of the blind will be opened, the ears of the deaf will be opened.

6   Then the lame will leap like the stag, and the tongue of the dumb will be freed,[2] for waters will burst forth in the wilderness, torrents in the plain.

7   There will be pools in the waste[3] place, springs of water in the dry places; grass will spring up, cane and reed in the dwelling-place of jackals.

8   There will be a path there, and it will be called 'the holy way'; no abomination[4] will pass by in it, there will be no path in it, and the foolish will not wander there.

9   There will be no lion(s) there, no evil animals will go there,[5] they will not be found there.

---

[1] 'An admonition and an encouragement of the weak: the savior is coming and redeems them': this is an addition to the Hebrew text, marking the midpoint of the Peshitta to Isaiah.

[2] 'freed': lit. 'made able to move'.

[3] 'waste' or 'desert'.

[4] 'abomination' or 'defilement'.

[5] 'go there': lit. 'go up'.

ܘܢܐܙܠܘܢ ܩܬܪܩܐ: ܩܬܢܩܪܘܣ ܘܩܪܙܢܐ. ܘܢܟܩܗܩ ܘܢܟܩ ܟܪܘܩ ܚܩܘܟܪܐ. 10 ـ
ܘܟܟܚܩܒ ܐܗܘܗܐ ܣܠܪܗܐܠ ܟܠܠ ܩܩܥܩܘܩ. ܚܘܩܩܐ ܘܣܠܪܗܐܠ ܝܒܘܩܩ.
ܘܢܟܝܩܩ ܦܘܗܘܢܠ ܗܐܩܣܟܠ.

10   The redeemed will go (there), the redeemed of the Lord; they will return, they will enter Zion with praise, joy will be upon their heads forever, they will attain delight and gladness, misery and groans will flee.

ܩܦܠܐܘܢ: ܠܗ.

ܟܘ ܚ

1 ܐ ܘܗܘܬ ܒܫܢܬ ܐܪܒܥܣܪܐ ܕܚܙܩܝܐ ܡܠܟܐ ܕܝܗܘܕܐ: ܣܠܩ ܣܢܚܪܝܒ ܡܠܟܐ
ܕܐܬܘܪ: ܥܠ ܟܠܗܝܢ ܩܘܪܝܐ ܥܫܝܢܬܐ ܕܝܗܘܕܐ. ܘܐܚܕ ܐܢܝܢ.

2 ܒ ܘܫܕܪ ܡܠܟܐ ܕܐܬܘܪ ܡܢ ܠܟܝܫ ܠܪܒ ܫܩܐ: ܠܘܬ ܚܙܩܝܐ ܡܠܟܐ
ܠܐܘܪܫܠܡ: ܒܚܝܠܐ ܥܫܝܢܐ. ܘܩܡ ܒܡܫܩܝܬܐ ܕܡܥܝܢܬܐ ܥܠܝܬܐ ܕܒܐܘܪܚܐ
ܕܚܩܠܗ ܕܩܨܪܐ.

3 ܓ ܘܢܦܩ ܠܘܬܗ ܐܠܝܩܝܡ ܒܪ ܚܠܩܝܐ ܪܒܒܝܬܐ: ܘܫܒܢܐ ܣܦܪܐ: ܘܝܘܐܚ ܒܪ
ܐܣܦ ܡܥܗܕܢܐ.

4 ܕ ܘܐܡܪ ܠܗܘܢ ܪܒ ܫܩܐ: ܐܡܪܘ ܠܚܙܩܝܐ: ܗܟܢܐ ܐܡܪ ܡܠܟܐ ܪܒܐ ܡܠܟܐ
ܕܐܬܘܪ: ܡܢܐ ܗܘ ܬܘܟܠܢܐ ܗܢܐ ܕܐܬܬܟܠܬ.

5 ܗ ܘܐܡܪܬ ܕܐܝܬ ܠܝ ܡܡܠܠܐ ܕܣܦܘܬܐ: ܘܡܠܟܐ ܘܓܢܒܪܘܬܐ ܠܩܪܒܐ. ܗܫܐ
ܥܠ ܡܢܘ ܐܬܬܟܠܬ: ܕܡܪܕܬ ܒܝ.

6 ܘ ܗܐ ܐܬܬܟܠܬ ܥܠ ܫܒܛܐ ܕܩܢܝܐ ܪܥܝܥܐ: ܥܠ ܡܨܪܝܢ. ܕܡܐ ܕܐܣܬܡܟ
ܓܒܪܐ ܥܠܘܗܝ: ܥܐܠ ܒܐܝܕܗ ܘܢܩܒ ܠܗ. ܗܟܢܐ ܗܘ ܦܪܥܘܢ ܡܠܟܐ
ܕܡܨܪܝܢ ܠܟܠ ܕܡܬܬܟܠܝܢ ܥܠܘܗܝ.

7 ܙ ܘܐܢ ܬܐܡܪ ܠܝ ܕܥܠ ܡܪܝܐ ܐܠܗܢ ܐܬܬܟܠܢ: ܗܢܐ ܗܘ ܚܙܩܝܐ ܕܐܥܒܪ
ܠܒܡܘܬܐ ܘܡܕܒܚܐ ܘܐܡܪ ܠܝܗܘܕܐ ܘܠܐܘܪܫܠܡ: ܕܩܕܡ ܡܕܒܚܐ ܚܕ ܬܣܓܕܘܢ.

Chapter 36

XVII

1 It happened in the fourteenth year of Hezekiah king of Judah that Sennacherib king of Assyria came up against all the fortified cities of Judah, and took them.

2 And the king of Assyria sent RabShakeh[1] from Lachish to Hezekiah the king, to Jerusalem, with a numerous army; he was standing at the upper part of the upper[2] pool, which was in the path of the fuller's field.

3 Eliakim, the son of Hilkiah, who is in charge of the household,[3] Shebna the scribe, and Joah the son of Asaph the recorder went out[4] to him.

4 RabShakeh said to them: Say to Hezekiah 'Thus says the great king, the king of Assyria: what is this (source of) confidence on which you have trusted?

5 I said that you have speech,[5] and intent, and fortitude to (go to) war; now, on what have you trusted, that you have rebelled against me?

6 See! you have put your trust in the support of a broken reed - in the Egyptian - which when a man has supported himself upon it, goes into his hand, piercing him: thus is Pharaoh king of Egypt to all who trust in him.

7 And if you should say to me that we have trusted in the Lord our God, how does it profit Hezekiah that he has taken away the high places and the altars, and has said to Judah and to Jerusalem: You will worship before a single altar?

---

[1] 'RabShakeh' or, literally translated, 'the chief butler'.

[2] 'upper ... upper': lit. 'ascent ... upper': two different Syriac roots.

[3] 'who is in charge of the household': lit. 'the great one of the house'. See 22:15, 36:22, 37:2.

[4] 'went out': sing. verb.

[5] 'speech': lit. 'speech of lips'.

8 ܚ ܘܗܘܐ ܐܬܡܠܟ ܥܡ ܡܪܝ ܡܠܟܐ ܐܬܘܪܝܐ. ܘܐܙܠ ܠܗ ܢܐܝܡ ܠܟܠܕܝܐ ܕܒܝܬܐ:
ܐܢ ܐܝܬ ܠܗ ܦܬܓܡܐ ܕܢܘܕܥ ܒܠܒܗܘܢ.

9 ܛ ܘܐܡܪܬ ܡܠܟܬܐ ܐܝܟ ܐܚܐ ܕܢܦܩ ܡܢ ܠܒܒܗܘܢ ܕܗܘܐ ܕܡܪܝ. ܘܐܬܐܡܪܬ ܠܗ
ܥܠ ܡܕܝܢܬܐ: ܕܢܐܬܐ ܠܗ ܡܬܡܟܢܐ ܘܦܬܓܡܐ.

10 ܝ ܗܘܐ ܕܝܢ ܟܕ ܢܦܩ ܡܢ ܡܕܝܢܬܐ ܫܟܠܬ ܠܐܪܥܐ ܗܘܐ ܠܡܣܒܪܘܬܗ. ܡܕܝܢܬܐ ܕܝܢ
ܐܡܪ ܠܗ ܕܐܬܐ ܠܐܪܥܐ ܗܘܐ ܘܐܣܬܟܠ.

11 ܝܐ ܘܐܡܪܘ ܠܐܠܗܝܢ ܘܟܗܢܐ ܘܩܘܡܘ ܠܘܬ ܥܡܐ: ܡܛܠ ܥܡ ܟܠܒܝܢ ܐܘܪܫܠܡ
ܡܫܠܛ ܕܡܟܢܝܢ ܚܝܠ. ܘܠܐ ܐܬܡܠܟ ܥܡ ܢܒܘܟܕܢܨܪ ܩܕܡ ܥܡܐ ܕܡܟܝܢ ܥܠ
ܫܘܪܐ.

12 ܝܒ ܘܐܡܪ ܠܗܘܢ ܙܟܝ ܥܡܐ: ܠܐ ܗܘܐ ܠܟܘܬܗܘܢ ܘܠܟܠܗ ܡܕܝܢܬܗܘܢ: ܡܬܚܫܒ ܡܕܝܢ
ܠܡܐܡܪ ܡܠܐ ܗܠܝܢ: ܐܠܐ ܠܒܝܬܐ ܕܐܬܟܢܫ. ܥܠ ܫܘܪܐ: ܘܠܐ ܢܐܬܘܢ
ܐܬܠܗܘܢ: ܘܢܦܠܘܢ ܐܢܫܝܗܘܢ ܥܡܗܘܢ.

13 ܝܓ ܘܩܡ ܙܟܝ ܥܡܐ. ܘܟܪܐ ܒܩܠܐ ܪܒܐ ܢܒܘܟܕܢܨܪ: ܘܐܡܪ: ܫܡܥܘ ܡܠܟܘܗܝ ܕܡܠܟܐ
ܪܒܐ ܡܠܟܐ ܕܐܬܘܪ.

14 ܝܕ ܗܟܢܐ ܐܡܪ ܡܠܟܐ ܕܐܬܘܪ: ܠܐ ܢܛܥܝܟܘܢ ܚܙܩܝܐ: ܡܛܠ ܕܠܐ ܡܫܟܚ
ܠܡܦܨܝܘܬܟܘܢ.

15 ܝܗ ܘܠܐ ܢܬܟܠܟܘܢ ܚܙܩܝܐ ܥܠ ܡܪܝܐ. ܕܢܐܡܪ ܕܡܦܨܐ ܡܦܨܐ ܠܢ ܡܪܝܐ: ܘܠܐ
ܡܫܬܠܡܐ ܡܕܝܢܬܐ ܗܕܐ ܒܐܝܕܘܗܝ ܕܡܠܟܐ ܕܐܬܘܪ.

16 ܝܘ ܠܐ ܬܫܡܥܘܢ ܠܚܙܩܝܐ. ܡܛܠ ܕܗܟܢܐ ܐܡܪ ܡܠܟܐ ܕܐܬܘܪ: ܥܒܕܘ ܥܡܝ
ܫܠܡܐ: ܘܦܘܩܘ ܠܘܬܝ. ܘܐܟܘܠܘ ܐܢܫ ܓܦܬܗ: ܘܐܢܫ ܬܐܢܬܗ. ܘܐܫܬܘ
ܐܢܫ ܡܝܐ ܕܓܘܒܗ.

17 ܝܙ ܥܕܡܐ ܕܐܬܐ ܘܐܕܒܪܟܘܢ ܠܐܪܥܐ ܕܐܝܟ ܐܪܥܟܘܢ: ܐܪܥܐ ܕܥܒܘܪܐ ܘܕܚܡܪܐ: ܐܪܥܐ ܕܠܚܡܐ
ܘܕܟܪܡܐ.

8   So now, ally yourself with my lord, the Assyrian king, and I will give you two thousand horses - if you have[1] horsemen that you can set upon them.

9   How can you turn (away) the face of one of the least servants of my lord, when you have trusted in the Egyptian, to give you chariots and horsemen?

10   For now, have I come up to this land to lay it waste, without the Lord? it is the Lord who said to me that I should go up against this land and lay it waste.

11   Eliakim, Shebna, and Joah said to RabShakeh: Speak with your servants in Aramaic, for we understand (it); do not speak with us in the Judean language[2] in front of the people standing on the wall.

12   RabShakeh said to them: It was not to you, nor to your lord, (that) my lord sent me to speak these words, but to the men who sit on the wall, so that they may not eat their own dung, and drink their own urine with you.

13   RabShakeh stood up, and called aloud,[3] in the Judean language, and said: Hear the words of the great king, the king of Assyria.

14   Thus says the king of Assyria: Do not let Hezekiah deceive you, for he cannot save you.

15   And may Hezekiah not make you trust in the Lord, for he will say: The Lord will surely save us, this city will not be handed over into the hands of the king of Assyria.

16   Do not listen to Hezekiah, for thus says the king of Assyria: Make a blessing with me,[4] and come out to me, and eat, each, from his own vines, and each, from his own fig trees, and drink, each, water from his own well.

17   Until I come, and I will lead you to a land which is like your land, a land of grain and of oil, a land of olive trees and of vineyards.

---

[1] 'if you have': lit. 'if there is to you'.

[2] 'Judean language': lit. 'Judean'.

[3] 'aloud': lit. 'in a loud voice'.

[4] 'Make a blessing with me' in the sense of 'make an agreement with me'.

18 ܝܚ ܠܐ ܢܛܥܝܟܘܢ ܚܙܩܝܐ ܘܢܐܡܪ ܕܡܪܝܐ ܡܦܨܐ ܠܟܘܢ. ܕܠܡܐ ܦܨܝܘ ܐܠܗܝܗܘܢ
ܕܥܡܡܐ: ܐܢܫ ܐܪܥܗ ܡܢ ܐܝܕܘܗܝ ܕܡܠܟܐ ܕܐܬܘܪ.

19 ܝܛ ܐܝܟܐ ܐܢܘܢ ܐܠܗܐ ܕܚܡܬ ܘܕܐܪܦܕ. ܘܐܝܟܐ ܐܢܘܢ ܐܠܗܐ ܕܣܦܪܘܝܡ. ܕܠܡܐ
ܦܨܝܘ ܠܫܡܪܝܢ ܡܢ ܐܝܕܝ.

20 ܟ ܡܢ ܡܢ ܟܠܗܘܢ ܐܠܗܐ ܕܐܪܥܬܐ ܗܠܝܢ ܦܨܝ ܐܪܥܗ ܡܢ ܐܝܕܝ: ܕܡܦܨܐ ܡܪܝܐ
ܠܐܘܪܫܠܡ ܡܢ ܐܝܕܝ.

21 ܟܐ ܘܫܬܩܘ ܠܗܘܢ: ܘܐܢܫ ܠܐ ܦܢܐ ܠܗ ܦܬܓܡ. ܡܛܠ ܕܦܩܕ ܡܠܟܐ
ܘܐܡܪ: ܠܐ ܬܬܠܘܢ ܠܗ ܦܬܓܡܐ.

22 ܟܒ ܘܐܬܐ ܐܠܝܩܝܡ ܒܪ ܚܠܩܝܐ ܪܒ ܒܝܬܐ: ܘܫܒܢܐ ܣܦܪܐ: ܘܝܘܐܚ ܒܪ ܐܣܦ
ܡܕܟܪܢܐ: ܠܘܬ ܚܙܩܝܐ ܟܕ ܡܨܪܝܢ ܢܚܬܝܗܘܢ ܘܚܘܝܘܗܝ ܡܠܘܗܝ ܕܪܒ ܫܩܐ.

18   May Hezekiah not deceive you and say: The Lord saves us. Have the gods of the nations saved (for any) man, his land from the hands of the king of Assyria?

19   Where are the gods of Hamath and of Arpad? where are the gods of Sepharvaim? Did they save Samaria from my hands?

20   Who of all the gods of these lands has saved his land from my hands, that the Lord might save Jerusalem from my hands?

21   But they kept silent,[1] and no man spoke a word to him, for the king had commanded and said: Do not speak a word to him.

22   Eliakim, the son of Hilkiah, who is in charge of the household,[2] came, and Shebna the scribe, and Joah the son of Asaph the recorder, to Hezekiah, their clothes torn, and told him what RabShakeh had said.[3]

---

[1] 'kept silent': lit. 'kept silent for themselves'. This use of the ethical dative is common in Syriac but should not be translated.

[2] 'who is in charge of the household': lit. 'the great one of the house'. See 22:15, 36:3, 37:2.

[3] 'what RabShakeh had said': lit. 'the words of RabShakeh'.

ܡܓܠܬܗ: ܒ.

1 ܐ ܘܗܘܐ ܕܟܕ ܫܡܥ ܚܙܩܝܐ ܡܠܟܐ: ܨܪܐ ܢܚܬܘܗܝ: ܘܐܬܟܣܝ ܣܩܐ. ܘܥܠ ܠܒܝܬܗ ܕܡܪܝܐ.

2 ܒ ܘܫܕܪ ܠܐܠܝܩܝܡ ܪܒܝܬܐ: ܘܠܫܒܢܐ ܣܦܪܐ: ܘܠܩܫܝܫܐ ܕܟܗܢܐ ܟܕ ܡܟܣܝܢ ܣܩܐ: ܠܘܬ ܐܫܥܝܐ ܢܒܝܐ ܒܪ ܐܡܘܨ.

3 ܓ ܘܐܡܪܘ ܠܗ: ܗܟܢܐ ܐܡܪ ܚܙܩܝܐ: ܝܘܡܐ ܗܘ ܕܐܘܠܨܢܐ: ܘܕܡܟܣܢܘܬܐ: ܘܕܪܘܓܙܐ: ܝܘܡܐ. ܡܛܠ ܕܡܛܘ ܚܒܠܐ ܕܒܢܝܐ. ܘܠܝܬ ܚܝܠܐ ܠܝܠܕܬܐ.

4 ܕ ܟܒܪ ܢܫܡܥ ܡܪܝܐ ܐܠܗܟ ܡܠܘܗܝ ܕܪܒ ܫܩܐ. ܕܫܕܪܗ ܡܪܗ ܡܠܟܐ ܐܬܘܪܝܐ: ܕܢܚܣܕ ܠܐܠܗܐ ܚܝܐ. ܘܢܟܣܝܘܗܝ ܒܡܠܐ ܕܫܡܥ ܡܪܝܐ ܐܠܗܟ. ܘܬܒܥܐ ܘܬܨܠܐ ܥܠ ܫܪܟܐ ܕܐܫܬܟܚܘ.

5 ܗ ܘܐܬܘ ܥܒܕܘܗܝ ܕܚܙܩܝܐ ܡܠܟܐ ܠܘܬ ܐܫܥܝܐ.

6 ܘ ܘܐܡܪ ܠܗܘܢ ܐܫܥܝܐ: ܗܟܢܐ ܐܡܪܘ ܠܡܪܟܘܢ: ܗܟܢܐ ܐܡܪ ܡܪܝܐ: ܠܐ ܬܕܚܠ ܡܢ ܡܠܐ ܕܫܡܥܬ: ܕܓܕܦܘ ܥܠܝ ܛܠܝܘܗܝ ܕܡܠܟܐ ܕܐܬܘܪ.

7 ܙ ܗܐ ܝܗܒ ܐܢܐ ܒܗ ܪܘܚܐ. ܘܢܫܡܥ ܫܡܥܐ: ܘܢܗܦܘܟ ܠܐܪܥܗ. ܘܐܪܡܝܘܗܝ ܒܚܪܒܐ ܒܐܪܥܗ.

8 ܚ ܘܗܦܟ ܪܒ ܫܩܐ. ܘܐܫܟܚ ܠܡܠܟܐ ܕܐܬܘܪ ܟܕ ܡܬܟܬܫ ܥܠ ܠܒܢܐ: ܟܕ ܫܡܥ ܕܫܩܠ ܡܢ ܠܟܝܫ.

9 ܛ ܘܫܡܥ ܥܠ ܬܪܗܩ ܡܠܟܐ ܕܟܘܫ: ܕܢܦܩ ܠܡܬܟܬܫܘ ܥܡܗ. ܘܫܡܥ ܘܫܕܪ ܐܝܙܓܕܐ ܠܘܬ ܚܙܩܝܐ.

Chapter 37

1 When Hezekiah the king heard, he tore his garments, clothed himself in sackcloth, and went to the house of the Lord.

2 He sent Eliakim who is in charge of the household,[1] Shebna the scribe, and the elders of the priests, clothed in sackcloth, to Isaiah the prophet, son of Amoz.

3 They said to him: Thus says Hezekiah 'This is the day of distress, of reproof, of anger, today, for the pains of childbirth[2] have come, but there is no strength in the woman giving birth'.

4 Perhaps the Lord your God will hear the words of RabShakeh, who was sent by his lord the king of Assyria,[3] that he might revile the living God, and might reprove him with the words which the Lord your God has heard: may you seek and pray concerning the remnant which has remained.[4]

5 The servants of Hezekiah the king came to Isaiah.

6 Isaiah said to them: Say thus to your lord 'Thus says the Lord. Do not fear the words which you heard, with which the messengers of the king of Assyria blasphemed before me.

7 See! I set a spirit in him: He will hear a report, and he will return to his land, and with the sword I will lay him low in his land.

8 RabShakeh returned, and found the king of Assyria fighting against Libnah, for he had heard[5] that he had marched from Lachish.

9 For he had heard concerning Tirhakah, the king of Cush,[6] that he had gone out to fight against him; he heard, and sent messengers to Hezekiah.

---

[1] 'who is in charge of the household': lit. 'the great one of the house'. See 22:15, 36:3, 22.

[2] 'childbirth': lit. 'children'.

[3] 'who was sent by his lord the king of Assyria': lit. 'whose lord the king of Assur has sent him'.

[4] 'remained': pl. verb.

[5] 'for he had heard': lit. 'when he heard'.

[6] 'Cush' or 'Ethiopia'.

10 ܝ ܗܳܟܰܢܳܐ ܐܶܡܰܪܘ ܠܚܶܙܩܝܳܐ ܡܰܠܟܳܐ ܕܝܗܘܕܳܐ ܠܡܐܡܰܪ: ܠܳܐ ܢܰܛܥܝܳܟ ܐܰܠܳܗܳܟ:
ܕܶܐܬܬܟܶܠܬ ܥܠܰܘܗܝ. ܘܳܐܡܰܪ ܐܢܬ ܕܠܳܐ ܡܶܫܬܰܠܡܳܐ ܐܘܪܫܠܶܡ ܒܺܐܝܕܰܘܗܝ ܕܡܰܠܟܳܐ
ܕܐܳܬܘܪ.

11 ܝܐ ܗܳܐ ܐܢܬ ܫܡܰܥܬ ܟܽܠ ܕܥܒܰܕܘ ܡܰܠܟܶܐ ܕܐܳܬܘܪ ܠܟܽܠܗܶܝܢ ܐܰܪܥܳܬܳܐ
ܠܡܰܚܪܳܒܗ ܐܶܢܶܝܢ. ܘܐܢܬ ܡܶܬܦܰܨܶܐ ܐܢܬ.

12 ܝܒ ܕܰܠܡܳܐ ܦܰܨܺܝܘ ܐܰܠܳܗܰܝܗܘܢ ܠܥܰܡܡܶܐ ܕܚܰܒܶܠܘ ܐܰܒܳܗܳܬܝ: ܠܓܽܘܙܰܢ ܘܠܚܳܪܳܢ
ܘܠܪܰܨܶܦ: ܘܠܒܢܰܝ ܥܶܕܶܢ ܕܒܬܠܰܣܰܪ.

13 ܝܓ ܐܰܝܟܘ ܡܰܠܟܳܐ ܕܚܡܳܬ: ܘܡܰܠܟܳܐ ܕܐܰܪܦܰܕ: ܘܡܰܠܟܳܐ ܕܡܕܺܝܢܬܳܐ ܣܦܰܪܘܳܝܡ: ܗܶܢܰܥ:
ܘܥܰܘܳܐ.

14 ܝܕ ܘܢܣܰܒ ܚܶܙܩܝܳܐ ܐܶܓܰܪ̈ܳܬܳܐ ܡܶܢ ܐܺܝܕܰܝ ܐܺܝܙܓܰܕ̈ܶܐ. ܘܩܪܳܐ ܐܶܢܶܝܢ
ܘܣܠܶܩ ܠܒܶܝܬܶܗ ܕܡܳܪܝܳܐ. ܘܦܰܪܣ ܐܶܢܶܝܢ. ܚܶܙܩܝܳܐ ܩܕܳܡ ܡܳܪܝܳܐ.

15 ܝܗ ܘܨܰܠܺܝ ܚܶܙܩܝܳܐ ܩܕܳܡ ܡܳܪܝܳܐ: ܘܳܐܡܰܪ.

16 ܝܘ ܡܳܪܝܳܐ ܚܰܝܠܬܳܢܳܐ ܐܰܠܳܗܳܐ ܕܐܝܣܪܳܝܶܠ ܕܝܳܬܶܒ ܥܰܠ ܟܪܘܒ̈ܶܐ. ܐܢܬ ܗܘ ܐܰܠܳܗܳܐ
ܒܰܠܚܘܕܰܝܟ ܥܰܠ ܟܽܠܗܶܝܢ ܡܰܠܟܘܳܬܳܐ ܕܐܰܪܥܳܐ. ܐܢܬ ܥܒܰܕܬ ܫܡܰܝܳܐ ܘܐܰܪܥܳܐ.

17 ܝܙ ܪܟܶܢ ܡܳܪܝܳܐ ܐܶܕܢܳܟ ܘܫܡܰܥ. ܦܬܰܚ ܡܳܪܝܳܐ ܥܰܝܢܰܝܟ ܘܚܙܺܝ. ܘܫܡܰܥ ܡܶܠܰܘܗܝ
ܕܣܰܢܚܶܪܺܝܒ: ܕܫܰܕܰܪ ܠܡܚܰܣܳܕܘ ܠܰܐܠܳܗܳܐ ܚܰܝܳܐ.

ܫܠ ܫܠ

18 ܝܚ ܫܰܪܺܝܪܳܐܝܬ ܡܳܪܝܳܐ: ܚܰܪܶܒܘ ܡܰܠܟܶܐ ܕܐܳܬܘܪ ܠܟܽܠܗܶܝܢ ܐܰܪܥܳܬܳܐ.

19 ܝܛ ܘܳܐܘܒܕܽܘܢ ܘܰܠܐܰܠܳܗܰܝܗܘܢ ܐܰܘܩܶܕܘ ܒܢܘܪܳܐ ܡܶܛܠ ܕܠܳܐ ܗܘܰܘ ܐܰܠܳܗܶܐ. ܐܶܠܳܐ ܥܒܳܕ ܐܺܝܕܰܝܳܐ
ܕܐܢܳܫܳܐ: ܕܩܺܝܣܳܐ: ܘܕܟܺܐܦܳܐ. ܘܳܐܘܒܕܽܘ ܐܶܢܘܢ.

20 ܟ ܘܗܫܳܐ ܡܳܪܝܳܐ ܐܰܠܳܗܰܢ: ܦܪܽܘܩܰܝܢ ܡܶܢ ܐܺܝܕܰܘܗܝ: ܕܢܶܕܥܽܘܢ ܟܽܠܗܶܝܢ ܡܰܠܟܘܳܬܳܐ ܕܐܰܪܥܳܐ:
ܕܐܢܬ ܗܘ ܐܰܠܳܗܳܐ ܒܰܠܚܘܕܰܝܟ.

21 ܟܐ ܘܫܰܕܰܪ ܐܶܫܰܥܝܳܐ ܒܰܪ ܐܳܡܘܨ ܠܘܳܬ ܚܶܙܩܝܳܐ: ܘܳܐܡܰܪ ܠܶܗ: ܗܳܟܰܢܳܐ ܐܳܡܰܪ ܡܳܪܝܳܐ
ܚܰܝܠܬܳܢܳܐ ܐܰܠܳܗܳܐ ܕܐܝܣܪܳܝܶܠ: ܗܳܝ ܕܨܰܠܺܝܬ ܩܕܳܡܰܝ ܥܰܠ ܣܰܢܚܶܪܺܝܒ ܡܰܠܟܳܐ
ܕܐܳܬܘܪ: ܫܶܡܥܶܬ.

10   Say thus to Hezekiah king of Judah, saying: Let him not deceive you, your god in whom you put your trust, for you say that Jerusalem will not be delivered up into the hands of the king of Assyria.

11   See! You have heard all that the kings of Assyria did to all the lands, to lay them waste: you, shall you be delivered?

12   Did they deliver (them), the gods of the nations which my fathers laid waste, Gozan, Haran, Rezeph, the children of Eden, and those in Telassar?

13   Where is the king of Hamath, and the king of Arpad, and the king of the city of Sepharvaim, and of Na, and of Aqa?

14   Hezekiah received the letters from the hand(s) of the messengers, read them, and went up to the house of the Lord; Hezekiah spread them out before the Lord.

15   Hezekiah prayed before the Lord, and said:

16   Mighty Lord God of Israel, who sits upon the cherubim, you alone are God,[1] over all the kingdoms of the earth; you made the heavens and the earth.

17   Bend your ear, Lord, and hear; open your eyes, Lord, and see; hear the words of Sennacherib, which he sent to revile the living God.

XVIII

18   Truly, Lord, the kings of Assyria have laid waste all lands.

19   And their land and their gods they have burned with fire because they were not gods, but the work of human hands - of wood, and of silver, and of stone - and they have destroyed them.

20   And now, Lord our God, save us from his hands, so that all the kingdoms of the earth will know that you alone are God.

21   Then Isaiah, son of Amoz sent[2] to Hezekiah, and said to him, Thus says the mighty Lord God of Israel 'All that you have prayed before me concerning Sennacherib king of Assyria, I have heard'.

---

[1] 'you alone are God': lit. 'you are God - only you'.

[2] 'sent': lit. 'was sent'.

22 ܕܟ ...

23 ܟܓ ...

24 ܟܕ ...

25 ܟܗ ...

26 ܟܘ ...

27 ܟܙ ...

28 ܟܚ ...

29 ܟܛ ...

22   This is the word which the Lord spoke concerning him: She treats you with contempt, she derides you, the virgin daughter of Zion; she tosses her head at[1] you, the daughter of Jerusalem,

23   Whom have you reviled and blasphemed, against whom have you lifted up your voice? You have lifted up your eyes on high against the Holy One of Israel.

24   By the hand of your messengers you have reviled the Lord; you said: With the multitude of my chariots I will go up to the summit of the mountains, and to the borders of Lebanon; I will hew down the tallest[2] of its cedars, and the choicest of its cypresses, and I will enter the summit of the furthest part of the forest of Carmel.

25   I will dig, and I will drink water, and with the hooves of my horses I will dry up all the mighty rivers.

26   Did you not hear that long ago I did it, that in days of old[3] I prepared it? now I have brought it (to pass) that you will be a waste place, a desolation, like the mighty cities.

27   Whose inhabitants grew weak[4] within them: they were broken and ashamed, they were like the grass of the field, like the herb(s) of springtime, like the blade(s of grass) on the rooftop, like the first growth of the crop[5] before the standing corn.[6]

28   I know your habitation, your coming in and your going out; and that you have been presumptuous in my presence.

29   Because you were presumptuous in my presence, and your blasphemy has reached[7] my ears, I shall put a ring in your nose, and a bridle in your lips, and I will make you return by the way in which you came.

---

[1] 'at': lit. 'after'.

[2] 'tallest': lit. 'heights'.

[3] 'days of old': lit. 'former days' as in 23:7.

[4] 'grew weak': lit. 'the hands were weakened'.

[5] 'first growth of the crop' or 'tender grass'.

[6] 'standing corn': 'corn' is here used as a generic term for a cereal crop.

[7] 'reached': lit. 'gone up to'.

30   This is the sign for you: you eat this year the crop that grows of itself, and the second year, the crop which grows from that, and the third year (you will be) sowing and reaping, planting vineyards, and eating their fruit.

31   And the remnant of the house of Judah that remained[1] will return, as a root that grows downwards yet makes fruits above.

32   For from Jerusalem the remainder goes forth, and will be delivered from the mountain of Zion; the zeal of the mighty Lord does this.

33   For thus says the Lord concerning the king of Assyria: He will not enter this city, he will not shoot an arrow there, he will not attack it with shields,[2] and he will not set ambushes for it.[3]

34   But he will return, by the way in which he came, and he will not enter this city, says the Lord.

35   I will protect this city and I will redeem it, for my sake, and for the sake of David my servant.

36   The angel[4] of the Lord went out, and killed, in the camp of the Assyrian, one hundred and eighty five thousand; they rose early in the morning: See! all corpses, dead.

37   Sennacherib broke camp; he went again, and dwelt in Nineveh.

38   And when he was worshipping in the house of Nisroch his god, Adrammelech and Sharezer his sons killed him with the sword, and they fled to the land of Qardawaye,[5] and Sarhadom[6] his son reigned after him.

---

[1] 'remained': pl. verb.

[2] 'shields' or 'bucklers'.

[3] 'set ambushes for it': lit. 'lie in wait against it (with) ambushes'.

[4] 'angel' or 'messenger'.

[5] 'Qardawaye': Hebrew 'Ararat'.

[6] 'Sarhadom': Hebrew 'Esarhaddon'.

ܩܦܠܐܘܢ: ܟܚ.

1 ܐ ܒܗܘܢ ܒܝܘܡܬܐ ܗܢܘܢ: ܐܬܟܪܗ ܚܙܩܝܐ ܠܡܡܬ. ܘܐܬܐ ܠܘܬܗ ܐܫܥܝܐ ܢܒܝܐ
ܒܪ ܐܡܘܨ: ܘܐܡܪ ܠܗ: ܗܟܢܐ ܐܡܪ ܡܪܝܐ. ܦܩܕ ܥܠ ܒܝܬܟ: ܡܛܠ ܕܡܐܬ
ܐܢܬ: ܘܠܐ ܚܝܐ ܐܢܬ.

2 ܒ ܘܐܗܦܟ ܚܙܩܝܐ ܐܦܘܗܝ ܠܫܘܪܐ. ܘܨܠܝ ܩܕܡ ܡܪܝܐ ܘܐܡܪ.

3 ܓ ܐܘ ܡܪܝܐ: ܐܬܕܟܪ ܕܗܠܟܬ ܩܕܡܝܟ ܒܩܘܫܬܐ: ܘܒܠܒܐ ܫܠܡܐ: ܘܕܫܦܝܪ
ܩܕܡܝܟ ܥܒܕܬ. ܘܒܟܐ ܚܙܩܝܐ ܒܟܝܐ ܪܒܐ.

4 ܕ ܘܗܘܐ ܦܬܓܡܗ ܕܡܪܝܐ ܥܠ ܐܫܥܝܐ ܢܒܝܐ: ܟܕ ܐܡܪ.

5 ܗ ܐܙܠ ܐܡܪ ܠܚܙܩܝܐ ܡܠܟܐ ܕܝܗܘܕܐ: ܗܟܢܐ ܐܡܪ ܡܪܝܐ ܐܠܗܗ ܕܕܘܝܕ ܐܒܘܟ:
ܫܡܥܬ ܨܠܘܬܟ: ܘܚܙܝܬ ܕܡܥܝܟ. ܗܐ ܡܘܣܦ ܐܢܐ ܥܠ ܝܘܡܝܟ ܚܡܫܥܣܪܐ
ܫܢܝܢ.

6 ܘ ܘܡܢ ܐܝܕܘܗܝ ܕܡܠܟܐ ܕܐܬܘܪ ܐܦܨܝܟ: ܘܠܡܕܝܢܬܐ ܗܕܐ. ܘܐܓܢ ܥܠ ܡܕܝܢܬܐ
ܗܕܐ: ܘܐܦܪܩܝܗ.

7 ܙ ܘܗܕܐ ܠܟ ܐܬܐ ܡܢ ܩܕܡ ܡܪܝܐ: ܕܥܒܕ ܡܪܝܐ ܦܬܓܡܐ ܗܢܐ ܕܐܡܪ.

8 ܚ ܗܐ ܡܗܦܟ ܐܢܐ ܠܛܠܠܐ ܕܕܪܓܐ ܕܢܚܬ ܒܕܪܓܐ ܕܒܝܬ ܐܚܙ: ܫܡܫܐ ܠܒܣܬܪܗ
ܥܣܪܐ ܕܪܓܝܢ. ܘܗܦܟ ܫܡܫܐ ܠܒܣܬܪܗ ܥܣܪܐ ܕܪܓܝܢ: ܒܕܪܓܐ ܕܢܚܬ.

9 ܛ ܟܬܒܗ ܕܚܙܩܝܐ ܡܠܟܐ ܕܝܗܘܕܐ: ܟܕ ܐܬܟܪܗ: ܘܚܝܐ ܡܢ ܟܘܪܗܢܗ.

Chapter 38

1   In those days, Hezekiah became mortally ill;[1] Isaiah the prophet, son of Amoz came to him, and said to him: Thus says the Lord 'Give the last commands concerning your house, for you are dying, you will not recover'.

2   Hezekiah turned his face to the wall; he prayed before the Lord, and said:

3   I implore you,[2] Lord: remember that I have walked before you in truth, and with a perfect[3] heart, and have done good before you; and Hezekiah wept bitterly.[4]

4   The word of the Lord came to Isaiah the prophet, saying:

5   Go, say to Hezekiah king of Judah: Thus says the Lord God of David your father: 'I have heard your prayer, and I have seen your tears. See! I am adding fifteen years to your life.[5]

6   I will deliver you from the hands of the king of Assyria, and this city; I will protect this city, I will save it.

7   This is a sign for you from before the Lord, that the Lord does this thing,[6] of which he has spoken.

8   See! I will turn back the shadow of the degrees,[7] which falls on the steps[8] of Ahaz your father, (turning) the sun back ten degrees'. And the sun turned back ten degrees, on the steps (on) which it fell.[9]

9   The writing of Hezekiah king of Judah, when he had been sick, and had recovered from his sickness.

---

[1] 'mortally ill': lit. 'sick to die'.

[2] 'I implore you': an interjection expressing pleading or sorrow.

[3] 'perfect' or 'whole'.

[4] 'wept bitterly'; lit. 'wept a great weeping'.

[5] 'life': lit. 'days'.

[6] 'thing' or 'word'.

[7] 'degrees': the markings of a sundial are meant.

[8] 'steps': the word for 'degree' can also mean 'step'.

[9] 'falls … fell': lit. 'goes down … went down'.

10   I said: in the midst of my days I will go, at the gate of Sheol I have left the remainder of my years.

11   I said: I will not see the Lord in the land of the living; no more will I see man with the inhabitants of the grave.

12   He has taken my generation;[1] it has passed away from me, like the shepherds' tent; they have cut short my life as (if it were) cords, as a web which is nearly finished;[2] you have delivered me over from day to night.[3]

14   Like a chirping swallow, I chirped; I moaned like a dove; I lifted up my eyes to the height(s); Lord, save me, give me cheer.

15   What shall I say? He spoke to me, he passed on, he woke me suddenly from all my sleep,[4] because of the bitterness of my soul. Lord, because of these things,[5] will they live?

16   For these things - the life of my spirit - heal me, make me live.

17   See! In peace bitter things were bitter to me; you delighted in my soul, that it would not wear away in corruption, for you have put[6] all my sins behind you.[7]

18   For Sheol will not give thanks to you, nor death praise you; they will not declare your truth, those who go down to the pit.

19   But the living, who are like me today, will give thanks to you; the father(s) will declare your truth[8] to the children..

20   The Lord will redeem us; we will sing his praises, all the days of our lives, in the house of the Lord.

21   Hezekiah said: What is it, the sign that I go up to the house of the Lord?

---

[1] 'generation' or 'time'.

[2] 'nearly finished': lit. 'near to being cut off'.

[3] 38:13 has been omitted by mechanical error: the closing words of the Hebrew of v.12 are the same as those of the Hebrew of v.13.

[4] 'he woke me suddenly from all my sleep': lit. 'he startled all my sleep'.

[5] 'these things': lit. 'them'.

[6] 'put': lit. 'cast'.

[7] 'you'3: lit. 'your body'.

[8] 'truth' or 'faithfulness'.

22 ܡܕ ܘܐܡܪ ܐܓܡܪܗ؛ ܢܗܘܝܘ ܘܟܠܝܗ ܘܒܐܘܬܐ. ܘܢܩܝܡܘܗ ܟܠܐ ܚܘܡܠܐ؛ ܘܩܚܝܡܠܗܡ.

XIX

22[1]   Isaiah said: Let them take a dried fig cake, and let them put (it) on the abscess, and it will be healed.[2]

---

[1] The MT order of the last two verses has been reversed in the Peshitta mss.

[2] 'and it will be healed' or 'and he will be healed'.

Chapter 39

1   At that time, Merodach-Baladan, son of Baladan, the king of Babylon, sent letters and gifts to Hezekiah, for he had heard that he had been sick, but had regained strength and been healed.

2   Hezekiah rejoiced in them, and he showed them his treasury,[1] the silver, the gold, the incense, the fine oil, all his store-rooms, and everything which was found in his treasuries; Hezekiah left nothing which he did not show them, in his house or in all his dominion.[2]

3   Isaiah the prophet came to Hezekiah the king, and said to him: What did these men say to you, and from whence did they come to you? Hezekiah said: From the distant land of Babylon they came to me.

4   He said: What did they see in your house? Hezekiah said: They saw everything which is in my house; I left nothing in my house that I did not show them.

5   Isaiah said to Hezekiah: Hear the word of the mighty Lord.

6   See! days are coming when everything which is in your house will be carried away: the treasure of your fathers, (laid up) until today, to Babylon will go; nothing will be left for you, says the Lord.

7   And some of your sons who will have come forth from you, whom you will have sired: they will be led away (captive), they will be eunuchs in the palace of the king of Babylon.

8   Hezekiah said to Isaiah: The word of the Lord that you have spoken is good. There will be peace and justice[3] in my days.

---

[1] 'treasury': lit. 'house of his treasury'.

[2] 'dominion: lit. 'house of his rule'.

[3] 'justice' or 'truth'.

1 ܟܢّܐܘܗܝ ܟܢّܐܘܗܝ ܠܣܡܝ: ܐܦܿܕ ܠܟّܘܦܿܗ.

2 ܗܟܕ ܚܠܟܬܐ ܕܐܘܿܡܚܟܡ: ܘܿܐܡܿܗ ܟـܗ. ܣܗّـܝܠ ܘܐܒّܐܚܟܡ ܣܢّܠܐ: ܘܿܪܟܚ ܬܣܠـܗܝܠܐ. ܘܿܡܚܟܝܗ ܡܢ ܐܦ̈ܗ ܘܓܕܢܐ ܐܚܩܐ ܘܩܚܕܗ ܣܗܼ̈ܩܗ ܣܗܿܩܿܗܗ.

3 ܗܠܐ ܘܗܕܐ ܓܩܿܒܿܝܚܕܐ: ܟܢّܗ ܐܘܙܢܐ ܠܚܿܕܢܐ: ܗܐܙܘܿܪܗ ܟܿܓܿܩܿܕܟܐ ܡܓّܢܠܐ ܠܐܿܟܿܕܗّ.

4 ܩܿܚܕܗ ܢܬܢܠܐ ܢܐܓّܩܚܗ. ܘܩܚܕّﻫ. ܝّﻫﺩّﺍ ﺩﻭّﻗﺩّﺍ ﻨّﺍ̈ﻗﺤﺟّﻫ. ﻭﻨّﻫﺩّﺍ ﺧّﺩﻧﺍ ﺣّﻗﺣّﻨﺍ: ﻫّﺍ̈ﺍ̄ﺯﺍ ﺧّﺩﻗّﺍ ﻛّﺟّﻗّﺪﻛّﺍ.

5 ܘّ̈ܢܓّـܠܐ ܐّܩّܩّﻫ ﻭّ̈ﻗّﺩﻧﺍ. ﻭّﻨّﺴّﺭﺍّﻧّﻫ ﺍّﺟّﺴﺍّﺍ ﺜّﻼ ﺣّﻗّﺰ. ﺳّﻫﻝ ﻭّﻗّﺍﻫّﺩّﻫ ﻭّﻗّﺪﻧﺍ ﻗّ̈ﻼﻻ.

6 ܗّﻠﺍ ﻭّﺍﻗّﺩ ﻋّﺰّ. ﻭّﺍﻗّﺩ ﺳّﻨﺍ ﺍّﻗّﺯﺍ. ﺜّﻼ ﺣّﻗّﺰ ﺣّﻗّﺪﻧﺍ: ﻭّﻗّ̈ﻛّﻫ ﺍّﺍ̈ﻧّﺪّﺍ̄ﻩ ﺍّﺳّﻮ ﺧّﻮﺟّﻨﺍ ﻭّﺳّﻤّﻼ.

7 ܢّﺟّ ﺣّﻗّﺪﻧﺍ: ﻭّﺳّﻨّ̈ﻗّﺍ ﺧّﻮﺟّﻨﺍ. ﺳّﻫّﻴّﻝ ﻭّﻭّ̈ﺍﻫّﻨّﻫ ﻭّﺧّﺪﻧﺍ ﻧّﻤّﺨّﻴّ ﺧّﻫ. ﻭّ̈ﻭّﺟّﻨّﺍ ﻫّﻩ ﺣّﻗّﻤّﺪّﻧّﻫ ﻭّﺧّﻘّﻨّﺍ ﻫّﻨّﻧّﺍ.

8 ܢّﺟّﻪ ﺣّﻗّﺪﻧﺍ: ﻭّﺳّﻨّﻗّﺍ ﺧّﻮﺟّﻨﺍ. ﻭّﺳّﻤّﺨّﻛّّﻫ ﻭّﺍ̈ﻟّﺪّﻫّ ﻗّﻨّﻗّﺍ ﺧّﻨّﻠّﻗّﻤّ.

9 ﺧّﻼ ﯾّﻫّﺩّﺍ ﻭّﻫّﺩّﺍ ﻫّﺴّﻴ ﺧّﺟّﺴّﻴ ﺯّﻫّﻨّﻫ ﻣّﺨّﻔّﻜّﻧّﺍ̈ﺍ. ﺍّ̈ﻭّﺳّﻴ ﻣّﺨّﺟّﻴ ﺣّﺴّﻤّﻼ: ﺍّﻭّﻣّﺨّﻛّﻡ ﻣّﺨّﻔّﻜّﻧّﺍ̈ﺍ. ﺍّ̈ﻭّﺳّﻴ: ﻭّﻻ ﺍّ̣ﻭّﺳّﻜّ. ﺍّﺧّﻨّﻴ ﺣّﻘّﻮّ̈ﺯّﺍ ﻭّﺴّّ̈ﻫّﻭّﺍ: ﻫّﺍ ﺍّﻛّﺪّﻭّﻗّﻴ.

10 ﻫّﺍ ﻫّﺪّﻧّﺍ ﺍّﻛّﺪّﺍ̈ﺍ ﺍّﻛّﺍ̄ ﺟّﻘّﻮّﻗّﻨّﺍ: ﻭّﻭّ̈ﻗّﺪّﻩ ﺣّﺴّﻤّﻼ: ﻫّﺍ ﺍّﻴّ̈ﺰّﻩ ﺧّﻘّﻩ: ﻫّﺧّﻮّ̈ﺟّﻭّﻩ ﻋّﻮّ̈ﻗّﺪّﻭّﻗّ.

11 ﺍّﺳّﻮ ﻭّ̈ﺧّﻨّﺍ ﻭّﻭّ̈ﺧّﻨّﺍ ﺧّﻴّ̈ﺍﺯّﻭّﻩ: ﻭّﺧّﻮّ̈ﻗّﺪّﻩ ﻣّﺟّﻨّﻩ ﺍّﻣّﺰّﺍ. ﻭّﺟّﺴّﻨّﻩ ﻋّﻘّﻼ ﺣّّ̈ﺪّﻩّﻩ. ﻭّﻛّﺟّﻗّﺪّﻧّﻴ ﻣّﺧّﺰّﻭّﻗّﻫّﺍ.

Chapter 40

1   Comfort, comfort my people,[1] says your God.

2   Console[2] Jerusalem, cry to her, for she was filled with strength, delighted in sin; and she has received from the hand of the Lord double for all her sins.

3   A voice that cries[3] in the wilderness: Restore a way for the Lord, make straight in the plain the pathways for our God.

4   All the valleys will be filled completely, all the mountains and hills will be brought low, the rugged place will be cleared, the rough place will be a plain.

5   And the glory of the Lord will be revealed, all flesh will see it together, for the mouth of the Lord has spoken.

6   A voice which says:[4] Cry! He said: What shall I cry? All flesh is grass, all its beauty as the blossom of the field.

7   The grass has dried up, the blossom has withered away, for the breath of the Lord has blown on it. So is the grass of this people.

8   The grass dries up, the blossom withers away, but the word of our God stands firm forever.

9   Go up to the high mountains, Zion who brings news. Lift up your voice with strength, Jerusalem who brings news. Lift up (your voice), do not fear. Say to the cities of Judah 'Behold your God'.

10   Behold, the Lord God comes in strength, his arm with power. Behold, his reward is with him, his work is before him.

11   As the shepherd who feeds his flock, gathers the lambs with his arm, carries them in his lap, nourishes those who suckle.

---

[1] 'Comfort, comfort my people' or 'Comfort him comfort him my people'.

[2] 'Console': lit. 'fill the heart of'.

[3] 'that cries' or 'of one who cries'. Similarly v.6.

[4] 'which says' or 'of one who says'. See v.3.

12 ܝܒ ܡܢܘ ܐܟܝܠ ܡܝܐ ܒܫܘܥܠܗ: ܘܫܡܝܐ ܡܫܚ ܒܙܪܬܗ. ܘܐܟܝܠ ܒܪܘܙܗ ܥܦܪܗ
ܕܐܪܥܐ. ܘܬܩܠ ܛܘܪܐ ܒܡܬܩܠܐ: ܘܪܡܬܐ ܒܡܣܐܬܐ.

13 ܝܓ ܡܢܘ ܬܩܢ ܪܘܚܗ ܕܡܪܝܐ. ܐܘ ܡܢܘ ܗܘܐ ܠܗ ܡܠܟ ܡܠܟܐ.

14 ܝܕ ܥܡܢܘ ܐܬܡܠܟ: ܘܐܠܦܗ. ܘܚܘܝܗ ܐܘܪܚܐ ܕܕܝܢܐ. ܘܐܠܦܗ ܝܕܥܬܐ. ܘܐܘܪܚܐ
ܕܣܘܟܠܐ ܚܘܝܗ.

15 ܝܗ ܗܐ ܥܡܡܐ ܐܝܟ ܢܘܛܦܬܐ ܡܢ ܩܕܣܐ: ܘܐܝܟ ܢܛܠܐ ܕܡܣܐܬܐ. ܘܓܙܪܬܐ ܐܝܟ ܕܩܝܩܐ
ܢܬܚܫܒܢ.

16 ܝܘ ܘܠܒܢܢ ܠܐ ܣܦܩ ܠܗ ܠܡܘܩܕܐ. ܘܚܝܘܬܗ ܠܐ ܣܦܩܐ ܠܗ ܠܥܠܬܐ.

17 ܝܙ ܘܟܠܗܘܢ ܥܡܡܐ ܐܝܟ ܠܐ ܡܕܡ ܚܫܝܒܝܢ ܠܗ. ܠܐܒܕܢܐ ܘܠܣܪܝܩܘܬܐ ܚܫܝܒܝܢ
ܠܗ.

18 ܝܚ ܠܡܢ ܕܡܝܬܘܢܝܗܝ ܠܐܠܗܐ. ܘܠܐܝܢܐ ܕܡܘܬܐ ܕܡܝܬܘܢܝܗܝ.

19 ܝܛ ܨܠܡܐ ܗܘ ܕܥܒܕ ܢܓܪܐ. ܘܩܝܢܝܐ ܒܕܗܒܐ ܩܪܡܗ. ܘܫܫܠܬܐ ܕܣܐܡܐ ܡܒܕ ܠܗ.

20 ܟ ܩܝܣ ܗܘ ܡܣܟܢܐ ܕܠܐ ܡܬܒܠܥ. ܘܓܒܐ ܢܓܪܐ. ܘܒܚܟܡܬܗ ܢܩܒܥܗ.
ܘܡܩܝܡ ܨܠܡܐ ܕܠܐ ܢܙܘܥ.

21 ܟܐ ܠܐ ܝܕܥܬܘܢ: ܘܠܐ ܫܡܥܬܘܢ. ܘܠܐ ܐܬܐܡܪ ܠܟܘܢ ܡܢ ܪܫܝܬܐ. ܘܠܐ
ܐܣܬܟܠܬܘܢ: ܫܬܐܣܘܗ ܕܐܪܥܐ.

12 Who has measured the waters in the hollow of his hand, stretched out the heavens in his span,[1] measured in his palm the dust of the earth, weighed the mountains in a balance, and the high places with scales?[2]

13 Who has established the spirit of the Lord, O[3] who was his counselor?[4]

14 By whom was he counseled, (who) taught him, made him understand the path of justice, taught him knowledge, showed him the path of understanding?

15 See, the nations are like a drop from a cauldron, like the dipping of scales, the islands like dust that may be thrown away.

16 And Lebanon is not adequate for burning for him, its animals (are) not adequate[5] for sacrifice to him.

17 And all the nations are counted as nothing (in comparison) to him, as ruin, as wasteland[6] they are counted (in comparison) to him.

18 To whom have you likened God, to what likeness have you likened him?

19 It is an image which the carpenter made, the smith plated with gold, and he has set in it refined silver.

20 He has set apart wood that is not rotten, the carpenter has selected, has carved it skillfully,[7] an image is constructed that does not move.

21 Did you not hear, did you not know, was it not told to you from the beginning, did you not understand (from) the foundations of the earth?

---

[1] 'span': the distance between the tip of the thumb and the tip of the little finger.

[2] 'scales': lit. 'a scale'.

[3] 'O' or 'or'.

[4] 'counselor': lit. 'who was for him one who counseled counsel'.

[5] 'adequate: lit. 'counted, reckoned'.

[6] 'wasteland' or 'a sword'.

[7] 'carved it skillfully': lit. 'with his skill he has carved it'.

22 ܟܒ ܘܠܗܘ ܕܝܬܒ ܥܠ ܚܘܕܪܗ ܕܐܪܥܐ: ܘܥܡܘܪ̈ܝܗ ܐܝܟ ܩܡܨܐ. ܕܡܬܚ ܫܡܝܐ ܐܝܟ ܩܛܝܪܐ. ܘܡܬܚ ܐܢܘܢ ܐܝܟ ܡܫܟܢܐ ܠܡܥܡܪܐ.

23 ܟܓ ܕܝܗܒ ܫܠܝ̈ܛܢܐ ܠܐ ܡܕܡ: ܘܕ̈ܝܢܐ ܕܐܪܥܐ ܐܝܟ ܕܠܝܬ ܐܢܘܢ.

24 ܟܕ ܠܐ ܢܨܒܘܢ: ܘܠܐ ܢܙܪܥܘܢ. ܘܠܐ ܢܫܪܫܘܢ ܥܩܪܐ ܒܐܪܥܐ. ܢܦܘܚ ܒܗܘܢ ܘܢܝܒܫܘܢ. ܘܥܠܥܠܐ ܬܫܩܘܠܝܘܢ ܐܝܟ ܕܠܬܒܢܐ.

25 ܟܗ ܠܡܢ ܕܬܕܡܘܢܢܝ ܕܫܘܐ ܐܢܐ ܠܗ: ܐܡܪ ܩܕܝܫܐ.

26 ܟܘ ܐܪܝܡܘ ܥܝܢ̈ܝܟܘܢ ܠܡܪܘܡܐ. ܘܚܙܘ ܡܢܘ ܒܪܐ ܗܠܝܢ. ܕܡܦܩ ܒܡܢܝܢܐ ܚܝܠܘܬܗܘܢ: ܘܠܟܠܗܘܢ ܡܢܐ ܫܡܗ̈ܬܐ. ܒܣܘܓܐ ܕܐܘܚܕܢܗ: ܘܒܥܘܫܢܐ ܕܚܝܠܗ ܐܢܫ ܠܐ ܛܥܐ.

27 ܟܙ ܠܡܢܐ ܡܡܠܠ ܐܢܬ ܝܥܩܘܒ: ܘܐܡܪ ܐܢܬ ܐܝܣܪܐܝܠ. ܕܐܬܛܫܝܬ ܐܘܪܚܝ ܡܢ ܡܪܝܐ: ܘܡܥܒܪ ܕܝܢܝ ܡܢ ܐܠܗܝ.

28 ܟܚ ܠܐ ܝܕܥܬ: ܘܠܐ ܫܡܥܬ: ܕܐܠܗܐ ܠܥܠܡ ܡܪܝܐ ܗܘ. ܕܒܪܐ ܣܘܦ̈ܝܗ ܕܐܪܥܐ. ܠܐ ܡܬܛܪܦ: ܘܠܐ ܠܐܐ: ܘܠܝܬ ܥܘܩܒܐ ܠܣܘܟܠܗ.

29 ܟܛ ܝܗܒ ܚܝܠܐ ܠܡܛܪ̈ܦܐ. ܘܠܡܚܝ̈ܠܐ ܬܩܦܐ ܡܣܓܐ ܚܘܣܢܐ.

30 ܠ ܢܫܠܗܘܢ ܛܠܝ̈ܐ ܘܢܠܐܘܢ. ܘܓܒܪ̈ܐ ܡܬܬܩܠܘ ܢܬܬܩܠܘܢ.

31 ܠܐ ܘܐܝܠܝܢ ܕܡܣܒܪܝܢ ܠܡܪܝܐ: ܢܚܠܦܘܢ ܚܝܠܗܘܢ. ܘܢܦܪܚܘܢ ܓܦ̈ܐ ܐܝܟ ܕܢܫܪܐ. ܘܢܪܗܛܘܢ: ܘܠܐ ܢܠܐܘܢ. ܘܢܗܠܟܘܢ: ܘܠܐ ܢܫܠܗܘܢ.

22 And to him who sits upon the circle of the earth, its inhabitants like the locust, who stretches out the heavens like a vault, stretches them like a tent for a dwelling-place.

23 Who made rulers (to be) nothing at all, earthly[1] judges as if they are not.

24 They will not plant, they will not sow, they will not set root in the earth; he will blow upon them and they will dry up, the whirlwind will carry them away like stubble.

25 To whom have you likened me, that I am comparable to him, says the Holy One?

26 Lift up your eyes to the height(s), see who created these, their hosts which he brings forth by number; he called all of them (by their) names, in the greatness of his glory and in the strength of his host not one is forgotten.

27 Why do you speak, Jacob, and you say, Israel, that my ways are hidden from the Lord, my judgment departed from my God?

28 Did you not know, did you not hear? that God is Lord forever, who created the ends of the earth, who does not tire, who is indefatigable, whose understanding is beyond comprehension.[2]

29 He gives might to the tired, greater strength[3] to those suffering pain.

30 Young men will grow tired and weary, youths will surely stumble.

31 Those who hope in the Lord will renew their strength, they will grow wings like doves, they will run and they will not weary, will walk and not be tired.

---

[1] 'earthly': lit. 'of the earth'.

[2] 'whose understanding is beyond comprehension': lit. 'there is no searching out of his understanding'.

[3] 'greater strength': lit. 'he increases strength'.

ܩܦܠܐܘܢ: ܡܐ.

1 ܐ ܫܬܘܩܘ ܠܝ ܓܙܪ̈ܬܐ. ܘܥܡ̈ܡܐ ܢܚܠܦܘܢ ܚܝܠܐ. ܢܬܩܪܒܘܢ: ܘܗܝܕܝܢ ܢܡܠܠܘܢ ܘܐܟܚܕܐ ܠܕܝܢܐ ܢܬܩܪܒܘܢ.

2 ܒ ܡܢܘ ܐܥܝܪ ܙܕܝܩܘܬܐ ܡܢ ܡܕܢܚܐ: ܘܩܪܝܗ ܠܪܓܠܗ. ܢܫܠܡܝܘܗܝ ܩܕܡܘܗܝ ܥܡ̈ܡܐ. ܘܡܠܟ̈ܐ ܢܫܥܒܕ. ܢܬܠ ܐܝܟ ܥܦܪܐ ܣܝܦ̈ܗ: ܘܐܝܟ ܩܫܐ ܕܢܫܒܐ ܩܫܬܗ.

3 ܓ ܢܪܕܘܦ ܐܢܘܢ: ܘܢܥܒܪ. ܒܫܠܡܐ. ܘܐܘܪܚܐ ܒܪ̈ܓܠܘܗܝ ܠܐ ܢܗܠܟ.

4 ܕ ܘܡܢܘ ܥܒܕ ܘܣܥܪ ܡܢ ܕܩܪܐ ܠܕܪ̈ܐ ܡܢ ܪܫܝܬܐ. ܐܢܐ ܐܢܐ ܡܪܝܐ ܩܕܡܝܐ ܘܐܚܪܝܐ: ܐܢܐ ܐܢܐ.

5 ܗ ܚܙܝ̈ ܓܙܪ̈ܬܐ. ܘܕܚܠܝ ܣܘ̈ܦܝܗ ܕܐܪܥܐ. ܕܚܠܝ ܘܩܪܒܝ ܘܐܬܝ.

6 ܘ ܓܒܪ ܠܚܒܪܗ ܡܥܕܪ. ܘܠܐܚܘܗܝ ܐܡܪ ܐܬܚܝܠ.

7 ܙ ܘܡܠܒܒ ܢܓܪܐ ܠܩܝܢܝܐ. ܕܐܪܝܡ ܒܡܩܘܒܬܐ: ܘܡܚܐ. ܘܐܡܪ ܥܠ ܕܒܩܐ ܕܫܦܝܪ ܗܘ. ܘܩܒܥܗ ܠܗ ܒܡܣܡܪ̈ܐ: ܕܠܐ ܢܬܬܙܝܥ.

ܪܫ ܩ

8 ܚ ܐܢ̱ܬ ܐܝܣܪܐܝܠ ܥܒܕܝ: ܝܥܩܘܒ ܕܓܒܝܬܟ: ܙܪܥܗ ܕܐܒܪܗܡ ܪܚܡܝ ܕܪܚܡܬܟ.

9 ܛ ܡܢ ܣܘ̈ܦܝܗ ܕܐܪܥܐ: ܘܡܢ ܙܘ̈ܝܬܗ ܩܪܝܬܟ. ܘܐܡܪܬ ܠܟ ܥܒܕܝ ܐܢ̱ܬ. ܓܒܝܬܟ ܘܠܐ ܐܣܠܝܬܟ.

10 ܝ ܠܐ ܬܕܚܠ ܡܛܠ ܕܥܡܟ ܐܢܐ. ܘܠܐ ܬܬܪܗܒ ܡܛܠ ܕܐܢܐ ܐܠܗܟ. ܚܝܠܬܟ: ܐܦ ܥܕܪܬܟ. ܐܦ ܣܡܟܬܟ ܒܝܡܝܢܝ ܙܕܝܩܬܐ.

11 ܝܐ ܢܒܗܬܘܢ ܘܢܚܦܪܘܢ ܐܝܠܝܢ ܕܡܬܚܪܝܢ ܠܟ: ܢܗܘܘܢ ܐܝܟ ܠܐ ܡܕܡ. ܘܢܐܒܕܘܢ ܒܥܠܕܒ̈ܒܐ ܕܕܝܢܝܢ ܥܡܟ.

Chapter 41

1 Be silent, islands, let the peoples renew might; let them draw near, then let them speak, let them draw near together to judgment.

2 Who has stirred up righteousness from the east, and called it to his foot? Nations will be delivered up before him, kings will be confounded, he will give (them) like dust to his sword, like the falling stubble (to) his bow.

3 He will pursue them, and he will make peace, he will not enter the way on foot.

4 Who prepared and effected, who called the generations from the beginning? I am the Lord, the first and the last, I am (he).

5 The islands saw me, the ends of the earth feared; they feared, they drew near, they came.

6 Each helps his companion, to his brother he says: Be strong.

7 The carpenter encouraged the smith, who strikes it with a mallet, labors, and says of the join that it is good; they fix it with nails, that it may not be moved.

XX

8 Now, Israel my servant, Jacob, you whom I have chosen,[1] the seed of Abraham my friend, you whom I have strengthened.[2]

9 From the ends of the earth, from its watchtowers I have called you. I said to you: You are my servant, I have chosen you, I will not reject you.

10 Do not fear, for I am with you, do not be troubled, for I am your God. I will strengthen you, I will truly help you, truly support you with my righteous right hand.

11 They will be ashamed, they will blush, those who look askance at you; they will be brought to naught,[3] they will perish, the men who contend with you.

---

[1] 'you whom I have chosen': lit. 'whom I have chosen you'.

[2] 'you whom I have strengthened': lit. 'whom I have strengthened you'.

[3] 'brought to naught': lit. 'be as nothing'.

12 ܝܒ ܬܒܥܐ ܐܢܘܢ: ܘܠܐ ܬܫܟܚ ܐܢܘܢ ܠܓܒܪ̈ܐ ܕܢܨܝܢ ܥܡܟ. ܢܗܘܘܢ ܐܝܟ ܕܠܐ
ܐܝܬܝܗܘܢ: ܓܒܪ̈ܐ ܕܡܬܟܬܫܝܢ ܥܡܟ.

13 ܝܓ ܡܛܠ ܕܐܢܐ ܐܢܐ ܡܪܝܐ ܐܠܗܟ: ܡܐܚܕܢܐ ܕܝܡܝܢܟ: ܐܡܪܢܐ ܠܟ ܠܐ ܬܕܚܠ. ܐܢܐ
ܐܢܐ ܥܕܘܪܟ.

14 ܝܕ ܠܐ ܬܕܚܠܝܢ ܬܘܠܥܬܗ ܕܝܥܩܘܒ: ܘܡܝܬܘܗ ܕܐܝܣܪܝܠ. ܐܢܐ ܐܢܐ ܥܕܘܪܟܝ: ܐܡܪ
ܡܪܝܐ. ܘܦܪܘܩܟܝ ܩܕܝܫܐ ܕܐܝܣܪܝܠ.

15 ܝܗ ܗܐ ܥܒܕܬܟ ܐܝܟ ܓܪܓܪܐ ܚܪܝܦܐ: ܕܕܝܫ ܘܡܕܩ. ܬܕܘܫ ܛܘܪ̈ܐ: ܘܬܕܩ.
ܘܪ̈ܡܬܐ ܬܥܒܕ ܐܝܟ ܥܘܪܐ.

16 ܝܘ ܬܕܪܐ ܐܢܘܢ. ܘܪܘܚܐ ܬܫܩܘܠܝܘܢ. ܘܥܠܥܠܐ ܬܒܕܪ ܐܢܘܢ. ܘܐܢܬ ܬܕܘܨ ܒܡܪܝܐ.
ܘܒܩܕܝܫܐ ܕܐܝܣܪܝܠ ܬܫܬܒܚ.

17 ܝܙ ܡܣܟܢ̈ܐ ܘܒܨܝܪ̈ܐ ܒܥܝܢ ܡܝ̈ܐ ܘܠܝܬ. ܘܠܫܢܗܘܢ ܒܨܗܝܐ ܝܒܫ. ܐܢܐ ܡܪܝܐ ܐܥܢܐ
ܐܢܘܢ. ܐܠܗܗ ܕܐܝܣܪܝܠ: ܘܠܐ ܐܫܒܘܩ ܐܢܘܢ.

18 ܝܚ ܐܦܬܚ ܢܗܪ̈ܘܬܐ ܒܛܘܪ̈ܐ: ܘܒܓܘ ܦܩܥܬܐ ܡܒܘ̈ܥܐ: ܐܥܒܕ ܡܕܒܪܐ ܠܐܓܡܐ
ܕܡܝ̈ܐ: ܘܐܪܥܐ ܨܗܝܬܐ ܠܡܒܘ̈ܥܐ ܕܡܝ̈ܐ.

19 ܝܛ ܐܬܠ ܒܡܕܒܪܐ ܐܪ̈ܙܐ ܘܐܫܟܪ̈ܐ: ܘܐܣܐ ܘܩܝܣܐ ܕܡܫܚܐ. ܐܣܝܡ ܒܥܪܒܬܐ
ܒܪ̈ܘܬܐ ܗܕܣ̈ܐ ܐܟܚܕܐ.

20 ܟ ܕܢܚܙܘܢ ܘܢܕܥܘܢ ܘܢܬܒܝܢܘܢ. ܘܢܣܬܟܠܘܢ ܐܟܚܕܐ: ܕܐܝܕܗ ܕܡܪܝܐ ܥܒܕܬ ܗܕܐ:
ܘܩܕܝܫܐ ܕܐܝܣܪܝܠ ܒܪܗ.

21 ܟܐ ܩܪܒܘ ܕܝܢܟܘܢ: ܐܡܪ ܡܪܝܐ. ܩܪܒܘ ܬܘܟܠܢܟܘܢ ܐܡܪ ܡܠܟܗ ܕܝܥܩܘܒ.

12   You will seek them, but you will not find them, the men who contend with you; they will be as if they had never been,[1] the men who fight with you.

13   For I am the Lord your God, who strengthens your right hand. I have said to you: Do not fear; I am your helper.

14   Do not fear, worm of Jacob, weevil of Israel. I am your helper, says the Lord, and your savior, the Holy One of Israel.

15   See! I have made you like a new threshing instrument that shatters, breaks into pieces: you will trample mountains, break (them) into pieces, you will make the high places as chaff.

16   You will winnow them, the wind will lift them up, the storm wind will scatter them: but you will exult in the Lord, you will glory in the Holy One of Israel.

17   The poor and the needy seek water, but there is none; their tongues are parched with thirst. I, the Lord, will answer them, the God of Israel; I will not forsake them.

18   I will open rivers in the mountains, springs in the midst of the plains, I will turn the wilderness into pools of water, the dry land into springs of water.

19   I will put in the wilderness cedars and acacias, myrtle and olive trees,[2] I will set in the plain beautiful cypresses (all) together.

20   So that they may see and know and consider,[3] and understand together, that the hand of the Lord did this, and the Holy One of Israel created it.

21   Bring near your contentions, says the Lord; bring near your arguments,[4] says the king of Jacob.

---

[1] 'as if they had never been': lit. 'as those who are not'.

[2] 'olive trees': lit. 'olive-wood'.

[3] 'and know and consider': lit. 'and they may know and they may consider'.

[4] 'arguments' or 'reflections, opinions'.

22   Let them come near, let them declare those things that are to come, the former things, what they (are); declare (them) to me so that we may set them in our heart(s), that we may know their latter end; or make us understand[1] the things which are coming.

23   Declare to me the signs that are to come, that we may know that you are gods, that you do both good and evil;[2] we will relate (it), we will see (it) together.

24   See! you, you are nothing, your works are in vain,[3] your election is an abomination.

25   I have awoken (one) from the north, who will come from the rising of the sun, and will call upon my name; rulers will come and be trodden down, like the clay that the potter treads down.

26   Who is it who will declare from the beginning, that we may know, we may say: (He is) righteous? There is none who declares, not even (one) to make heard, nor hears your words.

27   These are the first fruits of Zion, and I will give a messenger[4] to Jerusalem.

28   I looked, but there was no-one who reasons concerning these, so that I may question them, and they may give me an answer.

29   See! They are all nothing, their works are useless, their works are an empty wind.

---

[1] 'understand' or 'hear'.

[2] 'that you do both good and evil': lit. 'both those who do good are you and those who do evil are you'.

[3] 'in vain': lit. 'of naught'.

[4] 'messenger': usually a bearer of good rather than bad tidings.

ܩܦܠܐܘܢ: ܡܒ.

1 ܐ ܗܐ ܥܒܕܝ ܣܡܟܬܗ. ܘܓܒܝܝ ܕܨܒܬ ܢܦܫܝ. ܘܝܗܒܬ ܪܘܚܝ ܥܠܘܗܝ: ܕܢܦܩ ܕܝܢܐ ܠܥܡ̈ܡܐ.

2 ܒ ܠܐ ܢܩܥܐ: ܘܠܐ ܢܪܝܡ. ܘܠܐ ܢܫܡܥ ܩܠܗ ܒܫܘܩܐ.

3 ܓ ܩܢܝܐ ܪܥܝܥܐ ܠܐ ܢܬܒܪ. ܘܫܪܓܐ ܕܡܛܦܛܦ ܠܐ ܢܕܥܟ. ܒܩܘܫܬܐ ܢܦܩ ܕܝܢܐ.

4 ܕ ܠܐ ܢܕܥܟ ܘܠܐ ܢܬܡܚܠ: ܥܕܡܐ ܕܢܣܝܡ ܕܝܢܐ ܒܐܪܥܐ. ܘܠܢܡܘܣܗ ܓܙܪ̈ܬܐ ܢܣܟ̈ܝܢ.

5 ܗ ܗܟܢܐ ܐܡܪ ܡܪܝܐ ܐܠܗܐ: ܕܒܪܐ ܫܡܝܐ ܘܡܬܚ ܐܢܘܢ. ܘܩܒܥ ܐܪܥܐ ܘܥܒ̈ܕܐ ܕܒܗ̇. ܘܝܗܒ ܢܫܡܬܐ ܠܥܡܐ ܕܥܠܝܗ̇: ܘܪܘܚܐ ܠܕܡܗܠܟܝܢ ܒܗ̇.

6 ܘ ܐܢܐ ܡܪܝܐ ܩܪܝܬܟ ܒܙܕܝܩܘܬܐ: ܘܐܚܕܬ ܒܐܝܕܟ ܘܢܛܪܬܟ. ܘܝܗܒܬܟ ܩܝܡܐ ܠܥܡܐ: ܘܢܘܗܪܐ ܠܥܡ̈ܡܐ.

7 ܙ ܕܬܦܬܚ ܥܝ̈ܢܐ ܕܣܡ̈ܝܐ: ܘܬܦܩ ܠܐܣܝ̈ܪܐ ܡܢ ܒܝܬ ܚܒܘܫܝܐ: ܘܡܢ ܒܝܬ ܐܣܝ̈ܪܐ ܠܝ̈ܬܒܝ ܚܫܘܟܐ.

8 ܚ ܐܢܐ ܐܢܐ ܡܪܝܐ: ܘܗܢܘ ܫܡܝ. ܘܐܝܩܪܝ ܠܐܚܪܢܐ ܠܐ ܐܬܠ: ܘܐܦܠܐ ܬܫܒܘܚܬܝ ܠܓܠܝ̈ܦܐ.

9 ܛ ܩܕ̈ܡܝܬܐ ܐܢܐ ܡܚܘܝܬ. ܘܚܕ̈ܬܬܐ ܗܐ ܐܬ̈ܝܢ. ܘܥܕܠܐ ܢܕܢܚܢ: ܐܫܡܥܬ ܐܢܝܢ ܠܟܘܢ.

ܬܫܒܘܚܬܐ ܕܐܫܥܝܐ.

10 ܝ ܫܒܚܘ ܠܡܪܝܐ ܬܫܒܘܚܬܐ ܚܕܬܐ. ܬܫܒܘܚܬܗ ܡܢ ܣܘܦܝܗ̇ ܕܐܪܥܐ. ܢܚ̈ܬܝ ܝܡܐ ܘܡܠܝܘܬܗ: ܓܙܪ̈ܬܐ ܘܥܡܘܪ̈ܝܗܝܢ.

Chapter 42

1   Behold my servant, (whom) I have supported: in my chosen one my soul[1] has delighted. I have laid on him my spirit, that he may bring forth justice to the nations.

2   He will not cry out, he will not cry aloud, he will not make his voice heard in the street.[2]

3   The bruised reed he will not break, the flickering lamp he will not extinguish; in truth he will bring forth justice.

4   He will not be extinguished, he will not flicker, until he has set up justice on earth: the islands will await his law.

5   Thus says the Lord God, who created the heavens and stretched them out, who spread out the earth and all that is in it, gave breath to the people who are upon it, spirit to those who walk on it.

6   I, the Lord, called to you in righteousness, I took hold of your hand and strengthened you, I gave you as a covenant to the people, as a light to the nations.

7   So that you will open the eyes of the blind, bring forth the captives from the prison house,[3] and from the prison[4] those who dwell in darkness.

8   I am the Lord, and this is my name; and I will not give my glory to another, nor my praise to graven images.

9   The new things I make known; the former things - See! They have come. Before they appear I proclaim them to you.

The Praise of Isaiah

10   Praise the Lord with new praise, his praise from the ends of the earth, those who go down to the sea in its fullness, the islands and those who dwell in them.

---

[1] 'my soul' or 'I'.

[2] 'street' or 'market'.

[3] 'prison house': lit. 'house of confinement'.

[4] 'prison': lit. 'house of the bound'.

11 Let the wilderness and its cities rejoice, let Kedar become meadows, let the dwellers in the crags sing praises, let them cry out from the highest mountain.[1]

12 May they give praise to the Lord, may they proclaim his praises in the islands.

13 The Lord will go forth as a mighty man, as a warrior he will arouse zeal; he will cry out, he will conduct himself manfully, he will kill his enemies.

14 I have been silent; I will be silent forever; I have endured like a woman in labor. I will astonish, I will confound, at once.

15 I will lay waste the mountains and high hills, I will dry up all their strength, I will turn the rivers into islands, I will dry up the pools.

16 I will lead the blind in a way that they do not know; in pathways that they have not known, I will make them walk; I will turn darkness before them into light, I will make the rugged place smooth: these things I have done for them, I have not forsaken them.

17 They will turn back, they will be ashamed, in disgrace, those who put their trust in graven images, who say to molten images: You are our gods.

18 Deaf: listen! blind: understand and see!

19 Who is blind but my servant, deaf like my messenger whom I shall send? Who is blind like the ruler, blind like the servant of the Lord?

20 I have seen much, but you do not keep watch; I have opened ears, but you do not listen.

21 The Lord was pleased, in[2] his righteousness, that he would extol the law and praise it.

---

[1] 'highest mountain': lit. 'head of the mountains'.

[2] 'in': lit. 'because of'.

206

22 This is a people despoiled, downtrodden, they are traps for all their youths, and hidden in prisons; they were prey, with none to save,[1] trodden under foot,[2] with none to restore (them).[3]

23 Who is there among you who will hear this, who will give ear, hear (what comes) next?[4]

24 Who gives Jacob to be trodden under foot,[5] Israel for plundering? Was it not the Lord, because we sinned against him, we did not wish to walk in his ways, we did not obey his law.

25 He poured out upon them the heat of his wrath; with the strength of war he set fire to them from their surroundings, but they did not understand, the fire burnt them, but they did not take it to heart.[6]

---

[1] 'with none to save': lit. 'and there is no-one who saves'.

[2] 'trodden under foot': lit. 'for trampling under foot'.

[3] 'with none to restore (them)': lit. 'and there is no-one who restores'.

[4] '(what comes) next': lit. 'the next' or 'another'.

[5] 'trodden under foot': lit. 'for trampling under foot'.

[6] 'take it to heart': lit. 'bring (it) upon their heart'.

ܩܦܠܐܘܢ: ܡܓ.

ܩܕ ܥܒ

1 ܐ ܗܫܐ ܗܟܢܐ ܐܡܪ ܡܪܝܐ: ܕܒܪܟ ܝܥܩܘܒ ܘܓܒܠܟ ܐܝܣܪܐܝܠ. ܠܐ ܬܕܚܠ ܕܦܪܩܬܟ: ܘܩܪܝܬܟ ܒܫܡܟ: ܕܝܠܝ ܐܢܬ.

2 ܒ ܐܢ ܬܥܒܪ ܒܡܝܐ: ܥܡܟ ܐܢܐ. ܘܢܗܪܘܬܐ ܠܐ ܢܫܛܦܘܢܟ. ܐܢ ܬܗܠܟ. ܒܓܘ ܢܘܪܐ ܠܐ ܬܬܟܘܐ: ܘܫܠܗܒܝܬܐ ܠܐ ܬܘܩܕܟ.

3 ܓ ܡܛܠ ܕܐܢܐ ܐܢܐ ܡܪܝܐ ܐܠܗܟ: ܩܕܝܫܐ ܕܐܝܣܪܐܝܠ ܦܪܘܩܟ. ܝܗܒܬ ܠܡܨܪܝܢ ܚܠܦܝܟ: ܘܠܟܘܫ ܘܠܣܒܐ ܚܠܦܝܟ.

4 ܕ ܡܢ ܕܝܩܪܬ ܐܝܬ ܒܥܝܢܝ ܐܫܬܒܚܬ: ܘܐܢܐ ܪܚܡܬܟ ܝܗܒܬ ܐܢܫܐ ܚܠܦܝܟ: ܘܐܡܘܬܐ ܚܠܦ ܢܦܫܟ.

5 ܗ ܠܐ ܬܕܚܠ ܡܛܠ ܕܥܡܟ ܐܢܐ. ܡܢ ܡܕܢܚܐ ܐܝܬܐ ܙܪܥܟ. ܘܡܢ ܡܥܪܒܐ ܐܟܢܫܟ.

6 ܘ ܐܡܪ ܠܓܪܒܝܐ ܕܗܒܝ. ܘܠܬܝܡܢܐ ܕܠܐ ܬܟܠܐ. ܐܝܬܐ ܒܢܝ ܡܢ ܪܘܚܩܐ: ܘܒܢܬܝ ܡܢ ܣܘܦܝܗ̇ ܕܐܪܥܐ.

7 ܙ ܟܠ ܕܫܡܐ ܒܫܡܝ: ܠܐܝܩܪܝ ܒܪܝܬܗ ܘܓܒܠܬܗ ܘܥܒܕܬܗ.

8 ܚ ܐܦܩ ܥܡܐ ܥܘܝܪܐ: ܕܥܝܢܐ ܐܝܬ ܠܗܘܢ: ܘܐܕܢܐ ܐܝܬ ܠܗܘܢ ܘܚܪܫܝܢ.

9 ܛ ܟܠܗܘܢ ܥܡܡܐ ܢܬܟܢܫܘܢ ܐܟܚܕܐ. ܘܢܬܟܢܫܘܢ ܐܡܘܬܐ. ܡܢܘ ܐܝܬ ܒܟܘܢ ܕܢܚܘܐ ܗܕܐ: ܘܩܕܡܝܬܐ ܢܫܡܥܢ. ܢܝܬܘܢ ܣܗܕܝܗܘܢ ܘܢܙܕܕܩܘܢ: ܘܢܫܡܥܘܢ ܘܢܐܡܪܘܢ.

10 ܝ ܣܗܕܘܬܐ ܐܝܬܝܟܘܢ ܣܗܕܝ: ܐܡܪ ܡܪܝܐ: ܘܥܒܕܝ ܕܓܒܝܬ. ܘܬܕܥܘܢ ܘܬܗܝܡܢܘܢ ܒܝ. ܘܬܣܬܟܠܘܢ ܕܐܢܐ ܗܘ. ܘܩܕܡܝ ܠܐ ܐܬܒܪܝ ܐܠܗܐ. ܘܒܬܪܝ ܠܐ ܢܗܘܐ.

11 ܝܐ ܐܢܐ ܐܢܐ ܡܪܝܐ: ܘܠܝܬ ܦܪܘܩ ܠܒܪ ܡܢܝ.

Chapter 43

XXI

1 Now, thus says the Lord, who created you, Jacob, who formed you, Israel: Do not fear, for I have redeemed you, I have called you by your name, for you are mine.

2 If you should pass through the sea, I am with you; the rivers will not overwhelm you; if you should walk on fire you will not be scorched: the flame will not consume you.

3 For I am the Lord your God, the Holy One of Israel, your savior; I have given Egypt in your place, Kush and Sheba instead of you.[1]

4 Because you are honorable in my eyes you have been glorified, I have loved you; I have given a man in your place, peoples in place of your soul.

5 Do not fear, for I am with you; from the east I will bring your seed, from the west I will gather you.

6 Say to the north: Give; and to the south: Do not withhold; bring my sons from far away, my daughters from the ends of the earth.

7 All who call upon my name: to honor me I created him, I formed him, I made him.

8 Bring out the blind people who have eyes, (the people) who have ears yet are deaf.

9 All peoples will be gathered together, the nations will be gathered. Who is there among you will declare this, will make the former things heard? They will bring their witnesses and will be declared righteous, they will hear, they will speak.

10 In truth you are my witnesses, says the Lord, my servants whom I have chosen. You will know, you will believe in me, you will understand that I am he. Before me no God was created, after me there will be none.

11 I am the Lord; there is none other than[2] me.

---

[1] 'instead of you': lit. 'on account of your face'.

[2] 'other than': lit. 'again except for'.

12 ܝܒ ܐܢܐ ܚܘܝܬ ܘܦܪܩܬ ܘܐܫܡܥܬ: ܘܠܝܬ ܒܟܘܢ ܢܘܟܪܝܐ: ܘܐܢܬܘܢ ܣܗܕܝ: ܐܡܪ ܡܪܝܐ. ܘܐܢܐ ܐܠܗܐ.

13 ܝܓ ܘܐܦ ܡܢ ܝܘܡܐ ܩܕܡܝܐ ܐܢܐ ܐܢܐ: ܘܠܝܬ ܕܡܫܬܘܙܒ ܡܢ ܐܝܕܝ. ܘܡܥܒܕ ܕܥܒܕ ܐܢܐ: ܡܢܘ ܡܗܦܟ.

14 ܝܕ ܗܟܢܐ ܐܡܪ ܡܪܝܐ ܦܪܘܩܟܘܢ ܩܕܝܫܐ ܕܐܝܣܪܝܠ. ܡܛܠܬܟܘܢ ܫܕܪܬ ܠܒܒܠ. ܘܐܚܬܬ ܠܟܠܗܘܢ ܥܪܘܩܐ: ܘܟܠܕܝܐ ܕܒܣܦܝܢܐ ܡܫܬܒܚܝܢ.

15 ܝܗ ܐܢܐ ܐܢܐ ܡܪܝܐ ܩܕܝܫܟܘܢ: ܕܒܪܝܬ ܠܐܝܣܪܝܠ ܡܠܟܟܘܢ.

16 ܝܘ ܗܟܢܐ ܐܡܪ ܡܪܝܐ: ܕܝܗܒ ܐܘܪܚܐ ܒܝܡܐ: ܘܫܒܝܠܐ ܒܡܝܐ ܥܫܝܢܐ.

17 ܝܙ ܕܐܦܩ ܡܪܟܒܬܐ ܘܪܟܫܐ ܘܚܝܠܐ ܥܫܝܢܐ. ܘܐܟܚܕܐ ܢܫܟܒܘܢ ܘܠܐ ܢܩܘܡܘܢ. ܘܢܕܥܟܘܢ ܐܝܟ ܫܪܓܐ ܕܡܬܛܦܐ.

18 ܝܚ ܠܐ ܬܬܕܟܪܘܢ ܩܕܡܝܬܐ: ܘܥܬܝܩܬܐ ܠܐ ܬܣܬܟܠܘܢ.

19 ܝܛ ܗܐ ܥܒܕ ܐܢܐ ܚܕܬܐ. ܘܗܫܐ ܬܕܢܚ ܘܬܕܥܘܢܗ. ܘܐܥܒܕ ܐܘܪܚܐ ܒܡܕܒܪܐ: ܘܢܗܪܘܬܐ ܒܐܫܝܡܘܢ.

20 ܟ ܢܫܒܚܢܢܝ ܚܝܘܬܐ ܕܕܒܪܐ: ܬܢܝܢܐ ܘܒܢܬ ܝܥܢܐ: ܡܛܠ ܕܝܗܒܬ ܡܝܐ ܒܡܕܒܪܐ: ܘܢܗܪܘܬܐ ܒܐܫܝܡܘܢ: ܕܢܫܩܐ ܠܥܡܝ ܓܒܝܐ.

21 ܟܐ ܥܡܐ ܗܢܐ ܕܓܒܝܬ ܠܝ: ܢܫܒܚܘܢ.

22 ܟܒ ܠܐ ܗܘܐ ܠܝ ܩܪܝܬ ܝܥܩܘܒ: ܕܩܪܒܬ ܐܝܣܪܝܠ.

23 ܟܓ ܠܐ ܐܝܬܝܬ ܠܝ ܐܡܪܐ ܕܥܠܬܟ. ܘܒܕܒܚܝܟ ܠܐ ܐܝܩܪܬܢܝ. ܠܐ ܫܥܒܕܬܟ ܒܩܘܪܒܢܐ: ܘܠܐ ܐܠܐܝܬܟ ܒܠܒܘܢܬܐ.

24 ܟܕ ܠܐ ܙܒܢܬ ܠܝ ܒܟܣܦܐ ܩܢܝܐ ܕܒܣܡܐ. ܘܒܬܪܒܐ ܕܕܒܚܝܟ ܠܐ ܐܪܘܝܬܢܝ. ܐܠܐ ܫܥܒܕܬܢܝ ܒܚܛܗܝܟ: ܘܒܥܘܠܟ ܐܠܐܝܬܢܝ.

12   I have declared, I have saved, I have made heard; there is no stranger among you, you are my witnesses, says the Lord: I am God.

13   Even from the first day I am, there is none who delivers from my hands; anything that I make, who will overthrow?

14   Thus says, the Lord your savior, the Holy One of Israel: For your sake I have sent to Babylon, I have summoned all the fugitives; and to the Chaldeans who glory in ships.

15   I am the Lord, your Holy One, for I, your king, created Israel.[1]

16   Thus says the Lord, who set a way through the sea, a pathway through many waters.

17   Who brings forth chariots and horses and a mighty host; together they will lie down and not rise up, they will be extinguished like a flickering lamp.

18   Do not call to mind the former things; that which was first, do not consider[2].

19   See! I am making (something) new: now it will spring up, you will know it, I will make a way in the wilderness,[3] rivers in the wasteland.

20   The beast(s) of the field will praise me, the jackals and the ostriches, for I have given water in the wilderness, rivers in the wasteland, so that my chosen people may drink.

21   This people that I chose for myself: they will drink.

22   It was not me you called, Jacob, you whom I called 'Israel'.

23   You have not brought me the lambs of your burnt offerings, you have not honored me with your sacrifices; I have not enslaved you with offerings, nor wearied you with frankincense.

24   You did not buy with silver, for me, aromatic cane; you did not satiate me with the fat of your sacrifices: but you subjected me to your sins, you wearied me with your iniquity.

---

[1] 'I, your king, created Israel': lit. 'for I created Israel your king'.

[2] 'Do not call to mind … do not consider' or 'You will not remember … you will not understand'.

[3] 'wasteland' or 'desert'.

25 ܟܗ ܐܢܐ ܐܢܐ ܕܡܚܐ ܐܢܐ ܥܘܠܟܝ ܡܛܠܬܝ. ܘܚܛܗܝܟܝ ܠܐ ܐܬܕܟܪ.

26 ܟܘ ܐܬܕܟܪܢܝ: ܢܬܕܝܢ ܐܟܚܕܐ. ܐܫܬܥܐ ܕܬܙܕܕܩ.

27 ܟܙ ܐܒܘܟ ܩܕܡܝܐ ܚܛܐ. ܡܦܫܩܢܝܟ ܐܥܠܘ ܒܝ.

28 ܟܚ ܛܡܐܘ ܪܘܪܒܢܝ ܩܘܕܫܐ. ܘܐܫܠܡ ܠܝܥܩܘܒ ܠܚܪܡܐ: ܘܠܐܝܣܪܝܠ
ܠܚܣܕܐ.

25   I am he who blots out your iniquity, for my sake; I will not call to mind your sins.

26   Remember me; let us contend together: I have said that you will be justified.

27   Your first father sinned; your rulers have wronged me.

28   Your noblemen have defiled the sanctuary; I have given Jacob for a curse, Israel for a reproach.

ܩܦܠܐܘܢ: ܡܕ.

1 ܐ ܫܡܥ ܫܡܥܢܝ ܝܥܩܘܒ ܥܒܕܝ: ܘܐܝܣܪܐܝܠ ܕܓܒܝܬ.

2 ܒ ܗܟܢܐ ܐܡܪ ܡܪܝܐ: ܕܥܒܕܟ ܘܓܒܠܟ ܒܟܪܣܐ ܘܡܥܕܪܟ. ܠܐ ܬܕܚܠ ܥܒܕܝ ܝܥܩܘܒ: ܘܐܝܣܪܐܝܠ ܕܓܒܝܬ.

3 ܓ ܡܛܠ ܕܐܬܠ ܡܝܐ ܠܐܪܥܐ ܨܗܝܐ: ܘܢܗܪܐ ܒܝܒܫܐ. ܐܫܕ ܪܘܚܝ ܥܠ ܙܪܥܟ: ܘܒܘܪܟܬܝ ܥܠ ܒܢܝܟ.

4 ܕ ܘܢܥܒܘܢ ܡܢ ܒܝܢܝ ܥܣܒܐ: ܐܝܟ ܥܪܒܐ ܕܥܠ ܝܒܠܐ ܕܡܝܐ.

5 ܗ ܗܢܐ ܢܐܡܪ ܕܡܪܝܐ ܐܢܐ: ܘܗܢܐ ܢܩܪܐ ܒܫܡܗ ܕܝܥܩܘܒ. ܘܗܢܐ ܢܟܬܘܒ ܐܝܕܗ ܠܡܪܝܐ. ܘܒܫܡ ܐܝܣܪܐܝܠ ܢܬܟܢܐ.

6 ܘ ܗܟܢܐ ܐܡܪ ܡܪܝܐ ܡܠܟܗ ܕܐܝܣܪܐܝܠ ܘܦܪܘܩܗ: ܡܪܝܐ ܚܝܠܬܢܐ ܫܡܗ. ܐܢܐ ܐܢܐ ܩܕܡܝܐ: ܘܐܢܐ ܐܢܐ ܐܚܪܝܐ. ܘܠܝܬ ܐܠܗܐ ܠܒܪ ܡܢܝ.

7 ܙ ܘܡܢܘ ܐܟܘܬܝ ܢܩܪܐ: ܘܢܬܛܝܒ. ܘܢܚܘܐ: ܡܢ ܕܣܡܬ ܥܡܐ ܠܥܠܡ: ܘܐܬܘܬܐ ܕܐܬܝܢ ܢܚܘܘܢ.

8 ܚ ܠܐ ܬܕܚܠܘܢ ܘܠܐ ܬܬܪܗܒܘܢ: ܠܐ ܐܫܡܥܬܟܘܢ ܡܢ ܩܕܝܡ. ܘܐܘܕܥܬܟܘܢ ܘܐܢܬܘܢ ܣܗܕܝ. ܕܠܝܬ ܐܠܗܐ ܠܒܪ ܡܢܝ: ܘܠܝܬ ܕܬܩܝܦ ܕܠܐ ܝܕܥ ܐܢܐ.

9 ܛ ܥܒܘܕܝ ܐܢܘܢ ܟܠܗܘܢ ܦܬܟܪܐ ܕܥܒܕܝܢ ܣܪܝܩܐ. ܘܠܝܬ ܝܘܬܪܢ ܒܪܓܝܓܬܗܘܢ: ܘܣܗܕܝܗܘܢ ܐܘܡܢܐ ܕܥܒܕܘ ܐܢܘܢ: ܕܠܐ ܚܙܝܢ: ܘܠܐ ܝܕܥܝܢ: ܘܠܐ ܒܗܬܝܢ.

10 ܝ ܡܛܠ ܗܢܐ ܢܒܗܬܘܢ ܐܝܠܝܢ ܕܥܒܕܝܢ ܐܠܗܐ: ܘܡܬܟܝܢ ܦܬܟܪܐ ܕܠܐ ܡܘܬܪ ܠܗܘܢ.

Chapter 44

1　Now hear me, Jacob my servant, Israel whom I have chosen.

2　Thus says the Lord, who made you, formed you in the womb, helped you: Do not fear, my servant Jacob, Israel whom I have called.

3　For I shall give water in the parched place, streams in the dry land. I will pour out my spirit on your seed, my blessings on your children.

4　They will spring up from among the grass, like willows that are by streams of water.

5　This one will say 'I am the Lord's'; this one will call on the name of Jacob; this one will write with his hand to the Lord; and by the name of Israel he will be called.[1]

6　Thus says the Lord, the king of Israel, its savior, the mighty Lord is his name: I am the first, I am the last, there is no God other than me.

7　Who is like me? - let him proclaim, prepare himself, and declare; when I have set up the people for eternity, let them declare the signs that are coming.

8　Do not fear, do not be disturbed; did I not make you hear from the first, declared to you, for you are my witnesses: there is no God other than me, there is none who is powerful whom I do not know.

9　They are worthless, all the craftsmen who make images; there is no profit in their works that they desire to make: and the craftsmen that have made them witness that they do not see, nor hear, nor understand.

10　Therefore they will be ashamed, those who make gods, fashioning molten (images) in which there is no profit.

---

[1] 'call … called': two different roots are used in the Syriac.

11 ܝܐ ܗܐ ܟܠܗܘܢ ܐ̈ܘܡܢܝܗܘܢ: ܣܢ̈ܝܩܝܢ ܐܢܘܢ ܡܢ ܒܢ̈ܝܢܫܐ. ܢܬܟܢܫܘܢ ܟܠܗܘܢ
ܘܢܩܘܡܘܢ. ܘܢܕܚܠܘܢ ܘܢܒܗܬܘܢ ܐܟܚܕܐ.

12 ܝܒ ܕܠܛܫ ܦܪ̈ܙܠܐ ܢܓܪܐ: ܘܒܓܘܡܪ̈ܐ ܥܒܕܗ. ܘܒܡܩܒ̈ܐ ܓܠܦܗ. ܘܥܒܕܗ ܒܚܝܠܐ
ܕܕܪܥܗ. ܐܦ ܟܦܢ ܐܦ ܨܗܐ. ܘܠܐ ܐܫܬܝ ܡ̈ܝܐ ܘܐܬܠܐܝ.

13 ܝܓ ܓܒܐ ܢܓܪܐ ܩܝܣܐ: ܘܡܫܚܗ. ܘܒܓܠܠܐ ܪܫܡܗ. ܘܒܓܠܦܗ ܘܥܒܕܗ ܒܕܡܘܬܐ
ܕܓܒܪܐ: ܐܝܟ ܫܘܦܪܐ ܕܒܪܢܫܐ.

14 ܝܕ ܘܐܩܝܡܗ ܒܒܝܬܐ ܠܡܩܡܐ ܕܢܦܣܘܩ ܡܢ ܥܒܐ: ܕܒܩܠܬܐ ܐܪ̈ܙܐ. ܕܢܨܒܐ ܠܐܝܠܢܐ
ܠܡܛܪܐ.

15 ܝܗ ܘܢܣܒܘ ܡܢܗ: ܘܐܫܚܢܘ: ܘܐܦܘ ܠܚܡܐ. ܘܐܦ ܥܒܕܘ ܐܠܗܐ: ܘܣܓܕܘ ܠܗ.
ܥܒܕܘ ܨܠܡܐ ܘܣܓܕܘ ܠܗ.

16 ܝܘ ܦܠܓܗ ܐܘܩܕܘ ܒܢܘܪܐ. ܘܛܘܝܘ ܒܣܪܐ ܥܠ ܓܘܡܪ̈ܘܗܝ. ܘܐܟܠܘ ܘܣܒܥܘ
ܐܦ ܫܚܢܘ. ܘܐܡܪܘ ܐܘܗ: ܫܚܢܢ: ܘܚܙܝܢ ܢܘܪܐ.

17 ܝܙ ܘܫܪܟܐ ܥܒܕܘ ܐܠܗܐ ܠܨܠܡܐ: ܘܣܓܕܘ ܠܗ: ܘܨܠܝܘ ܠܗ: ܘܐܡܪܘ ܦܨܢ:
ܡܛܠ ܕܐܢܬ ܐܠܗܢ.

18 ܝܚ ܘܠܐ ܝܕܥܘ ܘܠܐ ܐܣܬܟܠܘ: ܕܛܡܥ ܗܘ ܚܙܘܐ ܕܥܝ̈ܢܝܗܘܢ. ܘܣܘܟܠܐ ܕܠܒܗܘܢ.

11   See! All their craftsmen: they are enchanters[1] of[2] mankind; let them all be gathered together, let them stand; they will be ashamed, will blush together.[3]

12   For the carpenter has sharpened an iron (tool), smoothed it with a scraping (tool), carved it with an auger, worked it with the might of his arm – he has also hungered, he has also thirsted, he did not drink water; he grew weary.

13   The carpenter has chosen wood and measured it, joined it with glue, carved it and worked it to the likeness of a man, like a comely person.[4]

14   He has placed in the house the wood that was cut from the forest, that grew in the rain, so that it would be fuel for man.

15   They took from it, they warmed (themselves), they baked bread; they also made a god and are worshipping it, they made a graven image and worshipped it.

16   Half of it they burned with fire, they roasted meat[5] upon its coals; they ate, were satisfied, and also warmed themselves;[6] they said: Aha! I have warmed myself, I have seen the fire.

17   And the rest they made a graven god, and worshipped it and prayed to it and said: Save us, for you are our god.

18   But they did not know, they did not understand, that their eyes[7] are stopped up, and the understanding of their mind.[8]

---

[1] 'enchanters' or 'dumb': the former fits the immediate context better, but the latter could have been intended as an addition to the sequence which closes v.9.

[2] 'of': lit. 'from'.

[3] 'let them all be gathered … let them stand … will be ashamed, will blush together': all four verbs are imperfect.

[4] 'person': lit. 'son of man'; it is not the form used when the term refers to Jesus.

[5] 'meat': lit. 'flesh'.

[6] 'warmed themselves': lit. 'grew warm'.

[7] 'their eyes': lit. 'the vision of their eyes'.

[8] 'mind': lit. 'heart'.

19   And they did not bring it to mind,[1] they did not know, they did not think, and they said: Half of it they burned with fire, upon its coals they baked bread, they roasted meat and ate; and with the rest they made themselves a wooden idol, and worshipped it.

20   Their heart feeds on ash, the wanderers go astray,[2] not saving themselves,[3] not saying: Our right hand has made a lie.

XXII

21   Remember these things, Jacob, and Israel, for you are my servant, I formed you to be a servant to me; therefore, Israel, do not forget me.

22   I have made your iniquity pass away like a mist, your sins like a cloud. Return to me, for I have saved you.

23   Sing praise(s), heaven, for the Lord has acted; make a joyful noise, foundations of the earth; rejoice with a hymn, mountains, forest, and all the trees within it: for the Lord has redeemed Jacob, he has been glorified in Israel.

24   Thus says the Lord who redeemed you, formed you in the womb, helped you: I am the Lord, for I made everything. Only I stretched out the heavens, I spread forth the earth, I alone.[4]

25   Bringing to naught the signs of the necromancers, I show their divinations to be foolish;[5] making the wise retire, I show their knowledge to be stupidity.[6]

26   And establishes the word of his servant, restores the counsel[7] of his messengers; who said to Jerusalem: She will be inhabited and to the cities of Judah: They will be rebuilt,[8] I will establish her desolate places.

---

[1] 'mind': lit. 'heart' as in v.18.

[2] 'wanderers … astray': the root ‫ל‬ is used for both. 'go astray' translates an infinitive absolute.

[3] 'saving themselves': lit. 'deliver their soul'.

[4] 'I alone': lit. 'from me and to me'.

[5] 'show their divinations to be foolish': lit. 'make their divinations appear foolish'.

[6] 'show their knowledge to be stupidity': lit. 'make their knowledge stupid'.

[7] 'counsel': lit. 'belief, mind'.

[8] 'rebuilt': lit. 'restored'.

27 ܙ ܘܟܐܕܢ ܠܟܢܘܡܟܐ ܣܒܝ. ܘܡܢܘܦܐܦܝ ܐܘܟܚ.

28 ܚ ܘܟܐܕܢ ܠܟܢܘܦܗ ܘܚܝ: ܘܦܠܗ ܙܪܝܣܝ ܢܟܠܡ: ܠܢܥܐܕܢ ܠܐܘܙܡܟܡ ܘܠܐܚܬܐ.
ܘܘܡܛܐ ܢܡܟܪܟܠܠ.

27   Who said to the deep: Be desolate, I will dry up your rivers.

28   Who said to Cyrus: My shepherd; for he will fulfill all my desire, to tell Jerusalem that she will be rebuilt, and the temple restored.

ܡܐܡܪܐ: ܟܗ.

1 ܐ ܩܠܐ ܐܡܪ ܡܪܝܐ ܠܡܫܝܚܗ: ܠܟܘܪܫ ܕܐܚܕܬ ܒܝܡܝܢܗ. ܢܫܬܥܒܕܘܢ ܩܕܡܘܗܝ ܥܡ̈ܡܐ. ܘܚܨܐ ܕܡܠ̈ܟܐ. ܐܫܪܐ ܠܡܦܬܚ ܩܕܡܘܗܝ ܬܪ̈ܥܐ: ܘܬܪ̈ܥܐ ܠܐ ܢܬܬܐܚܕܘܢ.

2 ܒ ܐܢܐ ܩܕܡܝܟ ܐܙܠ. ܘܛܘܪ̈ܐ ܐܫܘܐ. ܬܪ̈ܥܐ ܕܢܚܫܐ ܐܬܒܪ. ܘܡܘܟ̈ܠܐ ܕܦܪܙܠܐ ܐܓܕܥ.

3 ܓ ܘܐܬܠ ܠܟ ܣܝ̈ܡܬܐ ܕܚܫܘܟܐ: ܘܛܡ̈ܝܪܬܐ ܡܛܫܝܬܐ. ܕܬܕܥ ܕܐܢܐ ܐܢܐ ܡܪܝܐ ܕܩܪܝܬ ܒܫܡܟ: ܐܠܗܗ ܕܐܝܣܪܝܠ.

4 ܕ ܡܛܠ ܥܒܕܝ ܝܥܩܘܒ: ܘܐܝܣܪܝܠ ܓܒܝܝ: ܩܪܝܬܟ ܒܫܡܟ ܘܟܢܝܬܟ: ܘܠܐ ܝܕܥܬܢܝ.

5 ܗ ܐܢܐ ܐܢܐ ܡܪܝܐ: ܘܠܝܬ ܬܘܒ ܠܒܪ ܡܢܝ: ܘܠܝܬ ܐܠܗܐ. ܐܣܪܬܟ: ܘܠܐ ܝܕܥܬܢܝ.

6 ܘ ܕܢܕܥܘܢ ܡܢ ܡܕܢܚ̈ܝ ܫܡܫܐ: ܘܡܢ ܡܥܪ̈ܒܘܗܝ: ܕܠܝܬ ܠܒܪ ܡܢܝ. ܐܢܐ ܐܢܐ ܡܪܝܐ ܘܠܝܬ ܬܘܒ.

7 ܙ ܕܓܒܠ ܢܘܗܪܐ: ܘܒܪܐ ܚܫܘܟܐ. ܥܒܕ ܫܠܡܐ: ܘܒܪܐ ܒܝܫܬܐ. ܐܢܐ ܐܢܐ ܡܪܝܐ ܕܥܒܕ ܗܠܝܢ ܟܠܗܝܢ.

8 ܚ ܐܬܪܣܣܘ ܫܡܝܐ ܡܢ ܠܥܠ. ܘܥܢ̈ܢܐ ܢܪܣܘܢ ܙܕܝܩܘܬܐ. ܬܬܦܬܚ ܐܪܥܐ: ܘܬܥܒܕ ܦܘܪܩܢܐ. ܘܙܕܝܩܘܬܐ ܬܗܘܐ ܐܟܚܕܐ. ܐܢܐ ܐܢܐ ܡܪܝܐ ܕܒܪܝܬ ܗܠܝܢ.

9 ܛ ܘܝ ܠܕܐܢ ܥܡ ܓܒܘܠܗ: ܚܨܦܐ ܡܢ ܚܨܦ̈ܝܗ ܕܐܪܥܐ. ܕܠܡܐ ܐܡܪ ܛܝܢܐ ܠܦܚܪܐ ܡܢܐ ܥܒܕ ܐܢܬ. ܘܠܐ ܗܘܝܬ ܥܒܕܐ ܕܐܝܕ̈ܝܟ.

10 ܝ ܘܝ ܠܕܐܡܪ ܠܐܒܐ: ܡܢܐ ܡܘܠܕ ܐܢܬ. ܘܠܐܢܬܬܐ: ܕܡܢܐ ܡܚܒܠܬܝ.

Chapter 45

1 Thus says the Lord to his anointed, to Cyrus whom I have taken by his right hand: Nations will be subdued before him, and the loin(s) of kings; I will begin to open doors before him, doors will not be closed.

2 I will go before you, and make the rugged place smooth; I will shatter the brass doors, I will cut off the iron bars.

3 I will give you (the things) that are laid down in darkness, and the hidden (things which are) concealed, so that you may know that I am the Lord who called you[1] by your name, the God of Israel.

4 For, my servant Jacob, and Israel my chosen, I called you by your name, I named you, yet you did not know me.

5 I am the Lord, there is none other than me,[2] and no God; I strengthened you, yet you did not know me.

6 That they should know, from the rising of the sun and from its setting, that there is none other than me, I am the Lord, there is none other.[3]

7 Who formed the light, created darkness, made peace, created evil: I am the Lord who made all these.

8 Refresh yourself, heavens,[4] from above, clouds drop (down) righteousness; let the earth be opened, let redemption increase, and righteousness spring forth together: I am the Lord who created these.

9 Woe to him who contends with his maker, an earthen vessel from the earthen vessels of the earth. Shall[5] the clay say to the potter: What are you doing; I was not the work of your hands?

10 Woe to him who says to the father: What are you begetting? and to the woman: What have you borne?

---

[1] 'who called you': lit. 'for I have called you'.

[2] 'other than me': lit. 'again except me'.

[3] 'none other': lit. 'none again'.

[4] 'Refresh yourself, heavens' or 'Take delight in the heavens'.

[5] 'Shall': ܘܠܡܐ, is used for asking a question to which the answer will be in the negative.

11 ܝܐ ܗܳܟܰܢܳܐ ܐܳܡܰܪ ܡܳܪܝܳܐ ܩܰܕܺܝܫܳܐ ܕܺܐܝܣܪܳܝܶܠ ܘܰܓܒܳܠܶܗ. ܡܳܪܝܳܐ ܡܚܰܝܠܳܐ ܫܡܶܗ. ܫܰܐܶܠܽܘܢܝ ܐܳܬܘܳܬܳܐ ܥܰܠ ܒܢܰܝ̈. ܘܥܰܠ ܥܒܳܕ ܐܺܝ̈ܕܰܝ ܦܰܩܶܕܽܘܢܝ.

12 ܝܒ ܐܶܢܳܐ ܥܒܶܕܬ ܐܰܪܥܳܐ: ܘܒܰܪܢܳܫܳܐ ܥܠܶܝܗ̇. ܐܶܢܳܐ ܒܺܐܝ̈ܕܰܝ ܡܬܰܚܬ ܫܡܰܝܳܐ. ܘܦܰܩܶܕܶܬ ܠܟܽܠܶܗ ܚܰܝ̈ܠܰܘܗ̱ܝ.

13 ܝܓ ܐܶܢܳܐ ܐܰܩܺܝܡܬܶܗ ܒܙܰܕܺܝܩܽܘܬܳܐ. ܘܟܽܠܗܶܝܢ ܐܽܘܪ̈ܚܳܬܶܗ ܐܰܬܩܶܢ. ܗܽܘ ܢܶܒܢܶܐ ܡܕܺܝܢ̱ܬܝ. ܘܫܶܒܝܬܝ ܢܫܰܪܶܐ. ܠܳܐ ܒܰܫܘܳܕܳܐ: ܘܠܳܐ ܒܫܽܘܚܕܳܐ. ܐܡܰܪ ܡܳܪܝܳܐ ܡܚܰܝܠܳܐ.

14 ܝܕ ܗܳܟܰܢܳܐ ܐܳܡܰܪ ܡܳܪܝܳܐ: ܠܥܰܡܠܶܗ ܕܡܶܨܪܶܝܢ: ܬܶܐܓܽܘܪ̈ܶܐ ܕܟܽܘܫ ܘܣܒܳܝܶܐ. ܓܰܒ̈ܪܶܐ ܕܡܫܰܘܚܬܳܐ ܠܘܳܬܶܟܝ ܢܶܥܒܪܽܘܢ. ܘܕܺܝܠܶܟܝ ܢܶܗܘܽܘܢ: ܘܒܳܬܪܶܟܝ ܢܶܐܙܠܽܘܢ. ܘܒܫܶܫܠܳܬܳܐ ܢܶܥܒܪܽܘܢ. ܘܠܶܟܝ ܢܶܣܓܕܽܘܢ. ܘܒܶܟܝ ܢܶܒܥܽܘܢ. ܕܒܶܟܝ ܗܽܘ ܐܰܠܳܗܳܐ: ܘܠܰܝܬ ܬܽܘܒ ܐܰܠܳܗܳܐ ܐ̱ܚܪܺܝܢ.

15 ܝܗ ܫܰܪܺܝܪܳܐܺܝܬ ܐܰܢ̱ܬ ܗ̱ܘ ܡܫܰܡܠܝܳܐ: ܐܰܠܳܗܶܗ ܕܺܐܝܣܪܳܝܶܠ ܘܦܳܪܽܘܩܶܗ.

16 ܝܘ ܢܶܒܗܬܽܘܢ ܘܢܶܬܟܰܠܡܽܘܢ ܟܽܠܗܽܘܢ ܐܰܟܚܕܳܐ. ܕܡܶܬܥܰܒܕܺܝܢ ܒܨܰܠܡܶܐ: ܘܢܶܐܙܠܽܘܢ ܒܰܒܗܬ̈ܬܳܐ.

17 ܝܙ ܦܽܘܪܩܳܢܶܗ ܕܺܐܝܣܪܳܝܶܠ ܒܡܳܪܝܳܐ ܗ̱ܘ ܦܽܘܪܩܳܢܳܐ ܕܰܠܥܳܠܡܳܐ. ܠܳܐ ܬܶܒܗܬܽܘܢ: ܘܠܳܐ ܬܶܬܟܰܠܡܽܘܢ ܠܥܳܠܰܡ ܥܳܠܡܺܝܢ.

18 ܝܚ ܡܶܛܽܠ ܕܗܳܟܰܢܳܐ ܐܳܡܰܪ ܡܳܪܝܳܐ ܕܒܪܳܐ ܫܡܰܝܳܐ: ܘܗܽܘܝܽܘ ܐܰܠܳܗܳܐ ܕܓܒܰܠܳܗ̇ ܠܰܐܪܥܳܐ: ܘܥܒܰܕܳܗ̇. ܘܗܽܘܝܽܘ ܬܰܩܢܳܗ̇. ܠܳܐ ܗ̱ܘܳܐ ܣܪܺܝܩܳܐܺܝܬ ܒܪܳܗ̇ ܐܶܠܳܐ ܕܢܶܬܺܝܬܶܒ ܒܳܗ̇ ܒܪܳܗ̇. ܐܶܢܳܐ ܐ̱ܢܳܐ ܡܳܪܝܳܐ ܘܠܰܝܬ ܬܽܘܒ.

19 ܝܛ ܠܳܐ ܗ̱ܘܳܐ ܒܰܛܘܫܝܳܐ ܡܰܠܠܶܬ ܒܰܐܬܪܳܐ ܕܰܐܪܥܳܐ ܚܫܽܘܟܬܳܐ: ܘܠܳܐ ܐܶܡܪܶܬ ܠܙܰܪܥܳܐ ܕܝܰܥܩܽܘܒ ܕܡܶܫܬܰܐܠܺܝܢ ܒܣܪܺܝܩܽܘ. ܕܶܐܢܳܐ ܐ̱ܢܳܐ ܡܳܪܝܳܐ ܕܡܡܰܠܶܠ ܐ̱ܢܳܐ ܙܰܕܺܝܩܽܘܬܳܐ: ܘܡܚܰܘܶܐ ܐ̱ܢܳܐ ܬܪܺܝܨܽܘܬܳܐ.

20 ܟ ܐܶܬܟܰܢܰܫܘ: ܘܬܳܘ: ܘܶܐܬܩܰܪܰܒܘ ܐܰܟܚܕܳܐ: ܐܰܝܠܶܝܢ ܕܶܐܫܬܰܘܙܰܒܘ ܡܶܢ ܥܰܡ̈ܡܶܐ. ܘܠܳܐ ܝܺܕܰܥܘ ܕܫܳܩܠܺܝܢ ܩܰܝܣܳܐ ܓܠܺܝܦܳܐ. ܘܡܨܰܠܶܝܢ ܠܰܐܠܳܗܳܐ ܕܠܳܐ ܦܳܪܶܩ.

11 Thus says the Lord, the Holy One of Israel, its maker, the mighty Lord is his name: Ask of me signs concerning my sons, inquire of me concerning the work of my hands.

12 I made the earth, and mankind upon it; I with my hands stretched out the heavens; I ordered all their host.

13 I wakened him in righteousness, I will make all his ways smooth; he will build my city, he will let my captives go, not for ransom, and not for a bribe, says the mighty Lord.

14 Thus says the Lord: The labor of Egypt, the merchants of Cush and Sheba, the men of stature, will pass over to you, and they will be yours; they will follow after you, they will pass on in chains, they will bow down to you, they will pray to you, for God is with you, there is no other God.[1]

15 Indeed you are he who protects, the God of Israel and its savior.

16 Be ashamed, blush, all of them together, who walk in shame,[2] carving idols.

17 The salvation of Israel is through the Lord, the eternal savior:[3] you will not be ashamed, not blush, forever and ever.

18 For thus says the Lord who created the heavens, he is God who formed the earth, who made it, established it, he did not create it in vain, but so that his creation would inhabit it: I am the Lord, there is none other.

19 I did not speak in secret in the place of the darkened earth, I did not say to the seed of Jacob 'Seek me in vain', for I am the Lord, I speak (in) righteousness, I declare uprightness.

20 Gather together, come, draw near together, those who are delivered from the nations; they did not understand, those who raised up carved wood, prayed to a god that does not save.

---

[1] 'there is no other God': lit. 'there is again no other God'.

[2] 'shame' or 'a ditch'.

[3] 'eternal savior': lit. 'the savior of the ages'.

21 ܟܐ ܚܘܘ ܘܩܪܒܘ: ܘܐܬܡܠܟܘ ܐܟܚܕܐ. ܡܢܘ ܐܫܡܥ ܗܕܐ ܡܢ ܩܕܝܡ. ܘܡܢ ܕܫܘܪܝܐ
ܐܢܐ ܐܢܐ ܡܪܝܐ. ܘܠܝܬ ܬܘܒ ܐܠܗܐ ܠܒܪ ܡܢܝ. ܐܠܗܐ ܙܕܝܩܐ ܘܦܪܘܩܐ:
ܘܠܝܬ ܠܒܪ ܡܢܝ.

22 ܟܒ ܐܬܦܢܘ ܠܘܬܝ ܟܠܟܘܢ ܥܒܪܘܗ̇ ܕܐܪܥܐ: ܘܬܬܦܪܩܘܢ. ܡܛܠ ܕܐܢܐ ܐܢܐ ܡܪܝܐ:
ܘܠܝܬ ܬܘܒ.

23 ܟܓ ܒܝ ܝܡܝܬ: ܘܢܦܩܬ ܡܢ ܦܘܡܝ ܡܠܬܐ ܕܙܕܝܩܘܬܐ: ܘܠܐ ܬܗܦܘܟ. ܕܠܝ
ܬܟܘܦ ܟܠ ܒܘܪܟ. ܘܒܝ ܬܐܡܐ ܟܠ ܠܫܢ.

24 ܟܕ ܘܢܐܡܪܘܢ ܒܡܪܝܐ ܗܝ ܙܕܝܩܘܬܐ. ܘܥܫܝܢܐ ܠܘܬܗ ܢܐܬܘܢ. ܘܢܒܗܬܘܢ ܟܠ
ܕܡܚܪܝܢ ܒܗ.

25 ܟܗ ܒܗ ܢܫܬܒܚܘܢ ܘܢܙܕܕܩܘܢ ܟܠܗ ܙܪܥܗ ܕܐܝܣܪܝܠ.

21 Declare, approach, take counsel together. Who has made this heard from the first: I am the Lord from the beginning, there is no God other than me, the righteous God, the savior, there is none other than me?

22 Draw near to me, all you ends of the earth, that you may be saved, for I am the Lord, there is none other.[1]

23 By myself I have sworn. The word of righteousness has gone forth from my mouth, and it will not turn back: for to me every knee will bow, by me every tongue will swear.

24 They will say: Righteousness is in the Lord, strong men will go to him, all who spite[2] you will be ashamed.

25 In me will be praised, declared righteous, all the seed[3] of Israel.

---

[1] 'none other': lit. 'there is none again'.

[2] 'spite' or 'envy'.

[3] 'seed' or 'offspring'.

١ بِقَلا خَبلا: وَاصلاببِ نُجَه. وَهوَه هَوَمِبَبوَه، حِكْبِبْقَا لِمْنَا حِرْبِبَا:
حَسِبْبَابِلا وحكجَبِبَا جِقَبَبَا.

٢ اُصلابِبِبِ وبِقَبَ اُجبِبَا. ولا اُهقَسِ حَهمَحوَجُه لِمُهبِبْبوَه، وَاآلا حهمِبَا نَقَمَبِبوَه،

٣ هوَهمَحُبِبِ وَجِبِلَ مَحقوَب: وبُكَه هَبِبَه وَاصهَبِبْلا. وقمِعْبَاهمِبِ حَجَبِبِبِا: وقمِعْبَاهمِبِ حَجَبِبِبِا.

٤ حِبِبَعُبَا حَهمَبِبَابِلا اُبِلا هوَه. وَحِبِبَعُبَا حَهمَحَعوَبِلا اُبِلا اُهبِبِلا. اُبِلا حَجِبِبَا:
وَاُبِلا اُهقَهِبِلا. وَاُبِلا اُهبِبِلا وَاَقِبِلا.

٥ حَبِبَعِ وَقِمِبَاُوُبِبِ وقِمِعْبَاُوُبِبِ.

٦ حَبِبَهِبِ وهمِقَقَبِ وَوَجِبِلا مَنِ نَبِبَقَبِبِوَه، وهَاُهِبِلا حَقمِهَابِلا بِاُمَحَبِ. وَاُحِبِنِ
هَبِبْبَا. وحُجِبِبِ لِلْبِبَهُبِلا وهبِحِبِبِ لِلَه: وَاُوَه مَبِرِحَبِ لِلَه.

٧ وهَهمَحَبِ لِلَه بَلا بَلا قَبِرَقَبِبِوَه، وَهمِهَاحَجِبِ لِلَه. وهَبِبَعَبِ لِلَه بَلا
وَوَحَبِبِوَه. ولا مَهمَحَبَسِ حَهمَحَبِبِ مَبِ وَوَحَبِبِوَه. وَاُوَه مَبِرِحَبِ لِلَه: ولا حَبِبَا
حوَبِبوَه، ولا جِبِبَه حوَبِبوَه، مَبِ اُوَحِبِرِبِبِبِوَه،

٨ اُلاُوُجِبِبِ هوَحَبِ وَاصحَبِبِ. وَاُلابِلَه هَقَلا بَلا حَحجِبِبِ.

٩ اُلاُوُجِبِبِ هَبِبَعِبَابِا وهَبِ حَبِبَعِبِ. وَاُبِلا اُبِلا لِلَهُبِلا: وحَبِبِبَا لَاُوَ لِلَهُبِلا: وحَبِبِبَا
اُجِبِبَابِبِ.

١٠ وهمِعْقَا اُبِلا مَبِ وَبِمِبِبَا اِبِبِبِبَجِبَا: وهَبِ مَبِبِبِسِمِ اُمَحَبِ ولا اُلاُبِحَبِبِ اُهَبِ اُبِلا.
لاُوَحِبِبَبِ همِقَسِمِ اُبِلا. وبُكَه رِحِبِبِ حُجِبِ اُبِلا.

228

Chapter 46

1   Bel fell, Nebo was overthrown, their carved idols packed up (as) loads for the beast, for the hungry cattle.

2   They were overthrown, they fell together; they were not able to save those who carried them, they[1] were carried away[2] into captivity.

3   Hear me, (you) of the house of Jacob and all the remnant of Israel, who are borne in the womb,[3] carried in the womb.[4]

4   I am he unto old age, I will support unto the latter years; I made, I will carry, I will support and save.

5   To whom have you likened me and compared me?

6   To those who go astray, who bring out gold from their pouches, weigh silver in the scales, hire a smith, make a god and bow down to it, even pray to it.

7   Carrying it upon their shoulders, making it walk, setting it in its place: but it cannot get up from its place; they even pray to it: but it does not answer them, it does not save them from their afflictions.

8   Remember these things, and consider; wrongdoers, bring (them) to mind.[5]

9   Remember the former things which are everlasting;[6] for I am God, there is no other[7] God, there is none like me.

10   I declare, from the beginning, the latter things; from former times, I tell of those things which have not yet been effected; I establish my purpose, and all my will I bring to pass.

---

[1] 'they'[4]: lit. 'their souls, themselves'.

[2] 'were carried': lit. 'went'.

[3] 'borne in the womb': idiomatic.

[4] 'carried in the womb': P uses two words for 'womb', but only one is appropriate in English.

[5] 'mind': lit. 'heart', as in 44:18.

[6] 'everlasting': lit. 'from of old'.

[7] 'no other': lit. 'not again'.

11   I summon from the east a bird of prey, from a distant land a man of
      my counsel;[1] I speak, I bring, I have formed, I also bring to pass.

XXIII

12   Hear me, hard-hearted ones, far removed from righteousness.

13   I have brought my righteousness to come to pass, my redemption
      will not delay: I will give my redemption to Zion, my praise to Israel.

---

[1] 'counsel': lit. 'belief, mind'.

232

Chapter 47

1   Come down, sit in the dust, virgin daughter of Babylon; sit on the earth, daughter of the Chaldeans: there is no throne, for they will no more call you delicate, pampered.

2   Take a mill, grind flour, remove[1] your veil, cut[2] your white hair,[3] reveal your legs, pass through the rivers.

3   Your nakedness will be uncovered, your shame will be seen, I will exact vengeance from you, I will not cause a man to rush in upon you.

4   Our savior, the mighty Lord is his name, the Holy One of Israel.

5   Sit in confusion, go into the dark, daughter of the Chaldeans: for they will no more call you 'the mistress[4] of kingdoms'.

6   I was angry with my people, for they defiled my inheritance, I delivered them up into your hands; but you had no mercy on them, you set your yoke heavily[5] on the elders.

7   You said: I shall be the mistress forever: you did not take these to your heart, you did not call to mind the latter end.

8   Now hear these things, delicate one, who sits at peace, saying in her heart: I and no other,[6] I will not live[7] as a widow, I will not know bereavement.

9   They will come upon you, these two blows, in a single day: bereavement and widowhood will come upon you suddenly, in the multitude of your sorcerers,[8] in the multitude of your magicians.

---

[1] 'remove': lit. 'reveal'.

[2] 'cut': √ ܟܢ or 'lack' √ ܓܙ.

[3] 'white hair' or 'white clothes'.

[4] 'mistress' or 'heroine, champion'.

[5] 'set your yoke heavily': lit. 'greatly hardened your yoke'.

[6] 'I and no other': lit. 'I am and none again'.

[7] 'live': lit. 'sit'.

[8] 'sorcerers' or 'enchantments'.

10   For you put your trust in your wickedness, you said: There is no-one who sees me. Your wisdom and your knowledge have[1] led you astray; you said in your heart: I and no other.

11   Evil will come upon you in the early dawn, but you will not know it; confusion will fall upon you, and you will be unable to turn it aside; distress will come upon you suddenly, but you will not know it.

12   Stand up now with your magicians, with your many sorcerers, with whom you have labored[2] from your childhood: perhaps you will able to benefit, perhaps you will be strengthened.[3]

13   You have become weary with the multitude of your devices; let them stand up and save you, the Chaldeans who give heed to the heavens and the stars, who show you by the moon everything which comes upon you.

14   See! They are like straws that the fire burns up, they will not survive[4] the flame; there are no coals for their fire, nor brightness to settle before it.

15   So they were to you, your merchants with whom you have labored from your childhood; each turned aside to his own way, there is no-one who saves you.

---

[1] 'have': sing verb.

[2] 'labored' or 'become weary'.

[3] 'strengthened' or 'strengthen yourself'.

[4] 'survive': lit. 'save their soul from the hand of'.

Chapter 48

1   Hear these things, those of the house of Jacob who are called by the name of Israel, who have come forth from the waters of Judah, who swear by the name of the Lord, who make us think about[1] the God of Israel: not in truth, not in righteousness.

2   For they have called themselves 'of the city of holiness' and have supported themselves by the God of Israel: the mighty Lord is his name.

3   From the beginning I have declared the former things, they have[2] gone forth from my mouth; I have made you hear them:[3] suddenly I act, and they come to pass.[4]

4   I know that you are stubborn, that your neck is an iron sinew, your forehead brass.

5   I declared to you from the first, I made you hear before it had come to pass, so that you should not say 'My idols have acted, my graven images, my molten images, have saved me'.

6   I have heard, I have seen, all these things, will you not declare this?[5] I have made you hear new things (to be) kept in mind from now on, which you did not know.

7   They are created henceforth, not from of old; before (this) day you have not heard them, so you may not say 'I know them'.

8   You did not hear them, neither do you know them; from of old you would not take heed;[6] I know that you are very deceitful, you were called 'unrighteous' from the womb.[7]

---

[1] 'make us think about': lit. 'make mention of'.

[2] 'they have': lit. 'it has'.

[3] 'made you hear them': lit. 'I have made them heard by you'.

[4] 'come to pass' or 'they come'.

[5] 'will you not declare this?' or 'you will not declare this'.

[6] 'you would not take heed': lit. 'your ears have not been open'.

[7] 'womb': lit. 'belly'.

9 ܛ ܡܛܠ ܫܡܝ ܐܘܪܟ ܪܘܓܙܝ. ܘܬܫܒܘܚܬܝ ܐܚܕ ܠܟ: ܘܠܐ ܐܘܒܕܟ.

10 ܝ ܗܐ ܨܪܦܬܟ ܘܠܐ ܒܣܐܡܐ. ܘܒܚܢܬܟ ܒܟܘܪܐ ܕܡܣܟܢܘܬܐ.

11 ܝܐ ܡܛܠܬܝ ܐܥܒܕ ܕܠܐ ܐܬܛܘܫ. ܘܐܝܩܪܝ ܠܐܚܪܝܢ ܠܐ ܐܬܠ.

12 ܝܒ ܫܡܥܝܢܝ ܝܥܩܘܒ ܘܐܝܣܪܝܠ ܩܪܝܒܝ. ܐܢܐ ܐܢܐ ܩܕܡܝܐ: ܘܐܢܐ ܐܢܐ ܐܚܪܝܐ.

13 ܝܓ ܘܐܝܕܝ ܐܫܬܬ ܫܬܐܣܬܗ ܕܐܪܥܐ. ܘܝܡܝܢܝ ܛܦܚܬ ܫܡܝܐ. ܩܪܐ ܐܢܐ ܠܗܘܢ:
ܘܩܝܡܝܢ ܐܟܚܕܐ.

14 ܝܕ ܐܬܟܢܫܘ ܟܠܟܘܢ ܘܫܡܥܘ. ܡܢܘ ܐܝܬ ܒܟܘܢ ܕܚܘܝ ܗܠܝܢ. ܡܪܝܐ ܪܚܡܗ
ܘܢܥܒܕ ܨܒܝܢܗ ܒܒܒܠ: ܘܕܪܥܗ ܒܟܠܕܝܐ.

15 ܝܗ ܐܢܐ ܡܠܠܬ ܘܐܦ ܩܪܝܬ. ܘܐܝܬܝܬܗ ܘܐܨܠܚܬ ܐܘܪܚܗ.

16 ܝܘ ܩܪܘܒܘ ܠܘܬܝ ܘܫܡܥܘ ܗܕܐ. ܕܡܢ ܪܫܝܬܐ ܒܛܘܫܝܐ ܠܐ ܡܠܠܬ. ܘܡܢ ܙܒܢܐ
ܕܗܘܬ ܬܡܢ ܐܢܐ. ܘܗܫܐ ܡܪܝܐ ܐܠܗܐ ܫܕܪܢܝ: ܘܪܘܚܗ.

17 ܝܙ ܗܟܢܐ ܐܡܪ ܡܪܝܐ ܦܪܘܩܟ ܩܕܝܫܐ ܕܐܝܣܪܝܠ. ܐܢܐ ܡܪܝܐ ܐܠܗܟ ܡܠܦ ܐܢܐ
ܠܟ ܕܠܐ ܬܐܚܠܐ. ܘܡܕܪܟ ܐܢܐ ܠܟ ܐܘܪܚܐ ܕܬܐܙܠ ܒܗ.

18 ܝܚ ܠܘ ܕܝܢ ܨܬܬ ܐܝܬ ܦܘܩܕܢܝ. ܘܗܘܐ ܫܠܡܟ ܐܝܟ ܢܗܪܐ: ܘܙܕܝܩܘܬܟ ܐܝܟ
ܓܠܠܐ ܕܝܡܐ.

19 ܝܛ ܘܗܘܐ ܙܪܥܟ ܐܝܟ ܚܠܐ: ܘܝܠܕܐ ܕܡܥܝܟ ܐܝܟ ܚܨܪ̈ܘܗܝ. ܘܠܐ ܢܦܘܩ ܘܠܐ ܢܐܒܕ
ܫܡܗ ܡܢ ܩܕܡܝ.

20 ܟ ܦܘܩܘ ܡܢ ܒܒܠ: ܥܪܘܩܘ ܡܢ ܟܠܕܝܐ. ܒܩܠܐ ܕܬܫܒܘܚܬܐ ܚܘܘ ܗܕܐ.
ܘܐܫܡܥܘܗ ܘܐܦܩܘܗ ܥܕܡܐ ܠܣܘܦܝܗ ܕܐܪܥܐ. ܘܐܡܪܘ: ܦܪܩ ܡܪܝܐ
ܠܝܥܩܘܒ ܥܒܕܗ.

21 ܟܐ ܒܡܕܒܪܐ ܕܒܪ ܐܢܘܢ. ܘܡܝܐ ܡܢ ܛܪܢܐ ܐܪܕܝ ܠܗܘܢ. ܒܙܥ ܟܐܦܐ ܘܪܕܘ ܡܝܐ.

22 ܟܒ ܠܝܬ ܫܠܡܐ ܠܪܫܝܥܐ: ܐܡܪ ܡܪܝܐ.

9   For (the sake of) my name I will pause in[1] my anger, (for) my honor I will preserve you, I will not destroy you.

10   See! I have refined you, but not with silver; proved you in the furnace of want.

11   For my own sake I will act, so that it will not be defiled, I will not give my honor to another.

12   Hear me, Jacob and Israel (to) whom I have called: I am the first and I am the last.

13   My hand fashioned the foundations of the earth, my right hand spread out the heavens; I call (to) them, and they stand firm together.

14   Gather yourselves together, all of you, and listen. Who is (there) amongst you who declares these things? The Lord loved him who will do his will in Babylon, and among the seed of the Chaldeans.

15   I have spoken, even called, I have summoned her, I have made her way prosperous.

16   Draw near to me, and hear this: from the beginning, I spoke not in secret; from the time that was, I was there; now, the Lord God has sent me, and his spirit.

17   Thus says the Lord, your savior, the Holy One of Israel: I am the Lord your God, I teach you so that you will do no wrong,[2] I make known to you the way in which you should go.

18   But if only you would heed my commandments: then your peace would be as a river, your righteousness as the waves of the sea.

19   Your seed would be as the sand, the offspring of your bowels as pebbles; it should not come to an end, his name should not perish from my presence.

20   Go forth from Babylon, flee from the Chaldeans, with the sound of praise declare this; make it heard, bring it forth to the ends of the earth, say: The Lord has redeemed Jacob his servant.

21   He made them walk in the desolate waste, he made water flow for them from the flint, he cleaved the rock, the waters flowed.

22   There is no peace for the wicked, says the Lord.

---

[1] 'pause in': lit. 'delay'.

[2] 'that you will do no wrong'. See Introduction. Addendum 1.

ܩܦܠܐܘܢ: ܡܛ.

1 ܐ ܫܡܥܘ ܓܙܪ̈ܬܐ: ܘܨܘܬܘ ܐܡ̈ܘܬܐ. ܡܢ ܟܪܣܐ ܡܪܝܐ ܩܪܢܝ. ܘܡܢ ܡܪܒܥܐ ܘܡܢ ܟܪܣܗ ܕܐܡܝ ܕܟܪ ܫܡܝ.

2 ܒ ܘܥܒܕ ܦܘܡܝ ܐܝܟ ܣܝܦܐ ܚܪܝܦܐ: ܘܒܛܠܠܐ ܕܐܝܕܗ ܛܫܝܢܝ. ܘܥܒܕܢܝ ܐܝܟ ܓܐܪܐ ܓܒܝܐ: ܘܒܩܛܪܩܗ ܛܫܝܢܝ.

3 ܓ ܘܐܡܪ ܠܝ: ܥܒܕܝ ܐܢܬ: ܐܝܣܪܐܝܠ ܕܒܟ ܡܫܬܒܚ ܐܢܐ.

4 ܕ ܘܐܢܐ ܐܡܪܬ ܠܣܪܝܩܘ ܕܡܓܢ ܘܣܪܝܩܘܬܐ ܠܐܝܬ. ܘܫܘܝܬ ܚܝܠܝ ܠܣܪܝܩܘܬܐ. ܫܪܝܪܐܝܬ ܕܝܢܝ ܩܕܡ ܡܪܝܐ: ܘܥܒܕܝ ܩܕܡ ܐܠܗܝ.

5 ܗ ܗܫܐ ܗܟܢܐ ܐܡܪ ܡܪܝܐ: ܕܓܒܠܢܝ ܒܟܪܣܐ ܕܐܗܘܐ ܠܗ ܥܒܕܐ: ܘܐܦܢܐ ܠܝܥܩܘܒ ܠܘܬܗ: ܘܠܐܝܣܪܐܝܠ ܐܟܢܫ. ܐܫܬܒܚܬ ܩܕܡ ܡܪܝܐ. ܘܐܠܗܝ ܗܘܐ ܥܘܫܢܝ.

6 ܘ ܘܐܡܪ ܙܥܘܪܐ ܗܝ ܕܬܗܘܐ ܠܝ ܥܒܕܐ: ܘܬܩܝܡ ܫܒܛܐ ܕܝܥܩܘܒ: ܘܬܦܢܐ ܢܨܘܪ̈ܘܗܝ ܕܐܝܣܪܐܝܠ. ܝܗܒܬܟ ܢܘܗܪܐ ܠܥܡ̈ܡܐ: ܕܬܗܘܐ ܦܘܪܩܢܝ ܥܕܡܐ ܠܣܘܦ̈ܝܗ ܕܐܪܥܐ.

ܦܬ ܚܕ.

7 ܙ ܗܟܢܐ ܐܡܪ ܡܪܝܐ ܦܪܘܩܐ ܕܐܝܣܪܐܝܠ: ܘܩܕܝܫܗ: ܠܕܡܫܬܝܛܐ ܢܦܫܗ: ܠܕܡܣܠܝ ܡܢ ܥܡܐ ܘܡܢ ܥܒ̈ܕܐ ܕܫܠܝܛ̈ܢܐ: ܡܠ̈ܟܐ ܢܚܙܘܢ ܘܢܩܘܡܘܢ: ܘܫܠܝܛ̈ܢܐ ܢܣܓܕܘܢ ܠܗ. ܡܛܠ ܡܪܝܐ ܕܡܗܝܡܢ: ܩܕܝܫܐ ܕܐܝܣܪܐܝܠ ܕܓܒܟ.

8 ܚ ܗܟܢܐ ܐܡܪ ܡܪܝܐ: ܒܥܕܢܐ ܕܪܥܘܢܐ ܥܢܝܬܟ. ܘܒܝܘܡܐ ܕܦܘܪܩܢܐ ܥܕܪܬܟ. ܘܢܛܪܬܟ: ܘܝܗܒܬܟ ܩܝܡܐ ܠܥܡܐ: ܘܬܗܘܐ ܠܥܡ̈ܡܐ. ܕܬܩܝܡ ܐܪܥܐ: ܘܬܐܪܬ ܝܪ̈ܬܘܬܐ ܕܚܪ̈ܒܬܐ.

9 ܛ ܘܬܐܡܪ ܠܐܣܝܪ̈ܐ ܕܦܘܩܘ: ܘܠܕܒܚܫܘܟܐ ܕܐܬܓܠܘ. ܥܠ ܐܘܪ̈ܚܬܐ ܢܪܥܘܢ: ܘܒܟܠܗܘܢ ܫܒܝ̈ܠܐ ܡܪ̈ܥܝܬܗܘܢ.

Chapter 49

1   Listen, islands! Give ear, peoples! The Lord has called me from afar, from the womb, from the belly of my mother, he has been mindful of my name.

2   He has made my mouth like a sharp sword, he has hidden me in the shade of his hand; he has made me like a choice arrow, he has concealed me in his quiver.

3   He said to me: You are my servant, Israel, for in you I am glorified.

4   I did not say to the seed of Jacob that I had labored in vain, given my strength to vanity; truly my judgment is before the Lord, my work before my God.

5   Now thus says the Lord, who fashioned me in the womb so that I should be his servant, return Jacob to him, and gather Israel - I was glorified before the Lord, my God was my strength.

6   He said: It is a small thing, that you would be my servant, that you would establish the tribe of Jacob, return the scion of Israel; I have given you as a light to the nations, that you would be my redemption to the ends of the earth.

XXIV

7   Thus says the Lord, the Holy One of Israel, its savior, to him whose soul is despised, despised by the people and by the servants of rulers: Kings will see and stand up, rulers will worship him, because of the Lord who is faithful, the Holy One of Israel who chose you.

8   Thus says the Lord: In an favorable time I have answered you, on the day of salvation[1] I have helped you, I have formed you, I have given you as a covenant for the people, as a light to the nations, that you may establish[2] the land, and inherit the inheritance of the desolate wastes.

9   You will say to the bound: Go forth! and to the imprisoned: Be revealed! They will feed on the paths, all the pathways their pastures.

---

[1] 'salvation' or 'redemption'.

[2] 'establish' or 'raise up'.

10 ܝ ܠܐ ܢܟܦܢܘܢ: ܘܠܐ ܢܨܗܘܢ. ܘܠܐ ܢܡܚܐ ܐܢܘܢ ܫܘܒܐ ܘܫܡܫܐ. ܡܛܠ ܕܡܪܚܡܢܘܗܝ
ܢܕܒܪ ܐܢܘܢ. ܘܠܡܒܘ̈ܥܐ ܕܡܝ̈ܐ ܢܚܕܐ ܐܢܘܢ.

11 ܝܐ ܐܥܒܕ ܟܠܗܘܢ ܛܘܪ̈ܐ ܐܘܪ̈ܚܐ: ܘܫܒ̈ܝܠܐ ܢܬܬܪܝܡܘܢ.

12 ܝܒ ܗܐ ܗܠܝܢ ܢܐܬܘܢ ܡܢ ܪܘܚܩܐ: ܘܗܠܝܢ ܡܢ ܓܪܒܝܐ. ܘܗܠܝܢ ܡܢ ܝܡܐ: ܘܗܠܝܢ
ܡܢ ܐܪܥܐ ܕܣܝܢܝܡ.

13 ܝܓ ܫܒܚܝ ܫܡܝܐ: ܘܕܘܨܝ ܐܪܥܐ. ܐܬܦܨܚܘ ܛܘܪ̈ܐ ܒܬܫܒܘܚܬܐ. ܡܛܠ ܕܒܝܐ
ܡܪܝܐ ܠܥܡܗ: ܘܐܪܚܡ ܥܠ ܡܟܝ̈ܟܘܗܝ.

14 ܝܕ ܘܐܡܪܬ ܨܗܝܘܢ. ܕܫܒܩܢܝ ܡܪܝܐ: ܘܡܪܝܐ ܛܥܝܢܝ.

15 ܝܗ ܐܢ ܛܥܝܐ ܐܢܬܬܐ ܥܘܠܗ̇: ܘܠܐ ܡܪܚܡܐ ܥܠ ܒܪ ܡܥܝܗ̇: ܐܦ ܗܠܝܢ ܢܛܥܝܢ:
ܐܢܐ ܠܐ ܐܛܥܝܟܝ.

16 ܝܘ ܗܐ ܥܠ ܟܦ̈ܝ ܐܝܕܝ ܨܝܪܬܟܝ. ܘܫܘܪ̈ܝܟܝ ܩܕܡܝ ܐܢܘܢ ܐܡܝܢܐܝܬ.

17 ܝܙ ܥܓܠ ܒܢ̈ܝܟܝ ܡܣܬܪ̈ܩܝܟܝ. ܘܡܚܪ̈ܒܢܝܟܝ ܡܢܟܝ ܢܦܩܘܢ.

18 ܝܚ ܐܪܝܡܝ ܥܝ̈ܢܝܟܝ ܠܚܕܪ̈ܝܟܝ. ܘܚܙܝ ܕܟܠܗܘܢ ܡܬܟܢܫܝܢ ܘܐܬܝܢ ܠܟܝ: ܚܝ ܐܢܐ
ܐܡܪ ܡܪܝܐ: ܕܟܠܗܘܢ ܐܝܟ ܨܒܬܐ ܬܠܒܫܝܢ: ܘܬܬܟܠܠܝܢ ܐܝܟ ܟܠܬܐ.

19 ܝܛ ܡܛܠ ܕܚܪ̈ܒܬܟܝ: ܘܨܕܝ̈ܬܟܝ: ܘܐܪܥܐ ܕܡܚܒܠܘܬܟܝ. ܡܟܝܠ ܬܬܐܠܨܝܢ ܡܢ
ܥܡܪܐ: ܘܢܬܪܚܩܘܢ ܒܠܘ̈ܥܝܟܝ.

20 ܟ ܘܬܘܒ ܢܐܡܪܘܢ ܒܐܕ̈ܢܝܟܝ ܒܢ̈ܝ ܡܫܟܘܠܘܬܟܝ: ܐܠܝܨ ܗܘ ܠܝ ܐܬܪܐ. ܐܬܩܪܒ
ܠܝ: ܢܬܒ.

10   They will not hunger, they will not thirst, the parching heat and sun will not harm them; because of their compassion he will lead them, he will bring them to springs of water.

11   I will make all the mountains (into) paths, all the pathways will be lifted up.

12   These will come from afar, these from the north, these from the west,[1] and these from the sea of Sinim.

13   Sing praise, heavens! Exult, earth! Rejoice, mountains, with praise! For the Lord has comforted his people, has had mercy on his poor.

14   Zion said: The Lord has abandoned me, the Lord has forgotten me.

15   If a woman forgets her newborn baby, has no pity for the child of her womb,[2] even if these forget: I will not forget you.

16   See! I have engraved you on the palms of my hands, your walls are before me continually.

17   Directly,[3] your children are your destroyers; those who ravage you will go forth from you.

18   Lift up your eyes to your surroundings, and see all those who are gathered together, coming to you. As I live, says the Lord, you will clothe yourselves with them all as with an ornament, you will be adorned[4] like a bride.

19   For your desolate places, and your deserted places, the land of your destruction, from henceforth will be too narrow to be inhabited,[5] and those who devour you will flee.

20   Again they will say in your hearing, the children of your bereavement: The place is (too) narrow for us, bring us near, so that we may live.[6]

---

[1] 'west' or 'sea'.

[2] 'womb': lit. 'bowels'.

[3] 'Directly'. See Introduction. Addendum 3.

[4] 'adorned' or 'crowned'.

[5] 'too narrow to be inhabited': lit. 'restricted from an inhabitant'.

[6] 'live': lit. 'dwell'.

21 ܟܐ ܘܬܐܡܪܝܢ ܒܠܒܟܝ ܡܢܘ ܝܠܕ ܠܝ ܗܠܝܢ. ܕܗܐ ܐܢܐ ܡܬܟܠܬܐ ܐܢܐ ܘܡܫܒܝܬܐ:
ܓܠܝܬܐ ܘܡܛܪܕܬܐ. ܗܠܝܢ ܡܢ ܪܒܝ. ܐܢ ܐܢܐ ܗܐ ܐܫܬܚܪܬ ܒܠܚܘܕܝ: ܗܠܝܢ
ܐܝܟܐ ܗܘܘ.

22 ܟܒ ܗܟܢܐ ܐܡܪ ܡܪܝܐ ܐܠܗܐ: ܗܐ ܡܪܝܡ ܐܢܐ ܐܝܕܝ ܥܠ ܥܡܡܐ. ܘܠܥܡܡܐ ܐܩܝܡ
ܐܬܐ. ܘܢܝܬܘܢ ܠܒܢܝܟܝ ܒܥܘܒܝܗܘܢ. ܘܠܒܢܬܟܝ ܥܠ ܟܬܦܬܗܘܢ
ܢܫܩܠܘܢ.

23 ܟܓ ܘܢܗܘܘܢ ܡܠܟܐ ܡܪܒܝܢܝܟܝ: ܘܡܠܟܬܗܘܢ ܡܝܢܩܢܝܬܟܝ. ܘܥܠ ܐܦܝܗܘܢ
ܥܠ ܐܪܥܐ ܢܣܓܕܘܢ ܠܟܝ. ܘܥܦܪܐ ܕܪܓܠܝܟܝ ܢܠܚܟܘܢ. ܘܬܕܥܝܢ ܕܐܢܐ ܐܢܐ
ܡܪܝܐ: ܕܠܐ ܒܗܬܝܢ ܐܝܠܝܢ ܕܡܣܟܝܢ ܠܝ.

24 ܟܕ ܠܡܐ ܡܬܢܣܒܐ ܕܒܙܬܗ ܕܓܢܒܪܐ. ܐܘ ܫܒܝܬܗ ܕܥܫܝܢܐ ܡܬܦܪܩܐ.

25 ܟܗ ܡܛܠ ܕܗܟܢܐ ܐܡܪ ܡܪܝܐ: ܕܒܙܬܗ ܕܓܢܒܪܐ ܬܬܢܣܒ. ܘܫܒܝܬܗ ܕܥܫܝܢܐ
ܬܬܦܪܩ. ܘܕܝܢܝܟܝ ܐܢܐ ܐܕܘܢ. ܘܠܒܢܝܟܝ ܐܢܐ ܐܦܪܘܩ.

26 ܟܘ ܘܐܘܟܠ ܠܐܠܘܨܝܟܝ ܒܣܪܗܘܢ. ܘܐܝܟ ܡܪܘܬܐ ܢܪܘܘܢ ܡܢ ܕܡܗܘܢ. ܘܢܕܥܘܢ
ܟܠ ܒܣܪ ܕܐܢܐ ܡܪܝܐ ܦܪܘܩܟܝ: ܘܡܦܨܝܢܟܝ ܥܫܝܢܗ ܕܝܥܩܘܒ.

21   You will say in your heart: Who bore me these? For see! I am bereaved, I am deserted, exiled and troubled. Who reared these? See! If[1] I have been left alone, where were these?

22   Thus says the Lord God: See! I raise up my hand against the nations, I will raise a sign to the nations; they will bring your sons upon their hands, they will carry your daughters upon their shoulders.

23   Kings will be those who rear you, their princesses will suckle you; they will bow down to you with their faces on the ground, they will lick the dust of your feet; you will know that I am the Lord: those who wait for me are not ashamed.

24   Shall the prey of the mighty be carried off, or the captive of the strong be set free?

25   For thus says the Lord: The prey of the mighty will be carried off, and the captive of the strong will be set free, and I will judge your lawsuits, and I will redeem your children.

26   For I will feed your oppressors with their own flesh, they will be drunk with[2] their own blood as with the juice of the grape: and all flesh will know that I am the Lord your savior, the strong one of Jacob your helper.

---

[1] 'See! If': lit. 'If See!'.

[2] 'with'[2]: lit. 'from'.

ܩܦܠܐܘܢ: ܒ.

1 ܐ ܗܟܢܐ ܐܡܪ ܡܪܝܐ: ܐܝܢܘ ܟܬܒܐ ܕܫܘܒܩܢܐ ܕܫܒܩܬ ܠܐܡܟܘܢ. ܐܘ ܡܢܘ ܡܪܐ ܚܘܒܬܐ ܕܙܒܢܬܟܘܢ ܠܗ. ܗܐ ܒܚܛܗ̈ܝܟܘܢ ܐܙܕܒܢܬܘܢ. ܘܒܥܘܠ̈ܝܟܘܢ ܐܫܬܒܩܬ ܐܡܟܘܢ.

2 ܒ ܠܡܢܐ ܐܬܝܬ: ܘܠܝܬ ܐ̱ܢܫ. ܘܩܪܝܬ ܘܠܝܬ ܕܥܢܐ. ܡܚܕܐ ܚܕܒܐ ܐܝܕܝ ܘܦܪܩܐ. ܐܘ ܠܝܬ ܒܝ ܚܝܠܐ ܠܡܦܪܩܘ. ܗܐ ܒܟܐܬܝ ܡܚܪܒ ܐ̱ܢܐ ܝܡܐ. ܘܣܐܡ ܐ̱ܢܐ ܢܗܪ̈ܘܬܐ ܐܝܟ ܡܕܒܪܐ: ܘܡܣܪܝܢ ܢܘܢ̈ܝܗܘܢ ܡܢ ܕܠܝܬ ܡ̈ܝܐ: ܘܡܝܬܝܢ.

3 ܓ ܘܡܠܒܫ ܐ̱ܢܐ ܠܫܡܝܐ ܚܫܘܟܐ. ܘܣܩܐ ܣܐܡ ܐ̱ܢܐ ܬܟܣܝܬܗܘܢ.

4 ܕ ܡܪܝܐ ܐܠܗܐ ܝܗ̱ܒ ܠܝ ܠܫܢܐ ܕܝܘܠܦܢܐ. ܕܐܕܥ ܕܐܡܪ ܠܡܛ̈ܦܐ ܡܠܬܐ. ܐܥܝܪ ܒܨܦܪܐ. ܒܨܦܪܐ ܢܥܝܪ ܠܝ ܐܕܢܐ ܠܡܫܡܥ ܝܘܠܦܢܐ.

5 ܗ ܡܪܝܐ ܐܠܗܐ ܦܬܚ ܠܝ ܐܕܢܐ. ܘܐܢܐ ܠܐ ܗܦܟܬ ܠܒܣܬܪܝ: ܐܦܠܐ ܡܣܪܒ ܒܚܪܝܢܐ.

6 ܘ ܚܨܝ ܝܗܒܬ ܠܡܚ̈ܘܬܐ: ܘܦܟ̈ܝ ܠܡܡܪ̈ܛܐ. ܘܐܦ̈ܝ ܠܐ ܐܗܦܟܬ ܡܢ ܒܗܬܬܐ ܘܡܢ ܪܘܩܐ.

7 ܙ ܘܡܪܝܐ ܐܠܗܐ ܥܕܪܢܝ. ܡܛܠ ܗܢܐ ܠܐ ܒܗܬܬ: ܡܛܠ ܗܢܐ ܣܡܬ ܐܦ̈ܝ ܐܝܟ ܫܘܥܐ: ܘܝܕܥܬ ܕܠܐ ܒܗܬ ܐ̱ܢܐ.

8 ܚ ܕܩܪܝܒ ܗ̱ܘ ܡܙܕܩܢܝ. ܡܢܘ ܕܕܐܢ ܥܡܝ: ܢܩܘܡ ܐܟܚܕܐ. ܐܘ ܡܢܘ ܒܥܠ ܕܝܢܝ: ܢܬܩܪܒ ܠܘܬܝ.

Chapter 50

1   Thus says the Lord: Where is the bill of divorce[1] (with) which I repudiated your mother? Or who is my creditor,[2] to whom I sold you? See! In your sins you were sold, in your iniquity your mother was repudiated.

2   Why did I come? there was no-one (there); I called, and no-one answers. My hand reaped the harvest: did it fall short?[3] Or have I not the power to deliver?[4] See! With my rebuke I dry up the sea, I turn rivers into wilderness, their fish rot for lack of water, they die.

3   I clothe the heavens with darkness, I make sackcloth their garment.

4   The Lord God gave me a tongue of doctrine,[5] so that I may make known and declare the word to the weary;[6] he has awakened in the morning, in the morning he will make my ears[7] understand[8] doctrine.

5   The Lord God has opened my ears; I have not turned away,[9] nor have I stood firm in strife.

6   I gave my body to wounds, my cheeks to beating; I did not turn my face from shame, from spittle.

7   The Lord God helped me: therefore I was not ashamed, therefore I made my face like stone, I knew that I am not shamed.

8   For he is near, the one who justifies me; who contends with me? Let us stand up together; or who is my adversary?[10] Let him approach me.

---

[1] 'bill of divorce': lit. 'writing of release'.

[2] 'creditor': lit. 'lord of my debt'.

[3] 'did it fall short?' or 'it fell short'.

[4] 'have I not the power to deliver': lit. 'is there not might in me to redeem'.

[5] 'doctrine' or 'instruction, learning'.

[6] 'weary' or 'afflicted'.

[7] 'make my ears': lit. 'make for me ears to'.

[8] 'understand' or 'hear; obey'.

[9] 'away' or 'behind me'.

[10] 'my adversary': lit. 'the master of my contention'.

9 ܛ ܗܐ ܡܪܝܐ ܐܠܗܐ ܡܥܕܪ ܠܝ: ܡܢܘ ܡܚܝܒ ܠܝ. ܗܐ ܟܠܟܘܢ ܐܝܟ ܠܒܘܫܐ ܒܠܝܢ: ܘܣܣܐ ܢܐܟܘܠܝܘܢ.

10 ܝ ܡܢܘ ܒܟܘܢ ܕܕܚܠ ܡܢ ܡܪܝܐ: ܢܫܡܥ ܒܩܠܐ ܕܥܒܕܗ. ܕܗܠܟ ܒܚܫܘܟܐ: ܘܠܝܬ ܠܗ ܢܘܗܪܐ. ܢܬܬܟܠ ܒܫܡܗ ܕܡܪܝܐ: ܘܢܣܬܡܟ ܥܠ ܐܠܗܗ.

11 ܝܐ ܗܐ ܟܠܟܘܢ ܡܩܕܚܝ ܢܘܪܐ ܐܝܟܢܐ: ܘܡܚܕܪܝܢ ܫܠܗܒܝܬܐ. ܗܠܟܘ ܒܢܘܗܪܐ ܕܢܘܪܟܘܢ: ܘܒܫܠܗܒܝܬܐ ܕܐܘܩܕܬܘܢ. ܡܢ ܐܝܕܝ ܗܘܬ ܠܟܘܢ ܗܕܐ: ܕܒܟܪܝܘܬܐ ܬܫܟܒܘܢ.

9   See! The Lord God helps me: who condemns me? See! They are all like worn-out clothes, the moth will eat them.

10   Who among you (is there that) fears the Lord? May he hear the voice of his servant, who walks in darkness, and there is no light for him; may he hope in the name of the Lord, may he be redeemed by his God.

11   See! All of you, you all set on fire,[1] kindle flame: go, in the brilliance of your fire, in the flame of your fiery coal. This was yours from my hand: you will lie down in distress.

---

[1] 'you all set on fire': lit. 'are those who set on fire'.

مَجَّلَاهـ: با.

1 ، هُـوَمحـتوـهي بوُوهـُـهي حَرّوُـمُّهـبِأَ: وَحِـنّحِ حَـمُحـنّا. مُـوو حـلـهُـوزُا وِأَبِحِـرِّوَزّنَاهـ هُـنّه: هَـحـيّـوَحـا وِأَبِـهَـزّنَاهـ هُـنّه.

2 ، مُـوو لَاجـنّـوّهٍ أَجُـوّبِـهـ: هَـحـمُّـا وِجـلّـهَلّجـبِـهـ. وِمّـبِ هوا: هَـمّـنّـبِّهـه: وَحّـنَحّـبِّهـه: هَاهـيّـبِّهـه.

3 ، هَـهُلَا وِجـبُنا هُـدنا حَـزّومهـ: هَـمحـنا حـجُحـلّـهـي مُـنّحُـبِّهـ. وَحّـجِ هَـبِحـنّـه أَمـ حِـنِ: وَهّـجِحـبِّهـه أَمـ قَـنّوُمهـه وِهُـدنا. وِمّـرُّا مّـبِّـوّبِأَ لّـهـلّهّجـبِ حِـيّـهّـه: هَاهـوِّمبِأَ هَمُّلَا وِزّهِخّـا.

4 ، هُـوَمحـتوـهي حَـهِّـحهـا: وَزّوُّبِـمّـبِـي أَهِّوُـبِأَ. مُـهُلَا وِنّهُـوَمهـا هُـي هُـحُّـنّـحِ نُّهِّـحِ. وَوّـمبِ نّهـوّوَا هوا حـلّهِّـحهـا.

5 ، هَـنّـحـ أُوّـمُهـبِّأَ: هَـبِحـ قُـهّوُـمبِّي. وَحّـبِوُّوِّي حَـهِّـحهـا لّحّـلّأَوّـبِّهـه. حّـ مّـقّـبِحّـ حُـزّوِّبِأَ. وَحّـبِوّوِّي بِـقّـحّـبِّ.

6 ، أُوّـمحِـو حَـبِّـمّـحّـهّ حَـمّـمّـنا: مُـوو أَوّ حـحـبِّمّـهِ حّـأَوّحـا. مُـهُلَا وَحّـمّـمّـنا أَمـ نَّـبِّـنا بِـهّـبِّهّ: هَاوّـنّا أَمـ حـجُـهّـحـا بِـأَجـا. وَحّـهّـوّزّبِّهـه أَجـنّبِّأَ بِـهّـوَهّـبِ. وَقّـهّـوّمبِّي حـبِّـهّحّـ بِـهوّا: وَزّوُّمُهـبِّي لّا بِـأَحّـنِ.

7 ، هُـوَمحـتوـهي بِّـبِّحّـ أَوّـمُهـبِّأَ: حَـهّـا وِنّهُـوّمهـي حّـلّـحّـوّهـه: لّا بِـأَوّمحّهـ هّـ مّـحّـنّا وِأَبِّـنا: وَمّـ جّـهّـوّجّـهّه لّا بِـأَوّنّهـه.

8 ، هَـهُلَا وِأَمـ وَحّـهّـمّـنا هَأَمـ وِحّـلّجـهّمّـا نّأَجّـوّلّاـه مُّـمّـا. وِأَوّـمُهـبِّأَ حّـبِّـحّـ أَهوّا. وَحّـهّـوّمُهـي حّـزّوَّوَمبِ.

حّـهّ صّم

9 ، أَلّـلّاهّـنّـمبِ: أَلّـلّاهّـنّـمبِ: هَـحّـجّـحّـي هّـهّـنا وِبِّوَّوّحّـهـ وِهُـدنا. أَلّـلّاهّـنّـمبِ أَمـ وِجّـحّـبِّهّخّـا هّـمّـمّهّنا: هّأَمـ بِّوُّا وِمّـ حّـلّهّحّـي. أَبّـلّاي أَبّـلّاي وَحّـهّـمّهّي هّـهّـمّـا وَّخّـا: هَـمّـلّجّـحّـي حّـبّـأَبّـنّا.

250

Chapter 51

1   Hear me, (you) who pursue righteousness, and seek the Lord. Look to the mountain from which you were hewn, to the well from which you were hollowed out.

2   Look to Abraham your father, and to Sarah who bore you: for he was one, but I called to him, and I blessed him, and I multiplied him.

3   Because the Lord has built Zion, restores all her desolate wastes, turns her wilderness into Eden, makes her plain like the garden of the Lord: joy and gladness will be heard in her midst, thanksgiving and the sound of music.

4   Hear me, nations! Give ear, peoples! for the law goes forth from my presence, my judgment is a light to the nations.

5   My righteousness has drawn near, my salvation has gone forth: by my arm the peoples will be judged, the islands will await me, they will trust[1] in my arm.

6   Lift up your eyes to the heavens, look too beneath the earth: for the heavens will pass away like smoke, the earth will wear out like a garment, together with its inhabitants[2] - but my salvation will be eternal, my righteousness will not pass away.

7   Hear me, you who know righteousness,[3] people in whose heart is my law: do not fear the reproach of man, do not[4] tremble at their blasphemy.

8   For as wool, as a garment, the moth will eat them: but my righteousness is eternal, my salvation for generations.

XXV

9   Awake, awake! clothe yourself in the strength of the arm of the Lord; awake as in ancient days, as the generations of old: you are she who decreed the great decree, who killed the dragon.

---

[1] 'trust' or 'hope'.

[2] 'together with its inhabitants': lit. 'its inhabitants like it will be'.

[3] 'you who know righteousness': lit. 'knowers of righteousness'.

[4] 'do not ... do not' or 'you will not ... you will not'.

10 ܝ ܐܝܬܝܟܝ ܗܝ ܕܐܚܪܒܬܝ ܝܡܐ: ܘܡܝܐ ܕܬܗܘܡܐ ܪܒܐ. ܘܥܘܡܩܐ ܕܝܡܐ ܥܒܕܬܝ ܐܘܪܚܐ. ܕܢܥܒܪܘܢ ܦܪ̈ܝܩܐ ܦܪ̈ܝܩܘܗܝ ܕܡܪܝܐ.

11 ܝܐ ܘܢܬܦܢܘܢ ܘܢܐܬܘܢ ܠܨܗܝܘܢ ܒܫܘܒܚܐ. ܘܠܥܠܡܥܠܡ ܬܗܘܐ ܚܕܘܬܐ ܥܠ ܪ̈ܫܝܗܘܢ. ܒܘܣܡܐ ܘܚܕܘܬܐ ܢܕܪܟܘܢ. ܘܢܥܪܩܘܢ ܕ̈ܘܘܢܐ ܘܐܢ̈ܚܬܐ.

12 ܝܒ ܐܢܐ ܐܢܐ ܡܒܝܐܢܟܘܢ ܐܡܪ ܡܪܝܐ. ܡܢ ܐܢܬܝ ܕܕܚܠܬܝ ܡܢ ܐܢܫܐ ܕܡܐܬ: ܘܡܢ ܒܪܢܫܐ ܕܐܝܟ ܚܨܝܪܐ ܢܒܫ.

13 ܝܓ ܘܛܥܝܬܝ ܠܡܪܝܐ ܕܥܒܕܟܝ. ܕܡܬܚ ܫܡܝܐ: ܘܐܫܬܐܣ ܫܬܐܣܘܗܝ ܕܐܪܥܐ. ܘܕܚܠܬܝ ܐܡܝܢܐܝܬ ܟܠܝܘܡ ܡܢ ܩܕܡ ܚܡܬܗ ܕܐܠܘܨܐ: ܕܡܛܝܒ ܗܘܐ ܠܡܚܒܠܘ. ܐܝܟܐ ܗܝ ܚܡܬܗ ܕܐܠܘܨܐ.

14 ܝܕ ܕܡܣܬܪܗܒ ܗܘܐ ܚܒ̈ܝܫܐ ܠܡܫܪܝܘܬܗ. ܠܐ ܢܡܘܬܘܢ ܠܚܒܠܐ. ܘܠܐ ܢܚܣܪ ܠܚܡܗ.

15 ܝܗ ܐܢܐ ܐܢܐ ܡܪܝܐ ܐܠܗܟܝ. ܕܓܥܐ ܒܝܡܐ ܘܡܪܬܝܢ ܓܠ̈ܠܘܗܝ. ܡܪܝܐ ܚܝܠܬܢܐ ܫܡܗ.

16 ܝܘ ܕܣܡܬ ܡܠܝ ܒܦܘܡܟܝ. ܘܒܛܠܠܐ ܕܐܝܕܝ ܟܣܝܬܟܝ. ܒܗ ܕܡܬܚܬ ܫܡܝܐ: ܘܐܫܬܐܣܬ ܫܬܐܣܘܗܝ ܕܐܪܥܐ: ܘܐܡܪܬ ܠܨܗܝܘܢ ܕܥܡܝ ܐܢܬܝ.

17 ܝܙ ܐܬܬܥܝܪܝ ܐܬܬܥܝܪܝ: ܘܩܘܡܝ ܐܘܪܫܠܡ. ܕܐܫܬܝܬܝ ܡܢ ܐܝܕܗ ܕܡܪܝܐ ܟܣܐ ܕܚܡܬܗ. ܘܐܫܬܝܬܝ ܘܐܡܨܝܬܝ ܟܣܐ ܕܕܘܠܚܐ.

18 ܝܚ ܘܠܝܬ ܕܡܕܒܪ ܠܗ ܡܢ ܟܠܗܘܢ ܒܢ̈ܝܐ ܕܝܠܕܬ. ܘܠܝܬ ܕܐܚܕ ܒܐܝܕܗ ܘܡܩܝܡ ܠܗ: ܡܢ ܟܠܗܘܢ ܒܢ̈ܝܐ ܕܪܒܝܬ.

19 ܝܛ ܬܪܬܝܢ ܐܢܝܢ ܕܦܓܥܢܟܝ. ܠܡܢ ܢܬܬܥܝܩ ܥܡܟܝ. ܒܙܬܐ ܘܬܒܪܐ: ܘܟܦܢܐ ܘܚܪܒܐ. ܡܢ ܢܒܝܐܟܝ.

10   You it is who dried up the sea and the waters of the great deep: in the depths of the waters you made a pathway, that the redeemed might pass through, the redeemed of the Lord.

11   They will return, enter Zion with praise,[1] gladness on their heads forever; they will find delight and gladness, misery and groaning[2] will flee.

12   I am he who comforts you, says the Lord. Who are you, that you have been afraid of man who is mortal,[3] of mankind[4] that dries up as grass?

13   You have forgotten the Lord who made you, who stretched out the heavens, established the foundations of the earth; you have been afraid, continually, every day, of the rage of the oppressor, who was prepared to destroy: where is the rage of[5] the oppressor?

14   Who hastened to destroy the strong; they will not die by destruction,[6] his bread will not fail.

15   I am the Lord your God, who rebukes the sea, and its waves are still: the mighty Lord is his name.

16   For I set my words in your mouth, covered you with the shade of my hand, with which I stretched out the heavens, established the foundations of the earth. I said to Zion: You are my people.

17   Awake, awake, arise, Jerusalem! for you have drunk, from the hand of the Lord, the cup of his wrath, you have drunk, you have drained the cup of staggering.

18   There is none, of all the children that she bore, who comforts her, none who takes her hand and raises her up, of all the children that she reared.

19   These two (things) have come to you: who will grieve for you? Prey, ruin, famine, and the sword: who will comfort you?

---

[1] 'with praise' or 'in glory'.

[2] 'groaning': pl.

[3] 'is mortal': lit. 'dies'.

[4] 'mankind': lit. 'son of man'.

[5] 'of the rage of': lit. 'from before'.

[6] 'by destruction'. MT 'to the pit'. See Introduction. Addendum 1.

20   Your children are confounded, they lie down at the ends[1] of all the streets, like a flabby beet:[2] they are full of the anger of the Lord, the rebuke of your God.

21   Therefore, you who are humiliated,[3] hear these things, drunken (but) not on wine.

22   Thus says your Lord, the Lord: Your God will acquit[4] his people. See! I have taken from your hands the cup of staggering, not again will you drink[5] the cup of my wrath.

23   I will put it in the hand of those who humiliate you, who said to your soul: Lie down, we will pass over.[6] You have made your people like the earth, like a street for those who pass over.

---

[1] 'ends': lit. 'head'.

[2] 'flabby beet' or 'faded beet'. See Introduction. Addendum 1.

[3] 'you who are humiliated': lit. 'humiliated one'.

[4] 'acquit' or 'judge'.

[5] 'will you drink': lit. 'to drink'.

[6] 'Lie down, we will pass over' or 'Be humble, we will overcome'.

ܩܦܠܐܘܢ: ܢܒ.

1 ܐ ܐܬܥܝܪܝ: ܐܬܥܝܪܝ ܨܗܝܘܢ. ܘܠܒܫܝ ܠܒܘܫܐ ܕܬܫܒܘܚܬܐ: ܐܘܪܫܠܡ
ܡܕܝܢܬܐ ܩܕܝܫܬܐ. ܡܛܠ ܕܠܐ ܢܘܣܦ ܬܘܒ ܠܡܥܠ ܒܟܝ ܥܘܪܠܐ ܘܛܡܐܐ.

2 ܒ ܐܬܬܦܨܝ ܡܢ ܥܦܪܐ. ܘܩܘܡܝ ܬܒܝ ܐܘܪܫܠܡ. ܫܪܝ ܢܝܪܐ ܡܢ ܨܘܪܝܟܝ ܫܒܝܬܐ:
ܒܪܬ ܨܗܝܘܢ.

3 ܓ ܡܛܠ ܕܗܟܢܐ ܐܡܪ ܡܪܝܐ: ܡܓܢ ܐܙܕܒܢܬܘܢ: ܘܠܐ ܒܟܣܦܐ ܬܬܦܪܩܘܢ.

4 ܕ ܡܛܠ ܕܗܟܢܐ ܐܡܪ ܡܪܝܐ ܐܠܗܐ: ܠܡܨܪܝܢ ܢܚܬ ܥܡܝ ܒܩܕܡܝܬܐ
ܠܡܥܡܪ ܬܡܢ. ܘܐܬܘܪܝܐ ܒܡܓܢܐ ܕܒܪܗ.

5 ܗ ܘܗܫܐ ܡܐ ܠܝ ܗܪܟܐ ܐܡܪ ܡܪܝܐ: ܕܐܬܕܒܪ ܥܡܝ ܡܓܢ. ܡܫܬܠܛܢܘܗܝ
ܡܝܠܠܝܢ: ܐܡܪ ܡܪܝܐ. ܘܐܡܝܢܐܝܬ ܟܠܗܘܢ ܥܠ ܫܡܝ ܡܬܓܕܦ.

6 ܘ ܡܛܠ ܗܢܐ ܢܕܥ ܥܡܝ ܫܡܝ ܒܝܘܡܐ ܗܘ. ܡܛܠ ܕܐܢܐ ܗܘ ܡܡܠܠ:
ܘܐܬܝ.

7 ܙ ܡܐ ܝܐܝܢ ܥܠ ܛܘܪܐ ܪ̈ܓܠܘܗܝ ܕܡܣܒܪ ܫܠܡܐ: ܘܡܣܒܪ ܛܒܬܐ:
ܘܡܫܡܥ ܦܘܪܩܢܐ. ܕܐܡܪ ܠܨܗܝܘܢ: ܐܡܠܟ ܐܠܗܟܝ.

8 ܚ ܩܠܐ ܕܕܘ̈ܩܒܝܟܝ. ܐܪܝܡܘ ܩܠܐ. ܘܐܟܚܕܐ ܡܫܒܚܝܢ. ܡܛܠ ܕܥܝܢ ܒܥܝܢ ܢܚܙܘܢ ܟܕ
ܡܗܦܟ ܡܪܝܐ ܠܨܗܝܘܢ.

9 ܛ ܕܘܨܘ ܘܫܒܚܘ ܐܟܚܕܐ ܚܪ̈ܒܬܐ ܕܐܘܪܫܠܡ. ܡܛܠ ܕܒܝܐ ܡܪܝܐ ܠܥܡܗ:
ܘܦܪܩܗ ܠܐܘܪܫܠܡ.

10 ܝ ܓܠܐ ܡܪܝܐ ܕܪܥܗ ܩܕܝܫܐ ܠܥܝ̈ܢܝ ܟܠܗܘܢ ܥܡ̈ܡܐ. ܘܢܚܙܘܢ ܟܠܗܘܢ ܣܘܦܝܗ
ܕܐܪܥܐ ܦܘܪܩܢܗ ܕܐܠܗܢ.

Chapter 52

1   Awake, awake, Zion! clothe yourself with a garment of praise, Jerusalem, the holy city, for the uncircumcised and the unclean will not again enter you.

2   Shake the dust off yourself,[1] arise, sit down, Jerusalem; loosen the yoke from your neck, captive, daughter of Zion.

3   For thus says the Lord: You were sold without recompense - and not with money will you be redeemed.

4   For thus says the Lord God: My people went down first to Egypt, to live there; the Assyrian took him by force.

5   So now, what is (there) here for me, says the Lord, for my people was carried away without recompense; their rulers lament, says the Lord; continually, every day, they revile my name.

6   Therefore, on that day, my people will know my name, for I am he who speaks, it is I.

7   How fair upon the mountains are the feet of him who brings tidings of peace, who brings tidings of good,[2] who makes heard (my) salvation, who says to Zion: Your God reigns.[3]

8   The voice of your watchmen: they have raised a cry,[4] they sing praise(s) in unison: for face to face[5] they will see, when the Lord returns to Zion.

9   Rejoice, sing praise(s) in unison, desolate places of Jerusalem, for the Lord has comforted his people, he has redeemed Jerusalem.

10 The Lord has revealed his holy arm in the sight[6] of all peoples: all the ends of the earth will see the redemption of our God.

---

[1] 'Shake the dust off yourself': lit. 'Shake yourself from dust'.

[2] 'good': pl.

[3] 'reigns': perfect verb.

[4] 'a cry' or '(their) voice'.

[5] 'face to face': lit. 'eye with eye'.

[6] 'in the sight': lit. 'to the eye'.

11 ܝܐ ܥܒܪܘ: ܥܒܪܘ. ܦܘܩܘ ܡܢ ܬܡܢ: ܘܠܛܡ̈ܐܐ ܠܐ ܬܬܩܪܒܘܢ. ܦܘܩܘ ܡܢ ܓܘܗ:
ܘܐܬܕܟܘ: ܫܩ̈ܘܠܝ ܡܐܢ̈ܘܗܝ ܕܡܪܝܐ.
12 ܝܒ ܡܛܠ ܕܠܐ ܒܣܘܪܗܒܐ ܬܦܩܘܢ. ܘܒܥܪܘܩܝܐ ܠܐ ܬܐܙܠܘܢ. ܡܛܠ ܕܡܪܝܐ ܐܙܠ
ܩܕܡܝܟܘܢ: ܘܡܟܢܫܢܟܘܢ ܐܠܗܗ ܕܐܝܣܪܝܠ.
13 ܝܓ ܗܐ ܡܣܬܟܠ ܥܒܕܝ. ܘܡܬܬܪܝܡ: ܘܡܫܬܩܠ: ܘܡܬܥܠܐ ܛܒ.
14 ܝܕ ܐܝܟ ܕܬܗܪܘ ܥܠܘܗܝ ܣܓܝ̈ܐܐ. ܗܟܢܐ ܡܣܬܚܠ ܚܙܘܗ ܡܢ ܒܪ̈ܢܫܐ:
ܘܫܘܒܚܗ ܡܢ ܒܢ̈ܝܢܫܐ.
15 ܝܗ ܗܟܢܐ ܡܕܟܐ ܥܡ̈ܡܐ ܣܓܝ̈ܐܐ: ܘܥܠܘܗܝ ܢܐܚܕܘܢ ܡܠ̈ܟܐ ܦܘܡܗܘܢ. ܡܛܠ
ܕܠܐ ܐܬܐܡܪ ܠܗܘܢ ܚܙܘ: ܘܕܠܐ ܫܡܥܘ ܐܣܬܟܠܘ.

11 Pass on, pass on, go out from there, do not touch[1] the unclean;[2] go out from its midst, purify yourselves,[3] bearers of the vessels of the Lord.

12 For you shall not go out in haste, you shall not flee,[4] for the Lord goes before you, he who gathers you (up) is the God of Israel.

13 See! My servant understands, he is exalted, lifted up, raised up high.[5]

14 As many will be speechless concerning him:[6] so is his appearance distorted beyond that of man, his face beyond that of mankind.

15 This one purifies many nations; concerning him kings will shut their mouth(s): for what has not been told to them, they saw, and what they had not heard, they understood.

---

[1] 'do not touch' or 'do not approach'.

[2] 'the unclean': either things or people.

[3] 'purify yourselves' or 'be purified'.

[4] 'flee': lit. 'go in flight'.

[5] 'raised up high' or 'elevated greatly'.

[6] 'speechless concerning him' or 'struck dumb by him' or 'amazed by him'.

Chapter 53

1 Who has believed our report? To whom has the arm of the Lord been revealed?

2 He rose up before him as an infant, as a root from thirsty ground; he had no form, nor brilliance: we saw that he had no form,[1] and we denied him.

3 Despised and humiliated by man, a man of sorrows, acquainted with[2] suffering:[3] we turned our face away from him, we despised him, we did not value[4] him.

4 Truly, he has borne our sufferings, he has endured our sorrows; we saw[5] him as beaten, afflicted by God, humiliated.

5 Killed for our sins, brought low for our iniquity, chastised for our peace:[6] but by his wounds we will be healed.

6 We all like sheep have gone astray,[7] each man has gone his own way:[8] but the Lord has laid upon him the sins of us all.

7 He came near, and was brought low, but he did not open his mouth; he was led like a lamb to the slaughter, yet like a sheep before the shearer he kept silent, he did not open his mouth.

8 He was taken from imprisonment, from judgment: who of his generation will tell (of this)? For he was torn from the land of the living, some of the wicked of my people drew near to him.[9]

---

[1] 'he had no form'¹: lit. 'there was no (favorable) appearance to him'.

[2] 'acquainted with' or 'knowing'.

[3] 'suffering': pl.

[4] 'value': lit. 'count'.

[5] 'saw': lit. 'counted'.

[6] 'chastised for our peace': lit. 'the chastisement of our peace was on him'.

[7] 'have gone astray': lit. 'are going astray'.

[8] 'each man has gone his own way': lit. 'each to his way, we have turned'.

[9] 'some of the wicked of my people drew near to him' or 'from the wicked of my people they took him'.

9   A wicked man gave his grave, even a rich man at his death:[1] for he had done no wrong, there was no deceit in his mouth.

10   The Lord desired to afflict him, to cause him suffering; sin was laid on him[2] that he might see seed,[3] lengthen days; the will of the Lord will prosper in his hand.

11   In[4] the travail of his soul he will see, he will be sated with (his) knowledge, and he will acquit the righteous. He is the servant of many, their sins he will bear.

12   Therefore I will assign him to[5] the many, he will divide the spoil with the strong: for he cast himself down[6] to death, he was numbered with the wicked, he bore the sins of the many, he met with the wicked.

---

[1] 'A wicked man gave his grave, even a rich man at his death' or 'He set his grave (with) the impious, and the rich in his death'.

[2] 'on him': lit. 'on his soul'.

[3] 'that he might see seed' or 'that the offspring might see'.

[4] 'In' or 'From'.

[5] 'assign him to' or 'divide him with'.

[6] 'cast himself down': lit. 'threw his soul'.

Chapter 54

XXVI

1 Sing praise, (O) barren woman who has not given birth; exult with praise, rejoice, you who have not[1] labored: for the children of the deserted woman have multiplied, (are) more than the children of the married woman, says the Lord.

2 Enlarge the place of your tents, stretch out the hangings of your tents, do not refrain: lengthen your tent-cords, strengthen your stakes.

3 For you will increase on the right hand and on the left: your seed will inherit the nations, the deserted cities will be inhabited.

4 Do not fear, for you have not been shamed, you will not be overwhelmed, for you will not be put to shame, for you will forget the shame of your youth, you will no more call to mind the reproach of your widowhood.

5 For your Lord does so to you: the Mighty Lord is his name, your savior, the Holy One of Israel,[2] he will be called 'The God of all the earth'.

6 For the Lord called you as to a woman forsaken, distressed in spirit, as a wife of youth, forsaken, says your God.

7 In a moment of rage[3] I forsook you: but with my great mercy[4] I will gather you up.

8 In great rage I turned away my face from you; but in my eternal mercy[5] I took pity on you, says the Lord your savior.

9 This is to me like the days of Noah, when I swore that never again would the waters of Noah cover[6] the land: so have I sworn that I will not be angry with you, not reprove you.

---

[1] 'you who have not': lit. 'who has not'.

[2] 'your savior, the Holy One of Israel' or 'your savior is the Holy One of Israel'.

[3] 'moment of rage': lit. 'small rage'. See Introduction. Addendum 1.

[4] 'mercy': pl.

[5] 'mercy': pl.

[6] 'cover': lit. 'pass over'.

10 ܝ ܡܛܠ ܕܛܘܪܐ ܢܬܡܛܡܛܘܢ܆ ܘܪܡܬܐ ܢܬܪܟܢܢ܂ ܘܛܝܒܘܬܝ ܡܢܟܝ ܠܐ ܬܥܒܪ܂
ܘܩܝܡܐ ܕܫܠܡܟܝ ܠܐ ܢܙܘܥ܆ ܐܡܪ ܡܪܝܐ ܡܪܚܡܢܟܝ܂

11 ܐ ܡܣܟܢܬܐ ܘܡܬܛܠܛܠܬܐ ܘܠܐ ܡܬܒܝܐܢܝܬܐ܂ ܗܐ ܐܢܐ ܒܢܐ ܐܢܐ܆ ܟܐܦܝܟܝ ܒܟܘܚܠܐ܂
ܘܐܫܬܐܣܝܟܝ ܒܟܐܦܐ ܕܣܦܝܠܐ܂

12 ܒ ܘܐܥܒܕ ܫܘܪܝܟܝ ܒܟܐܦܐ ܕܐܣܦܝܣ܆ ܘܬܪܥܝܟܝ ܒܟܐܦܐ ܕܒܪܘܠܠܘܣ܆
ܘܬܚܘܡܝܟܝ ܒܟܐܦܐ ܓܒܝܬܐ܂

13 ܓ ܘܟܠܗܘܢ ܒܢܝܟܝ ܢܠܦܘܢܝ܂ ܘܣܓܝܐ ܫܠܡܐ ܕܒܢܝܟܝ܂

14 ܕ ܘܒܙܕܝܩܘܬܐ ܬܬܩܢܝܢ܂ ܐܬܪܚܩܝ ܡܢ ܥܘܠܡܐ܆ ܡܛܠ ܕܠܐ ܬܕܚܠܝܢ܂ ܘܡܢ ܬܒܪܐ܆
ܡܛܠ ܕܠܐ ܢܩܪܒ ܠܟܝ܂

15 ܗ ܘܟܠ ܕܡܬܢܩܦܝܢ ܡܢ ܐܚܪܢܐ܆ ܢܦܠܘܢ ܠܟܝ܂ ܘܬܗܘܐ ܥܡܟܝ ܓܘܣܐ
ܠܥܘܕܪܢܟܝ܂

16 ܘ ܗܐ ܐܢܐ ܒܪܝܬ ܢܦܚܐ ܕܢܦܚ ܒܢܘܪܐ ܓܘܡܪܐ܆ ܘܡܦܩ ܡܐܢܐ ܠܥܒܕܗ܂ ܘܐܢܐ
ܒܪܝܬ ܡܚܒܠܢܐ ܠܡܚܒܠܘ܂

17 ܙ ܟܠ ܡܐܢ ܕܡܬܛܝܒ ܥܠܝܟܝ܆ ܠܐ ܢܨܠܚ ܒܟܝ܂ ܘܟܠ ܠܫܢ ܕܢܩܘܡ ܥܡܟܝ
ܒܕܝܢܐ܆ ܬܚܝܒܝܢܗ܂ ܗܕܐ ܗܝ ܝܪܬܘܬܐ ܕܥܒܕܘܗܝ ܕܡܪܝܐ܂ ܘܙܕܝܩܘܬܗܘܢ ܡܢ
ܩܕܡܝ܆ ܐܡܪ ܡܪܝܐ܂

10 For the mountains may be flattened, the high places cast down: yet my loving-kindness will not pass away from you, the covenant of your peace will not pass away, says the Lord, the merciful one.

11 Humiliated, tempest-tossed, who has not been comforted: See! I turn[1] your stones into beryls, I will establish your foundations on[2] stones of sapphire.

12 I will build your walls with stones of jasper, your gates with stones of rock crystal, your boundaries with choice stones.

13 All your children will learn of me; the peace of your children will grow.

14 You will be restored[3] in righteousness: abstain from slander, in order that you may not be afraid, and destruction,[4] in order that it may not be near to you.

15 All who are returned by my hands will come to you, and you will be a house of refuge for your inhabitants.

16 See! I created the workman who blows on the fire with bellows, who perfects the instrument for his work: and I created the destroyer to destroy.

17 No instrument established against you will prosper;[5] every tongue that will arise against you in judgment, you will overcome.[6] This is the inheritance of the servants of the Lord: their righteousness is from me, says the Lord.

---

[1] 'turn': lit. 'make'.

[2] 'on' or 'with'.

[3] 'restored' or 'established'.

[4] 'destruction' or 'ruin'.

[5] 'No instrument established against you will prosper': lit. 'Any instruments that are established against you will not ascend to the top'.

[6] 'overcome' or 'declare guilty'.

ܩܦܠܐܘܢ: ܢܗ.

1 ܐ ܐܘ ܟܠ ܕܨܗܐ: ܐܙܠܘ ܠܡܝ̈ܐ: ܘܕܠܝܬ ܠܗ ܟܣܦܐ. ܐܙܠܘ ܙܒܘܢܘ: ܘܐܟܘܠܘ
ܕܠܐ ܟܣܦܐ: ܘܕܠܐ ܕܡܝ̈ܢ: ܚܡܪܐ ܘܚܠܒܐ.

2 ܒ ܠܡܢܐ ܬܬܩܠܘܢ ܐܢ̱ܬܘܢ ܟܣܦܐ ܕܠܐ ܠܠܚܡܐ: ܘܠܥܡܠܟܘܢ ܕܠܐ ܠܣܒܥܐ.
ܫܡܥܘܢܝ ܫܡܥܐ: ܘܐܟܘܠܘ ܛܒܬܐ. ܘܬܬܦܢܩ ܢܦܫܟܘܢ ܒܕܘܗܢܐ.

3 ܓ ܨܠܘ ܐܕܢ̈ܝܟܘܢ: ܘܬܘ ܠܘܬܝ. ܫܡܥܘܢܝ ܘܬܚܐ ܢܦܫܟܘܢ. ܘܐܩܝܡ ܠܟܘܢ
ܩܝܡܐ ܕܠܥܠܡ: ܛܝܒܘܬܗ ܕܕܘܝܕ ܡܗܝܡܢܬܐ.

4 ܕ ܗܐ ܣܗܕܐ ܠܥܡ̈ܡܐ ܝܗܒܬܗ: ܪܫܐ ܘܡܦܩܕܢܐ ܠܐܡ̈ܘܬܐ.

5 ܗ ܕܐܡܬܐ ܥܡ̈ܡܐ ܕܠܐ ܝܕܥܬ. ܘܥܡ̈ܡܐ ܕܠܐ ܝܕܥܘܟ ܠܘܬܟ ܢܪܗܛܘܢ. ܡܛܠ
ܡܪܝܐ ܐܠܗܟ: ܘܩܕܝܫܐ ܕܐܝܣܪܝܠ ܕܫܒܚܟ.

6 ܘ ܒܥܘ ܠܡܪܝܐ. ܘܡܐ ܕܐܫܟܚܬܘܢܝܗܝ: ܩܪܐܘܗܝ.

7 ܙ ܘܡܐ ܕܩܪܝܒ: ܢܫܒܘܩ ܚܛܝܐ ܐܘܪܚܗ: ܘܓܒܪܐ ܥܘܠܐ ܡܚܫܒܬܗ. ܘܢܬܦܢܐ
ܠܡܪܝܐ: ܘܢܪܚܡ ܥܠܘܗܝ: ܘܠܘܬ ܐܠܗܢ ܕܡܣܓܐ ܠܡܫܒܩ.

8 ܚ ܡܛܠ ܕܡܚܫܒ̈ܬܝ ܠܐ ܗܘ̈ܝ ܐܝܟ ܡܚܫܒ̈ܬܟܘܢ. ܘܐܘܪ̈ܚܬܝ ܠܐ ܗܘ̈ܝ ܐܝܟ
ܐܘܪ̈ܚܬܟܘܢ: ܐܡܪ ܡܪܝܐ.

9 ܛ ܡܛܠ ܕܐܝܟ ܕܪܡܝܢ ܫܡܝܐ ܡܢ ܐܪܥܐ: ܗܟܢܐ ܪܡܢ ܐܘܪ̈ܚܬܝ ܡܢ ܐܘܪ̈ܚܬܟܘܢ.
ܘܡܚܫܒ̈ܬܝ ܡܢ ܡܚܫܒ̈ܬܟܘܢ.

Chapter 55

1   Ho, all who thirst: go to the water! he who has no money,[1] go, buy (food)! take[2] wine and milk, he who has no money, no wage.[3]

2   Why do you weigh silver that is not for (buying) bread, and labor[4] for that which is not satisfying? Listen carefully to me - and you will eat good (food), your soul will delight itself in fatness.

3   Listen carefully,[5] come to me! Hear me, that your soul(s) may live! and I will establish for you an eternal covenant, the faithful goodness of David.

4   See! I have given you as a witness to the nations, a ruler and a leader to the peoples.

5   For you will call the nations that you did not know, and nations that do not know you will run to you, because of the Lord your God, the Holy One of Israel who has glorified you.

6   Seek the Lord! and when you have found him, call on him!

7   For when he has come near, the sinner will abandon his way, the unjust man his will;[6] he will turn to me, and I will have mercy on him; and to our God who abundantly forgives.

8   For my will is not like your will,[7] and my ways are not like your ways, says the Lord.

9   For as the heavens are higher than the earth, so my ways are higher than your ways, and my will than your will.

---

[1] 'he who has no money': lit. 'he who (is) without money (or 'silver')'.

[2] 'take': lit. 'eat'.

[3] 'wage': lit. 'hire' (pl.).

[4] 'labor': lit. 'your labor'.

[5] 'Listen carefully': lit. 'Incline your ears'.

[6] 'will' or 'thoughts'.

[7] 'will' or 'thoughts' as in v.7. So too v.9.

ـ 10 .

ـ 11 .

ـ.

ـ.

10 For as the rain falls, and the snow from the heavens, and (they) do not go back there but water the earth and make it fertile,[1] make it bear,[2] giving[3] seed to the sower and bread for food,

11 So my word will be, which came forth from my mouth: it will not return to me in vain, but only when it has done my will,[4] completed that for which I sent it.

12 For you will go forth in rejoicing, you will go in peace; the mountains and the high places will exult before you; in praise[5] all the trees of the field will clap their hands.[6]

13 Instead of the thorn, the cypress[7] will grow; instead of the wild thyme, the myrtle will grow:[8] and it will be as a name to the Lord, as an eternal, unfailing sign.[9]

---

[1] 'fertile': lit. 'generate'.

[2] 'bear' or 'bud'.

[3] '(they) do … water … make[1,2] … giving': sing. verbs.

[4] 'my will': lit. 'whatever I wish'.

[5] 'in praise': lit. 'the praise of'.

[6] 'clap their hands': lit. 'strike the palm'.

[7] 'cypress' or 'juniper'.

[8] 'grow': lit. 'shoot up'.

[9] 'sign': pl.

ܩܦܠܐܘܢ: ܢܘ.

1 ܐ ܗܟܢܐ ܐܡܪ ܡܪܝܐ. ܛܪܘ ܕܝܢܐ ܘܥܒܕܘ ܙܕܝܩܘܬܐ. ܡܛܠ ܕܩܪܝܒ ܗܘ ܦܘܪܩܢܝ ܠܡܐܬܐ: ܘܙܕܝܩܘܬܝ ܠܡܬܓܠܝܘ.

2 ܒ ܛܘܒܘܗܝ ܠܓܒܪܐ ܕܢܥܒܕ ܗܕܐ: ܘܒܪܢܫܐ ܕܢܬܚܝܠ ܒܗ. ܘܢܛܪ ܐܦ ܫܒܬܐ ܕܠܐ ܢܚܠܝܗ. ܘܢܛܪ ܐܝܕܘܗܝ ܕܠܐ ܢܥܒܕ ܕܒܝܫ.

3 ܓ ܘܠܐ ܢܐܡܪ ܒܪ ܢܘܟܪܝܐ ܕܡܬܠܘܐ ܠܡܪܝܐ: ܕܡܦܪܫܘ ܦܪܫܢܝ ܠܝ ܡܪܝܐ ܡܢ ܥܡܗ. ܘܠܐ ܢܐܡܪ ܡܗܝܡܢܐ: ܕܩܝܣܐ ܐܢܐ ܝܒܝܫܐ.

4 ܕ ܡܛܠ ܕܗܟܢܐ ܐܡܪ ܡܪܝܐ: ܠܡܗܝܡܢܐ ܕܢܛܪܘܢ ܫܒܬܝ: ܘܢܓܒܘܢ ܡܕܡ ܕܨܒܐ ܐܢܐ: ܘܡܬܚܝܠܝܢ ܒܩܝܡܝ.

5 ܗ ܐܬܠ ܠܗܘܢ ܒܒܝܬܝ ܘܒܫܘܪܝ ܐܬܪܐ. ܘܫܡܐ ܕܛܒ ܡܢ ܒܢܝܐ ܘܡܢ ܒܢܬܐ: ܫܡܐ ܕܠܥܠܡ ܐܬܠ ܠܗܘܢ ܕܠܐ ܢܦܣܘܩ.

6 ܘ ܘܠܒܢܝ ܢܘܟܪܝܐ ܕܡܬܠܘܝܢ ܠܡܪܝܐ ܠܡܫܡܫܘܬܗ: ܘܠܡܪܚܡܘ ܫܡܗ ܕܡܪܝܐ: ܘܢܗܘܘܢ ܠܗ ܥܒܕܐ. ܟܠ ܕܢܛܪ ܫܒܬܐ ܕܠܐ ܢܚܠܝܗ: ܘܡܬܚܝܠܝܢ ܒܩܝܡܝ.

7 ܙ ܐܝܬܐ ܐܢܘܢ ܠܛܘܪܐ ܕܩܘܕܫܝ ܘܐܚܕܐ ܐܢܘܢ ܒܒܝܬܐ ܕܨܠܘܬܝ. ܥܠܘܬܗܘܢ ܘܕܒܚܝܗܘܢ ܢܣܩܢ ܠܡܕܒܚܝ. ܡܛܠ ܕܒܝܬܝ: ܒܝܬ ܨܠܘܬܐ ܢܬܩܪܐ: ܠܟܠܗܘܢ ܥܡܡܐ.

8 ܚ ܗܟܢܐ ܐܡܪ ܡܪܝܐ ܐܠܗܐ: ܕܡܟܢܫ ܠܡܒܕܪܘܗܝ ܕܐܝܣܪܝܠ: ܬܘܒ ܐܟܢܫ ܥܠܘܗܝ ܠܡܟܢܫܘܗܝ.

9 ܛ ܟܠ ܚܝܘܬܐ ܕܕܒܪܐ: ܬܘ ܐܬܟܠܘ ܟܠܟܘܢ ܚܝܘܬܐ ܕܥܒܐ.

10 ܝ ܚܙܝ ܟܠܗܘܢ ܣܡܝܐ ܘܠܐ ܝܕܥܝܢ. ܟܠܗܘܢ ܟܠܒܐ ܐܠܡܐ ܐܢܘܢ: ܘܠܐ ܡܫܟܚܝܢ ܠܡܢܒܚ. ܚܙܝ ܘܕܡܟܝܢ: ܘܪܚܡܝܢ ܠܡܕܡܟ.

Chapter 56

1   Thus says the Lord: Guard justice, act with righteousness,[1] for my redemption is soon to come, my righteousness to be revealed.

2   Blessed is the man who will do this, and the son of man[2] who will be strengthened by it, who also guards the Sabbath so that he will not profane it, who guards[3] his hand so that he will not do evil.

3   And let him not say, the stranger[4] who is joined to the Lord: Indeed the Lord separates me from his people, and may the eunuch not say: I am (as) dry wood.

4   For thus says the Lord to the eunuchs who guard my Sabbaths, who choose what I wish, who are strengthened in my covenant,

5   I will give them, in my house, within my walls, a place; and a name better than 'sons' or 'daughters': an eternal name I will give them, that does not come to an end.

6   And to the strangers who are joined to the Lord, to serve him, to love the name of the Lord, who will be servants to him, all who guard the Sabbath so that they will not profane it, and are strengthened in my covenant,

7   I will bring them to my holy mountain, I will make them rejoice in my house of prayer, their offerings and their sacrifices (will be) acceptable at my altar, for my house will be called a house of prayer for all peoples

8   Thus says the Lord God, who gathers the dispersed of Israel: Again will I gather together, to him, those who are gathered together.

9   Every beast of the field: Come, eat, every beast of the forest.

10 All the blind see, but they do not know, they are all dumb dogs, they cannot bark; they see and sleep, they love to slumber.

---

[1] 'act with righteousness': lit. 'do righteousness'.

[2] 'son of man'. See 44:13.

[3] 'guards' or 'keeps'.

[4] 'stranger': lit. 'son of foreigners'.

11 ܝܐ ܘܟܠܒܐ ܐܢܘܢ ܕܡܚܝܐ ܢܦܫܗܘܢ: ܘܠܐ ܝܕܥܝܢ ܠܡܣܒܥܘ. ܗܢܘܢ ܒܝܫܝܢ ܘܠܐ
ܝܕܥܝܢ ܣܘܟܠܐ. ܟܠܗܘܢ ܠܐܘܪܚܗܘܢ ܦܢܘ: ܘܐܢܫ ܠܡܘܬܪܗ ܘܠܒܨܥܗ.

12 ܝܒ ܐܬܘ ܢܣܒ ܚܡܪܐ: ܘܢܣܒ ܫܟܪܐ. ܘܢܗܘܐ ܐܝܟ ܕܝܘܡܢܐ: ܘܢܬܪ ܠܢ ܫܘܒܚܐ
ܪܒ.

11 They themselves are greedy dogs, they cannot[1] be satisfied, they will be wicked, they have no[2] understanding, they have all turned to their (own) way, each to his (own) side, to his (own) place.

12 Come! let us take wine, let us take strong drink: (tomorrow) will be as today,[3] it will profit us greatly.[4]

---

[1] 'cannot' or 'do not know how to'.

[2] 'have no': lit. 'do not know'.

[3] '(tomorrow) will be as today' or 'let (tomorrow) be as today'.

[4] 'greatly': lit. 'much that is good'.

Chapter 57

1   See! The righteous has perished, and there is no man who takes (it) to heart;[1] the just men who do not understand are taken away, for from the presence of evil the righteous is taken away.

2   And peace will come, and they will rest on their beds, they will go before them.

XXVII

3   And you, approach here, sons of the afflicted woman, seed of the adulterer and the fornicator.

4   On what do you seize greedily? To what have you opened your mouth, lengthened your tongue? For see! You are the child of iniquity, false seed.

5   Who are comforted by idols, beneath every forest tree; you have slain the children in the valleys, beneath the crags of rock.

6   Your portion and your inheritance, it is with the portion of the valleys; you also poured out drink offerings upon them, you raised up offerings: shall I be comforted by these?[2]

7   Upon the high and lofty mountains you have made your bed; also there you have gone up to sacrifice sacrifices.

8   Behind the doors, upon the door-posts, you have engraved your remembrance: for from my presence you went into exile, you went up, you enlarged your bed, you were on their side,[3] you loved their bed, and the place that you saw.

9   You have adorned yourself for kings with ointment, taken more incense,[4] sent your messengers far away; you were brought low, unto Sheol.

---

[1] 'takes (it) to heart': lit. 'brings to his heart'.

[2] 'shall I be comforted by these?' or 'by these I shall be comforted'.

[3] 'you were on their side': lit. 'you were for yourself from them'.

[4] 'taken more incense': lit. 'increased your incense'.

10 ܝ ܒܣܘܓܐܐ ܐܘܪܚܬܟܝ ܠܐܝܬܝ. ܘܠܐ ܐܡܪܬܝ ܕܐܬܡܚܠܬ. ܚܝܘܬܐ ܕܐܝܕܝܟܝ ܐܫܟܚܬܝ. ܡܛܠ ܗܢܐ ܠܐ ܐܬܦܟܠܬܝ.

11 ܝܐ ܡܢ ܡܢ ܐܬܪܗܒܬܝ ܘܕܚܠܬܝ. ܕܟܕܒܬܝ ܒܝ. ܘܠܐ ܐܬܕܟܪܬܝܢܝ: ܘܠܐ ܣܡܬܝܢܝ ܒܠܒܟܝ. ܗܐ ܐܢܐ ܗܘ ܫܬܝܩܐ ܕܡܢ ܥܠܡ. ܘܡܢܝ ܠܐ ܕܚܠܬܝ.

12 ܝܒ ܐܢܐ ܐܚܘܐ ܙܕܝܩܘܬܟܝ. ܘܥܒܕܝܟܝ ܠܐ ܢܥܕܪܘܢܟܝ.

13 ܝܓ ܬܦܨܢܟܝ ܒܩܪܘܢܝܟܝ ܐܝܠܝܢ ܕܡܬܟܢܫܝܢ ܠܟܝ. ܠܟܠܗܘܢ ܢܫܩܘܠܝܢܘܢ ܪܘܚܐ. ܘܢܣܒ ܐܢܘܢ ܗܒܠܐ. ܘܐܝܠܝܢ ܕܡܬܬܟܠܝܢ ܥܠܝ: ܢܐܪܬܘܢ ܐܪܥܐ: ܘܢܐܪܬܘܢ ܛܘܪܝ ܩܕܝܫܐ.

14 ܝܕ ܘܢܐܡܪܘܢ ܟܒܘ ܟܒܘ: ܦܢܘ ܐܘܪܚܐ. ܘܐܪܝܡܘ ܬܘܩܠܬܐ ܡܢ ܐܘܪܚܗ ܕܥܡܝ.

15 ܝܗ ܡܛܠ ܕܗܟܢܐ ܐܡܪ ܡܪܝܡܐ ܘܡܥܠܝܐ: ܕܫܪܐ ܠܥܠܡܝܢ: ܘܩܕܝܫ ܫܡܗ: ܡܪܝܡܐ: ܘܩܕܝܫ ܡܫܪܝܗ: ܠܡܟܝܟܐ ܘܠܡܟܝܟܝ ܪܘܚܐ: ܠܡܚܝܘ ܪܘܚܐ ܕܡܟܝܟܐ: ܘܠܡܚܝܘ ܠܒܐ ܕܡܬܒܪܐ.

16 ܝܘ ܡܛܠ ܕܠܐ ܠܥܠܡ ܕܐܢ ܐܢܐ. ܘܠܐ ܠܥܠܡ ܪܓܙ ܐܢܐ. ܡܛܠ ܕܪܘܚܐ ܡܢ ܩܕܡܝ ܢܦܩܐ. ܘܢܫܡܬܐ ܐܢܐ ܥܒܕܬ.

17 ܝܙ ܒܥܘܠܐ ܕܒܨܥܗ ܪܓܙܬ ܘܡܚܝܬܗ. ܘܐܛܫܝܬ ܘܪܓܙܬ: ܘܐܙܠ ܡܬܚܒܠܗ ܒܐܘܪܚܐ ܕܠܒܗ.

18 ܝܚ ܐܘܪܚܬܗ ܚܙܝܬ: ܘܐܣܝܬܗ ܘܒܝܐܬܗ. ܘܦܪܥܬ ܒܘܝܐܐ ܠܗ ܘܠܐܒܝܠܘܗܝ.

10   You have grown weary in the multitude of your customs,[1] yet you did not say: I will desist. In the guilt[2] of your hands you wasted away: therefore you have not made supplication.

11   Of whom were you afraid, did you dread, that you were false to me, did not remember me, did not take me to your heart?[3] See! I am the Holy One forever,[4] yet you did not fear me.

12   I will declare my righteousness; your works will not profit you.

13   Let them save you when you call out,[5] those who are gathered to you; the wind will carry them all off, the whirlwind will take them; but those who hope in me will inherit the land, will inherit my holy mountain.

14   They will say: Make smooth, make smooth, restore the way, take away the stumbling-blocks from the way of my people.

15   For thus says the most high one, the uplifted one, the eternal one:[6] his name is holy, the uplifted one, his habitation is holy, for the humbled, the grieved of spirit, to restore to life the spirit of the humbled,[7] to restore to life the heart of those who suffer,

16   For I will not maintain anger forever, I am not enraged forever, for the spirit goes forth from my presence, and the soul[8] (that) I have made.

17   I was enraged by the iniquity of her deceit, I struck her; she turned, she was enraged, she journeyed on, groaning,[9] in the way of her heart.

18   I considered her ways, I healed her and comforted her, I consoled[10] her and those who mourn her.

---

[1] 'customs' or 'ways'.

[2] 'guilt': lit. 'debt'.

[3] 'take me to your heart': lit. 'take account of me in your heart'.

[4] 'forever': lit. 'who is from eternity'.

[5] 'when you call out': lit. 'in your shouting'.

[6] 'eternal one': lit. 'who dwells forever'.

[7] 'humbled … grieved of spirit … humbled': pl. nouns.

[8] 'soul' or 'breath'.

[9] 'groaning': lit. 'with her groaning'.

[10] 'consoled': lit. 'bestowed consolation'.

19   The speech of the lips is created:[1] Peace, peace, to those far away and to those near, says the Lord, I will heal them.

20   The wicked are troubled like the sea, for they cannot find calm, its waters return vermin and filth: there is no peace for the wicked, says my God.

---

[1] 'is created'. Pass. part. MT has an active part. as does the Leiden text. 7a1 itself and other mss have perfects.

282

Chapter 58

1   Cry aloud,[1] do not refrain, raise your voice like a trumpet, declare to my people their iniquity, to those of the house of Jacob their sins.

2   They seek me every day, wishing to know my ways, like a people that has acted righteously[2] and did not forsake the judgment of its God: asking of me judgment and righteousness, wishing to be brought near to God.

3   Why did we fast - and you did not see; why did we humble ourselves[3] - and you did not know?[4] See! On your fast day you did your will, coming near to all your idols.

4   See! You fast for strife, for contention, for smiting with the violence of iniquity; do not[5] fast as today; make your voice heard on high.

5   This is the fast that I have chosen: that a man should humble himself, [6] should bend his neck like a hook, humbling himself with sackcloth and ash: for this you should call a fast, the day of the Lord's will.

6   This is the fast that I have chosen: that you should loosen the bonds of iniquity, break the ties of deceit, free the downtrodden,[7] break all the ties.

7   You should break your bread for the hungry, bring the stranger[8] into your house; when you see the naked you should cover him, and not turn away from a human being[9].

8   Then your light will be opened, as the dawn, your righteousness will rise up speedily, your righteousness will go before you, and the glory of the Lord will gather you (in).

---

[1] 'aloud': lit. 'in your throat'.

[2] 'has acted righteously': lit. 'did righteousness'.

[3] 'ourselves': lit. 'our soul'.

[4] 'you did not see … you did not know': possibly, rhetorical questions.

[5] 'do not' or 'you will not'.

[6] 'himself': lit. 'his soul'.

[7] 'free the downtrodden': lit. 'loosen the downtrodden to freedom'.

[8] 'stranger' or 'foreigner'.

[9] 'human being': lit. 'son of your flesh'.

9 ܛ ܗܳܝܕܶܝܢ ܬܶܩܪܶܐ: ܘܢܶܥܢܶܝܟ ܡܳܪܝܳܐ. ܘܬܶܒܥܶܐ: ܘܢܶܐܡܰܪ ܗܳܐ ܐ̱ܢܳܐ. ܐܶܢ ܬܰܥܒܰܪ ܡܶܢ ܒܶܝܢܳܟ ܢܺܝܪܳܐ: ܘܬܶܐܡܰܪ ܠܒܺܝܫܳܬܳܐ. ܘܡܶܢ ܡܫܰܕܠܳܐ ܕܨܶܒܥܳܐ ܬܶܬܢܺܝܚ.

10 ܝ ܘܬܶܬܶܠ ܠܰܟܦܢܳܐ ܠܰܚܡܳܐ. ܘܬܣܰܒܰܥ ܢܰܦܫܳܐ ܕܟܰܦܢܳܐ: ܢܶܕܢܰܚ ܢܽܘܗܪܳܟ ܒܚܶܫܽܘܟܳܐ: ܘܚܶܫܽܘܟܳܐ ܐܰܝܟ ܛܰܗܪܳܐ.

11 ܝܐ ܘܢܕܰܒܪܳܟ ܡܳܪܝܳܐ ܐܰܡܺܝܢܳܐܺܝܬ. ܘܢܰܣܒܰܥ ܢܰܦܫܳܟ ܒܨܰܗܝܽܘܬܳܐ. ܘܓܰܪܡܰܝܟ ܢܶܬܥܰܫܢܽܘܢ. ܘܬܶܗܘܶܐ ܐܰܝܟ ܦܰܪܕܰܝܣܳܐ ܪܰܘܝܳܐ: ܘܐܰܝܟ ܡܰܒܽܘܥܳܐ ܕܡܰܝܳܐ ܕܠܳܐ ܦܳܣܩܺܝܢ ܡܰܝܘܗܝ.

12 ܝܒ ܘܢܶܒܢܽܘܢ ܡܶܢܳܟ ܚܰܪܒܳܬܳܐ ܕܡܶܢ ܥܳܠܡ. ܘܫܶܬܶܐܣܶܐ ܕܕܳܪ ܘܕܳܪܳܐ ܬܩܺܝܡ. ܘܢܶܬܩܪܶܐ ܠܳܟ ܓܳܕܶܪ ܬܰܪܥܳܐ: ܘܡܗܰܦܶܟ ܫܒܺܝܠܶܐ ܠܰܡܬܳܒܳܐ.

13 ܝܓ ܐܶܢ ܬܗܰܦܶܟ ܪܶܓܠܰܝܟ ܡܶܢ ܫܰܒܬܳܐ: ܕܠܳܐ ܬܶܥܒܶܕ ܨܶܒܝܳܢܳܟ ܒܝܰܘܡܳܐ ܕܩܽܘܕܫܝ. ܘܬܶܩܪܶܐ ܠܫܰܒܬܳܐ ܡܦܰܢܩܳܢܺܝܬܳܐ: ܘܩܽܘܕܫܶܗ ܕܡܳܪܝܳܐ ܡܝܰܩܪܳܐ. ܘܬܝܰܩܪܺܝܘܗܝ ܕܠܳܐ ܬܶܥܒܶܕ ܒܶܗ ܐܽܘܪܚܳܟ: ܘܠܳܐ ܬܶܥܒܶܕ ܒܶܗ ܨܶܒܝܳܢܳܟ: ܘܠܳܐ ܬܡܰܠܶܠ ܡܶܠܬܳܐ.

14 ܝܕ ܗܳܝܕܶܝܢ ܬܶܬܒܰܣܰܡ ܥܰܠ ܡܳܪܝܳܐ. ܘܐܰܪܟܒܳܟ ܥܰܠ ܥܽܘܫܢܶܗ ܕܐܰܪܥܳܐ. ܘܐܰܘܟܠܳܟ ܝܽܘܪܬܳܢܶܗ ܕܝܰܥܩܽܘܒ ܐܰܒܽܘܟ. ܡܶܛܽܠ ܕܦܽܘܡܶܗ ܕܡܳܪܝܳܐ ܡܰܠܶܠ.

9   Then you will call, and the Lord will answer you; you will call out, and he will say: See! (It is) I. If you will remove deceit from your midst, free[1] the downtrodden, depart from the perfidious word,

10   And you will give your bread to the hungry, and satisfy the soul of the hungry: your light will dawn in the darkness, your darkness (will be) as noon.

11   The Lord will guide you always, satisfy your soul with rich food, strengthen your bones, and you will be like a watered garden, like a spring of water whose waters do not fail.

12   And some of you will build[2] the desolate wastes of old, you will establish the foundations of generations; they will call you 'Repairer of breaches', who returns the paths to the dwelling-place.

13   If you will restrain your foot on[3] the Sabbath, so that you will not do your will on my holy day, and call the Sabbath 'delightful', and the holiness of the Lord 'honorable', and honor it so that you will not act during it in your (usual) way,[4] and not do your will during it,[5] and not speak a (vain) word,

14   Then you would trust in the Lord, so that I may make you ride upon the strength of the earth, consume the inheritance of Jacob your father: for the mouth of the Lord has spoken.

---

[1] 'free': lit. 'let loose'.

[2] 'some of you will build': lit. 'they will build, from you'.

[3] 'restrain your foot on': lit. 'turn your foot from'.

[4] 'act on it in your (usual) way': lit. 'do on it your way'.

[5] 'during it'[1]: lit. 'on it'.

ܩܦܠܐܘܢ: ܢܛ.

1 ܐ ܗܐ ܠܐ ܐܬܟܪܝܬ ܐܝܕܗ ܕܡܪܝܐ ܠܡܦܪܩ. ܘܠܐ ܝܩܝܪܐ ܐܕܢܗ ܠܡܫܡܥ.

2 ܒ ܐܠܐ ܚܛܗܝܟܘܢ ܗܢܘܢ ܦܪܫܘ ܒܝܢܝܟܘܢ ܠܐܠܗܟܘܢ. ܘܣܟܠܘܬܟܘܢ ܐܗܦܟܘ ܐܦܘܗܝ ܡܢܟܘܢ ܕܠܐ ܢܫܡܥ.

3 ܓ ܡܛܠ ܕܐܝܕܝܟܘܢ ܡܛܢܦܢ ܒܕܡܐ: ܘܨܒܥܬܟܘܢ ܒܥܘܠܐ. ܘܣܦܘܬܟܘܢ ܡܡܠܠܢ ܫܘܩܪܐ. ܘܠܫܢܟܘܢ ܪܢܐ ܒܥܘܠܐ.

4 ܕ ܘܠܝܬ ܕܩܪܐ ܒܙܕܝܩܘܬܐ. ܘܠܝܬ ܕܕܐܢ ܒܗܝܡܢܘܬܐ. ܐܬܬܟܠܘ ܥܠ ܣܪܝܩܘܬܐ: ܘܡܠܠܘ ܕܓܠܘܬܐ. ܒܛܢܘ ܥܡܠܐ: ܘܝܠܕܘ ܥܘܠܐ.

5 ܗ ܒܝܥܐ ܕܚܘܪܡܢܐ ܐܦܩܘ. ܘܩܘܠܐ ܕܥܟܒܝܫ ܙܩܪܘ. ܘܐܟܠ ܡܢ ܒܝܥܝܗܘܢ: ܢܡܘܬ. ܘܕܐܬܒܪܝܗ: ܢܦܩ ܐܟܕܢܐ.

6 ܘ ܢܚܘܗܘܢ ܠܐ ܢܗܘܐ ܠܠܒܘܫܐ. ܘܠܐ ܢܬܟܣܘܢ ܒܥܒܕܝܗܘܢ. ܥܒܕܝܗܘܢ ܥܒܕܐ ܐܢܘܢ ܕܥܘܠܐ. ܘܥܒܕܐ ܕܥܘܠܐ ܒܐܝܕܝܗܘܢ.

7 ܙ ܪܓܠܝܗܘܢ ܪܗܛܢ ܠܒܝܫܬܐ. ܘܡܣܬܪܗܒܝܢ ܠܡܐܫܕ ܕܡܐ ܙܟܝܐ. ܬܪܥܝܬܗܘܢ ܬܪܥܝܬܐ ܐܢܝܢ ܕܥܘܠܐ. ܘܬܒܪܐ ܘܬܒܪܐ ܒܫܒܝܠܝܗܘܢ.

8 ܚ ܐܘܪܚܐ ܕܫܠܡܐ ܠܐ ܝܕܥܘ. ܘܠܝܬ ܕܝܢܐ ܒܡܥܓܠܬܗܘܢ. ܫܒܝܠܝܗܘܢ ܡܥܩܡܢ. ܘܟܠ ܕܡܗܠܟ ܒܗܘܢ: ܠܐ ܝܕܥ ܫܠܡܐ.

9 ܛ ܡܛܠ ܗܢܐ ܐܬܪܚܩ ܡܢܢ ܕܝܢܐ. ܘܙܕܝܩܘܬܐ ܠܐ ܬܕܪܟܢ. ܣܟܝܢ ܠܢܘܗܪܐ:

ܢܫ ܒܫ

ܘܗܘܐ ܚܫܘܟܐ ܘܠܢܗܝܪܘܬܐ ܘܒܥܡܛܢܐ ܗܠܟܢ.

Chapter 59

1   See! The hand of the Lord is not feeble to save, his ear is not dull to hear.

2   But your debts have separated you from your God,[1] your sins have turned his face from you so that he will not hear.

3   For your hands are defiled with blood, your fingers with iniquity; your lips speak falsehood, your tongue devises iniquity.

4   There is none who invokes righteousness, none who judges in truth; they have put (their) trust in vanity, spoken emptiness; they have conceived deceit, they have begotten pains.

5   They have hatched the basilisk's eggs, they have woven the spider's web: whoever eats of their eggs will die; as they break,[2] a brood of vipers is found.

6   Their web will not be a garment, they will not cover themselves with their deeds; their deeds are deeds of depravity, deeds of iniquity are in their hands.

7   Their feet run to (do) evil, they hasten to shed innocent blood; their thoughts are thoughts of depravity, prey and destruction[3] in their paths.

8   They have not known the path of peace, there is no justice in their ways; their paths are perverted, all who walk in them know not peace.

9   Therefore justice has been removed from us, righteousness will not come to us; we expected light,

XXVIII

but there was darkness, brightness but we walked in thick darkness.

---

[1] 'separated you from your God': lit. 'separated between you with respect to your God'.

[2] 'as they break': lit. 'of her breaking'.

[3] 'destruction' or 'breaking'.

10 We have groped at the wall as the blind, we have groped as those who have no eyes; we have stumbled at noon as at evening, we have groaned as those who are brought near to death.[1]

11 We have roared, all of us, like bears, we have moaned[2] like doves; we waited for[3] justice but there was none, for salvation but it was far removed from us.

12 For our iniquity increased before you, our sins testified (against) us; for our iniquity is with us, our sins are known.

13 We have acted wickedly, been unfaithful to the Lord, we have turned away from following[4] our God; we have spoken unjustly,[5] we have rebelled; we have conceived, we have intended in[6] our hearts, affairs of falsehood.

14 We have turned justice around,[7] we have made righteousness stand afar off: for truth has stumbled in the open square,[8] reproof is unable to reach us.[9]

15 Truth was concealed, understanding had passed away from our mind(s); the Lord saw that there was no justice, it was evil in his eyes.

16 He saw that there was no man, he wondered that there was no-one to help: his arm redeemed him, his righteousness supported him.

17 He put on righteousness as with a breastplate, a helmet of redemption on his head; he put on the garment of retribution.

18 That he might be avenged on his adversaries, repay his enemies, repay retribution to the islands.

---

[1] 'death': lit. 'to die'.

[2] 'roared … moaned': both verbs √ המן; the translation varies for the appropriate animal.

[3] 'waited for' or 'expected'.

[4] 'following' or 'after'.

[5] 'unjustly': lit. 'injustice'.

[6] 'in': lit. 'from'.

[7] 'around': lit. 'behind it'.

[8] 'the open square' or 'an open space'.

[9] 'reach us': lit. 'come to'.

19 ܝܛ ܢܕܚܠܘܢ ܡܢ ܡܥܪܒܐ ܠܫܡܗ ܕܡܪܝܐ. ܘܡܢ ܡܕܢܚܝ ܫܡܫܐ ܠܐܝܩܪܗ. ܡܛܠ
ܕܬܐܬܐ ܐܘܠܨܐ ܐܝܟ ܢܗܪܐ. ܘܪܘܚܗ ܕܡܪܝܐ ܬܕܒܪܝܘܗܝ.

20 ܟ ܘܢܐܬܐ ܠܨܗܝܘܢ ܦܪܘܩܐ: ܘܐܝܠܝܢ ܕܡܬܦܢܝܢ ܥܘܠܐ ܡܢ ܝܥܩܘܒ: ܐܡܪ ܡܪܝܐ.

21 ܟܐ ܘܐܢܐ ܗܢܐ ܩܝܡܝ ܕܥܡܗܘܢ: ܐܡܪ ܡܪܝܐ: ܪܘܚܝ ܕܥܠܝܟ ܘܡܠܝ ܕܣܡܬ
ܒܦܘܡܟ: ܠܐ ܢܥܒܪܘܢ ܡܢ ܦܘܡܟ ܘܡܢ ܦܘܡܗ ܕܙܪܥܟ: ܘܡܢ ܦܘܡܐ ܕܙܪܥܐ
ܕܙܪܥܟ: ܐܡܪ ܡܪܝܐ: ܡܢ ܗܫܐ ܘܥܕܡܐ ܠܥܠܡ.

19   (Those) from the west will fear the name of the Lord, (those) from the rising[1] of the sun his honor: for the oppressor may come like a river, but the spirit of the Lord will humble him.

20   And a savior will come to Zion, and those (will come) who turn iniquity from Jacob, says the Lord.

21   And I (declare) this is my covenant with you, says the Lord: My spirit that is upon you, my words that I have put in your mouth, will not fail from your mouth, nor from the mouth of your seed, nor from the mouth of the seed of your seed, says the Lord, from now and forever.

---

[1] 'rising': pl.

ܩܦܠܐܘܢ: ܣ.

1 ܐ ܩܘܡܝ ܐܬܢܗܪܝ ܡܛܠ ܕܡܛܐ ܢܘܗܪܟܝ. ܘܐܝܩܪܗ ܕܡܪܝܐ ܥܠܝܟܝ ܕܢܚ.

2 ܒ ܡܛܠ ܕܗܐ ܚܫܘܟܐ ܡܟܣܐ ܠܐܪܥܐ: ܘܥܪܦܠܐ ܠܐܡܘܬܐ. ܘܥܠܝܟܝ ܢܕܢܚ ܡܪܝܐ.
ܘܐܝܩܪܗ ܥܠܝܟܝ ܢܬܚܙܐ.

3 ܓ ܘܢܐܬܘܢ ܥܡܡܐ ܠܢܘܗܪܟܝ: ܘܡܠܟܐ ܠܢܘܗܪܐ ܕܕܢܚܟܝ.

4 ܕ ܐܪܝܡܝ ܥܝܢܝܟܝ ܠܚܕܪܝܟܝ. ܘܚܙܝ ܕܟܠܗܘܢ ܡܬܟܢܫܝܢ ܘܐܬܝܢ ܠܟܝ. ܒܢܝܟܝ
ܡܢ ܪܘܚܩܐ ܐܬܝܢ. ܘܒܢܬܟܝ ܥܠ ܦܬܘܬܐ ܬܬܪܒܝܢ.

5 ܗ ܗܝܕܝܢ ܬܚܙܝܢ: ܘܬܬܢܗܪܝܢ. ܘܬܬܕܚܠܝܢ: ܘܢܪܘܚ ܠܒܟܝ. ܡܛܠ ܕܢܗܦܟ ܠܟܝ
ܥܘܬܪܗ ܕܝܡܐ. ܘܚܝܠܐ ܕܥܡܡܐ ܢܐܬܐ ܠܟܝ.

6 ܘ ܐܟܠܬܐ ܕܓܡܠܐ ܬܚܦܝܟܝ. ܒܟܪܐ ܕܡܕܝܢ ܘܥܝܦܐ: ܟܠܗܘܢ ܡܢ ܫܒܐ
ܢܐܬܘܢ. ܕܗܒܐ ܘܠܒܘܢܬܐ ܢܫܩܠܘܢ. ܘܬܫܒܚܬܗ ܕܡܪܝܐ ܢܣܒܪܘܢ.

7 ܙ ܟܠܗ ܥܢܐ ܕܩܕܪ ܢܬܟܢܫܘܢ ܠܟܝ. ܘܕܟܪܐ ܕܢܒܝܘܬ ܢܫܡܫܘܢܟܝ. ܘܢܣܩܘܢ
ܠܪܥܘܬܐ ܥܠ ܡܕܒܚܝ. ܘܒܝܬܐ ܕܬܫܒܘܚܬܝ ܐܫܒܚ.

8 ܚ ܡܢ ܐܢܘܢ ܗܠܝܢ ܕܐܝܟ ܥܢܢܐ ܦܪܚܝܢ: ܘܐܝܟ ܝܘܢܐ ܠܒܢܘܬܗܘܢ.

9 ܛ ܡܛܠ ܕܠܝ ܢܣܟܘܢ ܓܙܪܬܐ: ܘܐܠܦܐ ܕܬܪܫܝܫ ܐܝܟ ܕܒܩܕܡܝܬܐ. ܠܡܝܬܝܘ
ܒܢܝܟܝ ܡܢ ܪܘܚܩܐ: ܘܣܐܡܗܘܢ ܘܕܗܒܗܘܢ ܥܡܗܘܢ: ܠܫܡܗ ܕܡܪܝܐ
ܐܠܗܟܝ: ܘܩܕܝܫܐ ܕܐܝܣܪܝܠ ܕܫܒܚܟܝ.

Chapter 60

1   Arise, shine, for your light has come: the glory of the Lord will dawn upon you.

2   For see! Darkness covers the earth, thick darkness the peoples: yet the Lord will shine forth upon you, his glory will be seen upon you.

3   And the nations will come to your light, kings to the light of your brightness.

4   Lift up your eyes to your surroundings, see all who are gathered together and are coming to you: your sons will come from afar off, your daughters will be brought up on cradles.[1]

5   Then you will see, you will shine, you will rejoice; your heart will breathe freely; for the riches[2] of the sea return to you, the strength[3] of the nations will come to you.

6   A herd of camels will cover you, the firstborn of Midian and of Ephah; they will all come from Sheba, they will carry gold and frankincense, they will proclaim the praise[4] of the Lord.

7   All the flocks of Kedar will gather to you, the rams of Nebaioth will serve you, they will come up willingly to my altar, and I will praise the house of my glory.[5]

8   Who are they, these who fly like the clouds, like the doves to their dove-cotes?[6]

9   For the islands will wait for me, and the ships of Tarshish as of old, to bring your children from afar off, their silver and their gold with them, for the name of the Lord your God, the Holy One of Israel, who has praised you.

---

[1] 'cradles': litters for children.

[2] 'riches': sing.

[3] 'strength': pl.

[4] 'praise': pl.

[5] 'I will praise the house of my glory': 'praise' and 'glory' use the same Syriac root.

[6] 'their dove-cotes': lit. 'their windows in dove-cotes'.

10 ܝ ܘܢܒܢܘܢ ܒܢܝ ܢܘܟܪܝܐ ܫܘܪܝܟܝ. ܘܡܠܟܝܗܘܢ ܢܫܡܫܘܢܟܝ. ܡܛܠ ܕܒܪܘܓܙܝ
ܡܚܝܬܟܝ. ܘܒܪܚܡܝ ܪܚܡܬ ܥܠܝܟܝ.

11 ܝܐ ܢܬܦܬܚܘܢ ܬܪ̈ܥܝܟܝ ܐܡܝܢܐܝܬ: ܐܝܡܡܐ ܘܒܠܠܝܐ: ܘܠܐ ܢܬܐܚܕܘܢ. ܘܢܥܠܘܢ
ܠܟܝ ܚܝܠܐ ܕܥܡ̈ܡܐ: ܘܡܠܟ̈ܝܗܘܢ ܟܕ ܕܒܝܪܝܢ.

12 ܝܒ ܡܛܠ ܕܥܡܐ ܘܡܠܟܘܬܐ ܕܠܐ ܢܫܬܥܒܕܘܢ ܠܟܝ: ܢܐܒܕܘܢ. ܘܥܡ̈ܡܐ ܒܚܘܪܒܐ
ܢܬܚܪܒܘܢ.

13 ܝܓ ܐܝܩܪܐ ܕܠܒܢܢ ܢܐܬܐ ܠܟܝ: ܒܪܘܬܐ ܘܫܘܪܒܝܢܐ ܘܦܩܘܣܝܐ ܐܟܚܕܐ: ܠܫܘܒܚܗ ܕܐܬܪܐ
ܕܡܩܕܫܝ: ܘܠܐܬܪܐ ܕܪ̈ܓܠܝ ܐܝܩܪ.

14 ܝܕ ܘܢܐܬܘܢ ܠܟܝ ܟܕ ܡܬܟܦܝܢ ܒܢ̈ܝ ܡܡܟܟܢ̈ܝܟܝ. ܘܢܣܓܕܘܢ ܠܟܦ̈ܬܐ
ܕܪ̈ܓܠܝܟܝ ܟܠܗܘܢ ܡܨܥܪܢ̈ܝܟܝ. ܘܢܩܪܘܢܟܝ ܨܗܝܘܢ ܡܕܝܢܬܗ ܕܡܪܝܐ ܩܕܝܫܐ
ܕܐܝܣܪܝܠ.

15 ܝܗ ܚܠܦ ܕܗܘܝܬܝ ܫܒܝܩܬܐ ܘܣܢܝܬܐ ܘܠܝܬ ܕܥܒܪ ܒܟܝ: ܐܥܒܕܟܝ ܐܝܩܪܐ
ܠܥܠܡ: ܘܚܕܘܬܐ ܠܕܪܕܪܝܢ.

16 ܝܘ ܘܬܐܢܩܝܢ ܚܠܒܐ ܕܥܡ̈ܡܐ ܘܬܕ̈ܝܐ ܕܡ̈ܠܟܐ ܬܐܢܩܝܢ. ܘܬܕܥܝܢ ܕܐܢܐ ܐܢܐ ܡܪܝܐ
ܦܪܘܩܟܝ: ܘܡܦܨܝܢܟܝ ܥܫܝܢܗ ܕܝܥܩܘܒ.

17 ܝܙ ܚܠܦ ܢܚܫܐ ܐܝܬܐ ܕܗܒܐ. ܘܚܠܦ ܦܪܙܠܐ ܐܝܬܐ ܣܐܡܐ. ܘܚܠܦ ܩ̈ܝܣܐ ܢܚܫܐ.
ܘܚܠܦ ܟܐ̈ܦܐ ܦܪܙܠܐ. ܘܐܥܒܕ ܫܠܡܐ ܦܩܘܕ̈ܝܟܝ: ܘܫܠܝܛܢ̈ܝܟܝ ܙܕܝܩܘܬܐ.

18 ܝܚ ܘܠܐ ܢܫܬܡܥ ܬܘܒ ܚܘܠܐ ܒܐܪܥܟܝ: ܘܬܒܪܐ ܘܫܒܪܐ ܒܬܚܘܡ̈ܝܟܝ. ܘܢܩܪܘܢ
ܫܘܪ̈ܝܟܝ ܦܘܪܩܢܐ: ܘܬܪ̈ܥܝܟܝ ܬܫܒܘܚܬܐ.

19 ܝܛ ܘܠܐ ܢܗܘܐ ܠܟܝ ܬܘܒ ܫܡܫܐ ܠܢܘܗܪܐ ܕܐܝܡܡܐ. ܘܢܘܗܪܗ ܕܣܗܪܐ ܠܐ ܢܢܗܪ
ܠܟܝ. ܡܛܠ ܕܢܗܘܐ ܠܟܝ ܡܪܝܐ ܢܘܗܪܐ ܠܥܠܡ.

20 ܟ ܘܢܫܠܡܘܢ ܝܘ̈ܡܬܐ ܕܐܒܠܟܝ.

21 ܟܐ ܘܥܡܟܝ ܟܠܗܘܢ ܙܕܝܩܐ ܠܥܠܡ ܢܐܪܬܘܢ ܐܪܥܐ. ܢܨܒܬܐ ܕܢܨܒܬ: ܥܒܕ ܐܝܕܝ
ܢܬܝܩܪ.

10 Strangers[1] will build your walls, their kings will serve you, for in my anger I struck you, but according to my desire I have had mercy on you.

11 Your gates will be ever opened, by day and by night, they will not be closed; the hosts of the nations will come in to you, their kings will be led.[2]

12 For the nation and the kingdom that will not serve you will perish, the nations will be laid waste by the sword.

13 The glory of Lebanon will come to you, the beautiful[3] juniper and the cypress together, to glorify the place of my sanctuary, the place of my feet, my glory.

14 Humiliated they will come to you, the children of those who humiliated you; all those who provoked you will bow down to the soles of your feet, they will call you 'Zion, the city of the Lord, the Holy One of Israel'.

15 Instead of being forsaken and hated, with no-one passing through, I will make you a glory forever, a joy for the generations.

16 You will suck the milk of nations, you will suck the spoil of kings, you will know that I am the Lord your savior, your redeemer, the powerful one of Jacob.

17 Instead of brass I will bring gold; instead of iron I will bring silver; instead of wood, brass; instead of stones, iron; I will make peace your governor, righteousness your ruler.

18 Iniquity will no more be heard in your land, nor spoil and destruction within your borders; they will call your walls 'Redemption', your gates 'Praise'.

19 The sun will no more be a light for you by day, the light of the moon will not give light for you, for the Lord will be a light for you forever.

20 The days of your mourning will be completed.

21 All your righteous people will inherit the land forever: the shoot that I planted, the work of my hands, will be praised.

---

[1] 'Strangers': lit. 'Sons of foreigners'.

[2] 'will be led': lit. 'while being led'.

[3] 'beautiful': lit. 'adorned'.

22 ܡܢ ܐܝܟܘ ܢܗܘܐ ܠܐܝܬܝܗ: ܘܐܡܪܝܢ ܠܟܠܗܐ ܟܡܐܝܠܐ. ܐܢܐ ܡܕܢܐ ܟܪܝܗܢܗ ܐܝܗܬܐܘܘܢ.

22   The least will become a thousand, the deficient in people strong: I the Lord will guard it in its time.

Chapter 61

1   The spirit of the Lord God is upon me, for the Lord has anointed me and sent me, that I might bring hope to the afflicted, bind up the broken-hearted, proclaim freedom to the captives, free the bound.[1]

2   And I might proclaim the year of the Lord's intent,[2] the day of redemption by our God, to comfort all mourners.[3]

3   To give praise to the mourners of Zion: instead of ashes,[4] sweet-smelling oil; instead of mourning, clothing of glory; instead of a suffering spirit, they will be called 'The rams[5] of righteousness', the Lord's praiseworthy[6] plant.

4   They will build the desolate places of old, erect the places which were deserted from the beginning, renew the desolate cities, the deserted places of the generations.

5   Strangers will stand up and tend their flocks, strangers' children will be their ploughmen and vinedressers.

6   You will be called 'The priests of the Lord', 'Ministers of our God' will be said of you; you will consume the riches of the nations, with their glory you will be praised.

7   Instead of your disgrace, instead of your shame, you will inherit a double inheritance in their land; you will be glorified[7] by their portion, you will have everlasting joy.

8   For I am the Lord: I love justice, I hate rapine and injustice; I will set your toil in truth, I will establish an everlasting covenant for you.

9   Your seed will be known among the nations, the seed of your seed among the peoples; all who see you will recognize you, that you are the seed that the Lord has blessed.

---

[1] 'free the bound': lit. 'release to the bound'.

[2] 'intent' or 'will' or 'decision'.

[3] 'mourners' or 'who mourn'.

[4] 'ashes': sing.

[5] 'rams' or 'males'.

[6] 'praiseworthy': lit. 'praised'.

[7] 'you will be glorified' or 'glorify yourselves'.

XXIX

10   I will indeed take delight in the Lord, my soul will exult in my God, for he has clothed me with a garment of redemption, wrapped me in a mantle of righteousness, as the bridegroom is praised, as the bride is adorned.

11   As the earth which puts forth flowers, as a garden which brings forth seed, thus the Lord God brings forth righteousness, praise in the presence of all the nations.

ܩܦܠܐܘܢ: ܣܒ.

1 ܐ ܡܛܠ ܨܗܝܘܢ ܠܐ ܐܫܬܘܩ. ܘܡܛܠ ܐܘܪܫܠܡ ܠܐ ܐܫܠܐ. ܥܕܡܐ ܕܢܦܘܩ
ܙܕܝܩܘܬܗ ܐܝܟ ܢܘܗܪܐ: ܘܦܘܪܩܢܗ ܐܝܟ ܠܡܦܐܕܐ ܢܒܥܪ.

2 ܒ ܘܢܚܙܘܢ ܥܡܡܐ ܙܕܝܩܘܬܟܝ: ܘܟܠܗܘܢ ܡܠܟܐ ܐܝܩܪܟܝ. ܘܢܬܩܪܐ ܠܟܝ ܫܡܐ
ܚܕܬܐ: ܕܦܘܡܗ ܕܡܪܝܐ ܢܫܡܝܘܗܝ.

3 ܓ ܘܬܗܘܝܢ ܟܠܝܠܐ ܕܬܫܒܘܚܬܐ ܒܐܝܕܗ ܕܡܪܝܐ: ܘܬܐܓܐ ܕܡܠܟܘܬܐ ܒܐܝܕܗ
ܕܐܠܗܟܝ.

4 ܕ ܘܬܘܒ ܠܐ ܬܬܐܡܪܝܢ ܫܒܝܩܬܐ. ܘܐܪܥܟܝ ܬܘܒ ܠܐ ܬܬܐܡܪ ܨܕܝܬܐ. ܐܠܐ ܬܬܐܡܪܝܢ
ܨܒܝܢܝ: ܘܐܪܥܟܝ ܒܥܝܠܬܐ. ܡܛܠ ܕܨܒܐ ܒܟܝ ܡܪܝܐ. ܘܐܪܥܟܝ ܬܬܒܥܠ.

5 ܗ ܡܛܠ ܕܐܝܟ ܕܒܥܠ ܥܠܝܡܐ ܠܒܬܘܠܬܐ: ܗܟܢܐ ܢܒܥܠܘܢܟܝ ܒܢܝܟܝ.
ܘܐܝܟ ܕܚܕܐ ܚܬܢܐ ܒܟܠܬܐ: ܢܚܕܐ ܒܟܝ ܐܠܗܟܝ.

6 ܘ ܥܠ ܫܘܪܝܟܝ ܐܘܪܫܠܡ ܐܩܝܡܬ ܢܛܘܪܐ ܟܠܝܘܡ: ܒܐܝܡܡܐ ܘܒܠܠܝܐ
ܐܡܝܢܐܝܬ. ܘܠܐ ܢܫܬܩܘܢ: ܘܠܐ ܢܫܠܘܢ ܡܥܗܕܢܘܬܗ ܩܕܡ ܡܪܝܐ.

7 ܙ ܘܠܐ ܬܬܠܘܢ ܠܗܘܢ ܫܠܝܐ ܥܕܡܐ ܕܢܬܩܢܝܗ: ܘܥܕܡܐ ܕܢܥܒܕܝܗ ܐܘܪܫܠܡ
ܬܫܒܘܚܬܐ ܒܐܪܥܐ.

8 ܚ ܝܡܐ ܡܪܝܐ ܒܝܡܝܢܗ ܘܒܕܪܥܗ ܥܫܝܢܐ: ܕܠܐ ܐܬܠ ܬܘܒ ܥܒܘܪܟܝ ܡܐܟܘܠܬܐ
ܠܒܥܠܕܒܒܝܟܝ. ܘܠܐ ܢܫܬܘܢ ܒܢܝ ܢܘܟܪܝܐ ܚܡܪܟܝ ܕܠܐܝܬܝ ܒܗ.

9 ܛ ܐܠܐ ܡܟܢܫܢܘܗܝ ܢܐܟܠܘܢܗ. ܘܢܫܒܚܘܢ ܠܡܪܝܐ. ܘܡܟܢܫܢܘܗܝ ܢܫܬܘܢܗ ܒܕܪ̈ܬܐ
ܩܕܝܫܬܐ.

Chapter 62

1   On account of Zion I will not hold my peace, on account of Jerusalem I will not be silent, until her righteousness goes forth like a light, her redemption shines out[1] like a lamp.

2   The nations will see your righteousness, all the kings your glory; a new name will be invoked for you, that the mouth of the Lord will ordain.

3   You will be a crown of glory in the hand of the Lord, a diadem of the kingdom in the hand of your God.

4   No more will you be called 'Forsaken', your land will no more be called 'Deserted', but you will be called 'My Delight', and your land 'Married',[2] for the Lord has delighted in you, and your land will be married.

5   For as a youth marries a virgin, thus will your sons marry you, and as the bridegroom rejoices in the bride, your God will rejoice in you.

6   Upon your walls, Jerusalem, I have established watchmen every day, by day and by night continually, so that they will not hold their peace, and they will not be silent, who give an account of her[3] before the Lord.

7   You will give them no peace until he has established you, until he has made[4] you, Jerusalem, a praise in the land.

8   The Lord has sworn by his right hand and by his strong arm: No more will I give your produce as food for your enemies, the children of strangers will not drink your wine that you have labored to make.[5]

9   But his gatherers will eat it, and they will praise the Lord, his gatherers will drink it in my holy courts.

---

[1] 'goes forth … shines out': impf verbs.

[2] 'Married' or 'Taken as one's own'.

[3] 'who give an account of her': lit. 'her chroniclers'.

[4] 'has established … has made': impf verbs.

[5] 'to make': lit. 'in it'.

10 ܝ ܥܒܪܘ ܥܒܪܘ ܒܬܪ̈ܥܐ. ܦܢܘ ܐܘܪܚܐ ܠܥܡܐ. ܕܘܫܘ ܫܒܝܠܐ. ܘܓܒܘ
ܟܐ̈ܦܘܗܝ. ܐܪܝܡܘ ܐܬܐ ܠܥܡ̈ܡܐ.

11 ܝܐ ܗܐ ܡܪܝܐ ܐܫܡܥ ܠܣܘ̈ܦܝܗ ܕܐܪܥܐ. ܐܡܪܘ ܠܒܪܬܐ ܕܨܗܝܘܢ ܕܗܐ ܐܬܐ ܦܪܘܩܟܝ.
ܗܐ ܐܓܪܗ ܥܡܗ: ܘܥܒܕܗ ܩܕܡܘܗܝ.

12 ܝܒ ܘܢܩܪܘܢ ܐܢܘܢ ܥܡܐ ܩܕܝܫܐ: ܦܪ̈ܝܩܘܗܝ ܕܡܪܝܐ. ܘܐܢܬܝ ܬܬܩܪܝܢ ܒܥܝܬܐ:
ܩܪܝܬܐ ܕܠܐ ܐܫܬܒܩܬ.

10   Pass through, pass through, by the gate; restore the way to the people; prepare the path; clear[1] its stones; raise up a sign to the peoples.

11   See! The Lord has announced to the ends of the earth: Say to the daughter of Zion 'See! Your savior comes; See! His reward is with him, his work before him'.

12   And they will call them the Holy People, Redeemed of the Lord; and you will be called 'Desired', the city that is not forsaken.[2]

---

[1] 'clear': lit. 'lessen'.

[2] 'is not forsaken': perfect verb.

ܡܟܠܐܘ: ܡܝ.

1 ...

2 ...

3 ...

4 ...

5 ...

6 ...

7 ...

8 ...

9 ...

10 ...

Chapter 63

1   Who is this who comes from Edom, his garments blood-red from Bozrah, adorned by his clothing, mighty in his great strength?[1] I speak in righteousness, increasing salvation.[2]

2   Why are your garments, your clothing, blood-red, like one who has trodden in the wine-press?

3   I trod the wine-press alone, no-one from the nations was with me. I trampled them in my anger, I trod them in my fury; their blood splashed upon my clothing, I have bespattered all my garments.

4   For the day of vengeance was in my heart, the year of my redemption had come.

5   I looked, but there was none who helped, I wondered but there was none who supported:[3] my arm redeemed me, it was my fury that supported me.

6   I trod the nations in my anger, I laid them low in my fury, their strength I cast down to the ground.

7   I will call to mind the loving-kindness of the Lord, the praise of the Lord because of all that the Lord has bestowed on me: for he has magnified his loving-kindness to those of the house of Israel, which he has bestowed on me according to his mercy, according to the greatness of his loving-kindness.

8   For he said: They are my people, children who do not act deceitfully. He was their redeemer.

9   In all their afflictions, he did not afflict them; the angel[4] of his presence redeemed them; in his mercy, in his compassion he redeemed them, he raised them up, he lifted them up, all the days of old.

10   They embittered, they grieved, his holy spirit; so he had turned to them (as) an enemy, he himself fought against them.

---

[1] 'in his great strength': lit. 'with the multitude of his strength'.

[2] 'salvation': lit. 'to save'.

[3] 'helped ... supported': participles.

[4] 'angel' or 'messenger', as in 37:36.

11 ܝܐ ܘܐܬܕܟܪ ܝܘ̈ܡܬܐ ܕܥܠܡ ܕܡܘܫܐ ܥܒܕܗ: ܐܝܟ ܕܐܣܩ ܡܢ ܝܡܐ ܠܪ̈ܥܝܐ ܕܥܢܗ:
ܘܐܝܟ ܕܣܡ ܒܓܘܗ ܪܘܚܐ ܕܩܘܕܫܗ.

12 ܝܒ ܡܕܒܪ ܠܝܡܝܢܗ ܕܡܘܫܐ ܕܕܪܥܐ ܕܬܫܒܘܚܬܗ. ܨܪܐ ܝܡܐ ܡܢ ܩܕܡܝܗܘܢ.
ܘܥܒܕ ܠܗܘܢ ܫܡܐ ܠܥܠܡ.

13 ܝܓ ܕܒܪ ܐܢܘܢ ܒܬܗܘܡܐ ܐܝܟ ܣܘܣܝܐ ܒܡܕܒܪܐ. ܘܠܐ ܐܬܬܩܠܘ.

14 ܝܕ ܐܝܟ ܒܥܝܪܐ ܕܢܚܬܐ ܒܒܩܥܬܐ: ܪܘܚܗ ܕܡܪܝܐ ܕܒܪܐ ܐܢܘܢ. ܗܟܢܐ ܕܒܪܬ ܐܢܘܢ
ܠܥܡܟ: ܘܥܒܕܬ ܠܟ ܫܡܐ ܡܫܒܚܐ.

15 ܝܗ ܚܘܪ ܡܢ ܫܡܝܐ. ܘܚܙܝ ܡܢ ܡܕܝܪܟ ܩܕܝܫܐ ܘܡܫܒܚܐ. ܐܝܟܘ ܛܢܢܟ
ܘܓܢܒܪܘܬܟ: ܘܣܘܓܐܐ ܕܪ̈ܚܡܝܟ ܘܕܚܢܢܟ ܕܐܬܥܨܝܘ ܡܢܝ.

16 ܝܘ ܡܛܠ ܕܐܢܬ ܐܒܘܢ. ܐܒܪܗܡ ܠܐ ܝܕܥܢ. ܘܐܝܣܪܐܝܠ ܠܐ ܐܫܬܘܕܥܢ. ܐܢܬ ܗܘ
ܡܪܝܐ ܐܒܘܢ ܦܪܘܩܢ. ܘܡܢ ܥܠܡ ܫܡܟ.

17 ܝܙ ܠܡܢܐ ܐܛܥܝܬܢ ܡܪܝܐ ܡܢ ܐܘܪܚܟ. ܘܩܫܝܬ ܠܒܢ ܡܢ ܕܚܠܬܟ. ܐܬܦܢܝ
ܡܛܠ ܥܒ̈ܕܝܟ ܫܒܛܐ ܕܝܪܬܘܬܟ.

18 ܝܚ ܩܠܝܠ ܝܪܬܘ ܥܡܐ ܕܩܘܕܫܟ. ܒܥܠܕܒ̈ܒܝܢ ܕܫܘ ܡܩܕܫܟ.

19 ܝܛ ܗܘܝܢ ܡܢ ܥܠܡ: ܕܠܐ ܐܫܬܠܛܬ ܒܗܘܢ. ܘܠܐ ܐܬܩܪܝ ܫܡܟ ܥܠܝܗܘܢ.

11 He remembered the days of old, of Moses his servant, as (when) he brought up from the sea the shepherd of his flock, as (when) he set within him his holy spirit.

12 Guiding the right hand of Moses, the arm of his glory, he divided[1] the sea before them, he made them[2] a name forever.

13 He guided them in the depth(s) as a horse in the wilderness, and they did not stumble.

14 As cattle which descend into the valley, the spirit of the Lord guided them: thus you guided your people; you made for yourself a glorious name.

15 Look from heaven, see from your holy and glorious lofty dwelling: where are your zeal, your might, the intention of your bowels, of your mercy, which have yearned for us?[3]

16 For you are our father. Abraham did not know us, Israel did not recognize us. You are the Lord, our father, our redeemer, (this was) your name from old.

17 Why, Lord, have you made us stray from your way, hardened our heart so that we do not fear you?[4] Turn, for the sake of your servants, the tribe of your inheritance.

18 May they inherit a little,[5] your holy people;[6] our oppressors have trodden your holy place.

19 We were from of old, before you bore rule over them; your name was not invoked by[7] them.

---

[1] 'divided' or 'broke through'.

[2] 'made them' or 'made for them'.

[3] 'which have yearned for us': lit. 'which have returned upon us'.

[4] 'so that we do not fear you': lit. 'from your fear'.

[5] 'a little' or '(for) a little (while)'.

[6] 'May they inherit a little, your holy people' or 'Your holy people may inherit a little'.

[7] 'by': lit. 'on, over'.

Chapter 64

1 Did you did not open the heavens[1] and descend? The mountains quaked before you, they melted as wax is melted before a fire.

2 The fire will consume your enemies, and your name will be known to your enemies; the peoples will be disturbed before you.

3 When you did those terrible deeds,[2] which we did not hope for from you,[3] you came down, the mountains quaked before you.

4 From old, they have not heeded, they have not heard, no eye has seen a God other than you: that you make this for those who hope in you.[4]

5 You met with delight those who act righteously,[5] they will remember you by[6] your ways. See! You have been angry, we have sinned in them;[7] shall we ever[8] be saved?

6 For we were like the unclean, all of us; all our righteousness like a menstrous cloth; we have fallen like leaves, all of us; our sins have carried us (off), as a whirlwind.

7 There is no-one who calls on your name, who remembers to hold fast to you; for you have turned your face from us, you have delivered us into the hand of our sins.

8 Now, Lord, you are our father, we are the clay and you our potter; we are, all of us, the work of your hands.

9 Do not be very angry forever, Lord; do not remember our sins forever; see that we are, all of us, your people.

---

[1] 'Did you did not open the heavens?': The question could be read as a statement: 'You did not open the heavens'. MT 'Oh that you had torn open the heavens'. The translator read MT לוּא as a negative. See Introduction. Addendum 1.

[2] 'terrible deeds': lit. 'feared things'.

[3] 'hope for from you': lit. 'look to you for'.

[4] 'hope in you' or 'wait for you'.

[5] 'act righteously': lit. 'do righteousness'.

[6] 'by' or 'in'.

[7] 'them': refers to 'your ways'.

[8] 'ever': lit. 'in the age' or 'in eternity'.

10 ܝ ܩܘܪ̈ܝܐ ܕܩܘܕܫܟ ܗܘܝ ܡܕܒܪܐ. ܘܨܗܝܘܢ ܗܘܬ ܡܕܒܪܐ: ܘܐܘܪܫܠܡ ܚܪܒܬܐ.

11 ܝܐ ܒܝܬ ܩܘܕܫܢ ܘܬܫܒܘܚܬܢ: ܕܫܒܚܘܟ ܐܒܗ̈ܬܢ: ܗܘܐ ܠܝܩܕܢܐ ܕܢܘܪܐ. ܘܟܠܗ
ܪ̈ܓܝܓܬܢ ܗܘܬ ܠܚܘܪܒܐ.

12 ܝܒ ܥܠ ܗܠܝܢ ܐܬܚܣܢܬ ܡܪܝܐ. ܘܫܬܩܬ ܘܡܟܟܬܢ ܛܒ.

10   Your holy cities were a wilderness, Zion was a wilderness, Jerusalem a desolate waste.

11   Our holy house, our glory, (in) which our fathers praised you, was burnt by fire;[1] all our desire became a ruin.

12   Because of all these things you have held out (against us), Lord, you have kept silent, you have humbled us greatly.

---

[1] 'burnt by fire': lit. 'for the burning of fire'.

ܦܣܩܐ: ܣܗ.

ܢܘ ܠ

1 ܐ ܐܬܒܥܝܬ ܠܐܝܠܝܢ ܕܠܐ ܫܐܠܘܢܝ. ܘܐܫܬܟܚܬ ܠܐܝܠܝܢ ܕܠܐ ܒܥܘܢܝ. ܐܡܪܬ ܗܐ ܐܢܐ: ܠܥܡܐ ܕܠܐ ܩܪܐ ܫܡܝ.

2 ܒ ܦܫܛܬ ܐܝܕܝ ܝܘܡܐ ܟܠܗ: ܠܘܬ ܥܡܐ ܕܠܐ ܡܬܛܦܝܣ: ܕܡܗܠܟܝܢ ܒܬܪ ܐܬܪܥܝܬܗܘܢ: ܒܐܘܪܚܐ ܕܠܐ ܬܩܢܐ.

3 ܓ ܥܡܐ ܕܡܪܓܙܝܢ ܠܝ ܐܡܝܢܐܝܬ: ܕܕܒܚܝܢ ܒܓܢܬܐ: ܘܡܣܩܝܢ ܒܣ̈ܡܐ ܥܠ ܠܒܢ̈ܐ.

4 ܕ ܘܝܬܒܝܢ ܒܩܒܪ̈ܐ: ܘܒܝܬܝܢ ܒܡܥܪ̈ܬܐ. ܘܐܟܠܝܢ ܒܣܪܐ ܕܚܙܝܪܐ. ܘܡܬܛܡܐܝܢ ܒܡܪ̈ܩܐ ܡܐܢܝܗܘܢ.

5 ܗ ܘܐܡܪܝܢ ܩܪܘܒ ܠܘܬܟ: ܠܐ ܬܬܩܪܒ ܠܝ ܡܛܠ ܕܩܕܝܫ ܐܢܐ. ܗܠܝܢ ܗܘ̈ܝ ܬܢܢܐ ܒܪܘܓܙܝ: ܘܢܘܪܐ ܝܩܕܐ ܒܟܠܗܘܢ.

6 ܘ ܗܐ ܟܬܝܒܐ ܩܕܡܝ. ܠܐ ܐܫܬܘܩ: ܥܕܡܐ ܕܐܦܪܘܥ ܐܢܘܢ ܐܦܐ ܒܥܘܒܗܘܢ.

7 ܙ ܚܛܗܝܗܘܢ ܘܚܛܗ̈ܐ ܕܐܒܗܝܗܘܢ: ܐܟ ܚܕܐ ܐܡܪ ܡܪܝܐ. ܕܣܡܘ ܒܣ̈ܡܐ ܥܠ ܛܘܪ̈ܐ. ܘܥܠ ܪ̈ܡܬܐ ܨܥܪܘܢܝ. ܐܟܝܠ ܥܒܕ̈ܝܗܘܢ ܠܩܕܡܝܢ ܒܥܘܒܗܘܢ.

8 ܚ ܗܟܢܐ ܐܡܪ ܡܪܝܐ: ܐܝܟ ܕܡܫܬܟܚܐ ܛܘܛܝܬܐ ܒܣܓܘܠܐ: ܘܐܡܪ ܐܢܫ ܠܚܒܪܗ: ܠܐ ܬܚܒܠܝܘܗܝ: ܡܛܠ ܕܒܘܪܟܬܐ ܐܝܬ ܒܗ. ܗܟܢܐ ܐܥܒܕ ܡܛܠ ܥܒܕ̈ܝ: ܘܠܐ ܐܚܒܠ ܠܟܠܗܘܢ.

9 ܛ ܘܐܦܩ ܙܪܥܐ ܡܢ ܝܥܩܘܒ: ܘܡܢ ܝܗܘܕܐ ܝܪܬܐ ܕܛܘܪ̈ܝ. ܘܢܐܪܬܘܢܗ ܓܒ̈ܝܝ. ܘܥܒܕ̈ܝ ܢܥܡܪܘܢ ܬܡܢ.

10 ܝ ܘܢܗܘܐ ܫܪܘܢܐ ܕܝܪܐ ܠܥܢܐ. ܘܥܘܡܩܐ ܕܥܟܘܪ ܠܡܪܒܥܐ ܕܬܘܪ̈ܐ ܠܥܡܝ ܕܒܥܘܢܝ.

Chapter 65

XXX

1   I was sought by those who did not question me, I was found by those who did not seek me; I said: See! I (am here), to a people who did not call (on) my name.

2   I stretched out my hands every day to a disobedient[1] people, who persist in[2] their own opinions, in a way that is not right.

3   A people who anger me continually, who sacrifice in gardens, burn[3] incense upon stones.

4   Who sit among the graves, spend the night in caves, eat the flesh of pigs, pollute their utensils with dead bodies.

5   Who say: Stand back, do not approach me, for I am sanctified: these were (as) smoke in my anger,[4] a fire that is lit[5] every day.

6   See! It is written before me: I will not be silent until I have repaid them double in their bosom.

7   Their sins, and the sins of their fathers, are evident, says the Lord, for they have burnt incense upon the mountains, they have reviled me on the high places; I will measure their deeds first, in their bosom.

8   Thus says the Lord: As (when) a cluster of grapes is found in the bunch, and a man says to his friend 'Do not destroy it, for there is a blessing in it': thus I will do concerning[6] my servants, I will not destroy them all.

9   I will bring forth a seed from Jacob, the heir of my mountain from Judah; my chosen ones will inherit it, my servants will dwell there.

10   Sharon will be a dwelling for the flocks, the valley of Achor a fold for the herds, for my people who sought me.

---

[1] 'disobedient': lit. 'that does not obey'.

[2] 'persist in': lit. 'walk after'.

[3] 'burn': lit. 'set'. This is the usual idiom.

[4] 'in my anger'. MT 'in my nostrils'. A translation as 'anger' is technically correct but 'nostrils' fits the context better.

[5] 'is lit': lit. 'is burnt up, set on fire'.

[6] 'concerning' or 'because of'.

11 ܝܐ ܘܐܝܬܝܟܘܢ ܕܫܒܩܬܘܢ ܠܡܪܝܐ: ܘܛܥܝܬܘܢ ܠܛܘܪܗ ܩܕܝܫܐ. ܘܣܝܡܬܘܢ
ܦܬܘܪܐ ܠܓܕܐ: ܘܡܡܙܓܝܬܘܢ ܠܗܘܢ ܡܙܓܐ.

12 ܝܒ ܐܡܢܝܟܘܢ ܠܚܪܒܐ. ܘܟܠܟܘܢ ܒܩܛܠܐ ܬܬܪܟܢܘܢ. ܡܛܠ ܕܩܪܝܬܟܘܢ ܘܠܐ
ܥܢܝܬܘܢ. ܘܡܠܠܬ ܘܠܐ ܫܡܥܬܘܢ. ܘܥܒܕܬܘܢ ܕܒܝܫ ܩܕܡܝ. ܘܓܒܝܬܘܢ
ܡܕܡ ܕܠܐ ܨܒܐ ܐܢܐ.

13 ܝܓ ܡܛܠ ܗܢܐ ܗܟܢܐ ܐܡܪ ܡܪܝܐ ܐܠܗܐ. ܗܐ ܥܒܕܝ ܢܐܟܠܘܢ: ܘܐܝܬܝܟܘܢ ܬܟܦܢܘܢ.
ܗܐ ܥܒܕܝ ܢܫܬܘܢ: ܘܐܝܬܝܟܘܢ ܬܨܗܘܢ. ܗܐ ܥܒܕܝ ܢܚܕܘܢ: ܘܐܝܬܝܟܘܢ ܬܒܗܬܘܢ.

14 ܝܕ ܗܐ ܥܒܕܝ ܢܫܒܚܘܢ ܡܢ ܛܝܒܘܬܐ ܕܠܒܗܘܢ: ܘܐܝܬܝܟܘܢ ܬܒܟܘܢ ܡܢ ܟܐܒܗ
ܕܠܒܟܘܢ: ܘܡܢ ܬܒܪܗ ܕܪܘܚܟܘܢ.

15 ܝܗ ܘܬܫܒܩܘܢ ܫܡܟܘܢ ܠܡܘܡܬܐ ܠܓܒܝܝ. ܘܢܩܛܠܟ ܡܪܝܐ ܐܠܗܐ. ܘܠܥܒܕܘܗܝ
ܢܩܪܐ ܫܡܐ ܐܚܪܢܐ.

16 ܝܘ ܕܡܬܒܪܟ ܒܐܪܥܐ: ܢܬܒܪܟ ܒܐܠܗܐ ܐܡܝܢ. ܘܕܝܡܐ ܒܐܪܥܐ: ܢܐܡܐ ܒܐܠܗܐ
ܐܡܝܢ. ܡܛܠ ܕܢܬܛܥܝܢ ܐܘܠܨܢܐ ܩܕܡܝܐ: ܘܢܬܟܣܘܢ ܡܢ ܥܝܢܝ.

17 ܝܙ ܡܛܠ ܕܗܐ ܐܢܐ ܒܪܐ ܐܢܐ ܫܡܝܐ ܚܕܬܐ ܘܐܪܥܐ ܚܕܬܐ. ܘܠܐ ܢܬܕܟܪܢ ܩܕܡܝܬܐ.
ܘܠܐ ܢܣܩܢ ܥܠ ܠܒܐ.

18 ܝܚ ܐܠܐ ܢܚܕܘܢ ܘܢܪܘܙܘܢ ܠܥܠܡ ܥܠܡܝܢ ܕܒܪܐ ܐܢܐ. ܡܛܠ ܕܗܐ ܒܪܐ ܐܢܐ
ܠܐܘܪܫܠܡ ܕܘܨܐ: ܘܥܡܗ ܚܕܘܬܐ.

19 ܝܛ ܘܐܚܕܐ ܒܐܘܪܫܠܡ: ܘܐܪܘܙ ܒܥܡܝ. ܘܬܘܒ ܠܐ ܢܫܬܡܥ ܒܗ ܩܠܐ ܕܒܟܝܬܐ: ܘܩܠܐ
ܕܨܘܚܬܐ.

11   And you who forsook the Lord, forgot his holy mountain, filled tables for the gods of fortune, prepared[1] wine vessels[2] for them,

12   I will smite you with the sword, I will break you all in slaughter,[3] for I called to you but you did not answer, I spoke but you did not listen, you did evil before me, you chose that which I do not desire.

13   Because of this thus says the Lord God: See! My servants will eat, but you will hunger; See! My servants will drink, but you will thirst; See! My servants will rejoice, but you will weep.

14   See! My servants will give praise from the goodness[4] of their heart, but you will cry out from the pain of your heart, from the crushing of your spirit.

15   You will leave your name (as) a curse[5] for my chosen ones; the Lord God will slay you: but his servants he will call (by) another name.

16   He who blesses himself by[6] the earth blesses himself by the true God; he who swears by the earth swears by the true God; for the former troubles will be forgotten, they will be hidden from my presence.

17   For see! I create a new heaven and a new earth; the former things will not be remembered, they will not come to mind.[7]

18   But they will rejoice, they will exult forever and ever, (in) that which I create; for see! I create joy for Jerusalem, I will rejoice in her.

19   I will rejoice in Jerusalem, I will exult in my people; the sound of weeping will no more be heard in her, nor the sound of wailing.

---

[1] 'prepared'; lit. 'mixed': in the context of wine this means 'to mix with water'.

[2] 'wine vessels' or 'large bowls'.

[3] 'I will break you all in slaughter' (lit. 'and all of you in slaughter I will break you') √ ܟܬܫ or 'all of you in slaughter were blessed' √ ܒܪܟ (grammatically possible but poor sense). See Introduction. Addendum 2.

[4] 'goodness': pl.; or 'good things'.

[5] 'a curse': pl.

[6] 'by' or 'on'.

[7] 'come to mind': lit. 'go up to the heart'.

20 ܟ ܘܬܘܒ ܠܐ ܢܗܘܐ ܬܡܢ ܛܠܐ ܝܘܡܬܐ: ܘܣܒܐ ܕܠܐ ܢܡܠܐ ܝܘܡܬܗ. ܡܛܠ ܕܛܠܝܐ
ܒܪ ܡܐܐ ܫܢܝ̈ܢ ܢܡܘܬ. ܘܚܛܝܐ ܕܝܢ ܒܪ ܡܐܐ ܫܢܝ̈ܢ: ܢܬܠܛܡ.

21 ܟܐ ܘܢܒܢܘܢ ܒ̈ܬܐ: ܘܢܬܒܘܢ. ܘܢܨܒܘܢ ܟܪ̈ܡܐ ܘܢܐܟܠܘܢ ܦܐܪ̈ܝܗܘܢ.

22 ܟܒ ܠܐ ܢܒܢܘܢ: ܘܐܚܪ̈ܢܐ ܢܬܒܘܢ. ܘܠܐ ܢܨܒܘܢ: ܘܐܚܪ̈ܢܐ ܢܐܟܠܘܢ. ܡܛܠ ܕܝܘܡܬܗ
ܕܩܝܣܐ ܐܝܟ ܝܘܡܬܐ ܐܢܘܢ ܕܥܡܝ. ܘܥܒܕ ܐܝ̈ܕܝܗܘܢ ܢܒܠܘܢ ܓܒܝ̈ܝ.

23 ܟܓ ܠܐ ܢܠܐܘܢ ܠܣܪܝܩܘܬܐ: ܘܠܐ ܢܘܠܕܘܢ ܠܒܗܬܬܐ: ܡܛܠ ܕܙܪܥܐ ܐܢܘܢ ܕܒܪ̈ܝܟܘ
ܕܡܪܝܐ: ܗܢܘܢ ܘܒܢ̈ܝܗܘܢ ܥܡܗܘܢ.

24 ܟܕ ܘܥܕܠܐ ܢܩܪܘܢ: ܐܥܢܐ ܐܢܐ. ܘܥܕܠܐ ܢܡܠܠܘܢ: ܐܫܡܥ ܐܢܐ.

25 ܟܗ ܕܐܒܐ ܘܐܡܪܐ ܐܟܚܕܐ ܢܪܥܘܢ. ܘܐܪܝܐ ܐܝܟ ܬܘܪܐ ܢܐܟܘܠ ܬܒܢܐ. ܘܚܘܝܐ ܥܦܪܐ
ܠܚܡܗ: ܘܠܐ ܢܒܐܫܘܢ ܘܠܐ ܢܚܒܠܘܢ ܒܟܠܗ ܛܘܪܐ ܕܩܘܕܫܝ. ܐܡܪ ܡܪܝܐ.

20 No more will there be there an infant,[1] nor an old man who does not complete his days, for the child will die at one hundred years[2] old, but the one hundred year old man[3] who sins will be cursed.

21 They will build houses and dwell (in them), they will plant vineyards and eat their fruits.

22 They will not build (so that) others may dwell (there), they will not plant (so that)[4] others may eat: for the days of my people are as the days of trees; my chosen ones will eat the work of their own hands.

23 They will not labor in vain, they will not bring forth a curse: for they are the Lord's blessed seed, they and their children with them.

24 Before they call out, I will answer them; before they speak, I will hear them.

25 The wolf and the lamb will feed together; the lion like the ox will eat straw; the serpent will eat dust;[5] they will do no evil, they will not destroy, in all my holy mountain, says the Lord.

---

[1] 'infant': lit. 'young child (of) days'.

[2] 'one hundred years': lit. 'the son of a hundred years'.

[3] 'hundred year old man': lit. 'the son of a hundred years'.

[4] '(so that) … (so that)': lit. 'and … and'.

[5] 'the serpent will eat dust': lit. 'the serpent dust his food'.

ܩܶܦܳܠܐܘܿܢ: ܣܘ.

1 ܐ ܗܳܟܰܢܳܐ ܐܳܡܰܪ ܡܳܪܝܳܐ: ܫܡܰܝܳܐ ܟܽܘܪܣܝ: ܘܰܐܪܥܳܐ ܟܽܘܒܫܳܐ ܕܪ̈ܶܓܠܰܝ: ܐܰܝܢܳܐ ܒܰܝܬܳܐ ܕܬܶܒܢܽܘܢ
ܠܝ: ܐܰܘ ܐܰܝܢܳܐ ܐܰܬܪܳܐ ܕܢܝܳܚܬܝ.

2 ܒ ܗܳܠܶܝܢ ܟܽܠܗܶܝܢ ܐܺܝܕܝ ܥܒܶܕܬ݂: ܘܕܺܝܠܝ ܐܶܢܶܝܢ ܗܳܠܶܝܢ ܟܽܠܗܶܝܢ ܐܡܰܪ ܡܳܪܝܳܐ. ܘܰܒܡܰܢ
ܐܶܚܽܘܪ ܘܶܐܚܙܶܐ: ܐܶܠܳܐ ܒܡܶܣܟܺܢܳܐ ܘܰܒܡܰܟܺܝܟ ܪܽܘܚܳܐ ܕܙܳܐܰܥ ܡܶܢ ܡܶܠܰܝ.

3 ܓ ܕܢܳܟܶܣ ܬܰܘܪܳܐ ܐܰܝܟ ܗܰܘ ܕܩܳܛܶܠ ܓܰܒܪܳܐ: ܕܕܳܒܰܚ ܐܶܡܪܳܐ ܐܰܝܟ ܗܰܘ ܕܩܳܛܶܠ ܟܰܠܒܳܐ:
ܕܡܩܰܪܶܒ ܩܽܘܪܒܳܢܳܐ ܐܰܝܟ ܕܡܳܐ ܕܰܚܙܺܝܪܳܐ: ܕܡܩܰܪܶܒ ܠܒܽܘܢܬܳܐ ܐܰܝܟ ܗܰܘ ܕܰܡܒܰܪܶܟ
ܠܰܦܬ݂ܟܪ̈ܶܐ: ܐܰܦ ܗܶܢܽܘܢ ܐܶܬ݂ܪܥܺܝܘ ܒܐܽܘܪ̈ܚܳܬ݂ܗܽܘܢ: ܘܰܨܒ݂ܳܬ݂ ܢܰܦܫܗܽܘܢ ܒܛܰܢ̈ܦܳܬ݂ܗܽܘܢ.

4 ܕ ܐܰܦ ܐܶܢܳܐ ܐܶܨܒܶܐ ܒܒܽܘܙܳܚܗܽܘܢ: ܘܰܐܝܬܶܐ ܐܶܢܽܘܢ ܒܕܶܚܠ̈ܳܬ݂ܗܽܘܢ: ܥܰܠ ܕܩܪܺܝܬ݂ ܘܠܰܝܬ݂
ܕܥܳܢܶܐ: ܘܡܰܠܠܶܬ݂ ܘܠܳܐ ܫܡܰܥܘ: ܘܥܒܰܕܘ ܕܒܺܝܫ ܩܕܳܡܰܝ: ܘܰܓܒܰܘ ܡܶܕܶܡ ܕܠܳܐ ܨܒܺܝܬ݂.

5 ܗ ܫܡܰܥܘ ܦܶܬ݂ܓܳܡܶܗ ܕܡܳܪܝܳܐ ܐܰܝܠܶܝܢ ܕܙܳܝܥܺܝܢ ܡܶܢ ܡܶܠܬܶܗ. ܐܶܡܰܪܘ ܠܰܐܚܰܝܟ݂ܽܘܢ
ܣܳܢ̈ܐܰܝܟ݂ܽܘܢ ܡܣܰܠܝ̈ܳܢܰܝܟ݂ܽܘܢ ܡܶܛܽܠ ܫܡܺܝ. ܢܶܬ݂ܝܰܩܰܪ ܡܳܪܝܳܐ ܘܢܶܚܙܶܐ ܒܚܰܕ݂ܘܽܬ݂ܟ݂ܽܘܢ:
ܘܗܶܢܽܘܢ ܢܶܒ݂ܗܬ݂ܽܘܢ.

6 ܘ ܩܳܠܳܐ ܕܰܫܓ݂ܽܘܫܝܳܐ ܡܶܢ ܩܪܺܝܬ݂ܳܐ: ܘܩܳܠܳܐ ܡܶܢ ܗܰܝܟܠܳܐ: ܩܳܠܶܗ ܕܡܳܪܝܳܐ ܕܦܳܪܰܥ ܦܽܘܪܥܳܢܳܐ
ܠܒܥܶܠܕܒ݂ܳܒ݂ܰܘܗ݈ܝ.

7 ܙ ܥܕܠܳܐ ܬܶܚܒܰܠ ܝܶܠܕܰܬ݂: ܘܥܕܠܳܐ ܢܶܐܬܶܐ ܚܶܒܠܳܗ̇ ܐܶܬ݂ܦܰܠܛܰܬ݂ ܕܶܟܪܳܐ.

8 ܚ ܡܰܢ ܫܡܰܥ ܐܰܝܟ ܗܳܕܶܐ: ܘܡܰܢ ܚܙܳܐ ܐܰܝܟ ܗܳܠܶܝܢ: ܕܬܶܬ݂ܝܰܠܰܕ ܐܰܪܥܳܐ ܒܝܰܘܡܳܐ ܚܰܕ:
ܘܬܶܬ݂ܝܠܶܕ ܥܰܡܳܐ ܒܙܰܒܢܳܐ ܚܕܳܐ: ܡܶܛܽܠ ܕܚܶܒܠܰܬ݂ ܘܝܶܠܕܰܬ݂ ܨܶܗܝܽܘܢ ܠܒܢܰܝ̈ܗ̇.

Chapter 66

1 Thus says the Lord: Heaven is my throne, the earth is my footstool:[1] what is the house that you build for me, or what is the place of my repose?

2 All these my hand has made, they are mine, all these, says the Lord: to whom should I look, (with whom) should[2] I dwell, but to the quiet, to the humble of spirit, who trembles at my word?

3 He who slays an ox is like him who kills a man, he who sacrifices a lamb is like him who kills a dog; he who brings fine flour, (it is) like the blood of a pig, he who brings frankincense, he is like him[3] who blesses idols; truly, they have become reconciled to their ways, they delight in[4] their idols.

4 I will also consent to their delusion; I will repay them their deeds: for I called but no-one answered, I spoke but they did not hear. They did evil before me, they chose that which I did not desire.

5 Hear the word of the Lord, those who tremble at his word; say to your brothers (who) hate you, who reject you because of my name: May the Lord be praised, may he rejoice in your gladness, and may they be ashamed.

6 A sound of tumult from the city, a sound from the temple: the sound[5] of the Lord who requites vengeance[6] on his enemies.

7 Before she was in labor she gave birth, before her birth pains came she delivered a male.[7]

8 Who has heard (anything) like these, who has seen (anything) like these: that the earth labors for a single day, a people is born in a single[8] hour? For Zion has labored, she has borne her sons.

---

[1] 'footstool': lit. 'the footstool of my feet'.

[2] 'should … should' or 'will … will'.

[3] 'him … him … him': lit. 'he … he … he'.

[4] 'they delight in': lit. 'their soul has chosen'.

[5] 'sound … sound … sound' or 'voice … voice … voice'.

[6] 'vengeance' or 'retribution'.

[7] 'delivered a male': lit. 'she brought forth a male'.

[8] 'single day, a people born in a single': lit. 'one … one'.

9 ܛ ܐܢܐ ܡܘܠܕ ܫܘܦܪܐ ܗܘܝܬ: ܘܠܐ ܡܘܠܕ ܐܢܐ ܐܡܪ ܡܪܝܐ. ܕܥܩܪܐ ܠܐ ܗܘܝܬ ܐܢܐ
ܡܘܠܕ ܐܢܐ ܘܚܒܠܐ ܐܢܐ ܐܡܪ ܐܠܗܟܝ.

10 ܝ ܚܕܝ ܐܘܪܫܠܡ ܘܕܘܨܘ ܒܗ ܟܠ ܪܚܡܝܗ. ܐܬܒܣܡܘ ܥܡܗ ܒܒܣܝܡܘܬܐ ܟܠ
ܕܗܘܘ ܡܬܐܒܠܐ ܥܠܝܗ.

11 ܐ ܘܬܐܢܩܘܢ ܘܬܣܒܥܘܢ ܡܢ ܬܕܝܐ ܕܒܘܝܐܗ: ܘܬܐܢܩܘܢ ܘܬܬܦܢܩܘܢ ܡܢ ܒܘܣܡܐ
ܕܐܝܩܪܗ.

12 ܒ ܡܛܠ ܕܗܟܢܐ ܐܡܪ ܡܪܝܐ: ܕܗܐ ܡܨܠܐ ܐܢܐ ܠܘܬܗ ܫܠܡܐ ܐܝܟ ܢܗܪܐ: ܘܐܝܟ
ܢܚܠܐ ܕܫܛܦ. ܘܐܝܩܪܐ ܕܥܡܡܐ ܬܐܢܩܘܢ: ܘܥܠ ܟܬܦܬܐ ܬܬܛܥܢܘܢ: ܘܥܠ
ܒܘܪܟܐ ܬܬܦܢܩܘܢ.

13 ܓ ܐܝܟ ܓܒܪܐ ܕܡܒܝܐܐ ܠܗ ܐܡܗ: ܗܟܢܐ ܐܢܐ ܐܒܝܐܟܘܢ: ܘܒܐܘܪܫܠܡ ܬܬܒܝܐܘܢ.

14 ܕ ܘܬܚܙܘܢ ܘܢܚܕܐ ܠܒܟܘܢ: ܘܓܪܡܝܟܘܢ ܐܝܟ ܬܕܐܐ ܢܦܪܥܘܢ. ܘܬܬܝܕܥ ܐܝܕܗ
ܕܡܪܝܐ ܥܠ ܥܒܕܘܗܝ: ܘܢܪܓܙ ܥܠ ܒܥܠܕܒܒܘܗܝ.

15 ܗ ܡܛܠ ܕܗܐ ܡܪܝܐ ܒܢܘܪܐ ܐܬܐ: ܘܐܝܟ ܥܠܥܠܐ ܡܪܟܒܬܗ. ܕܢܦܢܐ ܒܚܡܬܐ
ܪܘܓܙܗ. ܘܟܐܬܗ ܒܫܠܗܒܝܬܐ ܕܢܘܪܐ.

16 ܘ ܡܛܠ ܕܒܢܘܪܐ ܕܐܢ ܡܪܝܐ: ܘܒܚܪܒܗ ܠܟܠ ܒܣܪ: ܘܢܣܓܘܢ ܩܛܝܠܘܗܝ
ܕܡܪܝܐ.

17 ܙ ܕܡܬܩܕܫܝܢ ܘܡܬܕܟܝܢ ܒܓܢܬܐ: ܚܕ ܒܬܪ ܚܕ ܒܡܨܥܬܐ: ܘܐܟܠܝܢ ܒܣܪܐ
ܕܚܙܝܪܐ: ܘܫܩܨܐ ܘܥܘܟܒܪܐ. ܐܟܚܕܐ ܢܣܘܦܘܢ ܐܡܪ ܡܪܝܐ.

18 ܚ ܘܐܢܐ ܝܕܥ ܐܢܐ ܒܥܒܕܝܗܘܢ ܘܒܡܚܫܒܬܗܘܢ: ܗܐ ܕܐܬܐ ܠܡܟܢܫܘ ܠܟܠܗܘܢ
ܥܡܡܐ ܘܠܫܢܐ: ܘܢܐܬܘܢ ܘܢܚܙܘܢ ܐܝܩܪܝ.

9   I have given this expectation, but I do not cause birth,[1] says the Lord; is it I who causes birth, I who withholds?[2] says your God.

10   Rejoice in Jerusalem, exult in her, all who love her; delight in her with gladness, all who were in[3] mourning for her.

11   You will suck, you will be satisfied, at the breast of her consolation; you will suck, you will delight in[4] the power of her glory.

12   For thus says the Lord: See! I set in her peace like a river, like an overflowing torrent; you will suck the glory of the peoples, you will be carried upon cradles, you will grow strong[5] at her knees.[6]

13   Like a man whose mother comforts him, thus will I comfort you: you will be comforted in Jerusalem.

14   You will see, your heart will rejoice, your bones[7] will flourish like the tender grass; the hand of the Lord upon his servants will be known, it will destroy his enemies.

15   For see! The Lord comes in fire, his chariot like a whirlwind, for he will return in the heat of his anger, his rebuke a flame of fire.

16   For the Lord judges in fire, in it he tries all flesh, and the slain of the Lord will multiply.

17   Those who sanctify themselves, who purify themselves in gardens, one after another in the center, eating the flesh of pigs, of vermin, and mice: together they will perish, says the Lord.

18   For I know their deeds and their minds: when I have come to gather all peoples, all tongues, they will come, they will see my glory.

---

[1] 'I have given this expectation, but I do not cause birth' or 'Have I given this expectation, but do not cause birth?'

[2] 'is it I … I who withholds?': ܠܡܐ is used where a negative answer is expected.

[3] 'in'[1,2] or 'with'.

[4] 'at … in': lit. 'from … from'.

[5] 'grow strong' or 'grow up'.

[6] 'at her knees': lit. 'on knees'.

[7] 'your bones' or 'you yourselves'.

19 ܝܛ ܘܐܣܝܡ ܒܗܘܢ ܐܬܐ: ܘܐܫܕܪ ܡܢܗܘܢ ܡܫܘܙܒ̈ܐ ܠܥܡ̈ܡܐ: ܠܬܪܫܝܫ:
ܘܠܦܘܠ : ܘܠܠܘܕ: ܕܢܓܕܝܢ ܒܩܫܬܐ: ܘܠܬܘܒܠ : ܘܠܝܘܢ: ܘܠܓܙܪ̈ܬܐ
ܪ̈ܚܝܩܬܐ: ܕܠܐ ܫܡܥܘ ܫܡܥܝ ܘܠܐ ܚܙܘ ܐܝܩܪܝ: ܘܢܚܘܘܢ ܐܝܩܪܝ ܒܥܡ̈ܡܐ.

20 ܟ ܘܢܝܬܘܢ ܠܟܠܗܘܢ ܐܚܝܟܘܢ ܡܢ ܟܠܗܘܢ ܥܡ̈ܡܐ ܩܘܪܒܢܐ ܠܡܪܝܐ:
ܒܪ̈ܟܫܐ: ܘܒܡܪ̈ܟܒܬܐ: ܘܒܡ̈ܛܘܬܐ: ܠܛܘܪܐ ܕܩܘܕܫܝ: ܠܐܘܪܫܠܡ ܐܡܪ ܡܪܝܐ:
ܐܝܟ ܕܡܝܬܝܢ ܒܢ̈ܝ ܐܝܣܪܝܠ ܩܘܪܒܢܐ ܒܡ̈ܐܢܐ ܕܟ̈ܝܐ ܠܒܝܬܗ ܕܡܪܝܐ.

21 ܟܐ ܐܦ ܡܢܗܘܢ ܐܣܒ ܠܟܗ̈ܢܐ: ܘܠܠܘ̈ܝܐ: ܐܡܪ ܡܪܝܐ.

22 ܟܒ ܐܝܟ ܕܫܡܝܐ ܚ̈ܕܬܐ ܘܐܪܥܐ ܚܕܬܐ ܕܥܒܕ ܐܢܐ: ܕܩܝܡܝܢ ܩܕܡܝ ܐܡܪ ܡܪܝܐ: ܗܟܢܐ
ܢܩܘܡ ܙܪܥܟܘܢ ܘܫܡܟܘܢ.

23 ܟܓ ܘܢܗܘܐ ܡܢ ܝܪܚ ܒܝܪܚ: ܘܡܢ ܫܒܬܐ ܠܫܒܬܐ: ܢܐܬܘܢ ܟܠ ܒܣܪ
ܠܡܣܓܕ ܩܕܡܝ ܐܡܪ ܡܪܝܐ.

24 ܟܕ ܘܢܦܩܘܢ ܘܢܚܙܘܢ ܦܓܪ̈ܝܗܘܢ ܕܓܒܪ̈ܐ ܕܐܡܪܕܘ ܒܝ: ܕܠܐ ܡܝܬܐ ܬܘܠܥܬܗܘܢ:
ܘܢܘܪܗܘܢ ܠܐ ܕܥܟܐ: ܘܢܗܘܘܢ ܕܘܡܪܐ ܠܟܠ ܒܣܪ.

19   I will set a sign in them, I will send from them a remnant[1] to the peoples, to Tarshish, to Pul, to Lud, who draw the bow, to Tubal, to Javan, to the distant islands, who have not heard my name, have not seen my glory: and they will declare my glory among the peoples.

20   They will bring all your brethren from all the peoples, (as) an offering to the Lord, on horses, in chariots, in two-horse chariots, to my holy mountain, to Jerusalem, says the Lord, as the children of Israel bring fine flour in pure vessels to the house of the Lord.

21   I will also take the priests and the Levites from them, says the Lord.

22   As the new heavens and the new earth that I am making, that stand firm before me, says the Lord, thus will your seed and your name be established.

23   And it will be, month by month, and Sabbath by Sabbath,[2] that all flesh will come to worship before me, says the Lord.

24   They will go out and they will see the dead bodies of the men who sinned against me, whose worm does not die, and whose fire is not quenched, and they will be a wonder to all flesh.

---

[1] 'remnant': lit. 'refugees'.

[2] 'month by month, Sabbath by Sabbath': lit. 'from the time of a month by a month, and from the time of a Sabbath to a Sabbath'.